Canada: The State of the Federation 1997

D0217438

Non-Constitutional Renewal

Edited by

Harvey Lazar

Institute of
Intergovernmental
Relations

Institut des
relations
intergouvernementales

Canadian Cataloguing in Publication Data

The National Library of Canada has catalogued this publication as follows:

Main entry under title:

Canada, the state of the federation

Annual
1985-
Vols. for 1997-   have also a distinctive title.
ISSN 0827-0708
ISBN 0-88911-767-5 (bound : 1997) ISBN 0-88911-765-9 (pbk. : 1997)

1. Federal-provincial relations – Canada – Periodicals. 2. Federal government –
Canada – Periodicals. I. Queen's University (Kingston, Ont.). Institute of
Intergovernmental Relations.

JL27.F42   332.02'3'0971   C86-030713-1

The Institute of Intergovernmental Relations

The Institute is the only organization in Canada whose mandate is solely to promote
research and communication on the challenges facing the federal system.

Current research interests include fiscal federalism, constitutional reform, the reform of federal political institutions and the machinery of federal-provincial relations,
Canadian federalism and the global economy, and comparative federalism.

The Institute pursues these objectives through research conducted by its own staff
and other scholars through its publication program, seminars and conferences.

The Institute links academics and practitioners of federalism in federal and provincial governments and the private sector.

L'Institut des relations intergouvernementales

L'Institut est le seul organisme canadien à se consacrer exclusivement à la recherche
et aux échanges sur les questions du fédéralisme.

Les priorités de recherche de l'Institut portent présentement sur le fédéralisme fiscal,
la réforme constitutionnelle, la modification éventuelle des institutions politiques
fédérales, les nouveaux mécanismes de relations fédérales-provinciales, le fédéralisme
canadien au regard de l'économie mondiale et le fédéralisme comparatif.

L'Institut réalise ses objectifs par le biais de recherches effectuées par son personnel et par des universitaires de l'Université Queen's et d'ailleurs, de même que par
des conférences et des colloques.

L'Institut sert de lien entre les universitaires, les fonctionnaires fédéraux et
provinciaux et le secteur privé.

CONTENTS

FOREWORD

This year's edition of *Canada: The State of the Federation* represents a departure from past editions in that it was conceived with the idea of providing an integrated view on a selected theme. Hence, the longer-than-usual title to this the twelfth edition in this annual series.

This year's theme is non-constitutional renewal of the federation. From the time of the collapse of the Charlottetown Accord to the 1997 federal election there was a widespread conviction among political leaders at both the federal and provincial levels, and from both official language groups, that further efforts at constitutional reform would not be productive. This was reflected, for example, in the 1993 election platform of the federal Liberal Party and the 1995 platform of the Ontario Conservative Party. In both cases, the platforms were silent on the constitutional issue and the growing political gulf between a Quebec that had not yet signed on to the 1982 constitutional amendments and the remaining regions of the country.

This focus on non-constitutional strategy merits attention on two separate scores. First, it deserves attention in that it affects things that matter in the daily lives of Canadians, including policy goals and outcomes, democratic processes and the way our federalism functions. It is also important to know whether, and to what extent, it may have implications for a longer term political reconciliation between Quebec and the wider Canadian polity.

To shine light on these questions, two types of essays were commissioned. One was on policy issues that were selected as representative of the range of items that had been on the intergovernmental agenda over the last several years. Hence, the volume includes three chapters on social policy renewal, two on internal trade, one on the environment, and another on aboriginal affairs.

The second was on the intergovernmental strategies of individual governments. Alberta was selected because it has played a larger role in intergovernmental relations in Canada in recent years than its size alone would dictate. The election of the Conservative Party in Ontario has resulted in a radical reform agenda in that province with resulting consequences on intergovernmental relations. The change of premiership in Quebec also merits attention considering the state of political relations between Quebec and other parts of the country. An assessment of federal government strategy is also provided.

v

As is the tradition with this series, this volume also provides a chronology of major events in the federation from July 1996 to June 1997.

In keeping with the idea of this volume being more thematically organized, the work has already begun on the 1998 edition. The collection will serve as an examination of the changing political, social, economic, and cultural contexts in which Canadians find themselves at the end of the twentieth century. The redefinition of the state's role, changing conceptions of citizenship, the globalization of markets, new technologies, and the increased permeability of domestic cultures all combine to pose new challenges to the Canadian federation. These challenges have the potential to reorient the way in which Canadians articulate their more traditional political concerns such as language, federal-provincial relations, and social policy. The contributors to the 1998 volume will explore these challenges from a variety of perspectives and offer insight into how or if the federation will meet them.

As in previous years, this volume has been a product of team effort. I wish to thank the authors for their work and cooperation. Each chapter has been read by at least two independent readers and I would like to thank them also for their significant contribution. Thanks also to Mary Kennedy, Patti Candido and Tom McIntosh at the Institute, Marilyn Banting for copyediting, Valerie Jarus and Mark Howes of the Desktop Publishing Unit of the School of Policy Studies, as well as Michel Labbé and Chris Page for assistance with the translation.

Harvey Lazar
December 1997

CONTRIBUTORS

Keith G. Banting is Stauffer-Dunning Professor of Policy Studies, and Director of the School of Policy Studies at Queen's University, Kingston, Ontario. During 1997-98 he is a Visiting Scholar at the Center for European Studies, Harvard University, Boston.

Audrey Doerr is a political scientist, former Regional Director, Ontario Region, Department of Indian and Northern Development (1991-96).

Patrick Fafard is Assistant Professor in the School of Policy Studies, Queen's University, Kingston, Ontario.

Roger Gibbins is Professor of Political Science at the University of Calgary, Alberta, where he has taught since 1973.

Robert Howse is Associate Director of the Centre for the Study of State and Market at the University of Toronto, Toronto, Ontario.

Melissa Kluger is completing an honours degree in Political Studies and English at Queen's University, Kingston, Ontario.

Robert H. Knox is the former Executive Director of the Internal Trade Secretariat and is now associated with TCI — Convergence Consultants of Toronto.

Harvey Lazar is Director of the Institute of Intergovernmental Relations, Queen's University, Kingston, Ontario.

Sid Noel is Professor of Political Science at the University of Western Ontario, London, Ontario.

Réjean Pelletier is Professor of Political Science, Laval University, Ste-Foy, Quebec.

John Richards teaches public policy at Simon Fraser University, Burnaby, British Columbia, and is an analyst at the C.D. Howe Institute, Toronto, Ontario.

Daniel Schwanen is a senior policy analyst at the C.D. Howe Institute, Toronto, Ontario.

I

Overview

1

Non-Constitutional Renewal:
Toward a New Equilibrium in the Federation

Harvey Lazar

Le rejet de l'accord de Charlottetown en 1992 et les élections du gouvernement Libéral fédéral en 1993, fut un point tournant dans la gestion de la fédération. Entre 1993 et 1997, les gouvernements fédéral et provinciaux on placé les grandes réformes constitutionnelles de coté. Au lieu, souvent sans la participation du gouvernement du Québec, ils se sont concentrés sur des méthodes non-constitutionnelles pour tenter de renouveler la fédération. Ce chapitre donne une vue d'ensemble de ce qui a été accomplie par cette méthode non-constitutionnelle. Il explique pourquoi les gouvernements ont choisi cette stratégie et évalue sont impact en relation avec quatre critères: l'efficacité des politiques et ses effets sur le fédéralisme, la démocratie et la réconciliation politique à l'intérieur du Canada. Il note que cette concentration sur les méthodes non-constitutionnelles a coïncidé avec la croissance de collaboration entre les gouvernements fédéral et provinciaux. Il suggère que cette croissance dans cette collaboration fédéraliste a du mérite. Il conclu qu'il a des influences qui travaillent pour et contre la continuation de cette approche collaborationniste, et que la façon dont ces forces se dérouleront auront des implications profondes pour le futur de la fédération.

INTRODUCTION

The failure of the Charlottetown Accord and the election of the federal Liberals in 1993 marked a turning point in intergovernmental relations in Canada. Whereas constitutional reform was the centrepiece of federal-provincial relations in the 1980s and early 1990s, the period since then has been overwhelmingly focused on the idea that the Canadian federation can continuously reinvent itself through non-constitutional means. The assumption has been that Canadian federalism has the capacity to adapt to changing needs and evolving circumstances regardless of the difficulty in implementing formal constitutional amendments. The purpose of this volume is to take stock of what has been achieved through non-constitutional mechanisms during this period (1993-97) and to assess the nature and extent of federation reform and renewal that has occurred.

This first essay, which constitutes Part I, provides an overview of the effects of the non-constitutional approach. In so doing, of course, it draws heavily on the other authors. Accordingly, it is necessary to indicate briefly the scope and structure of the book.

Part II includes seven essays that concentrate on different aspects of the renewal process. Three of the chapters offer perspectives on social policy renewal, which has been at the heart of recent interprovincial and federal-provincial dialogue. Two chapters assess progress in implementing the Agreement on Internal Trade. The others deal with federal-provincial relations in environmental matters and federal-provincial-aboriginal relations. This selection of essays is not random. They were commissioned on the basis that they include some of the most difficult and current files in federation management and cover a large proportion of public expenditure and a wide range of intergovernmental practice.

Part III contains four essays. The first three examine the recent intergovernmental diplomacy of three provinces with a particular focus on the non-constitutional dimension of their policies. It concludes with a chapter on the non-constitutional approach of federal progress in implementing the Agreement on Internal Trade.

CHOOSING THE NON-CONSTITUTIONAL ROUTE: OTTAWA'S MOTIVES

The decision of the Canadian people to reject the Charlottetown Accord in 1992 put major constitutional reform into the political deep freeze. Leaders in the English-speaking regions of the country were of the view that further efforts to provide constitutional recognition of Quebec's distinctiveness would provoke an adverse political reaction that would further damage national unity. Within Quebec nationalist circles, both federalist and indépendentist, there was a belief that the rest of Canada had neither the interest nor the inclination to respond favourably to Quebec's constitutional aspirations. Constitutional fatigue was the order of the day.

Nowhere was the ennui more evident than in the federal Liberal Party's 1993 election platform — its famous *Red Book*. Reminiscent of the Sherlock Holmes' dog that did not bark, in over one hundred pages of carefully drafted analysis and undertakings, the *Red Book* chose to stay silent on the constitutional impasse and the seemingly widening political gulf between a Quebec government that had still not signed on to the 1982 *Constitution Act* and the remainder of the country. The Liberals believed that their electoral prospects would be enhanced by being as different as possible from the Tories, and the Conservatives were identified with two failed efforts at megaconstitutional reform. Time and again, the Liberal leader, Jean Chrétien, expressed his disdain for the "C" word and argued instead that what Canadians wanted, more than anything else, was integrity in government and the dignity of work.

The electoral result seemed to justify this strategy. The Liberals swept to power with a substantial majority, winning 98 of 99 seats in Ontario and 30 of 31 in Atlantic Canada. In Manitoba they secured all seats but two. While the result was in many respects a handsome victory for Chrétien — the Liberals had won no less than four seats in each of the provinces — it was also noteworthy that the most politically disaffected regions had sent large majorities from regionally-based parties to represent them in Parliament. In Quebec the Bloc Québécois took 54 of 75 ridings while in the three western-most provinces the Reform Party was returned in 50 of 72 constituencies.

During the Liberals' first two years in office, the official antidote for Quebec's demands, and the alienation in western Canada, was "good government." The fiscal situation was tackled forcefully, especially through Paul Martin's 1995 budget and a comprehensive "program review." The latter put all departments through the financial wringer asking hard questions about whether it was necessary for government to be involved, whether the federal government was the appropriate order of government to be doing it and whether the job could be done more economically.

To be sure, the Liberals talked about the importance of job creation. In a speech in Quebec City on 18 September 1994, Prime Minister Chrétien remarked that it was unacceptable that unemployed Canadians who wished to work were unable to experience the dignity of putting bread and butter on the family table. There was the infrastructure program to at least give symbolic recognition to the weight that the prime minister attached to meeting his electoral commitments on job creation. But in Ottawa, restoring federal finances was seen to be inconsistent with the federal pump priming that might have otherwise helped to drive down the unemployment rate quickly. At the beginning of his term of office, the prime minister doubtless hoped that his government would identify the "silver bullet" that would enable both the deficit and unemployment to be reduced simultaneously. But gradually he and his government became reconciled to the idea that really substantial progress on the jobs front would require that the government first get its books in order; and by the time of the run-up to the Liberal's second budget, Paul Martin and the fiscal agenda ruled supreme in Ottawa.[1]

As for constitutional reform, in an interview in December of 1993, the prime minister declared that his government would not hold constitutional talks with the Government of Quebec even if there were a majority vote in Quebec in favour of sovereignty. Five months later, during a visit through western Canada, he repeated that he was elected to put people back to work, not to discuss a hypothetical separation. "If everyone were to shut up on that, I would be very happy," he was reported to have said. He continued: "The people of Canada, the people of Quebec included, are fed up with talking about the constitution."[2]

The election of the Parti Québécois (PQ) in September 1994 did little to change the position of the federal government on the merits of a new constitutional initiative. In the immediate aftermath of the election, Prime Minister Chrétien urged the PQ to hold its sovereignty referendum as soon as possible and reiterated that there would not be another round of constitutional talks. A month later he stated publicly that the federal government had no backup plan in the event of a "yes" in the coming referendum. In a speech in Montreal in February 1995 he dwelled on the achievements of the Team Canada trade missions overseas and the gains that this brought to Quebec, and all of Canada, noting at the same time Premier Parizeau's non-participation.

From time to time, the federal government criticized the ambiguities in the Parti Québécois' position regarding both the timing and wording of the promised referendum on separation. These occasional interventions suggested, however, that Ottawa was confident that the federalist side could handily win the referendum. This strategy was maintained up to the last few days of the Quebec referendum campaign when, in an apparently panicky effort to stem a tide in favour of those promoting Quebec secession, the federal government gave undertakings that it would, within the limits of its constitutional authority, recognize Quebec's distinctiveness and assure Quebec of a *de facto* veto over future constitutional amendments. In the event, the federalist side won the 30 October 1995 referendum by the slimmest of majorities.

The referendum results altered Ottawa's approach to national unity in some ways while leaving it unscathed in others. The consistency was reflected in the Liberal government's determination not to open the constitutional file.[3] It remained closed during the last two years of Chrétien's first term of office, the Liberals being convinced that the consensus did not exist in the country for satisfactory constitutional resolution of various grievances, whether from Quebec, western Canada or Aboriginal Peoples. In this view, opening the file was bound to lead to failure and thus further damage national unity.

The prime minister acted swiftly to fulfill a number of commitments that he made to the people of Quebec toward the end of the referendum campaign. Thus, the House of Commons and Senate passed a motion recognizing Quebec as a distinct society within Canada in December 1995. Parliament also passed a bill in February 1996 guaranteeing that the Government of Canada would not make any constitutional changes affecting Quebec or any of the other major regions of the country without their consent (in effect lending the federal government's veto to the five regions). Although neither of these measures entailed constitutional change, they were an expression of the federal government's good faith to work toward an eventual constitutional amendment in these two subject areas. For purposes of this volume, therefore, they are not treated as part of Ottawa's non-constitutional strategy.

Finally, the prime minister committed his government to renewal of the federation by specifying the roles and responsibilities of the two orders of government, by finding new models of federal-provincial cooperation in order to bring services and decisions closer to citizens, by making the federation more efficient, and by better reflecting the specific needs of the different regions of the country. It was this undertaking that was at the heart of Ottawa's non-constitutional approach.

In one sense, this latter commitment was simply an extension to the intergovernmental policies pursued in the first half of the mandate. The approach remained pragmatic and step-by-step, rather than a single large-scale package. But in another sense, there was a difference. The difference was in the breadth, intensity and determination with which the "renewal of the federation" through non-constitutional means was pursued. Increasingly, a litmus test for policy initiatives in Ottawa was whether they would help in the renewal of the federation

"Renewal" had no precise meaning in the federal government's lexicon but it was clear that it did not include the transfer of authority to some provinces that would not be available to other provinces. Renewal accordingly excluded formal asymmetries. Moreover, while there was occasional talk that renewal could include moving powers to the federal government from the provinces in order to achieve economies of scale (an example often cited was securities regulation), this did little to obscure the fact that much of the debate was about which powers Ottawa was prepared to devolve to the provinces and under what terms and conditions.

A hypothesis of this essay is that the federal government's focus on non-constitutional renewal was motivated by a set of forces that may have made this approach the only politically viable option for managing the federation during the period under review here. One consideration was Ottawa's need to be able to show Quebecers that, contrary to the charges of the PQ and Bloc Québécois (BQ) and regardless of the difficulties in securing constitutional amendments, the country was not stuck with *status quo* federalism. Canada's system of governance was able to respond and adapt to changing needs and circumstances. In this perspective, agreements between Ottawa and one or more provinces that provided better policy, improved service delivery, reduced waste or clarified effective decisionmaking authority between orders of government understandably received increasing priority.

But improving federal-provincial relations for its demonstration effect was by no means the only influence on the federal government. As already noted, restoring the fiscal house was the overriding priority of the first Chrétien government; and since a substantial proportion of federal spending involved transfers to provinces, this led the federal government to open up its fiscal arrangements with the provinces. Also, political leaders of virtually all party stripes and at both orders of government appeared to believe that extensive "overlap and duplication" between the provinces and Ottawa implied a large waste of taxpayer dollars and that a cleaner and clearer division of responsibility would accordingly save significant sums of money.[4] This, too, pointed to a large change in the nuts and bolts of federal-provincial relations. But there was more. Voices from western Canada frequently carried a decentralizing tone or at least a demand for greater respect for the existing division of powers. New theories of public management were emphasizing a larger role for markets, for partnerships and for communities. At the same time, public opinion polls showed declining respect for government, including especially the federal government.[5] In short, for Prime Minister Chrétien and his government, the need for a new set of relations with the provinces was driven by fiscal pressures and a government-reform agenda, neither of which required opening up the constitution, at least as much as it was by the Quebec factor.

Indeed, since a number of Quebec's traditional demands required constitutional amendment, the federal government's choice of a non-constitutional strategy was far from the ideal response to Quebec's aspirations. In some sense, it simply reflected Ottawa's judgement that other strategic options for responding to Quebec's disaffection were not practicable while, at the same time, some of the non-constitutional dossiers had to be dealt with for reasons largely unrelated to Quebec. In the circumstances, the best that could be done by Ottawa was to implement its non-constitutional approach with some sensitivity to Quebec's needs.

Alternative strategies were theoretically available and some were suggested. There were calls for radical decentralization, for example, from the Reform Party in western Canada and the Allaireists in the provincial Liberal Party in Quebec. But this was not in the cards for at least three reasons. The federal government perception was that Canada was already heavily decentralized in comparison to other federations.[6] Second, the federal Liberals did not believe that the Canadian public wanted a radical decentralization.[7] There may have also been a belief in Ottawa that such an approach would simply lead to a new and more radical set of demands.

A more centralized approach was if anything less viable. For one thing, it would have required dollops of federal money and Ottawa was in the process of withdrawing dollars from the system of intergovernmental transfers, not adding to them. Even with new money, several and perhaps most provinces would have been reluctant partners, having learned painfully over a period of years that Ottawa can be an unreliable funding partner. Moreover, several of the provinces were elected with mandates that indicated their strong commitment to the idea that the existing division of powers must be better respected (at a minimum). Such an approach would have also given excellent political ammunition to supporters of Quebec secession.

As for the constitutional approach, as already noted, opinion in Canada outside Quebec meant that a comprehensive constitutional strategy would be stillborn; and once the PQ was elected provincially there was even less reason to give attention to this option.

In short, the federal government believed that, at least for the period of its electoral mandate, it had little choice but to concentrate on the non-constitutional approach and to advance it in a way that best balanced the various factors noted above. Effectively, this meant dealing with issues, one at a time, employing legislative or administrative solutions, on the basis of the concrete circumstances of each file. In this sense, it was less an explicit strategy for winning the hearts and minds of the people of Quebec than an approach that presumed that good government and good policy would be as attractive to Quebecers as it would be to all other Canadians.

This strategy also fit well with the prime minister's preferred way of working. Jean Chrétien was more at home with an approach that promised concrete deliverables in bite-sized chunks than with more comprehensive schemes that required grand vision and that risked grand failure.

In this context, while the signals from the Prime Minister's Office in the aftermath of the Quebec referendum made it clear to federal ministers that new arrangements with the provinces were needed in order to demonstrate the "flexibility" of the federal system, the evidence does not suggest that any deal which could be sold to the provinces would necessarily win the personal support of the prime minister. The new arrangements had to provide better policy or better ways of implementing policies and therefore better government — not simply a federal-provincial deal for the sake of showing change.

A few examples, discussed more substantively later in this chapter or elsewhere in this volume, will illustrate the point that flexibility in federal-provincial relations was not given undue weight in the federal government's deliberations. Replacing the Established Programs Financing (the transfers for health care and postsecondary education) and the Canada Assistance Plan with the Canada Health and Social Transfer (CHST) was perhaps the most important decision taken by the federal government affecting relations with the provinces. With that decision, Ottawa eased up a little on the existing conditions that were attached to those transfers and committed itself not to establish any new conditions without the support of the provinces. But more significantly, the decision also enforced large reductions in planned transfers to the provinces reflecting the omnipresent federal fiscal agenda. These federal expenditure cuts were bound to play havoc with provincial finances and contribute to politically very difficult and sensitive reductions in provincial health, education, and social service budgets. For this reason, the federal government recognized that the CHST decision could not be helpful to its cause in the Quebec referendum. Yet, it announced the CHST decision before referendum.

In the case of labour market training, mainly due to political pressures from Quebec, the federal government agreed to transfer funds to the provinces. But it did not do so unconditionally. Rather, Ottawa insisted that the provinces recognize its role in the pan-Canadian dimensions of the labour market and it required provincial undertakings concerning language of service. A results-based accountability structure was also implemented for monies turned over to the provinces. Federal labour-market policy goals were therefore not abandoned although the way of reaching them led to a much larger provincial role.

The federal government refused to negotiate new fiscal arrangements with the Government of Ontario, notwithstanding strong and justified pressures from that province that Ottawa rectify past inequities. Here, too, the fiscal agenda won out, in this case over improved relations with Ontario. Also, the federal-provincial agreement to amend the Canada Pension Plan required large increases in contribution rates, indicating that Ottawa was not simply using intergovernmental agreements as a route to enhancing its popularity.

For Ottawa, therefore, federation renewal meant case-by-case management of individual files under which improved relations with provinces, including Quebec, were an important determinant of the federal approach but by no means the sole or even the overriding consideration. In that sense, the non-constitutional approach was less a strategy than an umbrella under which it was possible to group many federal initiatives and activities. What these measures all had in common was that they did not entail constitutional change, they generally involved less spending and they required new understandings between the two orders of government. This approach was characterized also by the idea that the kind of intergovernmental relationship that is appropriate will vary according to the functional realities and specific circumstances of each file.

The implications of this approach to public policy are mixed. On the favourable side, the flexibility that attaches to it allows for the specific facts of each case to be taken into account in improving policy outcomes. A diverse range of intergovernmental processes and institutional structures is at the disposal of governments to find the best possible solution and there is no dogmatism from the top that limits the scope for creativity. The result will frequently be "custom built," since the facts surrounding many files are unique.

There are also risks in this approach. Since the facts vary from file to file — and there will always be room for arguing about which facts are most relevant — it is difficult for provincial governments, and indeed the public, to understand Ottawa's overall sense of where the Canadian federation is or should be headed. No overarching view of federalism appears to underlie the government's approach. No deeply rooted set of principles is guiding its decision-making processes, through good times and bad. The result is that the federal government's behaviour is difficult to predict, making it an uncertain and at times unreliable partner for the provinces.

Of course, were there an intellectually rigorous philosophy from the federal government, and political discipline in adhering to it, the result would almost certainly be insufficient flexibility to accommodate adequately the diversity of provincial views and the differences across files. Therefore, this is not a plea for a single comprehensive theory of federalism as a basis for action by Ottawa. Rather, it is a caution that, in balancing the pressures that it has to deal with, there may be a need for a larger measure of coherence in the federal government's approach to the management of the federation. This is especially true to the extent that the government's strategy acknowledges the growing interdependence among orders of government and therefore requires an increased reliance on partnerships.

THE NON-CONSTITUTIONAL ROUTE AND THE PROVINCES

The federal government alone could not implement an effective non-constitutional strategy and the provinces and territories — with the frequent exception of Quebec after the election of the PQ — were at least as strongly committed to this strategy as was Ottawa. Accordingly, it is equally vital to understand what prompted the provinces to fasten onto this approach and to work with Ottawa on a wide range of issues.

The first point to note here is that provincial government leaders outside Quebec were reading the same polls as their counterparts in Ottawa. During the period under review here, they recognized that people in the English-speaking regions of the country were not prepared to support the kinds of constitutional amendments that might have been helpful to the federalist side in Quebec. For example, during the 1995 provincial election campaign in Ontario, the Conservative Party platform was as silent on issues of national unity as the federal Liberals had been in the federal campaign two years earlier. Second, like the federal government, the provinces were also faced with harsh fiscal circumstances and in some cases they were faster off the mark in making fiscal restraint a priority. The effect of this fiscal priority was to ensure their opposition to any possible enhancement of federal spending that might have privileged Quebec at the expense of other regions, reinforcing what Ottawa already knew about the non-viability of spending its way to national unity. At the same time, it helped to make them relatively understanding of the federal decision to cut back sharply on transfers to the provinces.[8]

Provincial leaders were motivated by other factors also. They wished to improve policy outcomes on some files (e.g., child poverty). They sought redress on others (e.g., Ontario's complaint about the unfairness of the way in which federal transfers to provinces are allocated). They apparently also believed that presumed economies could be achieved in still others (e.g., Alberta's and Quebec's claims for exclusive authority in labour market training).

They may have judged as well that a period of federal fiscal weakness was a good time to roll back perceived federal intrusions into their areas of jurisdiction (e.g., the concern of a number of provinces regarding the federal role in interpreting and enforcing the provisions of the *Canada Health Act*).

The extensive agenda and the scope of decisions flowing from the Annual Premiers' Conference in 1995 at St. John's and 1996 at Jasper are testimony to the provincial commitment to renewing the federation through non-constitutional means. The St. John's conference focused heavily on "social policy reform and renewal" and emphasized the "commitment to the objective of reducing and eliminating barriers to the free movement of persons, goods, services and investments among provinces and territories" under the framework of the Agreement on Internal Trade.

The communiqué from Jasper focused on jobs and growth and reaffirmed the importance to all governments of eliminating deficits and reducing debt. Premiers tackled the renewal agenda under a number of headings, including "rebalancing roles and responsibilities" and "social policy reform and renewal." The agreement among premiers on many issues excluded Premier Parizeau, emphasizing the gap between the Government of Quebec and other governments in Canada. The agenda and decisions of the 1997 Annual Premiers' Conference in New Brunswick indicated that there has been no change in approach since Jasper.

While provincial governments outside Quebec understood well the potential importance of federation renewal for national unity, and were sensitive to the need to act in a way that took account of Quebec politics, their change agenda was developed mainly on the basis of their own circumstances and needs.

ASSESSING THE NON-CONSTITUTIONAL STRATEGY

Nation-building, whether in the political or sociological sense, is never complete. Assessing progress normally entails a series of interim report cards rather than a "once and forever" measure of whether the nation has somehow "passed" of "failed" the test. What follows is, therefore, an interim evaluation of what was achieved during the life of the first Chrétien government (although the text occasionally reports on events prior to or after this period).

Four assessment criteria are used below. The non-constitutional strategy is considered initially in relation to the impact on three factors: policy effectiveness, the kind of federalism being practised in Canada, and democratic values. Finally, some preliminary consideration is given to the effects of the strategy for political reconciliation between Quebec and the wider Canadian polity.

POLICY EFFECTIVENESS

Given the weight attached to fiscal matters by federal and provincial governments, the analysis begins there and then deals separately with the four areas that are covered in the later chapters: social policy, internal trade, environmental policy, and aboriginal policy.

THE FISCAL AGENDA

The main policy priority during the review period was the need to improve public finances at both the federal and provincial levels. The record of success here, among both federal and provincial governments, was quite outstanding by virtually any standard. There is no extensive public record of the private discussions of the meetings of federal and provincial finance ministers. Nonetheless, it is evident from the annual budgets of each of the ministers that they were in broad agreement about the necessity of eliminating annual deficits and restoring the nation's finances. Progress was also discussed and reviewed periodically by federal and provincial leaders, as at the First Ministers' Meeting in 1995.

As for that part of the fiscal retrenchment that was imposed by the federal government through the cutbacks associated with the introduction of the CHST, this was implemented with rather less controversy in federal-provincial relations than might have been expected given the extent of the "hit" on the provinces. In some small measure, this may have been because the federal finance minister gave fair warning, almost 18 months, of what was coming. Partly it may have been due to the election of a number of provincial governments that made fiscal discipline a central feature of their policies. In his chapter, "Ontario and the Federation at the End of the Twentieth Century," for example, Sid Noel points to the fact that in its early months in office the Harris government was remarkably accepting of the CHST cuts. But it also had something to do with the fact that provincial governments recognized the inevitability of some large reductions (even if not as large as those that were imposed), that they lacked the power to prevent them and that somehow they would have to muster the political leadership to move beyond them. To be sure, some provincial leaders suggested that provinces were unfairly singled out in the federal cutbacks, leading to the usual exchange of numbers among the experts in fiscal federalism. Some premiers argued that if the federal government paid less for provincial programs, Ottawa should have less say about their content. But at least in the initial few years following the introduction of the CHST, these criticisms did not so dominate provincial reaction that it was impossible for the two orders of government to work together.[9]

The priority attached to improving public finances included wealthier and poorer provinces and governments that ranged from social democratic to radically conservative. After Premier Bouchard replaced Premier Parizeau, Quebec also committed to this goal. Overall, the extent of consensus and solidarity on the issue of public finances was quite remarkable.

Federal-provincial relations on taxation issues also received some attention during the review period. The Chrétien Liberals were elected in 1993 on a platform that included a promise to rescind the Goods and Services Tax. Not long after it was elected, the federal government began to interpret its electoral commitment as one that would be satisfied by a harmonizing of federal and provincial sales taxes. By the end of the federal mandate, however, harmonization agreements had been signed with three provinces only and to achieve these Ottawa had found it necessary to use costly fiscal incentives that had the effect of irritating non-signing provinces.

On a more positive note, the federal finance minister announced in late 1997 that Ottawa had agreed, after many years of federal-provincial discussion, to much enhanced flexibility for the provinces in the design of their income tax systems within the framework of the federal-provincial tax collection agreements. Whereas Ottawa's traditional position was that provinces would have to levy their taxes as a percentage of the federal tax payable, it appears that in the future provinces will be free to impose their tax directly on income and still use the federal government as tax collector.[10]

SOCIAL POLICY

The volume offers three chapters on social policy renewal — by Keith Banting, John Richards, and Harvey Lazar. While each author takes a somewhat different approach, all three touch in varying ways on the effects of the social policy renewal process on the first three of our assessment criteria, that is, policy effectiveness, federalism, and democracy. It is what they have to say about policy effectiveness that forms the basis for our remarks here.

Banting's focus is on the lessons learned from the post-World War II experience during which the modern welfare state was constructed.[11] The essence of his argument is that the combined federal and provincial postwar welfare state gave Canada, *de facto,* many of the elements of a social union; and that in relation to the equity and efficiency criteria that are usually associated with social policy, what was created merits high marks.

One of the few programs to receive enhanced funding during the first Chrétien administration was fiscal equalization. While Richards, "Reducing the Muddle in the Middle" is generally critical of intergovernmental transfers, he argues in favour of a strong equalization program. He also applauds the reduced conditionality associated with the CHST, although he would prefer that it eventually be phased out and replaced with an income tax point transfer to the provinces. Richards similarly supports the direction of the most recent set of federal-provincial bilateral labour market agreements and is even firmer in his backing of the new National Child Benefit.

Lazar argues that federal-provincial relations became increasingly collaborative in the last two and a half years of the first Chrétien government following the enforcement of the CHST and that, in general, this has resulted in policy moving in desirable directions. In child benefits, the outcome should be some progress in reducing poverty among working families with young children while strengthening the efficiency of the labour market. The outcome of federal-provincial negotiations on the Canada Pension Plan was an enhanced level of funding for the CPP that should serve to improve its political sustainability. As for the new labour market agreements, which eight provinces signed with the federal government, they include an accountability structure that may serve as a prod on governments to improve results. Without wishing to be "Pollyannish," it is arguable that the public will, over time, be better served by the new arrangements in these three areas than those they have replaced.[12]

More generally, this was a period in which provincial and federal governments began to reconsider how to preserve the Canadian social union in the light of the damage done to the social safety net as a result of expenditure reductions. The provinces were initially (1994-95) skittish of venturing into this territory with the federal government, fearing that Ottawa would attempt to tarnish them with the political costs of the federal fiscal cutbacks that were then widely expected. But soon after Ottawa imposed the CHST, the provinces, except Quebec, took the initiative and have since been playing a major role in shaping the intergovernmental social policy agenda. As this volume was being finalized, at the urging of the provinces, debate was beginning about the possibility of a federal-provincial framework agreement on social policy. This has the potential to strengthen the social union and extend the social rights of citizenship.

Since the fiscal agenda trumped social policy over these years, there is no doubt that at the end of the review period, Canada had a weaker safety net at both federal and provincial levels than it did earlier in the decade. Within the new fiscal context, however, the intergovernmental process led to a number of measures that were, or had the potential to be, genuine improvements in policy, including in child benefits, CPP, equalization, and labour market training; and a federal-provincial dialogue had started for a framework agreement on social policy.

INTERNAL TRADE POLICY IMPLEMENTATION

The Agreement on Internal Trade (AIT) was signed in 1994 and it came into force a year later. There are widely divergent views as to whether the agreement

is a significant step forward in promoting a more perfect economic union and
the economic rights of citizenship or simply a weak imitation of an international trade agreement. This dispute, for the most part, reflects differences of
opinion about the provisions of the agreement as originally written, not observations about its practical effects on the behaviour of governments and
other economic agents.[13] This is a particularly relevant here for two reasons:
the AIT contains numerous undertakings by governments to implement various commitments according to agreed timetables; and the way in which
commitments are honoured also affects the ease with which its provisions can
be used. Accordingly, the manner in which the AIT is being implemented is
an appropriate test of policy effectiveness.

The heart of the AIT is the sector chapters that set out the various obligations to both reduce explicit barriers across borders and promote positive
economic integration. One of the sectors most amenable to more integration
is the government procurement market since it is directly within the control
of the signatories to the agreement. Since the signing of the AIT, progress
here has been significant. Non-discriminatory rules have been established and
a common tendering system is expected to be operational within the next two
years so that businesses anywhere in Canada will be able to access most public sector tenders on that single system. Schwanen, "Canadian Regardless of
Origin," provides details regarding the implementation status of each of the
commitments that governments have entered into noting which deadlines have
been met and which ones have not. While Knox, "Economic Integration in
Canada through the Agreement on Internal Trade," reports shortcomings with
the bid-protest system, he concludes that "procurement at the federal and provincial level is more open and accessible across the country and, imperfect as
it may be, Canada has an undertaking in place for a national public sector
procurement market that was not there before."

In the case of labour mobility, the agreement requires that qualifications of
certified workers from other jurisdictions be recognized and differences in
occupational standards reconciled. At least 400 non-governmental occupational licensing bodies have been requested to participate and Schwanen reports
that 300 have become engaged. Procedures are also now in force to remove
barriers that individual Canadians face as they move from one region of the
country to another. Knox cites several examples of individuals who were initially barred from practising their occupation in another province but who
have used the consultation mechanisms of the AIT to resolve their disputes to
their satisfaction. While it is too soon to know the extent of the actual progress
that will be realized in this area, the early signs are promising.

The AIT facilitates economic integration by lowering the costs for firms
doing business outside their home province. One example of progress is that
the registration and reporting burdens have been eased for firms doing business

in more than one jurisdiction. A second relates to consumer protection where harmonization has been achieved in several areas (e.g., cost of credit). In several other sectors, the implementation process has been slower.

The report card on the AIT's dispute resolution provisions is mixed. The arrangements have proved effective in some cases. But the agreement and its provisions are poorly publicized. Solutions are too slow in coming and, if only for that reason, discourage those who have a need to resolve immediate problems.

The operating structures of the agreement are also weak. Knox observes that the Committee on Internal Trade (CIT) lacks authority relative to the numerous ministerial level intergovernmental committees that have grown up over the years in virtually all subject areas (sectors/chapters) of the agreement. This difficulty is compounded by the requirement that CIT decisions be made by consensus.

The agreement is a work in progress. Notwithstanding some achievement, the pace of implementation has been slower than originally planned. In part this may be because the attention of political leaders was diverted to more pressing matters, in particular, the fiscal agenda and the need for social policy renewal that came in its wake. Implementation also requires careful attention to thousands of small details, which is painstaking work that cannot realistically command the attention of first ministers.

This then suggests the need for stronger institutions at both the ministerial and secretariat levels to get the job done. The time has come for a set of decision rules that would enable the agenda to be advanced with something less than a unanimity rule. More transparency is also required if citizens, both individual and corporate, are to maximize their rights of citizenship under its provisions.

ENVIRONMENTAL POLICY

The record of policy achievement on the environmental front was disappointing. The Canadian Council of Ministers of the Environment (CCME) launched a major negotiating effort to better harmonize federal and provincial policy. The initial outcome was a comprehensive and complex Environmental Management Framework Agreement (EMFA) that would have devolved some authority from Ottawa, but the ministers ultimately decided not to proceed with this initiative. This was followed by a Canada-wide Accord on Environmental Harmonization under which subagreements were to be concluded on all areas of environmental management "that would benefit from Canada-wide coordinated action" and three such subagreements were developed on environmental assessment, standards, and inspection. While the Canada-wide accord was approved in principle in November 1996 by the CCME, the signing date has been deferred twice since then and the House of Commons Standing Committee on Environment and Sustainable Development has recommended further delay (December 1997). Thus, at the end of the review period covered in this volume, it was not clear that this second arrangement would be ratified. In the meantime, events in the run-up to the 1997 Kyoto Conference suggested that both federal government and federal-provincial policymaking on major files like greenhouse emissions are inadequate.

Patrick Fafard, "Green Harmonization," documents a very extensive federal-provincial effort "marked by a considerable degree of cooperation" but with few tangible results. Since many groups with an interest in environmental matters are critical of the Canada-wide accord, as they were of the earlier EMFA, the delays are not necessarily a bad thing for environmental policy. But they also suggest a lack of accomplishment.[14]

POLICIES RELATED TO ON-RESERVE ABORIGINALS

Constitutional reform with respect to First Nations also remained on the back burner during this period and Ottawa instead chose to follow an incremental agenda of making agreements with aboriginal groups, and wherever possible, provincial governments. It refused to move away from this approach even after the report of the Royal Commission on Aboriginal Relations was released. Dealing with practical problems, one at a time, was as much the hallmark of the federal government approach to relations with First Nations as it was on the social, economic, and environmental agendas discussed above.

This strategy is documented by Audrey Doerr, "Federalism and Aboriginal Relations," whose method is to illustrate it by referring to agreements reached between Ottawa and various First Nations, often with the relevant province also involved. The focus is on three broad subject areas: land claims, education, and economic development.

On land claims in southern Canada, substantive progress has long been slow. There was, however, an increase in federal-provincial-aboriginal activity, especially in British Columbia — where with few exceptions land treaties were never signed with First Nations — and in Manitoba and Saskatchewan — where specific land claims required resolution. Accomplishments include the agreement-in-principle signed with the Nisga'a in British Columbia in 1996 and an agreement-in-principle among federal, Manitoba, and 19 First Nations in that province. Land claims settlements offer the potential of a stronger economic base for Aboriginal People and, for non-Aboriginal People, the prospect of greater certainty over the status of lands and in addressing third-party issues. While it may be many years before the outcome of this stepped-up activity bears fruit, these developments are encouraging. The recent Supreme Court ruling on the non-extinguishing of aboriginal title is a new development in this process, however, and it remains to be seen how it will affect the settlement process.

In on-reserve education, the federal government legislates on schools and their operations and the provinces have effective responsibility for curriculum, standards, and teacher certification. Accordingly, to the extent that First Nations wish to assume jurisdiction and control over education, they need to deal with both the provinces and Ottawa. The potential benefit is that it simplifies the provision of educational services and places responsibility with the local community. Doerr provides recent examples of where this is occurring.

Economic development for on-reserve peoples remains a huge challenge for public policy. The rate of population growth is considerably faster than for the wider population and, on average, Aboriginal Peoples are much younger. Federal and federal-provincial policies, in conjunction with First Nations, emphasized institution-building in such diverse areas as aboriginal banking, oil and gas development, and property taxation as well as the more traditional federal-provincial-aboriginal joint development agreements.

Where policy is consciously developed in small chunks, it is difficult to generalize about effectiveness since the impact of those policies may be impossible to disentangle from the various other factors influencing outcomes for the target population. Moreover, where initiatives have a long time fuse, as is the case with land claims and education, there is yet a further barrier to commenting on policy effectiveness. Still, if the counterfactual to the kind of approaches described above is the traditional policymaking of Indian and Northern Affairs Canada, and the federal government's poor record in solving serious aboriginal social and economic problems, the direct participation of First Nations as equal partners in an intergovernmental process may be a genuine step forward.

SUMMARY ON POLICY EFFECTIVENESS

In summary, both orders of government agreed on the priority to be attached to restoring of public finances and made excellent progress on that goal. The finance ministers had less success in harmonizing sales taxes but, at the end of the review period, there were indications that long-standing federal-provincial differences regarding the amount of flexibility available to the provinces within the framework of federal-provincial income tax collection agreements might be resolved. There is a major work program under way to reconstruct the Canadian social union with provincial governments playing a leading role. Quebec has remained outside this initiative, illustrating the earlier argument that the non-constitutional strategy is not being motivated principally by concerns for political reconciliation with that province. Modest progress has been achieved in implementing the AIT. A variety of initiatives are being developed and implemented in relation to aboriginal policy. While achievements are still small relative to what needs to be done, there were some steps forward in limited areas. The environmental area was the weakest area among those considered here. On that front, it was the failures that stood out.

THE EFFECTS OF NON-CONSTITUTIONAL RENEWAL ON CANADIAN FEDERALISM

The second criterion for assessing the effectiveness of the non-constitutional approach is its effect on the kind of federalism being practised in Canada. In this regard, it is important to recall that this recent focus has an honourable lineage. During the century following the Confederation of 1867, important adjustments were made in the way effective power was distributed between federal and provincial governments on a number of occasions in response to changing needs and circumstances; and these were generally implemented without constitutional amendment.[15]

In the decades prior to World War II, the two orders of government acted largely independently of one another in a relatively decentralized federation. The war years saw power centralized in Ottawa. In the immediate aftermath of the war, there was a short period of decentralization followed by a couple of decades of centralization in which the federal government used its spending power both to create federal-provincial shared-cost programs and to transfer money directly to individuals. These initiatives were often in areas of what would have otherwise been exclusive provincial jurisdiction. While both co-operation and conflict between Ottawa and the provinces marked this period, most provinces for most of the time were prepared to tolerate the larger federal role in return for the additional funding provided. The Government of Quebec did not share this view, however, consistently rejecting the political legitimacy of the federal spending power.

By the early 1970s, provincial governments were becoming increasingly concerned that shared-cost programs were distorting their priorities. As a result, block funding began to replace matching funds. This was also a period when areas of provincial jurisdiction became increasingly important public priorities (e.g., education, health care) and areas of federal jurisdiction less important (e.g., defence). Centralization peaked and there was once more a trend toward decentralization. But the size of the state remained far larger than was the case in the prewar years and so, despite the decentralization, the character of the federation was much different than the period of watertight compartments. The "mutual independence" of the prewar years was giving way to "mutual interdependence."

In short, prior to the period of intensive constitutional focus that began in the late 1960s and that came to dominate federal-provincial relations during the 1980s and the early 1990s, there were ebbs and flows in the effective distribution of power in the federation. It is also arguable that during these years, especially until the period of constitutional emphasis, Canada was one of the world's most successful federations. All of this suggests that the obsession with constitutional change that characterized the quarter century prior to the election of the Liberals in 1993 was in some sense a unique chapter in Canadian history. In this perspective, the recent focus on non-constitutional methods for dealing with pressures for change is a return to methods that have served Canadians well in the past.

How then do we characterize the federalism of the 1993-97 period under review? When examining the seven chapters in Part II as a whole, what emerges strongly is the *increase* in the extent of the *collaboration* between the two orders of government as well as the *diversity* in the methods of collaboration. This is not to suggest that these years were marked exclusively by such collaboration. To the contrary, the workings of the federal system remained an amalgam of arrangements that included a wide variety of federal-provincial, and in a few cases interprovincial, relationships. These included examples of classical federalism in which the two orders of government acted within their own jurisdiction largely independently of one another with no suggestion of hierarchy (e.g., both orders of government provided income support to unemployed people under certain conditions). They included as well cases of the federal government imposing conditions associated with shared-cost programs in areas of exclusive provincial jurisdiction (e.g., the federal requirement that provinces adhere to the conditions of the *Canada Health Act* to avoid financial penalty) and of non-hierarchical collaboration (e.g., the National Child Benefit).

But none of this was new. The architecture of the federation has long been based on a variety of different designs. What was new was the greater emphasis on collaboration by which I mean governments working together on a *non-hierarchical* basis in a way that reflects their *interdependence*. In this regard, the most effective work was found in the social area but only after a period of considerable tension when the provinces were suspicious that Ottawa would act unilaterally through its Social Security Review Process and indeed did act unilaterally through the CHST. After CHST, however, there was extensive federal-provincial collaboration on several social issues. There was, as well, the beginning of a debate regarding the possibility of national leadership in areas of exclusive provincial jurisdiction through interprovincial leadership.[16] Collaboration did not always mean policy success. But even in the environmental area, the possibility of collaborative national decisionmaking through a formally integrated federal-provincial process was

explored via the EMFA. In the case of internal trade, there was much constructive work of a "nuts and bolts" nature going on but more might have been
achieved with stronger institutions. As for the federal-provincial-First Nation
relations, they were as diverse as the diversity that characterizes the circumstances from region to region.

The growth in collaborative federalism during this period may at first glance
seem surprising. Much of the rhetoric from western Canada, as reflected in
the federal Reform Party and the Klein government in Alberta, was suggestive of the disentanglement of classical federalism. The 1995 election of the
Conservatives in Ontario resulted in another powerful voice apparently committed to such an agenda. In conjunction with a PQ government in Quebec
and a large Bloc Québécois contingent in the House of Commons, it might
have been thought that the political basis for enhanced collaboration would
be lacking.

Yet underneath the rhetoric, the reality was sometimes different. In "Alberta's Intergovernmental Relations Experience," Gibbins notes that the
Government of Alberta has had a long tradition of intergovernmentalism as a
strategy for offsetting Alberta's weak representation in national institutions.
In fact, Alberta was and remains a leader in the federal-provincial collaboration surrounding internal trade and it was the first of the provinces to enter
into a bilateral labour market agreement with Ottawa in 1996. It also played a
leadership role in the early work of the Provincial-Territorial Ministerial Council on Social Policy Reform and Renewal which, while calling for the end of
federal unilateralism in social policy, at the same time acknowledged the federal government as a legitimate player in national social policy.

Spooked perhaps by the electoral price paid by the Peterson and Rae governments for their constitutional strategies, Premier Harris initially
de-emphasized federal-provincial relations and focused his intergovernmental efforts on domestic policy (e.g., rationalizing roles with municipalities,
school boards). But when his government did turn its attention to federal-
provincial matters, it might have been expected to avoid the collaborative
approach. Its rhetoric was small government and disentanglement whereas
collaboration creates the image of complexity. The government also had a
grievance against Ottawa because of its continued *de facto* financial discrimination against Ontario in a number of large programs. Further, with Ontario's
economy continuing to integrate north-south, its self-interest in east-west
collegiality might be declining.

Yet, Ontario recognized the pan-Canadian dimension in social policy and
commissioned the Courchene report that in turn has helped to promote the
idea of social union run collectively by the provinces. While relations with
Ottawa were tense following a short honeymoon (e.g., Ontario Budget, 1997),
Ontario nonetheless participated in collaborative efforts like the National Child

Benefit and current joint work on disability. The fact that collaborative federalism at the strategic policy level can lead to disentanglement at the program level may help to explain the interest of the Harris government.

As Réjean Pelletier shows in his chapter, Quebec has also been willing to participate in some collaborative activities especially under Premier Bouchard. This participation has stretched from Team Canada trade missions to a federal-provincial labour market agreement and included the internal trade and environmental files. At the same time, other provinces were strong supporters of collaboration. Both Saskatchewan and British Columbia, for example, played lead roles in creating the momentum to achieve the National Child Benefit.

When comparing the "collaborative" federalism of 1993-97 to the "cooperative federalism" of the 1960s, the fiscal context is an important distinction. Whereas the earlier period was one of rapidly rising public expenditure, and Ottawa was able to encourage provincial participation in national programs by undertaking to cover half the costs of the provincially delivered programs, the more recent period was within a framework of shrinking resources. Yet the intergovernmentalism that marked the years of the first Chrétien administration was if anything wider in scope than was the case two and three decades ago.

Two factors appear to be at play here. First, the incentive to collaborate does not disappear during tough fiscal times. It does, of course, decline in respect of shared-cost programs to the extent that Ottawa withdraws money from them. But shared-cost programs are not the only way in which the two orders of government impact one another and there are influences that work in the opposite direction. For example, fiscal tightness creates incentives for both orders of government to maximize the results from their expenditures and tax incentives but this may be difficult to achieve in areas where both orders of government are active unless they are cooperating with one another. In this regard, it is not uncommon for federal programs to operate through tax law or cash benefits and for provincial programs to operate through services, regulation or cash benefits in the same area. In these kinds of situations, either order of government may be able to thwart the effectiveness of the other unless they cooperate. The case of child benefits was an illustration prior to the recent creation of the National Child Benefit.

Fiscal tightness also increases incentives for downloading and uploading. But such gamesmanship also entails wasteful administrative costs that ultimately fall on the taxpayer unless governments work together to avoid such incremental costs. Even where there is no program overlap, the actions of one government can affect the other. Changes to the criminal code can influence provincial costs of administering the justice system and international trade or environmental commitments by Ottawa may force adjustments that affect provincial revenues or expenditures. While all of these examples also apply during periods of fiscal plenty, the incentive to do something about them is stronger in tough times. All these factors have been at work in the period under review.

When comparing recent years to earlier periods of cooperation there is a second distinction worth noting. International borders matter less now in the economic, social, cultural, and environmental areas than they did three decades ago with consequences for internal borders as well. One result is a much bigger role for the provinces in areas that were once more or less exclusive federal domains. For example, globalization has led to international trade negotiations that involve items of provincial jurisdiction and therefore require provincial collaboration if international agreements signed by Ottawa are to be implemented. A second example is that growing numbers of Aboriginal People have left their reserves (crossed borders) and effectively become subject to provincial programming. These developments more than anything else reflect the increasing interconnectedness of what once were distinct activities and the consequential overlap of governmental roles with these changing circumstances.

While this interdependence has led to collaboration, it is different than the cooperative federalism of the Pearson era and the early Trudeau years. Existing shared-cost programs are much less conditional now than they were then. (The only large remaining shared-cost program with significant federally imposed conditions is, in effect, the health component of the CHST.) Also, Ottawa has undertaken to start no new shared-cost programs in areas of exclusive provincial responsibility without the agreement of most of the provinces and to compensate any provincial government that opts out of such agreements provided that province introduces a comparable program. This reduces significantly the amount of *hierarchy* between orders of government associated with shared-cost programs. Many of the other areas of recent collaboration, such as internal trade, CPP, and child benefits, involve partnership, not hierarchy.

The Canadian federalism of the interwar years was in significant measure characterized by *independence and non-hierarchy* between orders of government. The centralization of the war years entailed *independence and hierarchy*, with Ottawa in charge. The centralization of the 1950s and 1960s was something different because, by then, the role of the peacetime state was much larger than it had been in earlier decades and the relationship between orders of government had come to involve greater *interdependence* with significant elements of *hierarchy*. The non-constitutional focus of the years that coincided with the first Chrétien government, and especially the second half of that era, involved growing *interdependence* but with a greater respect for the idea that the two orders of government should relate to one another on a *non-hierarchical* basis.

THE EFFECT OF NON-CONSTITUTIONAL RENEWAL ON CANADIAN DEMOCRACY

With a substantial array of intergovernmental activity underway, and a case to be made that it should receive even more priority (see above comments on internal trade and the environment), a question that arises is whether so much intergovernmentalism is consistent with democratic processes and values. In his chapter, Banting suggests that concerns about "democratic deficits" in Canada have historically been linked mainly to big constitutional packages, not administrative arrangements. Indeed, there is no evidence that the public is about to reject politically the outcomes of recent federal-provincial agreements on child benefits, the Canada Pension Plan, or labour market training for such reasons. In these cases, however, governments have undertaken initiatives to reduce concerns about democratic deficits (e.g., through commitments to regular public reporting within a published accountability structure). In the case of environmental policy, Fafard reports that the failings were not attributable to a lack of openness in government. As for the implementation process around internal trade, these remain opaque, which has detracted from their effectiveness. Better and more regular information here would simultaneously serve policy goals and democratic values.

Overall, the more that governments use intergovernmentalism to solve problems, and the more these processes generate hard outcomes that matter to people, the more governments will need to give attention to democratic concerns. Among other things, this will require enhanced transparency on how intergovernmental decisions are made. Clearer lines of accountability regarding the responsibilities of the two orders of government (the more integrated the decisionmaking process of the two orders of government the more important to spell out what each has committed to do) will similarly be needed. And more attention will also have to be paid to more fully involving both legislatures and the wider public in the intergovernmental decisionmaking processes.

EFFECTS ON POLITICAL RECONCILIATION WITHIN CANADA

The effects of the non-constitutional strategy on the prospects for a political reconciliation between Quebec and the rest of Canada are difficult to assess. Accordingly, my remarks here will be both tentative and cautious.

The first observation is that the non-constitutional strategy has generally avoided the irritations that periodically serve to fuel support for the sovereignty side. This may be a "plus" for reconciliation. The strategy has also shown that serious policy challenges that involve both orders of government can be managed well, as on the fiscal front and child benefits. To the extent that this illustrates a functional polity, this too may encourage a political environment that is conducive to reconciliation.

However, it is also worth noting that the areas of federal-provincial relations where Quebec was participating fully, including internal trade and environmental issues, have received relatively little high level attention from the federal government during the years under review. This lack of attention was understandable. From a national unity viewpoint, no special political sensitivity attached to these items because the Government of Quebec saw them as "business as usual." Moreover, there was arguably a more pressing set of issues that both orders of government had to tackle.

One of these pressing issues was social policy renewal. The Quebec government position on social policy is that it is an overwhelmingly provincial jurisdiction and that the federal role is based, for the most part, on what it considers to be an illegitimate use of the federal spending power (see the joint communiqué from the First Ministers' Meeting, 12 December 1997). To the extent that this view is widely shared by Quebecers, or that disputes about technical issues like the spending power are simply hard to understand, this social policy focus entails risk from the perspective of political reconciliation. This helps to explain why the federal government has pledged not to create new shared-cost programs in areas of exclusive provincial jurisdiction without broad provincial support and to provide financial compensation to those provinces that opt out if they create similar programs. It may also help to account for the interest of some provinces in promoting interprovincial, rather than federal-provincial, frameworks for national programs.

The spending power is not only used by the federal government, however, for shared-cost programs but also to effect cash transfers to individuals. Notwithstanding the Quebec government's view, Ottawa's constitutional authority to use this power appears strong, its political legitimacy generally accepted in much of Canada and it is an efficient way for the federal government to connect directly with citizens. It is not yet clear how far Ottawa intends to shift in this direction although the limitations the federal government has placed on itself with regard to shared-cost programs suggest the possibility of significant movement.[17] Since the likely effects of such a movement on Quebec public opinion are uncertain, this issue is a "wild card" in relation to political reconciliation.

The discussion about social policy leads to a consideration of the effects of Ottawa and the provinces working together without Quebec at the table as a participating partner. In earlier periods, Ottawa and at least some of the provinces would have gone to great lengths to avoid "isolating Quebec." Today, governments appear to have reluctantly accepted that they must get on with business even if Quebec absents itself or assumes observer status only. The issue here has less to do with the pros and cons of this practice on any single issue than its cumulative effects over time. While in no way intended as a training ground for operating a Canada without Quebec, other governments are learning how to do business with one another without Quebec's active participation much of the time.

The Quebec government may have its own reasons to find these developments attractive. They may help over time, for example, to support the nation-to-nation objectives of the Parti Québécois by effectively legitimizing the idea that the other provinces collectively, or some combination of the other provinces and Ottawa, are the embryo from which an "English Canada" might be born and with which Quebec may one day be able to negotiate the economic association or political partnership that Premier Bouchard has promised.

In brief, from a political reconciliation perspective, the recent heavy intergovernmental focus on social policy is high risk. At a minimum, therefore, relatively more high level attention than has been the case over the last four years should be devoted to items where there are convergent interests between Quebec and other parts of Canada. In "Searching for Plan A," Robert Howse states that this would nurture the "community of association" by thickening the economic and other ties across regions and language groups and without raising troublesome identity politics. With more progress on convergent interests, then areas of divergence might loom less significant.

It is also desirable to clarify what the roles and responsibilities of the provincial and federal governments will be in a new social union. The 1997 First Ministers' Meeting states that it will be developed in a way that respects the constitutional responsibilities of the different orders of government. Yet, it has been portrayed by the Quebec government as an assault on provincial powers. Since it is evident that larger provinces like Ontario and Alberta have no intention of agreeing to any such outcome, and a number of other provinces are also likely to be recalcitrant, the political risks of this initiative from a unity viewpoint seem larger than the substantive reality. This argues that, to the extent that social policy renewal remains high priority, there is urgency in defining with great clarity what is intended in this area so that individual Quebecers will be better able to appreciate what is being considered. For what it may be worth, one view of these discussions is that, contrary to what Quebec asserts, they do not indicate a new federal government unilateralism in which provinces would become more dependent on Ottawa. Rather, they reflect the idea that the Canadian federation cannot avoid the "mutual interdependence" of the modern world and that the "mutual independence" or watertight compartments of earlier periods in Canadian history are increasingly dysfunctional in a world of growing interconnectedness.

The non-constitutional approach of the 1993-97 period was never, of course, seen as a complete strategy for promoting political reconciliation within

Canada. It did not address either the symbolic or practical issues relating to the protection and promotion of the French language, for example. Nor did it address some of the symbolic and practical concerns of Canadians in the western-most provinces. But it has been about more than good government. It has also been about buying time while public finances were being restored, making progress on issues that required the attention of both orders of government, and allowing some of the emotions, on both sides of the language divide, to cool in the aftermath of the failures of both the Meech and Charlottetown Accords.

The fact that the pro-sovereignty side came so close to winning the 1995 Quebec referendum indicates that as a way of buying time it has been far from a complete success. Yet, the federalists did receive more than half the votes in the referendum; and it is possible, if less than certain, that there is greater openness in the other regions of Canada than there was two or three years ago to finding some basis for reconciliation. Since reconciliation depends as much on opinion in the provinces outside Quebec as it does on events within that province, this is noteworthy. The readiness of the nine premiers to re-open the constitutional file, as reflected in the Calgary Declaration, speaks directly to this point.

At this juncture, therefore, the mundane conclusion to be drawn about the effects of the non-constitutional approach is that it was a necessary step for healing the wounds of the country. It has helped to create the preconditions for another effort at reconciliation. But in and of itself, it is unlikely to be sufficient for that purpose.

An issue worth reflecting on in this context is the effect of Plan "B" on the non-constitutional approach. It was suggested above that the non-constitutional strategy has been developed in a generally non-provocative way. Recently, however, at least as seen through the media, it has received far less attention than the federal government's Supreme Court reference regarding the constitutionality of a unilateral declaration of independence by Quebec. Similarly, it has attracted less attention than Stéphane Dion's letters to Quebec government ministers about this same issue and the possibilities of Quebec being partitioned in the event of independence. In this sense, Plan "B" and the so-called "provocations" it creates may detract from the non-constitutional approach.

Yet, the interaction of the two strategies can be overstated. Even without a Plan "B" the non-constitutional files would not be headline material. They are too complex and technocratic. Also, in the delicate balancing act that Ottawa must attempt, Plan "B" has two distinct target audiences. In addition to persuading Quebecers that secession is an unnecessary, dangerous, and potentially very costly adventure, it is directed also at reassuring Canadians who live outside Quebec that their national government is not standing by idly in the face of the threat of Quebec secession. To the extent that Plan "B" causes Canadians outside Quebec to believe that their interests are being protected, this may help to encourage them to be more open to some of Quebec's demands.

The non-constitutional strategy has not yet run its course from a reconciliation perspective. To the contrary, a strategy for reconciliation among Canadians that relies exclusively on constitutional reform smacks too much of recent failures. When the federal and provincial governments chose the non-constitutional approach, it was for all practical purposes all that was available. Such a declaration may be less true today. But an approach that demonstrates the ability of the federal system to adapt without constitutional amendment remains an essential ingredient to the process of renewing the federation. And the record of the last few years involves considerable achievement.

LOOKING AHEAD

Whether the collaborative federalism that has emerged in recent years should or will continue is an open question. The normative aspect of this issue is considered first.

There is much diversity in the functions of government. At the broadest level, governments set the public agenda by choosing priorities and creating general frameworks within which those priorities are pursued. Governments also do more pedestrian things like designing the details of programs and administering them. Given this diversity, it follows that collaborative federalism can operate at several levels that range all the way from strategic policy frameworks to program administration.

As society and economy become increasingly specialized and interdependent, it is difficult to imagine a world of watertight compartments at the strategic level. By strategic, in this context, we mean several things: the need for the two orders of government to exchange views regarding priorities; the need to identify the areas of overlap in their activities, and to understand the ways in which the behaviours of each may impact on the activities of the other; the need to exchange information regularly about their respective activities in the overlapping areas, and to seek agreement about relative roles and responsibilities in relation to the overlap. In some cases, even more will be needed including agreement about national objectives so that the discussion about roles and responsibilities is taken within the context of a specific public purpose.

The years under review suggest some movement toward this kind of collaboration, including agreement on national objectives. Federal and provincial governments made fiscal restraint a genuine priority during these years.

Through meetings of federal and provincial ministers of finance and their officials, a number of the activities noted in the paragraph immediately above were wholly or partly carried out. More to the point, had there been large differences between the two orders of government on the importance of the fiscal goal, it would have been close to impossible to achieve the success that was experienced in restoring public finances. Note that this conclusion did not require governments to agree on the specifics of how to achieve the desired results. The neighbouring provinces of Alberta and Saskatchewan used quite different methods, for instance, to reach their balanced budget goals.

A second example is in the fairly broad agreement among governments over the last couple of years about the priority attached to social policy renewal. Without such agreement, efforts at protecting and promoting the idea of the social union would have been dysfunctional, as was the case early in the life of the Chrétien government when it attempted to initiate a national social security review. Once again, the more recent agreement did not, and does not, presume collaboration on all aspects of government activity in pursuit of that priority. Moreover, the fact that Quebec remains outside the agreement may eventually limit what is achieved in this broad area.

The principal point here is that in the absence of some measure of cooperation in priority setting, and activities linked to the priorities, public policy risks gridlock. When the role of the state was tiny, as at the time of Confederation, this may not have been true. But the time is long passed when the world of watertight compartments was functional. The Rowell-Sirois report that was published more than a half-century ago chronicled the huge differences between the size of the state in the 1930s and what it had been in 1867. What they found then is, of course, far truer today.

The reality of a PQ government in Quebec City imposes a strain on priority setting nationally. Yet setting aside the PQ's sovereignty project, Quebec's priorities were not noticeably different from those of other Canadian governments. Notwithstanding its apparent disdain for fiscal priorities during the 1994 Quebec general election campaign, the PQ subsequently decided to make a balanced budget a priority. Under Premier Bouchard it has participated in Team Canada trade missions. The Quebec government even agreed with other governments regarding the priority of social policy, including the components of social policy identified by the Federal-Provincial-Territorial Ministerial Council on Social Policy Renewal. This was reflected in the news release from the December 1997 First Ministers' Meeting in which Quebec went on record as "sharing essentially the same concerns" about social policy (even though it did not agree that this priority should be part of the intergovernmental agenda). The fact that the PQ had similar broad priorities may help to explain why, despite some huge political differences with the rest of Canada, the practical "on the ground" policy impact was somehow manageable.

The view that collaboration is a corollary of modern governance in Canada is not intended to suggest that all issues, which in some way involve either directly or indirectly the two orders of government, are best handled through collaboration. There are and will remain areas where the classical model of federalism will continue to serve Canadians well.

Within Canada, however, at the strategic level, the number of areas where governments act completely independently of one another is more likely to decline rather than increase and for much the same reason that national governments find that they must increasingly deal with cross-border issues. The real world is becoming more and more interconnected across geographic regions and subject areas. Accordingly, the need for collaborative federalism can be expected to grow.

Collaboration can be managed well or badly and not all forms of collaboration are equal. Collaboration that requires the agreement of both orders of government on a regular basis, or that requires the agreement of all provincial governments, as well as Ottawa, risks inaction. For example, the decision rule for the AIT, which appears to require a consensus of all governments, is one reason that governments are not moving as swiftly as they had undertaken to meet the various milestones for AIT implementation. Second, collaborative arrangements frequently lack transparency and clear lines of public accountability and this raises questions of both democratic legitimacy and policy effectiveness. Third, intergovernmental arrangements that require all provincial governments to follow the same rules and the same approaches in areas of provincial jurisdiction, perhaps because of some federal government carrot or stick, risk losing the experimentation that federal systems can offer. Such an approach should be the rare exception. Indeed, involuntary collaboration that imposes this kind of commonality in provincial programming is based on the idea that Ottawa is the senior partner in the federation. As such, it offends the federalism principle that is a bedrock of the Canadian compact and is certain to weaken further the fragile political consensus on which the Canadian polity now depends. This list of dangers is not an argument against collaborative federalism so much as it is a set of cautions as governments navigate through its many shoals.

Finally, while collaboration at the strategic policy level may be increasingly necessary, this observation does not in any way presume the need for more collaboration in respect of program design or administration. At this level of governmental activity, we can reasonably expect to see a diversity of programmatic specifics that include both disentangled and collaborative approaches and, even occasionally, federal government unilateralism. Where there is also collaboration at the programmatic or administrative levels, however (for instance, where federal and provincial governments create a "single window" so that citizens can obtain both federal and provincial programs from a common office), it is reasonable as well to expect a clear delineation of exactly which government is responsible for what. Where that occurs, collaboration and disentanglement may be as much complementary activities as they are ideas in conflict.

Leaving aside arguments about the merits and demerits of collaborative federalism, questions also arise about the likelihood that it will continue. It was noted above that Quebec remains a limited partner preferring a more disentangled approach to many issues. Some provinces, notably Ontario and Alberta, may also wish to continue testing the scope for collaboration at the interprovincial level where the issues involve exclusive provincial jurisdiction only.

The emerging position of Ontario merits particular consideration here, not only because it is the largest province but also because, among the provinces, its intergovernmental strategy is the one that is undergoing the largest transformation. Ontario's economy has become more dependent on trade with the United States. Its government was elected following a commitment to shrink and simplify government and cut taxes (in contrast to its predecessor). It also has large grievances against the federal government. Taken together, these factors point to a government with an incentive structure in transition. Where Ontario was once likely to equate its interests with the national interest, the new context suggests more weight on regional, particularly regional economic, interests.[18]

Three conclusions flow from these considerations. First, although Ontario has participated fully in collaborative intergovernmentalism, its enthusiasm for this approach will almost certainly be conditioned by the readiness of Ottawa to respect provincial jurisdiction and the degree to which the approach generates outcomes that address Ontario's priorities. Second, by virtue of its growing dependence on international trade, Ontario has less economic reason than it once did to tolerate the current federal-provincial fiscal arrangements and the amount of implicit equalization that now flows either directly (e.g., CHST, labour market training) or indirectly (e.g., unemployment compensation) from Ontario via Ottawa to the less prosperous regions of the country. It will therefore be a more demanding partner in future federal-provincial negotiations. Yet, and this is the third point, it is also in Ontario's interest to encourage the new collaboration. The more effective that collaboration is, and the better Canada functions, the less the risk that Ontario will have to deal with the disruptive economic and other effects of the secession of a large economic neighbour and partner.

Policy statements by the federal government in the 1997 Throne Speech and the second *Red Book* suggest that the second Chrétien administration may remain on the collaborative course. The circumstances that led the federal Liberals to pursue a collaborative approach in the first mandate, however, are not identical to those that prevail today, suggesting that a change of strategy is within the realm of possibility. In particular, the federal fiscal situation has improved, thus opening the door to Ottawa using financial resources to exercise leadership, which in turn raises questions about the mechanisms it might use for this purpose. Given the federal commitment to not introduce new shared-cost programs in areas of exclusive provincial jurisdiction without a wide measure of provincial support, this suggests direct transfers to individuals or creative use of the income tax system. To the extent that such direct federal initiatives are possible without thwarting or complicating provincial programs in overlapping areas, there can be little objection to them.

But the areas that Ottawa targeted in the 1997 Throne Speech — children, youth employment, health care, and innovation — all involve matters where there is extensive provincial programming. Unilateral federal initiatives in these fields run the risk of generating policy outcomes that are at cross purposes with provincial measures; and in that event, there is an even larger risk of reducing the fragile trust between most of the provinces and the federal government. New unilateral spending initiatives by the federal government in the education or health areas are likely to be particularly unhelpful, in this regard. It is the provincial governments that are now paying the political price for higher postsecondary tuition fees and reduced levels of health-care services which flowed in significant measure from the federal reductions in transfer payments to provinces just a couple of years ago.

These items were discussed at the First Ministers' Meeting in December 1997 suggesting that the federal government has not fixed on a unilateral course. There are different explanations, however, about what is motivating the federal government. It may have avoided new spending initiatives in the above-noted areas mainly because there is still considerable fiscal caution in Ottawa. In this sceptic's view of federal government motives, further spending initiatives are simply being deferred until the second half of that government's electoral mandate when Ottawa's fiscal position is likely to be stronger and the temptation to spend or to reduce taxes for partisan purposes even greater.

The alternative view is that Ottawa, while still less than fully coherent in its federalism strategy, is nonetheless groping toward a more collaborative vision of the federation. *Accordingly, on matters where the federal government has an interest, but there is also undeniable provincial jurisdiction,* it will stay on the table with the provinces until there is agreement among governments.

Collaboration requires provincial support and at times their leadership. The provincial initiative in social policy suggests that most provinces are open to this strategy for managing the federation. If this is so, this leaves much of the onus on the way Ottawa responds.

Collaboration requires hard work and patience, without any certainty of agreement on the issue under discussion. For the federal government, therefore, there is always the risk of gridlock and missing out on short-term political gains. Where there appears to be a public appetite for action, and Ottawa has the tools to act alone, the temptation to act unilaterally will be great.

The dilemma for the federal government is that the short-term gain on any single file may be at the price of long-term pain in terms of federation management. For without increasing collaboration in the areas of overlap, there is the virtual certainty of deteriorating relations between the federal government and the larger English-speaking provinces, as a minimum. If this occurs, then the impact on future efforts at political reconciliation within Canada can only be damaged.

The challenge for the federal and provincial governments is to find a new equilibrium point in federation management. Growing interdependence is a reality of modern society. Managing that interdependence with sensitivity to the federal structure of the polity is crucial to what lies ahead.

NOTES

1. See Edward Greenspon and Anthony Wilson-Smith, *Double Vision: The Inside Story of the Liberals in Power* (Toronto: Doubleday Canada, 1996).

2. The references to statements by the prime minister, on this page and the next, are drawn from Anne Poels, "Chronology of Events 1993-94," in *Canada: The State of the Federation 1994*, ed. Douglas M. Brown and Janet Hiebert (Kingston: Institute of Intergovernmental Relations, Queen's University, 1994); Andrew C. Tzembelicos, "Chronology of Events 1994-95," in *Canada: The State of the Federation 1995*, ed. Douglas M. Brown and Jonathan W. Rose (Kingston: Institute of Intergovernmental Relations, Queen's University, 1995).

3. I am referring here to large-scale constitutional reform.

4. I am aware of no objective evidence to support this claim by political leaders.

5. Ekos Research Associates Inc., *Rethinking Government,* 95-1 (Toronto: Ekos Research Associates, 1995), p. iv.

6. Ronald Watts, *Comparing Federal Systems in the 1990s* (Kingston: Institute of Intergovernmental Relations, Queen's University, 1997), pp. 69-73.

7. Ekos Research Associates Inc., *Rethinking Government 1995, Final Report* (Toronto: Ekos Research Associates, 1996), pp. xx-xxi.

8. I am not arguing here that the provinces accepted easily the cutbacks imposed by the federal government, as will be evident later in this essay. Rather, the point being made is that, given the magnitude of the federal cutbacks, the provincial reaction was remarkably tepid.

9. In the discussions of federal and provincial finance ministers in December 1997, the distribution of the anticipated federal "fiscal dividend" was a significant controversy. Provincial ministers told the media that Ottawa should give higher priority to restoring transfers for existing provincial programs rather than starting new programs that would deliver benefits directly to individuals in areas that

the provinces argue to be in their jurisdiction. See *The Globe and Mail* 10 December 1997, pp. A1 and A10.

10. The statements were reported widely in the media during the meeting of federal and provincial finance ministers in December 1997.

11. Banting's contribution was designed to create the historical context for the other two social policy chapters (and for that reason it concentrates on a time period that is outside the years mainly under review here).

12. Collaborative work is also under way to improve programs to bring persons with disabilities further into the mainstream and to extend the children's agenda beyond the National Child Benefit. In areas of health policy as well, there is a substantial intergovernmental agenda. In these latter three cases, it is too soon to know what the policy results will be, but it is noteworthy that the intergovernmental collaboration appears to be systematic.

13. Michael J. Trebilcock and Daniel Schwanen, *Getting There: An Assessment of the Internal Trade Agreements* (Toronto: C.D. Howe Institute, 1995).

14. A harmonization agreement was signed in early 1998 between the federal government and nine provinces. Quebec did not sign.

15. Richard Simeon and Ian Robinson, *State, Society, and the Development of Canadian Federalism* (Toronto: University of Toronto Press, 1990).

16. Provincial-Territorial Council on Social Policy Renewal, "Progress Report to Premiers No. 2," (mimeo), 1997. Institute of Intergovernmental Relations, *Assessing ACCESS: Towards a New Social Union* (Kingston: Institute of Intergovernmental Relations, Queen's University, 1997).

17. This issue was a significant point of controversy in the public communications of Premier Bouchard at the time of the December 1997 First Ministers' Conference.

18. Thomas J. Courchene with Colin R. Telmer, *From Heartland to North American Region State* (Toronto: Centre for Public Management, Faculty of Management, University of Toronto, 1997).

II

Major Policy Files

2

The Past Speaks to the Future:
Lessons from the Postwar Social Union

Keith G. Banting

Ce chapitre s'appui sur le passé pour informer le futur, en se demandant quelles aperçus peuvent être gagnées de la période après-guerre pour nos débats courants au sujet de l'union sociale. Il examine la structure de l'union sociale mise en place par la génération après-guerre, en mettant l'accent sur les instruments à travers lesquels le gouvernement fédéral appuya l'émergence de programmes sociaux à travers le Canada et les diverses relations fédéral-provincial qui les ont étayées. Le chapitre alors évalue le système après-guerre en termes de trois séries de valeurs de base: les valeurs de politique sociale, les valeurs démocratiques, et les valeurs fédéralismes. Il argumente que l'union sociale après-guerre a contribué fortement à l'accomplissement de valeurs politiques sociales clefs, que ses références démocratiques étaient plus ambiguës, et que le principal défi à l'union social était encré dans les valeurs fédéralismes. Par conséquent, l'histoire de la période après-guerre confirme la dure nature des échanges dont nous faisons face aujourd'hui. La question clef est à savoir quelle série de valeurs prédominera au moment où nous reconcevons notre union sociale pour le prochain siècle.

INTRODUCTION

During the postwar years, Canadians built their own version of the welfare state, establishing a new social contract between citizens and the state.[1] This process was underway throughout the western world, as all countries experienced similar pressures to protect citizens from the social insecurities inherent in industrial society. Canada, however, faced the additional challenge of fashioning its social programs in the context of a federal state and a society divided along linguistic and regional lines. Constructing the welfare state therefore also involved building what would now be called a *social union*, a set of understandings about the balance between federal and provincial social programs, and a set of intergovernmental arrangements to give those understandings life.

The postwar generation had to decide whether there would be a *pan-Canadian* welfare state or a series of distinctive *provincial* welfare states. The social union that emerged in those years was a compromise between these two poles. The system was significantly more decentralized than that in many other federal systems, including countries such as Australia and the United States, but it did incorporate critical pan-Canadian dimensions. Major social programs operated across the country as a whole and established a set of social benefits that Canadians held in common, irrespective of the region in which they lived. In this way, Canadian experience reflected the larger historical trend identified by T.H. Marshall, who argued that the modern welfare state was adding a new dimension to citizenship in western nations, a new set of social rights that individuals hold, not because of their status, class, or region, but by virtue of their common position as citizens.[2]

In the postwar social union, the pan-Canadian elements of the welfare state were associated strongly with the role of the federal government. As the political and economic strength of the federal government has declined in recent years, and as our constitutional tensions have grown, the original social union has come under strain. Increasingly, Canadians are being forced back to first principles in social debate. What is the appropriate balance between pan-Canadianism and regional diversity in the construction of the welfare state? If pan-Canadianism is an important value, are there mechanisms other than federal power through which it can be sustained?

The purpose of this chapter is to draw on the experience of the postwar social union, and to ask what insights, if any, it offers for our current debates about the future accommodation between federalism and the welfare state. The following section examines the basic architecture of the postwar social union, focusing on the instruments with which it was constructed and the diversity of federal-provincial relationships embedded in it. The next section evaluates the postwar system in terms of three sets of core values: social policy values, democratic values, and federalism values. The final section then attempts to distil some tentative lessons from the history of the postwar system that might assist us as we redefine the social union for the next generation.

THE STRUCTURE OF THE POSTWAR SOCIAL UNION

The "social union" is a relatively new concept in Canadian political discourse. Not surprisingly, therefore, there is no consensus on its meaning, and the varied definitions that are emerging invite us down quite different pathways. For some analysts, the social union is essentially a broad social contract, a unifying vision of the social role of the state and a grand design for major social programs.[3] To be successful and durable over time, such a social contract would need to be grounded in a broad consensus on key parameters: the basic relationships among citizens, social groups, and the state; the values that should animate social programs; and the political processes through which social programs are to be designed. This definition of the social union suggests that the current challenge before us is to develop a new collective vision of our social future, a new blueprint for social policy which will replace the vision developed by the postwar generation.

There is no doubt that governance in Canada would be enhanced by a new consensus on social policy. However, a social union in this sense is a dauntingly ambitious project, requiring agreement on an enormous range of ideologically charged issues that go well beyond the relationship between federalism and the welfare state. Our recent constitutional history suggests that comprehensive packages can be sunk by the cumulative political damage inflicted by a wide range of interests each of which is primarily concerned about quite specific component of the total design. Defining a new social contract would certainly test Canadians' collective capacity for consensus and compromise.

For these reasons, this chapter adopts a narrower conception of the social union, one more analogous to the concept of the economic union which is already well established in our political discourse. The core issue from this perspective is the accommodation between the welfare state on the one hand and federalism on the other, and the focus is on the pan-Canadian reach of social programs and the federal-provincial relationships that structure the sector. As we shall see, the issues involved are complex, and securing a consensus on even this conception of the social union is a challenge, requiring hard choices among core values on which contemporary Canada is built.

To understand the basic architecture of the postwar social union, it is useful to examine its basic components: (a) the instruments that the federal government utilized to build a pan-Canadian structure, and (b) the diverse federal-provincial relationships that underpinned the key social programs.

FEDERAL INSTRUMENTS

The federal government utilized three critical policy instruments in developing pan-Canadian social programs: the provision of benefits directly to citizens, federal shared-cost programs in areas of provincial jurisdiction, and equalization grants to poorer provinces.

Direct Federal Programs

Although it is sometimes argued casually that social policy generally is a provincial responsibility, the federal government's own jurisdiction in social policy is substantial, especially in the area of income security. During the middle decades of this century, three formal amendments to the constitutional division of powers gave the federal government complete authority over Unemployment Insurance, and substantial authority in the area of pensions. In addition, under the doctrine of the spending power, the federal government claimed an untrammeled right to make payments to individuals, institutions or other governments for any purpose, and argued that such transfers do not represent an invasion of provincial jurisdiction as long as they do not constitute regulation of the sector.[4] Finally, the federal role in taxation constitutes a powerful instrument in redistributive policies, especially with the development of a fuller array of refundable tax credits and benefits.

On these constitutional footings, the federal government developed a significant direct presence in social policy. In 1940, it introduced Unemployment Insurance, which was later complemented by training and other labour market programs. The federal government also established two universal programs: Family Allowances (1944) which were paid to all families with dependent children; and Old Age Security (1951), which provided a basic pension to all elderly Canadians. In the mid-1960s, the federal government enriched pensions with two additional programs: the Canada Pension Plan, a contributory plan providing earnings-related pensions, and the Guaranteed Income Supplement, an income-tested benefit for the elderly poor. Finally, a Spouse's Allowance for younger spouses of pensioners was added in 1975.

These initiatives established a direct federal presence in the lives of Canadians, and made Ottawa the dominant government in income security. Provincial governments delivered Workers' Compensation and social assistance programs; and Quebec chose to operate its own Quebec Pension Plan, which is closely aligned with the Canada Pension Plan operating throughout the rest of the country. Nevertheless, the federal role was dominant. Figure 1 measures the intergovernmental balance in terms of which government delivered income security payments to citizens. Even though these calculations ignore all federal contributions to the financing of provincial benefits, the preponderant role of Ottawa is clear: the federal government paid out between 70 and 80 percent of all income security dollars directly to Canadians for the entire period from the late 1950s to the early 1990s.

Direct federal delivery created pan-Canadian social programs that, with one significant exception, treated Canadians equally, irrespective of where they lived. Old Age Security, the Canada Pension Plan, the Guaranteed Income Supplement, the Spouse's Allowance, and Family Allowances established uniform benefits and conditions that did not vary from region to region. As such, they represented social rights of the type described by Marshall and other students of the social dimension of citizenship that was emerging in Western nations during the twentieth century. Canadians shared this network

**Figure 1: Federal-Provincial Balance in Income Security
Expenditures**

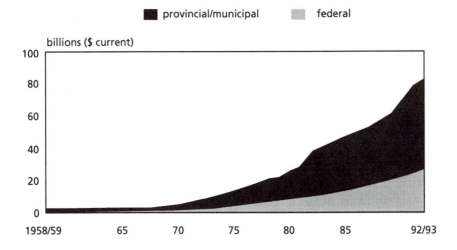

Source: Data supplied by the Caledon Institute of Social Policy.

of benefits and obligations irrespective of the language they spoke or the region in which they lived.

Exceptions to the uniform application of federal income transfers did creep in over time. A minor exception emerged in the mid-1970s when the federal government agreed to vary Family Allowance payments among families of different sizes within a particular province at the request of the provincial government. However, average benefits were to remain equal in all provinces, and in the end only Alberta and Quebec took up this opportunity. The significant exception was Unemployment Insurance. In 1957, coverage was extended to self-employed fishermen, the only category of self-employment so covered, a provision that was particularly important to Atlantic Canada. Later the program was amended such that both eligibility criteria and benefit periods varied according to regional differences in unemployment rates. Although the definition of region for UI purposes did not correspond with provincial boundaries, in practice the level of generosity came to vary significantly by province, especially in later years when cuts to the program fell most heavily on areas with lower unemployment rates. By the mid-1990s, an unemployed person in Newfoundland was twice as likely to be receiving unemployment benefits as an unemployed person in Ontario.[4] Unemployment insurance thus stood out as a regionalized income-security program, and an exception to the general pattern of federal programs contributing to a pan-Canadian definition of the social rights of citizenship.

Shared-Cost Programs

In other parts of the welfare state, the constitution and political realities pointed to provincial responsibility and delivery. In such areas as health care, social assistance and postsecondary education, the federal government therefore relied on the spending power to make shared-cost grants to provincial governments. Under these programs, Ottawa provided substantial financial support to any province mounting a program that met conditions or standards specified in federal legislation. In this way, the federal government stimulated the expansion of key social services, and established a common framework for program design from coast to coast.

The pan-Canadian nature of these programs turned to a significant degree on the terms and conditions attached to federal funding, especially in their developmental stages. The level of specificity in shared-cost programs varied considerably, both over time and from program to program. For example, some of the early shared-cost programs, such as the categorical social assistance programs that were the precursors to the Canada Assistance Plan, did establish relatively detailed conditions, including maximum shareable benefit levels. However, provincial resistance, especially from Quebec, changed that practice, and federal conditions became less detailed. Nevertheless, the federal conditions that were attached to shared-cost programs were important in giving broad shape to provincial programs:

- The most specific and detailed conditions were reserved for medicare. Five principles were embedded in the legislation, requiring provincial health-care programs to provide comprehensive medical coverage, universality, portability, accessibility, and public administration. The federal role, especially when reinforced by the 1984 *Canada Health Act,* was most important in preserving equality of access to health care, and preventing the introduction of user fees in provincial plans. Otherwise, the federal principles left considerable scope for provincial variations in the range of medical services covered and the mix of delivery systems in place.

- In the case of social assistance and welfare services, the Canada Assistance Plan imposed fewer conditions. To qualify for federal support, provinces did have to establish a program that assisted all needy persons, a provision that prevented the exclusion of specific categories of poor people on the US model.[5] Provinces were also required to create formal appeal procedures for beneficiaries, and to agree not to establish provincial residency requirements for social assistance. Within this basic framework, however, there was substantial room for provincial discretion. For example, there were no national standards for actual benefit levels, and provincial generosity has varied significantly.[7]

• Postsecondary education represented the least intrusive federal program, as no conditions were attached to the federal transfer. Provinces were free to spend the money as they saw fit and, after the adoption of block funding in 1977, were even free to divert the money to other sectors. Nevertheless, the funding certainly facilitated the expansion of postsecondary institutions across the country, and it is difficult to believe that smaller provinces in particular would have established substantial university and college systems without the support. Some analysts have also argued that federal funding represented an implicit constraint on provincial discretion, for example, by forestalling the introduction of higher tuition fees for out-of-province students in universities and colleges.

Equalization Grants

Federal equalization grants to poorer provinces constituted the third instrument that sustained pan-Canadianism. These grants were designed to enable the seven poorer provinces to provide average levels of public services without having to resort to above-average levels of taxation. Equalization grants have always been unconditional, and in theory could be used to reduce provincial taxes rather than enhance provincial programs. In practice, however, the equalizing of fiscal capacity among provincial governments led to a more common level of public services generally across the country than would have been possible if provinces had to rely on their own revenues alone.

The power of the equalization system is illustrated by Tables 1 and 2. Table 1 shows the equalizing effects of these federal grants on the fiscal position of the provincial governments. Table 2 illustrates the implications of equalization for health-care, albeit somewhat indirectly. As the first two columns indicate, federal health-care transfers to the provinces are broadly similar across the country, both in per capita terms and as a proportion of provincial health expenditures. Moreover, as the third column indicates, actual provincial health expenditures are also reasonably similar in per capita terms; the differences between high- and low-spending regions are consistent with differences in the cost of providing services in different parts of the country. Yet the fourth column demonstrates that health expenditures represent a much larger proportion of the gross domestic product in poorer provinces than in rich ones, a difference that is only sustainable in the context of a strong equalization program that reduces differences in the fiscal capacity of provincial governments.

Table 1: **Provincial Per Capita Revenues Before and After Equalization as a Percentage of the National Average for Own-Source Revenues, 1987-1988**

	Nfld.	P.E.I.	N.S.	N.B.	Que.	Ont.	Man.	Sask.	Alta.	B.C.
Before	60	64	76	71	85	108	80	90	146	104
After	98	98	98	98	98	108	98	98	146	104

Source: R. Boadway and P. Hobson, *Intergovernmental Fiscal Relations in Canada* (Toronto: Canadian Tax Foundation, 1993), Table 4.7.

Table 2: **Federal Health Transfers and Provincial Health Spending, 1994**

Province	Federal Health Transfer: per capita ($)	Federal Transfer: % of Provincial Health Spending	Provincial Health Spending: per capita ($)	Public Health Spending: % of Provincial GDP
Newfoundland	553	34.3	1,613	10.3
Prince Edward Island	551	37.8	1,457	8.7
Nova Scotia	543	38.2	1,442	8.1
New Brunswick	541	34.1	1,589	8.6
Quebec	543	34.7	1,568	7.2
Ontario	541	31.8	1,702	6.6
Manitoba	535	34.5	1,553	8.3
Saskatchewan	535	36.3	1,474	7.6
Alberta	542	34.7	1,563	5.9
British Columbia	536	30.0	1,787	7.1

Source: Health Canada, *National Health Expenditures in Canada: 1975-1994: Full Report* (Ottawa: Minister of Supply and Services, 1996).

Thus three key policy instruments — direct federal programs, shared-cost programs, and equalization grants — contributed to a pan-Canadian structure of social programs in the postwar social union.

MODELS OF FEDERALISM IN THE POSTWAR SOCIAL UNION

The second basic component of the postwar social union was the complex set of federal-provincial relations underpinning core social programs. Canada did not develop a single, integrated philosophy of federalism to give shape to intergovernmental relations during the postwar period. Instead, the country proceeded in a quintessentially Canadian manner, through incremental, and often ad hoc arrangements for particular programs. In so doing, governments borrowed freely from a number of distinctive conceptions of federalism, and embedded a variety of different models in federal-provincial relations in the social union:

- *Classical federalism:* Some aspects of social policy were delivered by the federal or provincial governments acting independently within their own jurisdiction: Unemployment Insurance, Family Allowances, Old Age Security, and the Guaranteed Income Supplement at the federal level; Workers' Compensation at the provincial level. Historically, this model involved minimal efforts to coordinate the decisions of the two levels of government, even when decisions at one level had significant implications for programs at the other level.

- *Cooperative Federalism*: This term was associated with the traditional shared-cost model that was central to health insurance, welfare, and postsecondary education. Formally, this model involved each government making separate decisions: the federal government deciding to offer financial support to provinces on certain terms; and the provinces deciding whether to accept the money and the terms. In practice, considerable intergovernmental bargaining preceded the introduction of the major shared-cost programs, and the substance of many social programs was hammered out in the crucible of the federal-provincial conference. Nevertheless, these agreements are formally the result of independent decisions, and contain the potential for unilateralism, as became clear as the federal government began to cut its financial commitments to the programs from the mid-1970s on.

- *Co-determination:* In a co-determination model of federalism, the formal agreement of both levels of government is required before any action is possible. Unilateralism is not an option here. In the social policy sector, the strongest example is the Canada Pension Plan, which can be amended only with the agreement of the federal government

and two-thirds of the provinces representing two-thirds of the population of the country. This approach to formal rules-based joint
decisionmaking reflects yet another model of federalism, one much
more analogous to the German system. The institutions differ, since
the provincial governments are not represented in the upper chamber
of the national parliament, as in Germany. But the central dynamic is
similar: nothing happens unless formal approval is given by both levels of government.

- *Confederalism:* This model is purely interprovincial. Although the federal government may play a facilitating role, final agreements are made
  and managed by the provincial governments. In the social sector, the
  initiatives of the Council of Ministers of Education of Canada on comparative testing and other matters reflect this basic approach.[8]

Thus at least four distinct models of federalism were embedded in the postwar social union. Another view of the diversity of intergovernmental relations
in that period can be seen in Figure 2, which displays variations in the extent
and nature of intergovernmental collaboration associated with different programs. The horizontal access measures levels of agreement among provinces,
while the vertical axis measures levels of agreement between the federal and
provincial governments. The lower left corner represents unilateral decisionmaking by governments, as reflected in the classical model of federalism. The
upper right corner represents the co-determination model of federalism, with
its emphasis on formal joint decisionmaking by both federal and provincial
governments according to established rules.

This figure not only highlights the considerable diversity in federal-
provincial relations, but also their dynamic nature. Programs shift from one
pattern of interaction to another over time. The case of health insurance is
particularly revealing here, with the high level of intergovernmental collaboration that eased the introduction of hospital insurance in the mid-1950s fading
somewhat into the more conflictual debate over the introduction of medicare
in the 1960s, and dropping further with the introduction of the *Canada Health
Act* in 1984 against the virtually unanimous opposition of the provinces. A
similar figure capturing trends in the 1980s and 1990s would also reflect an
evolutionary process, with further drift toward unilateralism in the context of
federal budgetary reductions, followed by a reverse trend toward higher levels of intergovernmental collaboration more recently. Federal-provincial
relations in the social policy sector are constantly being reshaped by the wider
political and economic currents in the country.

In summary, the architecture of the postwar social union was complex. The
federal government relied on three major instruments in building pan-Canadian
social programs; and the federal-provincial relationships underpinning those
programs reflected a range of models of federalism. This internal complexity
makes any evaluation of the postwar social union a challenging undertaking.

Figure 2: *Intergovernmental Relations in the Postwar Social Union: Forms and Levels of Collaboration*

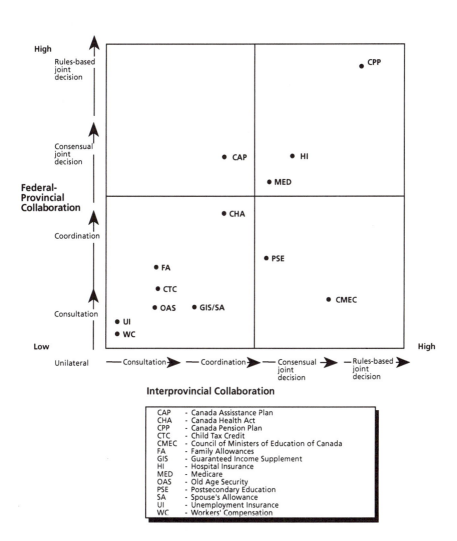

Source: Adapted from M. Biggs, *Building Blocks for Canada's New Social Union,* Working Paper no. F-02 (Ottawa: Canadian Policy Research Networks, 1996).

EVALUATING THE POSTWAR SOCIAL UNION

A comprehensive evaluation of the postwar model turns on both the nature of the social programs that it sustained and on its implications for Canadian governance more broadly. Building on Biggs,[9] one can identify three sets of values central to an assessment of the social union: social policy values, democratic values, and federalism values. Each of these values generates a series of questions that can be used to probe the strengths and weaknesses of the edifice of programs and intergovernmental agreements constructed during and after the Second World War:

- What were the implications of the social union for *social policy values*, such as equity and efficiency, in the design of social programs? In addition, did the social union enhance or frustrate coordination among different programs?

- What were the implications of the social union for *democratic values*? Did it preserve clean lines of accountability between individual governments and their electorates? Was the process sufficiently transparent to inform public debate? Did citizens and social interests believe that the process was accessible to them? Was the process sufficiently flexible to ensure that social programs could be responsive to changes in public preferences?

- What were the implications of the social union for *federalism values*? Did the social union strike an appropriate balance between regionalism and pan-Canadianism? Did the social union contribute toward national unity by building a common vision of the country, or erode that unity by imposing a centralized approach too rigid for its diversity?

This is clearly a sweeping set of questions and, as we shall see, different questions tend to point to different conclusions. In the final analysis, which set of values is to predominate becomes a critical issue.

In using these questions to assess the postwar accommodation between federalism and the welfare state, it is important to compare the results with the outcomes that would likely have flowed from the other historical choice available to the country at the time, which was a more decentralized system. As the Tremblay Commission in Quebec observed in the mid-1950s, expanding the role of the federal government was not the only possible response to at least some of the imbalances that constrained provincial governments during the interwar era. "It is no more difficult," the commission argued, "to add new taxes to the powers of the provinces than to transfer unemployment insurance and old age pensions to the central government."[10] What, then, were the consequences of choosing a semi-centralized welfare state in the postwar period?

THE SOCIAL UNION AND SOCIAL POLICY VALUES

The strongest case for the postwar social union can be made in terms of social policy values. The pan-Canadian dimensions of the postwar social union contributed to higher levels of equity and efficiency in the design of the welfare state than could have been reasonably expected from a more decentralized regime.

Analysts of social programs normally distinguish between two dimensions of equity: *vertical* equity, which involves narrowing the range of inequality between rich and poor; and *horizontal* equity, which involves ensuring that individuals in similar circumstances are treated similarly by public programs. The postwar settlement enhanced both dimensions.

The social union contributed to stronger vertical equity by reducing economic and political obstacles that would have constrained the development of powerful social programs under a more decentralized regime. On the *economic* side, the stronger federal role reduced constraints implicit in fiscal competition among provinces. During the interwar era, provincial and municipal political leaders were very conscious of the implications of the mobility of both capital and labour for social programs. In 1927, for example, the premier of Manitoba wrote to the prime minister on the subject of unemployment in the following terms: "If any City or Province singly adopted plans to solve unemployment, that City or Province would become the mecca to which the unemployed in other cities or provinces would drift."[11] In 1933, the Quebec Social Insurance Commission argued that although family allowances were desirable, a provincial program "would perhaps place our manufacturers in a disadvantageous position with reference to other provinces."[12] The commission went on to argue that:

> ordinary prudence suggests that unemployment insurance should be federal in character. It is very advisable to spread the social responsibilities over the whole country, for otherwise the provinces which participate will find themselves in a condition of inferiority with respect to the non-participants. It must not be forgotten that the expenses involved in social legislation would be incorporated in the net cost of production.... Moreover, the establishment of unemployment insurance in only one province would prove a great attraction to the unemployed in other provinces.[13]

The Rowell-Sirois Commission later summed up the case for federal action on unemployment insurance and old age pensions in almost identical words. "The principal reason ... lies in the readiness of industry in one province to complain if it is taxed for social services which are provided out of general taxation in other provinces or are not provided at all in other provinces.... The employer is placed in a position of competitive disadvantage in comparison with employers where there are not contributory social services."[14]

Clearly, policymakers at both levels of government were impressed by the logic of the mobility of the factors of production in the Canadian economy. The expansion of federal programs in the postwar period offset these constraints by creating the conditions for a broadly comparable tax and benefit regime across the country. None of this implies that provincial welfare states were an impossibility. The mobility of the factors of production did not prevent the diffusion of a number of provincial initiatives in the interwar years, such as workers' compensation and mothers' allowances, across much of the country. Nevertheless, it is unlikely that provincial diffusion would have created as complete or powerful a system as emerged under the postwar social union.[15]

The enhanced federal role also reduced *political* barriers to the expansion of social programs and their diffusion across the country. Throughout much of the postwar era, the federal government played a critical role in forging an ideological compromise among provincial governments on the main directions of social policy. In some cases, such as health care, Ottawa largely adopted a model already proven in one province, and became the instrument of its extension across the country; in other cases, federal leadership in program design was stronger. Its most important political role, however, was to force a pan-Canadian compromise. Although the outcome was not always as robust as more reformist provinces might have wished, it often went far beyond the initial preferences of more conservative provincial governments.

Pensions and medicare provide examples. In his analysis of federal-provincial diplomacy in the 1960s, Richard Simeon concludes that if contributory pensions had been an exclusively provincial jurisdiction in the 1960s, "it is most unlikely that a plan comparable to the CPP would have been enacted."[16] Contributory public pensions were not a provincial priority at the time, and many provinces would undoubtedly have followed Ontario's plan to rely on regulation of the private sector, with employers of a certain size being required to provide occupational pensions.[17] However, federal leadership catapulted a public plan to the top of the national agenda; and in the final bargaining, Ottawa played a critical role in forging a compromise between Quebec's preference for an expansive, redistributive plan and the more conservative design favoured by Ontario.[18]

Similarly, medicare would almost certainly not have spread from Saskatchewan across the country in the absence of federal action. Although Ontario's decision in 1956 to opt for universal coverage of hospital services was important in spurring Ottawa to action, Alberta, British Columbia, and Ontario opposed extending universal public insurance to include physician services in the mid-1960s. These governments sided with the private insurance industry and the medical profession in insisting that public coverage be restricted to the hard to insure, such as the elderly and the poor. Premier Robarts of Ontario went so far as to denounce the new medicare program as "a Machiavellian scheme that is ... one of the greatest frauds that has ever been perpetrated on the people of this country."[19] In the absence of federal action, these provinces would have opted for a more restricted public role in health insurance and, faced with the opposition of the medical profession, several other provinces would likely have followed their lead. However, once the federal shared-cost program was in place and their residents were paying federal taxes to support the program elsewhere, even these conservative governments had little choice but to join the national scheme.

Thus, the federal role overcame important economic and political barriers that would have faced a decentralized welfare state. Undoubtedly, regional pockets of radicalism would still have emerged in a decentralized system. However, diffusion across the country would have been more limited by fiscal and ideological constraints, and the resulting pattern would have not only been more regionally diverse but also less powerful on average. Almost certainly, programs such as the Canada Pension Plan and medicare would not have emerged on a country-wide basis. In effect, a decentralized Canada would have been a more conservative Canada.

The postwar social union also enhanced *horizontal* equity by increasing the extent to which citizens in similar situations were treated similarly by the public sector, irrespective of the region in which they lived. Powerful inter-regional transfers flowed explicitly through equalization grants and implicitly through direct federal benefits to individuals and shared-cost payments to provincial governments, narrowing regional differences in the quality of social benefits that would have emerged from a purely provincial system. The power of this dimension of the social union became apparent even in the early stages of the expansion of the federal role. Table 3 illustrates the impact in the late 1930s and the 1940s by comparing benefit levels in provincial programs that received federal support with provincial programs that did not. Mothers' Allowances, which were financed exclusively from provincial and municipal revenues, did not exist at all in two provinces, and average benefits where they did exist varied by a ratio of almost three to one. In contrast, pensions for the blind and elderly, for which Ottawa shared the costs and set a maximum shareable benefit level, existed in all provinces and average benefits across the country were much more equal. A more contemporary illustration of the importance of the interregional role of the federal government can be seen in the similarity in levels of inequality between rich and poor within the different provinces. As Table 4 indicates, the gini coefficients measuring income inequality within provinces were remarkably similar across the country, and became more so between the mid-1970s and the early 1990s. It is difficult to believe that a more decentralized system would have generated such a pan-Canadian pattern.

Table 3:   **Average Monthly Benefit Levels under Provincial Programs, 1938-1949**

	Mothers' Allowances 1942	Blind Pensions 1938	Old Age Pensions 1938	Old Age Pensions 1949
Prince Edward Island	–	$14.07	$10.63	$34.46
Nova Scotia	$28.55	19.08	14.64	35.33
New Brunswick	–	19.34	13.68	36.01
Quebec	26.64	19.57	17.84	37.63
Ontario	28.91	19.48	18.43	38.05
Manitoba	35.79	18.68	18.66	38.36
Saskatchewan	13.77	19.79	16.45	37.29
Alberta	22.96	–	18.30	37.87
British Columbia	39.19	17.52	19.18	37.26

Source: K.G. Banting, *The Welfare State and Canadian Federalism,* 2d ed. (Montreal: McGill-Queen's University Press, 1987).

Table 4:   **Disposable Personal Income Inequality Across Provinces**

	1975	1987	1991	% Change 1975-1991
Canada	0.293	0.289	0.286	-2.4
Alberta	0.328	0.288	0.284	-13.3
British Columbia	0.289	0.306	0.278	-3.9
Manitoba	0.288	0.279	0.278	-3.5
New Brunswick	0.288	0.283	0.266	-7.8
Newfoundland	0.300	0.284	0.265	-11.6
Nova Scotia	0.286	0.276	0.266	-7.0
Ontario	0.277	0.272	0.273	-1.4
Prince Edward Island	0.284	0.277	0.270	-4.8
Quebec	0.284	0.292	0.273	-4.0
Saskatchewan	0.342	0.298	0.286	-16.5

Note: Data are derived from the Luxembourg Income Study.
Source: T.M. Smeeding, "Trends in Income Inequality: New Evidence from the Luxembourg Income Study," presentation to Queen's International Institute on Social Policy, Kingston, 25-30 August 1996).

Horizontal equity contributes not only to a fairer distribution of public benefits across the country, but also to the *efficiency* of the Canadian economy. Pan-Canadian social programs should constrain economic distortions by reducing formal barriers to mobility in the form of residency requirements on one hand, and by reducing inefficient incentives to mobility in the form of sharply different benefit levels on the other. In effect, a strong social union reinforces the internal economic union. In the postwar version of the social union, formal barriers to mobility were reduced by the prohibition on provincial residency requirements for social assistance in the Canada Assistance Plan and the portability provisions of the *Canada Health Act*. In addition, the pan-Canadian application of federal programs such as Family Allowances, OAS and the GIS, as well as the close integration of the CPP and the QPP foreclosed residency barriers that might otherwise have emerged. Of course, the contribution of the postwar social union to economic efficiency was far from complete. As Courchene and others have argued, the social union established negative prohibitions of certain forms of provincial barriers, but it did not create positive incentives for integration in other areas more fully under provincial jurisdiction, such as the transferability of educational and technical qualifications.[20] Moreover, the increasingly marked regional discrepancies that crept into the federal Unemployment Insurance program over time have weakened the economic pressures for adjustment in labour markets in poorer parts of Canada, indicating that federal jurisdiction is not always a guarantee of equal treatment of Canadians from coast to coast. On balance, however, the postwar social union complemented and reinforced the Canadian economic union more completely than a purely provincial system is likely to have done.

The social union thus scores reasonably well in terms of the values of equity and efficiency. However, when attention shifts to other social policy values, such as the level of coordination among social programs, the record is less positive. Administrators and front-line social service officials regularly despair over the lack of a single, integrated *system* that is rationally designed and easy to administer. This professional orientation received an early expression in the 1943 Marsh Report, which insisted that "the task is to visualize the system as a whole, and to integrate the component units" in a unified structure through strong central leadership.[21] Indeed, Marsh argued that it would be a "catastrophe" if the federal government dominated some programs and the provinces dominated others.[22] However, Marsh's centralized blueprint crashed on the constitutional and regional realities of the country, and the divided jurisdiction described above fell into place.

As a result, problems of coordination and integration across programs were a recurring theme in the postwar politics of social policy. Some of the tensions in health care and other social services were eased in 1978 with the adoption of block-funding for health care and postsecondary education. However, the quest for closer integration of income security programs remained a holy grail throughout the postwar period. Citizens faced a maze of programs offered by federal, provincial, and sometimes municipal agencies; and as a federal policy paper admitted, "somehow the poor citizen is expected to coordinate all of these bureaucracies — a degree of coordination which even governments themselves have been unable to achieve."[23] In addition, as governments increasingly sought to reform income security programs in the 1970s, divided jurisdiction became a major stumbling block.[24] Quebec emphasized the need for provincial control to ensure the *planification* of a single, integrated system. The theme was central to the report of a major provincial commission released in 1971, the Castonguay-Nepveu Report,[25] and the issue figured prominently in the political battles that led to the collapse of the constitutional package negotiated at the Victoria Conference in the same year. Frustration spread to other provinces as well during the subsequent decade, as federal waves repeatedly rocked provincial boats. In 1980, an interprovincial task force complained that provinces had spent most of the decade responding to repeated revisions to Unemployment Insurance, four changes in Family Allowances, the introduction of the Child Tax Credit, and the enrichment of the GIS — each of which had an impact on the management and costs of provincial social assistance programs.[26]

Despite the recurring tensions, little progress was made in developing a mechanism for closer integration of the income-security system. As the interprovincial report emphasized, "there is no agreement on what level of government should co-ordinate and integrate social security programs."[27] In the context of a continuing struggle over jurisdiction, it was difficult to build a culture of intergovernmental collaboration, a step that would have implied the acceptance of the legitimacy of the role of both levels of government in the system. As a result, there was no intergovernmental mechanism in place to help manage the much more serious cuts and program changes in the 1980s and the first half of the 1990s. The resulting damage both to program design and to the federation more widely, as well as the more recent efforts to repair some of the damage through intergovernmental collaboration are discussed elsewhere in this volume.

On balance, the postwar social union contributed powerfully to critical social policy values. It facilitated the emergence of a stronger and more powerful welfare state, enhancing equity in both its vertical and horizontal dimensions; and it reinforced the efficiency of the internal economic union. The failure to develop coordination mechanisms was an important limitation, which became increasingly evident as governments sought to redesign the system they had created in earlier decades. In a wider social calculus, however, the contribution to social policy values was still a positive one.

THE SOCIAL UNION AND DEMOCRACY

The postwar social union also has implications for the democratic values of accountability, transparency, and openness. Here the evaluation is much more mixed, as the implications varied considerably with the different intergovernmental relationships embedded in postwar programs. The classical model of federalism generates fewest objections on democratic grounds: when each government operates independently in its own jurisdiction, accountability is less compromised than in other intergovernmental models. Admittedly, citizens in federal states are often confused about which level of government is responsible for any particular program, even when governments are operating independently in their own jurisdiction. Nevertheless, Family Allowances, the OAS and GIS at the federal level, and Workers' Compensation at the provincial level represented reasonably faithful approximations of the canons of parliamentary democracy. There is a continuing debate about which level within a classical federation is most responsive to its electorate. Some political theorists suggest that provincial governments are inevitably "closer" to the public; but many social groups, at least in English Canada, insist, often vociferously, that the federal government is far more open and responsive than the provinces. The response of disability groups to the Federal Task Force on Disability Issues is simply the most recent example.[28] The federal electorate is inevitably more diverse than that of any single provincial electorate, but there seems to be no particular reason for assuming that federal politicians are less attentive to their electors than their provincial counterparts.

In comparison to the clean lines of classical federalism, models involving stronger forms of intergovernmental collaboration generate tensions with democratic values. Many of the postwar social programs, such as the Canada and Quebec Pension Plans, medicare and the Canada Assistance Plan, were hammered out in the closed world of federal-provincial bargaining. As with international treaties, the resulting agreements represented complex sets of compromises that could not be changed without unraveling completely, and they were normally presented to legislatures, interest groups and the wider public as a *fait accompli*. Moreover, given their intergovernmental parentage, it was difficult for citizens to understand which government should be held accountable on a continuing basis. At the provincial level, priorities and design choices were constrained to some degree by federal policies. On the federal level, Ottawa was transferring substantial sums to provincial governments, for which it often received little visibility and credit, and over which it exercised a decidedly imperfect policy control. Only very knowledgeable citizens could understand the complex interplay of governments that shaped important social programs, and even they would have difficulty in deciding whom to hold accountable for policy failures.

Although these democratic tensions appear in the cooperative model of federalism, they are accentuated in the model of formal co-determination. The Canada Pension Plan is more difficult to amend than most parts of the constitution of the country. Under the existing rules, the federal government, the Ontario government, and a number of combinations of other provinces have a formal veto; moreover, the need for harmonization with the Quebec Pension Plan gives the province of Quebec a special role in the process.[29] As a result, amending the Canada Pension Plan requires a super consensus of the governments of Canada. The result has been a process that is partially insulated from the normal dynamics of democratic politics, and a program that is slow to adapt to changing conditions.[30]

Clearly, one of the lessons that Canada learned in the postwar period is the tension between intergovernmentalism and democratic values. However, the weight of these criticisms should not be overstated. By its very nature, parliamentary democracy concentrates power, and most decisions made by governments within their own jurisdiction are hardly models of open, participatory policymaking. Indeed, in some cases, vigorous intergovernmental conflict over social programs probably enhanced public awareness and debate. Moreover, it is important not to impose contemporary concerns and standards on earlier historical periods. There is little evidence that the Canadian public was upset about the federal-provincial nature of the process that led to the Canada and Quebec Pension Plans, medicare and the Canada Assistance Plan. The danger that the intergovernmental bargaining might mute a wider politics raised few objections beyond the rarified confines of academic discourse; and the remarkably closed nature of the Social Security Review of the mid-1970s sparked remarkably little comment.[31] The contemporary critique of intergovernmentalism is a more recent phenomenon, which was fueled by public reactions to the process of constitutional reform, not the politics of social policy. Overall, the theoretical tensions between collaborative forms of federalism and the canons of democratic theory did not unduly trouble either the Canadian public or their governments in the postwar period.

THE SOCIAL UNION AND FEDERALISM

The deepest challenge to the postwar social union did not flow from concerns about social policy values or democratic values but from the federal nature of the country. From one perspective, the social union seemed to be built on strong federalist foundations. Federalism is not only an instrument for accommodating regional diversity but also for reflecting commonalities; and there was considerable evidence in the postwar period that Canadians across the country shared increasingly similar values about the critical social issues that they confronted in their daily lives. The traditional divide on such issues between Quebec and the rest of Canada narrowed rapidly with the secularization of Quebec society in the 1950s; and public opinion data provided evidence of a broad interregional consensus in public attitudes on social policy. Canadians were divided, to be sure, over the scope and generosity of social programs, but the distribution of opinion did not differ dramatically among regions. Further, the minor regional variations that did exist were not particularly surprising since, with few exceptions, the greatest support for social programs was found in Quebec and Atlantic Canada, the regions with the greatest needs.[32] In effect, pan-Canadian social policy seemed to rest on a pan-Canadian consensus on the social role of the state.

However, the politics of Canadian federalism since the mid-1960s has taught us that a growing interregional consensus on policy does not guarantee agreement on jurisdiction. The last 30 years have been marked by recurring intergovernmental warfare over which level of government should be responsible for social programs. On the surface, some of these battles were about coordination and planning, as we have seen. At a more fundamental level, however, conflict was rooted less in differences over the substance of policy than in diverging conceptions of the nature of Canadian federalism and the appropriate balance between the federal and provincial governments in the lives of citizens. The real challenge was rooted in conflicting conceptions of community. An analysis of questions asked by the Canadian Gallup Poll organization between the years 1949 and 1975 found that regional differences in attitudes were much less pronounced on social issues than on issues relating to the nature of the Canadian community, such as language policy, relations with Britain, and federal-provincial relations.[33] These public orientations were reflected in, and reinforced by, the more general political conflicts within the federation. The rise of the sovereignist movement in Quebec and the wider conflicts among the regions of the country increasingly strained the sense of a common political community on which pan-Canadian social programs were premised.

The crisis of political community and identity gave a new significance to social policy, transforming it into an instrument of statecraft as well as an instrument of social justice. As the regional tensions built up in the federation in the 1960s and 1970s, the federal government argued that a strong federal presence in social policy was an instrument of national unity.[34] Medicare, pensions and unemployment insurance created a set of benefits and rights founded not on region or language but on a common Canadian citizenship. They represented spheres of shared experience in a society marked by considerable regional diversity, and they tied the interests of individuals across the country to the federal state. Given the economic structure of the country, monetary policy, trade policy, and energy policy tended to pit one region of the country against another; given the ethnic and linguistic structure of the country, cultural policies can generate similar conflicts. On social policy, however, Ottawa could fashion appeals that cut across territorial divides, reinforce the legitimacy of the role of the federal government and strengthen Canadians' sense of attachment to their country. In addition, the interregional transfers embedded in the social union represented a shared commitment spanning the continent, serving much the same symbolic function that was served by the railroads in the nineteenth century.

The reaction of provincial governments to this dimension of social policy varied between Quebec and the rest of the country. Provincial governments other than Quebec did not evidence a strong interest in defending their jurisdiction in the postwar years. They lobbied the federal government throughout the 1950s and 1960s to expand its contributions to their social assistance programs, and they generally supported the expansion of the federal government's own income-security programs, which further eased provincial welfare burdens. As we have seen, there were conflicts, sometimes sharp ones, over the design of new social policy programs, such as Ontario's resistance to universal medicare in the mid-1960s; and the provinces expressed frustration over coordination problems in the income-security sector. In addition, provinces complained that federal shared-cost programs introduced rigidities into program design, although the shift to block-funding in 1977 eased many of the irritants, at least in the case of the health sector. In general, however, these conflicts did not congeal into fundamental battles over jurisdiction during the postwar years, and these provinces did not seek to recapture jurisdiction occupied by Ottawa in the heyday of federal influence.

This pattern remained largely intact as long as the federal government remained a substantial financial partner. The dynamic was seriously eroded in the 1980s and 1990s, however, when Ottawa began to reduce its financial transfers without significantly loosening the conditions attached to them. Indeed, the 1984 *Canada Health Act* tightened federal standards in the health sector by establishing penalties for provinces that allowed extra-billing. The legislation was passed in the face of almost unanimous provincial opposition and, although the popularity of the legislation with the public ensured provincial compliance, the tensions simply mounted. As the federal cuts continued year after year, Ottawa's share of the costs of critical provincial services such as health care fell from half to less than a quarter. Provincial governments were left to cope with the intense financial pressure on popular programs, and to face the political fallout from voters when benefits were cut. Not surprisingly, provincial leaders came increasingly to resent federal conditions supported by fewer and fewer federal dollars, and by the mid-1990s many of them began to challenge the basic legitimacy of the federal role.

In contrast, the primary issue for the government of Quebec has always been jurisdiction. Quebec never fully accepted the semi-centralized welfare state that emerged in the postwar era. In 1956, the Tremblay Commission described federal social programs as a form of "federal imperialism" that would erode the province's distinctive character,[35] and this view has been maintained by virtually every provincial premier since then. Successive governments — federalist and sovereignist alike — have sought to capture the full domain of social policy from the federal government. This drive went well beyond the desire of other provinces for release from the constraints inherent in traditional shared-cost programs. Successive Quebec governments also demanded that a wide range of federal programs, including the full range of income-security programs, be transferred to Quebec jurisdiction, and constitutional negotiations from the Victoria Charter to the Charlottetown Accord have turned in part on this demand. Quebec has long been committed to the goal of a Quebec welfare state.

In effect, both the federal government and the Quebec government saw social programs as instruments of community-building and state-building. The political importance of these battles was highlighted by referendums on Quebec sovereignty conducted by the Quebec government in 1980 and 1995. During the 1980 campaign, federal ministers charged that independence would threaten the standard of living of Quebecers, and that a sovereign Quebec would not be able to sustain the social programs that Quebecers enjoyed as citizens of Canada. The federal minister of national health and welfare pointed to the interregional transfers implicit in federal programs that would be lost and told elderly voters that some of their pensions would probably disappear. The contrast with the 1995 referendum could not have been greater. The serious cuts to federal programs meant that federal ministers could no longer pose as defenders of popular benefits, and the separatist forces took the offensive. During the first weeks of the campaign, the *Parti Québécois* charged that only sovereignty could save pensions and other social benefits, and the leadership of the federalist forces in Quebec politics was left trying to explain why Quebecers should stay in a federation that reduced their social benefits. Obviously, the shift from a decisive federalist win in 1980 to a near loss in 1995 cannot be attributed solely or even primarily to the weakening of the federal role in social policy. However, the two battles highlighted the strategic role that social benefits play in some of the most intense moments in Canadian federalism.

MAKING THE PAST SPEAK TO THE FUTURE

Making the past speak to the future is never easy. History speaks with as many voices as there are listeners to hear, and each of us hears those parts of the story that resonate with our own concerns. We are unlikely, therefore, to draw conclusions that will answer definitively contemporary questions about how to build a new social union for Canada. Nevertheless, the history of the postwar social union does at least help to clarify the issues at stake in the current debates.

The basic architecture of the postwar social union leaves lessons. The simple recognition that there were multiple sources of pan-Canadian social policy in the postwar period reminds us that the issues go well beyond the traditional debate about national standards in provincial areas of jurisdiction. Shared-cost programs were only one of the arrows in the federal quiver. If the role of shared-cost programming is increasingly constrained in the future, the federal government can extend pan-Canadianism through the judicious use of other instruments, especially the direct delivery of benefits to citizens through the tax and transfer system. This option becomes increasingly plausible, at least in an incremental way, with the dawning of post-deficit politics in Ottawa. This is not to suggest that instruments are perfectly substitutable, and that direct transfers to Canadians can achieve precisely the same ends as shared-cost programs. But the multiple sources of pan-Canadianism in the postwar model stand as a reminder that the federal role in social policy does not rise and fall exclusively with the shared-cost mechanism.

The diversity of federal-provincial relationships embedded in the postwar social union points in a similar direction. As we have seen, the postwar generation did not elaborate an integrated philosophy of federalism, and the welfare state was undergirded by a diverse set of federal-provincial relationships, reflecting quite varied conceptions of the ideal federal state. Such complexity may be seen as a sign of confusion and weakness by those burdened with excessively ordered minds. But from the perspective of learning from the past, the diversity of relationships and models has important advantages. First, it suggests alternatives to which we might turn when individual approaches, such as cooperative federalism, fall into disfavour. Second, it creates a natural laboratory in which to assess the relative strengths and weaknesses of different approaches to federalism.

An evaluation of the strengths and weaknesses of the postwar social union also leaves lessons. Clearly, the strongest contribution of the postwar social union was in terms of social policy values. The semi-centralized system facilitated the development of a stronger set of social programs across the country as a whole than would have emerged from a decentralized system. Pockets of radicalism, such as Saskatchewan in the health-care sector, would presumably still have developed. But the diffusion of major innovations across the country would have been deeply constrained by the mobility of capital and labour, the ideological diversity of governments across the country, and the inequality in the fiscal capacity of rich and poor provinces. The expansion of the federal role facilitated a common tax and benefit regime across the country, forged ideological compromises among key provinces, and substantially equalized the fiscal capacity of provincial governments. Without that presence, major programs such as the Canada Pension Plan and medicare would not have emerged on a pan-Canadian basis. A decentralized Canada would have been a more unequal Canada.

In theory, one of the problems confronting a decentralized system — the inequality in the fiscal capacity of provincial governments — could have been offset by a system of equalization grants sufficiently powerful to compensate for the interregional transfers implicit in direct federal benefits to citizens and shared-cost payments to provinces. Indeed, the Tremblay Commission, which recommended the transfer of social programs to the provincial level in the 1950s, was quite sanguine about the prospects of such equalization emerging from a confederal compact among the provinces themselves.[36] Even if one sets aside that option as unrealistic, could federally-delivered equalization grants compensate for the transfers implicit in other federal programs? The problem here would be the political durability of one large, consolidated equalization grant. By making explicit all of the implicit transfers, such a grant would certainly attract much more political attention, and probably more criticism from citizens and politicians in rich regions receiving no significant social benefits from the federal government under the decentralized approach. Decentralization plus interregional transfers would have been a high risk strategy for poor regions in the 1950s, and would be today as well.

The only qualification to the largely positive relationship between the postwar social union and social policy values concerns the failure to coordinate federal and provincial programs. The institutional barriers to treating social policy as an integrated system were real, and became more obvious as governments sought to redesign postwar programs. The failure to establish an intergovernmental culture of collaboration in the postwar era is not an inevitable consequence of a federal state, as the current efforts to build a national child benefits program suggest. However, serious and continuing dispute over the division of power between levels of government does complicate the prospects, since the building of systems of collaboration does imply an acceptance of the legitimacy of the role of the two levels of government in social policy, something that Quebec has been unwilling to do.

Despite coordination failures, the overall contribution of the postwar balance in the federation contributed powerfully to social policy values. Not surprisingly, therefore, the weakening of the federal government has triggered anxious questions about the future. In part, the issue is how to preserve existing pan-Canadian social programs such as medicare; and in part, the issue is how to ensure that the country can devise equally effective responses to major social problems that emerge in the future. In the early 1990s, attention focused on the idea of a social charter;[37] and in the mid-1990s attention has shifted to the idea of a confederal model, represented by an interprovincial compact on social policy.[38] Debate on both of these options has been intense, focusing in both cases on the nature of the enforcement mechanism. Unfortunately, the history of the postwar social union offers few insights into instruments that were marginal or non-existent at the time.

   In comparison to its contribution to social policy values, the postwar social
union receives more mixed reviews in democratic terms. Programs reflecting
the classical approach to federalism continued to approximate the canons of
parliamentary democracy, but stronger forms of intergovernmentalism, such
as cooperative federalism and co-determination, created problems for the openness, transparency, accessibility, and clear lines of accountability. The current
shift toward stronger intergovernmental collaboration raises these issues once
again. Informal forms of federal-provincial coordination, such as practised in
the recent reforms to child benefits, are less problematic, although even here
the process was marked by closed negotiations between governments.[39] However, the country may be inching toward the strongest form of executive
federalism, the co-determination model. The commitment in the 1995 Speech
from the Throne that the federal government will not initiate any new shared-
cost programs without the formal support of a majority of the provinces
represents a move in this direction, as does the pressure from provincial governments for a joint process of interpretation and enforcement of the *Canada
Health Act.* The practical limitation on this approach is that it imports into the
social policy sector all of the conflicts that have surrounded recent debates
over the amending formula for the constitution as a whole. The formula governing reforms to the Canada Pension Plan was established in a period when
such issues were much less charged, and it would be extremely difficult to get
agreement on a similar formula today.[40] However, even if this practical limitation could be overcome, it is worth remembering the democratic critique of
such potent intergovernmentalism.
   Having said that, the seriousness of the democratic indictment of
intergovernmentalism in social policy should not be overstated. Canadian
governments are hardly paragons of openness even when operating exclusively
in their own jurisdiction; and certainly in the postwar period Canadians were
not particularly troubled by federal-provincial processes. Contemporary dis-
content with the elitist nature of executive federalism seems to focus primarily
on the process of constitutional reform, and it is striking how few objections
were raised to the largely closed negotiations that have moved forward the
national child benefits program in recent months. In theory, the tension between intergovernmentalism and democracy is clear. In practice, it has not
been the source of the primary challenges to the social union we inherited
from the postwar generation.
   The real challenge comes from the federal nature of Canada. The postwar
social union has important lessons for the ways in which we debate the allocation of responsibilities between levels of government. Historically, theorists
of federalism suggested that matters on which the population across the country largely agreed should be allocated to the central government, while matters
on which regional populations tended to disagree should be allocated to provincial governments. More recently, theorists have also debated the question

in terms of the relative effectiveness of different levels of government. For example, advocates of decentralization often argue in terms of the greater flexibility of the system, with regional governments serving as sources of experimentation in the system; and opponents of decentralization have pointed to the dangers of triggering a race to the bottom, and so on.

The postwar tension between federalism and the welfare state points to a more complicated discourse. In the long term, substantial consensus in regional views on social policy was not enough to sustain the federal role at the heart of the postwar social union. The centrifugal pressures that weakened the postwar structure were not rooted primarily in regional differences over the substance of social policy. Rather they grew from two other sources: fragmenting conceptions of political community and political identity, most obviously in the challenge of Quebec nationalism; and the erosion of federal fiscal strength. Each of these crises had different but powerful consequences for the postwar social union.

The crisis of political identity transformed the debate about the division of powers from a discourse about effectiveness into a discourse about community and national unity. Social programs became cultural instruments, and controversies over jurisdiction took on a political symbolism that has made their resolution more difficult. Advocates of the decentralization of social programs see greater provincial jurisdiction as a means of accommodating centrifugal pressures and preserving the unity of the country. Critics counter that the decentralization of social programs diminishes the presence of the central government in the daily lives of Canadians, and erodes the underlying sense that, at some level, all citizens are part of a common political community with shared commitments and a collective future. Unfortunately, the postwar experience does not offer much evidence on the long-term effectiveness of either of these two strategies. Critics of the decentralist strategy might question whether successive past reductions in the federal role have actually undercut the appeal of sovereignty in Quebec, or whether a uniform decentralization to all provinces can really respond effectively to a challenge rooted in the need for a recognition of the distinctiveness of Quebec. Such critics might also argue that pan-Canadian social programs contribute to francophone Quebecers' sense of attachment to the country.[41] Nevertheless, this is one issue on which history speaks with many voices, and different analysts hear different lessons.

History speaks more definitively about the corrosive effects of the erosion of federal fiscal strength. Provinces other than Quebec did not challenge the fundamental legitimacy of the expanded federal role as long as the federal government was a serious funding partner. It was the long series of reductions in federal financial transfers that slowly eroded provincial acceptance of the federal role. Deep and rapid cuts, such as those in the mid-1990s, were particularly deadly. In the long term, the fiscal crisis may not prove terminal to the federal role, as Ottawa's financial position strengthens slowly in coming years. At a minimum, however, this experience speaks to the need for greater comity and predictability in funding arrangements, to be achieved through a set of ground rules concerning advance notice, consultation, transparency, and publicly discussed formula for the allocation of federal transfers among provinces.

In the final analysis, the experience of the postwar social union confirms the hard nature of the trade-offs before us. Strong pan-Canadian programs proved important to achieving key social policy values; the democratic credentials of the postwar social union were more ambiguous; and the primary challenge was rooted in federalism values. The central issue, therefore, is which set of values are to dominate as we refashion our social union. For some social policy groups, social policy values are fundamental, democratic values such as an accessible policy process represent a close second, and federalism ranks as a very distant third. From this perspective, federalism values should adjust to accommodate other social values. For other critics, federalism is the primary or primordial value, and other concerns must be adjusted accordingly. What is the purpose of a federal state, they ask, if we then create program structures that emulate a unitary state? There is no silver bullet, no magic solution that can easily reconcile such diverse views, and much will depend on the relative weight to be given to the three sets of values. History is silent on the balance that should give shape to a new social union for the decades to come, and the current generation of Canadians must find their own answer to this most fundamental of questions.

NOTES

1. This chapter builds on Keith G. Banting, "Institutional Conservatism: Federalism and Pensions," in *Canadian Social Welfare Policy: Federal and Provincial Dimensions,* ed. J.S. Ismael (Montreal: McGill-Queen's University Press, 1985); *The Welfare State and Canadian Federalism*, 2d ed. (Montreal: McGill-Queen's University Press, 1987); "The Welfare State as Statecraft: Territorial Politics and Canadian Social Policy," in *European Social Policy: Between Fragmentation and Integration,* ed. S. Leibfried and P. Pierson (Washington, DC: The Brookings Institution, 1995); and "The Social Security Review: Policy-Making in a Semi-Sovereign Society," *Canadian Public Administration* 38, 2 (1995): 283-90. The text has been significantly enhanced by excellent research assistance provided by Kate Brown, and by helpful comments on an early draft provided by Harvey Lazar and an anonymous reviewer.

2. Thomas H. Marshall, "Citizenship and Social Class," in *Class, Citizenship and Social Development,* ed. T.H. Marshall (New York: Doubleday, 1964).

3. Margaret Biggs, *Building Blocks for Canada's New Social Union*, Working Paper no. F-02 (Ottawa: Canadian Policy Research Networks, 1996).

4. Canada, *Federal-Provincial Grants and the Spending Power of Parliament: Working Paper on the Constitution* (Ottawa: Information Canada, 1970).

5. Timothy Sargent, *An Index of Unemployment Insurance Disincentives,* Working Paper no. 95-10 (Ottawa: Department of Finance, Fiscal and Economic Analysis Branch).

6. In the US, the AFDC program generally provided support to mothers with dependent children only, excluding single people and childless couples.

7. National Council of Welfare, *Welfare Incomes, 1995* (Ottawa: National Council fo Welfare, 1996).

8. Tom Courchene's recent proposal for an interprovincial accord among provincial governments to sustain pan-Canadian social values represents another example of the confederal model. See Thomas Courchene, "ACCESS: A Convention on the Canadian Economic and Social Systems," Working Paper prepared for the Ministry of Intergovernmental Affairs (Toronto: Government Printers, 1996); and *Assessing ACCESS: Towards a New Social Union* (Kingston: Institute of Intergovernmental Relations, Queen's University, 1997).

9. Margaret Biggs, *Building Blocks for Canada's New Social Union.*

10. Quebec, Royal Commission of Inquiry on Constitutional Problems, *Report* (Quebec: Éditeur officiel, 1956), vol. 2, p. 320.

11. Banting, *The Welfare State and Canadian Federalism*, p. 64.

12. Quebec, Social Insurance Commission, *Report* (Quebec: Éditeur officiel, 1933), p. 108.

13. Ibid., p. 203.

14. Canada, Royal Commission on Dominion-Provincial Relations, *Report* (Ottawa: King's Printer, 1940), vol. 2, pp. 36, 40-1.

15. For an analysis in terms of rational choice theory that points in the same direction, see Dan Usher, "How Should the Redistributive Power of the State be Divided between Federal and Provincial Governments?" *Canadian Public Policy/ Analyse de Politiques* 6 (1980): 16-29.

16. Richard Simeon, *Federal-Provincial Diplomacy: The Making of Recent Policy in Canada* (Toronto: University of Toronto Press, 1970), p. 270.

17. Quebec was the only province to have shown any interest in contributory pensions, but such a program was not a priority of the Quebec government until Ottawa launched its initiative, see Simeon, *Federal-Provincial Diplomacy*, pp. 45-46; Kenneth Bryden, *Old Age Pensions and Policy-Making in Canada* (Montreal: McGill-Queen's University Press, 1974), p. 164.

18. Banting, "Institutional Conservatism"; Bryden, *Old Age Pensions and Policy-Making in Canada.*

19. Quoted in Malcolm G. Taylor, *Health Insurance and Canadian Public Policy: The Seven Decisions that Created the Canadian Health Insurance System* (Montreal: McGill-Queen's University Press, 1987), p. 375.

20. Courchene, "ACCESS."

21. Marsh, *Report on Social Security in Canada* (Toronto: University of Toronto, [1943] 1975), pp. 52-55 and *passim.*

22. Ibid., p. 251.

23. Canada, *Working Paper on Social Security* (Ottawa: Information Canada, 1973), p. 15.

24. Rodney Haddow, *Poverty Reform in Canada, 1958-1978: State and Class Influences on Policy Making* (Montreal: McGill-Queen's University Press, 1993); Christopher Leman, *The Collapse of Welfare Reform: Political Institutions, Policy and the Poor in Canada and the United States* (Cambridge, MA: The MIT Press, 1980).

25. Quebec, Commission of Inquiry on Health and Social Welfare, *Report* (Quebec: Éditeur officiel, 1971).

26. Interprovincial Conference of Ministers Responsible for Social Services, *The Income Security System in Canada* (Ottawa: Canadian Intergovernmental Conference Secretariat, 1980), ch. 4 provided an excellent analysis of the administrative tensions among income security programs.

27. Ibid., p. 113.

28. Canada, Federal Task Force on Disability Issues, *Equal Citizenship for Canadians with Disabilities: The Will to Act* (Ottawa: Minister of Supply and Services, 1996).

29. Although the Canada Pension Plan does not operate generally in Quebec, a number of Quebec residents do contribute to the fund, and the government of Quebec counts in the amending formula for the CPP itself. Thus, a combination of Quebec and another smaller province could conceivably also block a change.

30. Banting, "Institutional Conservatism: Federalism and Pensions."

31. The contrast with the process of the social security review initiated by the federal government in 1994 in the context of wider public dissatisfaction with intergovernmental elitism was dramatic. See Keith G. Banting, "The Way Beavers Build Dams: Social Policy Change in Canada," in *A New Social Vision for Canada: Perspectives on the Federal Discussion Paper on Social Security Reform,* ed. K. Banting and K. Battle (Kingston: School of Policy Studies, Queen's University, 1994) and "The Social Security Review: Policy-Making in a Semi-Sovereign Society."

32. For a review of public opinion data in this period, see Banting, *The Welfare State and Canadian Federalism,* ch. 8.

33. Donald Blake and Richard Simeon, "Regional Preferences: Citizens' View of Public Policy," in *Small Worlds: Provinces and Parties in Canadian Political Life,* in D. Elkins and R. Simeon (Toronto: Methuen, 1980).

34. See, for example, Canada, *Income Security and Social Services* (Ottawa: Information Canada, 1969), especially p. 68. For a wider discussion of social policy as an instrument of social integration, see Banting, "The Welfare State as Statecraft."

35. Quebec, Royal Commission of Inquiry on Constitutional Problems, *Report.*

36. Ibid., vol. 2, pp. 288-94.

37. Ontario, *A Canadian Social Charter: Making Our Shared Values Stronger* (Toronto: Ministry of Intergovernmental Affairs, 1991).

38. Courchene, "ACCESS."

39. Richard Zucker has labelled this form of collaboration "reciprocal federalism" in Richard Zucker, "Reciprocal Federalism: Beyond the Spending Power,"1995, mimeo.

40. The CPP formula gives a formal veto to Ontario but to no other single province.

41. Keith G. Banting, "Cultural Diversity, Citizenship and Social Rights," paper presented to the Conference on Citizenship, Diversity and Pluralism, University of Saskatchewan, 31 October – 1 November 1997.

3

Reducing the Muddle in the Middle:
Three Propositions for Running the Welfare State

John Richards

Cet article essaie de répondre à la question à savoir comment mieux gérer les programmes sociaux dans un état fédéral. En résumé, l'article avance trois propositions.

La première insiste sur des budgets balancés en utilisant des procédures comptables crédibles. La politique sociale repose sur le consentement de la majorité. Une condition nécessaire pour le consentement est que les citoyens aient une idée juste au sujet des coûts des programmes, en termes des taxes qui devront être payées.

La seconde proposition concerne la responsabilité. Seul un niveau de gouvernement devrait en général être responsable pour un domaine particulier de politique sociale, et le gouvernement responsable devrait se procurer les revenus nécessaires selon ses propres sources de taxation. La responsabilité veut dire que le gouvernement responsable peut simultanément présenter de nouveaux programmes et enlever les vieux qui relèvent de son domaine, et que les citoyens par des élections démocratiques peuvent récompenser le gouvernement pour de bons résultats et punir pour les mauvais.

Un corollaire est de minimiser le rôle des cours et des agences coordinatrices intergouvernementales compliquées dans la politique sociale. Inévitablement, des programmes défieront l'affectation à l'un ou l'autre des niveaux de gouvernement. Par conséquent, il y aura toujours "un désordre dans le milieu." Un autre corollaire est que l'organisation de ce milieu sera compliquée, et sa taille devrait être gardée au minimum.

La troisième proposition concerne l'avantage comparatif. Ottawa a un avantage comparatif dans la livraison de programmes qui redistribuent le revenu selon des règles relativement directes, mais la plupart des programmes sociaux impliquent une administration complexe et, dans ces cas, la juridiction provinciale devrait primer. Qu'arrivera-t'il des provinces plus pauvres? Un programme d'égalisation fiscale à travers les provinces est une contribution fédérale valable à la politique sociale. À part l'égalisation, les transferts intergouvernementaux sont de façon générale à être évitées.

INTRODUCTION

From the beginning of civilized discourse people have disagreed, often passionately, over what mutual obligations they owe to their community — over what, in our secular age, is called social policy. This chapter contains little advice on what social policy should be. Instead, it provides advice on how to organize passionate disagreement. That advice is summarized in three propositions and the bulk of this chapter makes the case for these propositions which, in the interest of providing an outline, are listed below:

- *Proposition One: Never separate the case for generous social policy from the case for balanced budgets.* The welfare state rests on the democratic assent of the majority. A necessary condition for that assent is that citizens have a fair idea of both program benefits and their costs, in terms of taxes to be paid.

- *Proposition Two: Accountability matters. One — and only one — level of government should in general be responsible for any particular domain of social policy, and the responsible government should be required to raise necessary revenues via own-source taxation.* In a federation, as in any other form of government, accountability is crucial to the long-run success of government initiatives. Accountability means that the responsible government can simultaneously introduce new policies in its domain and scrap old ones, that citizens know the tax cost of social programs, and that citizens have a clear means — democratic elections — whereby they can reward their governments for good outcomes and punish them for bad. The first corollary is to minimize the role of the courts and of complex intergovernmental coordinating agencies in social policy. Successful welfare states require good politicians and administrators, not good judges or diplomats. They need good administrators to run a respectable welfare state, and good politicians to lead and heed public debate over social policy. Even the best of judges and intergovernmental diplomats are poor substitutes. Inevitably, some programs defy allocation to one or other level of government. Hence, there will always be a "muddle in the middle." A second corollary is that organization of this middle will be convoluted, and its size should be kept to a minimum.

- *Proposition Three: Respect comparative advantage, and celebrate competitive federalism. Ottawa has a comparative advantage in delivery of programs that redistribute income according to relatively straightforward rules, but most social programs entail complex administration and, in such cases, provincial jurisdiction should prevail.* Reconciling provincial paramountcy in most areas of social policy with the requirements of accountability poses a problem: What about poor provinces with insufficient fiscal capacity to raise sufficient revenue for a reasonable set of social programs? A program of fiscal equalization across provinces is a valuable federal contribution to social policy. Beyond equalization, intergovernmental transfers are generally to be avoided.

Before proceeding with the main argument, however, it is useful to digress briefly on the nature of social policy. It entails three dimensions.

THE THREE DIMENSIONS OF SOCIAL POLICY

The first and most obvious dimension of social policy is the extent to which the non-poor should redistribute income to the poor. Social assistance programs use general tax revenue to provide targeted benefits for the poor. Hence the first source of debate: how much redistribution to undertake? If social policy concerns only this dimension, and if people across the country give similar answers to this question, then the central government has a comparative advantage over subnational units. The central government can assure redistribution corresponds to citizen preferences. Furthermore, uniform tax and benefit rules avoid inefficient migration of people out of high-tax regions and into high-benefit regions.

Most social programs do more than redistribute income. Many simultaneously improve economic efficiency by overcoming a "failure" inherent in particular markets. To illustrate, in Canada, as in most industrial countries, health insurance is funded primarily from general tax revenue; citizens do not pay actuarially fair premiums. Accordingly, this is a social program that redistributes, in the form of health services, toward low-income and high-risk citizens. (These two groups overlap but are not identical.) It is also an example of using social policy to correct several market failures, one of which is the inefficiency associated with the buying and selling of private health insurance. In a private market, insurees want maximum coverage at the lowest possible cost and have a strong incentive to hide risk factors that point to a high probability of expensive claims. Insurers have a strong incentive to deny liability. The result is cheating by both parties, costly monitoring to discourage cheating and far-from-universal insurance coverage for high-risk patients. Pooling everyone into a universal health insurance plan can dramatically lower such costs. According to a US Congressional study,[1] the per capita cost of insurance overhead under the Canadian system, where provinces operate "single-payer" insurance systems for their entire populations, is approximately one-fifth the per capita cost in the United States where private health insurance is the norm.

That Canada has addressed the "failures" of health markets more aggressively than in the US is shown by the post-1960 divergence in health-care costs between the two countries. Prior to adopting "socialized medicine,"

Canada and the United States both spent about 6 percent of GDP on health care. By the mid-1990s, Canada was spending below 10 percent, and the US above 14 percent. Incidentally, by simple measures of health status (infant mortality and average life expectancy), Canada has maintained a slight but consistent edge over the US throughout the last three decades.[2]

Debating health policy accordingly entails debate over at least two dimensions: the extent to which government should redistribute, and the extent to which it can improve economic efficiency in an important sector of the economy.

That is not all. Health care is a social policy that embodies the third and most controversial dimension: use of government to realize certain widely shared values. The majority in most industrial countries insist everyone must have basic health insurance; they treat it as a "merit good." Regardless of the wealth or poverty of my neighbour, regardless of his or her preferences, regardless of the relative efficiency of market versus single-payer insurance systems and independent of whether the illness is communicable to me, I do not want him or her to face significant financial costs in seeking health care if and when it is needed. Accordingly, I am not prepared to let them choose to spend their money freely in this instance. I vote for a political party that obliges us to pay taxes that support a universal health insurance program.[3]

In summary, it is useful to think of social programs as government activities having one or more of the following goals: to redistribute income, to redress market "failures" where redress has a major redistributive effect, and to realize certain widely shared values concerning distribution of "merit goods." Once we allow that social programs entail the second and third dimensions, it is not surprising that social policy is contentious. It cannot be reduced to rules incorporated in an income tax system; it inevitably entails complex administrative and policy decisions that in turn require responsible politicians, professional administrators and dedicated service providers.

Proposition One: Never separate the case for generous social policy from the case for balanced budgets. It would have been far, far better for Canadian social policy if Canadian senior governments had engaged in fiscal restraint earlier — before the demand placed on social programs by the early 1990s recession forced spending up and, given high debt, also forced governments to raise taxes; and before debt-service costs became a cancerous growth squeezing the fiscal resources required for other programs. No one can be certain as to what would have happened had some particular event in the past been different. But, had the political leadership of the centre and left, federally and provincially, not succumbed so completely to an opportunistic Keynesian discourse that ridiculed the task of balancing the books, Canadian senior governments would probably have eliminated deficits much earlier, with less disruption to social programming.

For illustrative purposes, I pick on the federal Liberals. They are not the only set of Canadian politicians to have ignored this first proposition and, by 1997, the majority of Liberals had learned to respect it. The great irony of the 1997 general election is that many Canadians voted Liberal because the party did what, in 1993, it had ridiculed the Tories for having promised. Starting with the 1995-96 budget, Ottawa credibly set about the task of cutting its coat to the size of the available cloth.

I start with the Liberals' 1993 election manifesto, the famous *Red Book*. In it they quoted James Tobin, a prominent elder statesman among Keynesian economists, on the potential economic costs that deficit reduction might induce and they dismissed the Tory target for balancing the budget:[4]

> the Conservatives have set another unrealistic target [in the 1993-94 budget] by promising to eliminate the deficit in the next five years.... Any responsible government must have as a goal the elimination of the deficit. That is our goal. Given the current state of the economy, a realistic interim target for a Liberal government is to seek to reduce the federal deficit to three percent of [GDP] by the end of its third year in office [i.e., by the 1996-97 budget]. To achieve this target, cutting expenditures alone, as the Conservatives are proposing, will not be sufficient. Faster economic growth and reduction of unemployment is a prerequisite for sustained deficit reduction.[5]

Were the *Red Book* merely election propaganda, such waffle would be unsurprising. But it was more than propaganda; it was an earnest attempt among policy-oriented Liberals to synthesize their ideas. On fiscal matters, this amounted to an opportunistic Keynesianism which, reduced to its core, goes roughly as follows. Faced with recession and unemployment, governments should stimulate demand by deficit spending and by expansionary monetary policy which lowers interest rates; a resurgent economy will generate the revenues necessary to eliminate the deficit. Cutting expenditures is inevitably counter-productive: it will lower aggregate demand, exacerbate unemployment and the demand for redistributive social programs.

The prevalence of this discourse distorted macroeconomic debate far too long. In 1993, John Crow (champion of restrictive monetary policy) and Ralph Klein (premier of a province actually engaged in fiscal restraint) were the personification of error for Liberals. The only other senior government which, at the time, had a credible fiscal program to restore balance was Saskatchewan, led by Roy Romanow. The anomaly of a NDP government reducing spending was beyond the ken of conventional wisdom; it was politely ignored.

I do not want to use irony to gloss over the complexity of debates surrounding appropriate macroeconomic policy. Here, I make a simple observation. Tight monetary policy becomes a logical outcome in a country whose political leadership refused the discipline required to balance budgets. Variants of this opportunistic Keynesianism were practised by most senior Canadian governments over the two decades prior to 1995.

Take as example the economic boom in the late 1980s. Both the federal and provincial governments — here the Liberal government at Queen's Park was the prime culprit — should have dampened aggregate demand by aggressive fiscal restraint. Had this occurred, inflation would probably not have increased in the final years of the decade, and the case for restrictive monetary policy would have been less convincing. Far from assessing the possibility of renewed inflation, the federal Liberals congratulated their provincial colleagues for new spending programs at Queen's Park, and did their utmost to undermine the modest exercise in fiscal restraint being practised by their Conservative opponents in Ottawa. John Crow's policies undoubtedly amounted to overkill; they unnecessarily increased interest rates in 1990 and deepened the ensuing recession. Intellectual honesty demands, however, that any critique of monetary restriction be accompanied by a critique of the failure of Canadian politicians to respect this first proposition.

Opportunistic Keynesians sin by omission. They ignore the politically painful half of fiscal stabilization: that governments must run fiscal surpluses to damp the inflationary potential of economic booms and to maintain the financial capacity to run deficits during recessions. When the majority of the political elite subscribe to some variant of opportunistic Keynesianism, the exercise of fiscal discipline becomes highly controversial. It requires more political courage than the typical government is capable of mustering. When, for whatever reason, inflation worsens and people call on governments for a response, most perceive monetary policy as the only feasible option.

The federal Liberals' 1995-96 budget marks a genuinely important break with past Canadian practice. We can trace the evolution of official Liberal thinking via a series of major documents, each identifiable by the colour of its cover. The appropriate point of departure is the scarlet-coloured *Red Book*. There followed the Grey and Purple Papers, the Green Paper, and the collected White Papers.

By the time the Liberals began preparing their first budget, 1993's scarlet maple leaves were buried beneath the snow. In January 1994 the Department of Finance published three sober documents on the state of the country's finances.[6] These background documents and the 1994-95 budget[7] were all bound in white covers. A neutral white symbolized that the Liberals' initial intent was, in aggregate, to change little. The Liberals projected an identical spending level for the next two years (1994-95 and 1995-96) to that undertaken by their predecessors in their previous two budgets.

Financial markets responded sceptically. Bankers discussed the possibility of a collapse in demand for bonds issued by Canadian senior governments (similar to what had occurred in Mexico in late 1994). Interest rates on Canadian public debt rose in spring 1994, and it became clear that debt-servicing costs would exceed budget projections. Finally, to use an appropriate image, the penny dropped. Cabinet agreed to abandon the *Red Book's* waffle and actually balance the books. Given already high tax rates, this required lower program expenditures.

As was to be expected, the government was less than perfectly consistent in its conversion to fiscal rectitude. In the fall of 1994, for example, the Liberals continued with its major social policy review by publishing a Green Paper which contained a number of sensible reforms.[8] But, in it, the Cabinet avoided costing social programs and establishing priorities appropriate to a smaller total budget. Shortly after the Green Paper, the Department of Finance published its Grey and Purple Papers.[9] Here were two blunt policy statements, clothed in suitably subdued colours, intended to prepare Canadians for the 1995-96 budget.

Via the Grey Paper, the Liberals admitted that, using the Finance Department's base-case projection (the "prudent scenario"), realizing even the modest *Red Book* target of a deficit below 3 percent of GDP by fiscal 1996-97 required a combination of tax increases and program expenditure cuts not envisaged in the 1994-95 budget. The Grey Paper also undertook a useful disaggregation and description of the major categories of public spending. Using a definition consistent with the above discussion, social spending accounted for nearly two- thirds of the total.[10] The message was clear: any serious exercise in deficit elimination meant cuts to social programs.

The most ambitious of all these documents was undoubtedly the Purple Paper. Here was a well argued attempt to provide what the title promised — "a new framework for economic policy." No one could accuse the Finance Department of opportunistic Keynesianism. It bluntly argued the antithesis, calling for an end to deficit spending as the prerequisite for good social policy:

> The debt and deficit are often portrayed as issues primarily of concern to financial markets and ideologues. The truth is that those who suffer most immediately from Canada's fiscal deterioration are the unemployed, the poorer regions of the country, and the average young to middle-aged family with a mortgage and other debt incurred to raise and educate their children. The unease of financial markets in the face of Canada's debt spiral translates directly to higher loan and mortgage payments for the average Canadian. And the relentless compounding pressure of interest costs on the public debt is severely eroding the abiity of the government to provide for Canada's less advantaged citizens and regions. The social consequences of debt are every bit as grim as the economic.[11]

Beyond making the case to end deficit spending, the fundamental recommendation was that government policy be judged on its ability to help Canadians adapt to market change, as opposed to its ability to protect Canadians from change. For example, the Purple Paper stressed government's role in helping workers acquire new skills, as opposed to its role in providing passive income support. On the subject of UI reform, it stated bluntly: "more will be needed to return UI closer to insurance principles and to create programs that improve job readiness."[12]

The final document in this kaleidoscope is the actual 1995-96 budget, with its suitably sober dark grey cover.[13] The budget reduced by a quarter inter-governmental transfers and transformed all remaining transfers into block grants; it cancelled the century-old Crowsnest Pass transportation subsidy to prairie farmers; it reduced the dairy subsidy and international aid; it required significant civil servant layoffs. It announced further cuts to UI and hinted at future reductions in pension benefits. Relative to the past generation of Canadian federal budgeting, all this was a radical departure. Admittedly, relative to the wrenching fiscal adjustments undergone by some other industrial countries — from Sweden to the UK and New Zealand — the changes were modest. And the net result was no more than a lowering, by 1996-97, of the projected federal deficit below the threshold of 3 percent of GDP.

One means to appreciate quantitatively the significance of the watershed 1995 budget is to compare the revenue and expenditure projection made by the Tories in their last budget,[14] tabled in 1993, with actual outcomes. Here, in point form, are a few observations based on Figure 1 and Table 1 and the 1997 budget.[15]

- Relative to 1994-95 levels, the Liberals expect to have lowered (nomi-nal dollar) program spending by 11 percent in 1998-99. The key break occurred obviously in 1995.

Figure 1.1: Overcoming Debt Denial, Program Spending

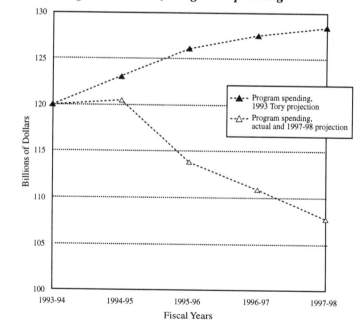

Figure 1.2: Overcoming Debt Denial, Debt-Service Costs

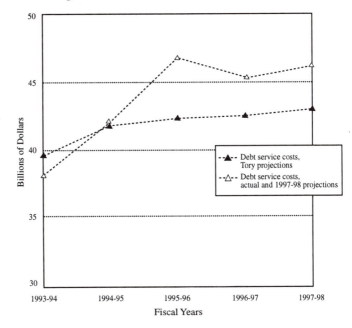

Figure 1.3: Overcoming Debt Denial, Revenues

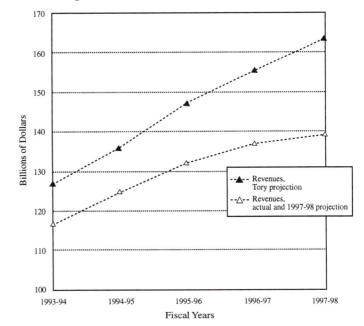

- The Liberals accepted that public resistance to discretionary tax increases is sufficiently potent that federal tax revenues cannot be
  increased faster than GDP. The federal tax-GDP ratio accordingly remained constant throughout the Liberals' first term in office. It ranged
  between 16.5 percent and 17 percent of GDP.[16]

- Even with the recent decline in interest rates and federal expenditure
  restraint, federal debt-service costs are well above levels projected by
  the Tories in 1993, and are approaching one-half the total of all program spending. For 1997, federal debt-service costs are now greater
  than the value of all program spending by the Government of Ontario.

- Despite this exercise in fiscal redress, the net federal debt as a share
  of GDP continued to rise until 1996-97, at which point it reached 74.4
  percent,[17] four times the corresponding statistic in the early 1970s.
  Finally, in 1997-98, this ratio began to decline.

In concluding discussion of this proposition, a final argument is addressed
to those who instinctively mistrust the linking of social policy to the setting of
fiscal limits. If Ottawa balances its budget by fiscal 1998-99, as appears likely,
and if Ottawa accepts that the tax-GDP ratio has reached a ceiling, does that
mean such a large contraction in per capita program spending as to threaten
the health of Canadian social programs?

By way of answer, I refer to a modest study published by the C.D. Howe
Institute in 1994. With the inspirational title, "The Courage to Act," it was
published after the Liberals' first do-nothing budget and before the do-
something-serious 1995 budget.[18] The study undertook a simple exercise to
estimate the magnitude of federal program spending cuts required, assuming
that Ottawa would balance its budget in fiscal 1998-99, (which is effectively
the projection of the 1997 budget),[19] and assuming that revenues would rise in
proportion to GDP, that is, no increase in the tax-GDP ratio would take place.
The conclusion was that program spending would need to be about 12 percent
below 1994 levels, a reduction similar to current projections for fiscal 1998-
99. (Table 1 shows the magnitude of program expenditures in 1994-95 and
current projections for 1998-99. We shall return to the disaggregated figures
below.)

If the Canadian population grows by 5 percent between 1994 and 1998, a
cut of 12 percent in program spending implies an average per capita cut of
17 percent. This may appear draconian. It is not if placed in historical perspective. If both the federal *and* provincial governments reduce 1994 program
spending by that amount by 1998, per capita program spending in constant
dollars will be at levels prevailing in the early 1980s, hardly a time of the
minimal state in Canada.

A corollary to this proposition is that governments must present budgets to
their respective legislatures in a transparent manner that allows legislators

Table 1: The Liberals' Exercise in Fiscal Restraint: Changes in Federal Program Spending, 1994-95 to 1998-99

		1994-95	1998-99	Change	
		($ billion)		$	%
1	Elderly benefits	20.5	22.9	2.4	12
2	Labour adjustment	14.8	14.1	-0.7	-5
3	Indian and Inuit	3.7	4.4	0.7	19
4	Canada Health and Social Transfer (CHST)[a]	19.3	12.5	-6.8	-35
5	Other transfers to territories and provinces	0.7	1.1	0.4	57
6	Equalization	8.5	8.4	-0.1	-1
7	Business subsidies and other transfers	16.3	10.1	-6.2	-38
8	Crown corporations	5.0	3.8	-1.2	-24
9	Defence	10.7	8.5	-2.2	-21
10	Other[c]	21.0	21.0	0.0	0
11	Total, program spending	120.5	106.8	-13.7	-11
12	Total, major program spending to individuals (1.+2.+3.)	39.0	41.4	2.4	6
13	Total cash transfers to other governments (4.+5.+6.)	28.5	22.0	-6.5	-23
14	Total, program spending less major program spending to individuals and transfers to governments (11.-12.-13.)	53.0	43.4	-9.6	-18
15	Total, program spending excluding CHST (11.-4.)	101.2	94.3	-6.9	-7
16	Debt-service charges	42.0	46.5	4.5	11
17	Budgetary revenues[b]	125.0	146.2	21.2	17
18	Deficit (-)/surplus (+) (17.-11.-16.)	-37.5	-7.1	30.4	

Notes:

a. This figure includes cash transferred plus the value of Quebec's extra tax points which serve to lower what otherwise would be federal transfers to that province. The value of these extra tax points is deducted from the cash transfer to Quebec. Hence, the figures shown exceed actual cash transferred. The 1994-95 figure includes the cash transfers (plus value of Quebec's extra tax points) under the Canada Assistance Plan and Established Program Financing; the 1998-99 figure includes the cash transfer (plus value of Quebec's extra tax points) under the Canada Health and Social Transfer. The figure cited, $12.5 billion, includes the electoral promise of an additional $0.7 billion made by the Liberals during the 1997 election campaign.

b. By an argument analogous to that in note a, this value exceeds actual revenues received by an amount equal to the value of Quebec's extra tax points.

c. The figure cited, $21.0 billion, includes $0.3 billion, the estimated cost of electoral promises other than the $0.7 billion increase to the CHST.

Source: adapted from Canada, Department of Finance, *Budget Plan* (Ottawa: Department of Finance, 1997), p. 64.

and citizens to engage in intelligent debate over levels of taxation and public expenditures. This may appear a banal matter, but it is not. Governments attempting to avoid fiscal discipline are always tempted to "cook the books." The devices used rarely confuse professional accountants engaged by bond rating agencies to assess government indebtedness, but they can readily frustrate public debate.

Proposition Two: Accountability matters. One — and only one — level of government should in general be responsible for any particular domain of social policy, and we should require the responsible government to raise necessary revenues via own-source taxation. Lord Durham and de Tocqueville made their respective observations on Canada and the United States during the 1830s. Had they returned from the grave a century later to observe once again the state of North American society, they would probably have concluded the United States would be more likely than Canada to generate a generous welfare state. Washington, with the blessing of the majority of Americans, was launching major new social programs. Prior to World War II, the United States enjoyed more generous social security legislation than did Canada. Central to the New Deal was the willingness of Americans at all levels — from the Supreme Court to ordinary citizens — to blur the fundamental principle of federalism, which is a sharply etched division of jurisdiction between levels of government. Washington was able to use a number of heads of federal jurisdiction to intervene in domains that formerly had been considered exclusive matters of state jurisdiction. In terms of the continuum Harvey Lazar constructs in his contribution to this volume, the Americans moved decisively from "classical federalism" in the direction of "federal unilateralism."

For Canada, the final arbiter of constitutional matters remained in London until appeals to the Judicial Committee of the Privy Council were abolished in 1947. Until then, this group of judges had the final say on Canadian squabbles over which set of politicians, federal or provincial, could intervene in any matter. The Judicial Committee represented the pinnacle of administrative wisdom distilled from British imperial rule and, in general, its members opted for strict accountability. If one level of government was responsible for a particular function, so be it. For example, inspired by the New Deal, Ottawa attempted to legislate on hours of work and minimum wage, matters generally deemed to fall under provincial jurisdiction. Ottawa justified its legislation on the grounds of implementing an International Labour Organization treaty to which Canada was a party. In 1937, the Privy Council overturned the legislation, refusing to allow Ottawa to use its treaty-making powers as means to blur provincial responsibility for labour law. In a famous line from his decision, Lord Atkin used a maritime image: "While the ship of state now sails on larger ventures and into foreign waters she still retains the watertight compartments which are an essential part of her original structure."[20]

The sceptic's response to Lord Atkin's "watertight compartments" doctrine is to ask: Are contemporary elected governments — in particular provincial governments — worthy of such trust? Sceptics worry that allocation of particular social policy programs to the provincial level will result in a checkerboard of uneven social policy across Canada. Better to promote some variant of collaborative federalism that constrains provincial variation. Some prefer a model whereby Ottawa constrains the provinces by a set of conditional grants and imposition of national standards. Some want power in the hands of the courts — perhaps via an explicit social charter — to overlook the performance of both Ottawa and the provinces. But, having placed some agency in a position of overseer, the question then becomes, can we trust the overseer? The key problem is worth emphasizing: all variants of collaborative federalism entail shared jurisdiction and reduce political accountability of any one government for the quality of social programming.

Ultimately, the sceptic's question is an empirical one. Which generates better social policy: respect for "watertight compartments" or, on the other hand, the logic of collaborative federalism? The evolution of social policy north and south of the 49th parallel over the twentieth century has provided a prolonged large-scale social experiment. Canada and the United States are similar along many dimensions. Both are federations of continental size. Both are prosperous industrial societies whose dominant cultural roots are in Western Europe. At the end of the century, the conclusion is, I think, inescapable: the Canadian greater reliance on "watertight compartments" contributed to realizing a European-style welfare state, whereas the American emphasis on collaborative federalism retarded the Americans from making similar progress.

Canadians should not be smug about the better quality of our social programs. That we maintained a more precise division of responsibilities is due to a variety of factors having little to do with the search for good social policy. Overshadowing any other is the strength of the dual loyalty among francophone Quebecers. For reasons of culture and language, the majority among them want a powerful government in Quebec City. They have refused any Canadian equivalent to the New Deal transformation in American politics. While not as powerful as in Quebec City, other provincial capitals (such as Edmonton) also have a tradition of resisting an expanded federal role. And, so long as the Judicial Committee of the Privy Council was the final arbiter of our constitution, the courts played a role in preserving Canada as a classic federation.

The Americans, on the other hand, essentially abandoned classic federalism in the 1930s. During the Great Depression, the New Deal Congress established the pattern: those interested in active social policy concentrated on generating influence in Washington which, in turn, cajoled state and local governments via a combination of conditional grants, mandated programs and judicial overview. The strategy entailed the carrot of Washington's providing cash on a conditional basis, and the stick of intervention by activist courts in the case of recalcitrance. The high point of American social policy innovation came in the 1960s, at the time of President Johnson's War on Poverty.

Undeniably, there have been successes. The courts played the lead role in obliging conservative states to desegregate within their jurisdictions. Washington shared in the cost of providing social assistance in poor states, and pioneered innovative programs such as early education for poor children. Washington successfully implemented programs of universal health care for the old (Medicare) and for the poor (Medicaid). And, despite the heavy hand of Washington and the courts, certain states (for example, Wisconsin) have established a reputation for continuous independent social policy innovation.

But, since the 1960s, there have been more failures than successes. Public enthusiasm for social policy has waned. Conservative Congressional leaders have damned the undeniable inefficiencies of many federally mandated social programs. They are right inasmuch as Medicare and Medicaid are inordinately expensive. In 1996, Congress abolished the long-standing Aid to Families with Dependent Children (AFDC) and substituted block grants to the states. AFDC contained many perverse incentives that perpetuated single parenthood and welfare dependency.

Among American liberals, some have been interested in rehabilitation of a Jeffersonian version of "states' rights" — the American equivalent of the watertight compartments doctrine. An example is the Democratic Leadership Council, an important lobby of senior Democratic politicians. But, it is fair to say the dominant view of social policy among US liberals remains the New Deal legacy.[21]

The natural instinct among social policy advocates is to refuse this second proposition. If one agency of government is, for whatever reason, resistant to social policy innovation, then lobby another. At this point, I introduce two cases. The first illustrates the value of strict accountability in generating good social policy; the second illustrates the damage done by lack of accountability.

Case One: Sakatchewan and the arrival of universal health insurance in Canada. In an evolutionary sense one can trace the origins of medicare back through the fossil remains of policy initiatives dating from the early twentieth century. But the key events all took place in a short space of time in the 1960s, starting with the 1960 provincial election in Saskatchewan. That election was effectively a referendum on the promise of Premier Tommy Douglas that, if reelected, his government would introduce a mandatory form of medical care insurance during its 1960-64 term of office.[22]

The campaign was heated. The principal opposition party (the Liberals) adamantly opposed the idea of "socialized medicine," as did the province's physicians. Douglas won reelection, whereupon he launched a public enquiry on the matter, and his Cabinet and senior bureaucrats devoted their energies to the design and launch of an insurance agency capable of integrating the existing private insurance companies and of insuring all uninsured provincial residents. Political controversy was intense. On the left, the government faced demands for more radical reorganization of ambulatory health care into a series of cooperatively organized community health centres. On the right, the physicians took their opposition to the point of calling a provincewide strike in the summer of 1962. In order to maintain health services the government found itself engaged in strike-breaking. It hired a hundred foreign doctors to practise on salary throughout the province. To mediate the strike, the government engaged a senior British Labour Party official who had participated in the launch of the British National Health Service in the late 1940s. After three weeks, the doctors and government came to an agreement. The doctors achieved a few concessions: a decrease in direct government control and increase in professional overview of the insurance agency but, on the essentials, the physicians conceded. They accepted that the government could introduce a mandatory form of medical care insurance. The government paid for the new service via general revenue and a premium which was, in effect, a poll tax varying by family size. There was no short-run prospect of federal cost-sharing.

Very quickly, the value of a universal medicare program became evident. The provincial government's insurance agency ran its affairs competently. The government did not interfere — any more than before — in the freedom of practice of physicians. Patients no longer had to concern themselves with the complexities of buying health insurance for basic services or, if previously uninsured, no longer worried about large medical bills. Doctors experienced higher incomes and simpler accounting procedures since their patients were, all of them, now insured and, all of them, able to pay for services. In 1964 Saskatchewan voters decided that, after 20 years, they had had enough of the socialists. They elected the opposition Liberals whose ideologically conservative leader (Ross Thatcher) had earlier vowed to dismantle medicare. He quickly realized the program's popularity and broke his vow.

Simultaneous with Douglas's initiative, John Diefenbaker's Conservatives had established the Royal Commission on Health Services (chaired by Judge Emmett Hall). The basic recommendation of this commission, delivered to Lester Pearson's newly elected Liberals in 1964, was to encourage adoption by all provinces of health insurance plans based on that in Saskatchewan. Ottawa utilized its spending power to inaugurate a highly popular cost-sharing venture that induced even the most conservative provincial governments to do precisely that. By the early 1970s, all ten provinces had set up equivalents to Saskatchewan's universal medical insurance plan.

The federal Liberals had promised universal health-care insurance from time-to-time since the end of World War I. It required, however, a successfully functioning provincial experiment before Ottawa and the other provinces acted. Cumulatively, Saskatchewan's health insurance reforms over the two decades of CCF rule (1944-64) demonstrated the feasibility of realizing in North America universal hospital and medical insurance systems comparable to those in Western Europe.

The case of medicare in Saskatchewan illustrates nicely the value of strict accountability: the freedom of a duly elected government to introduce and scrap social programs within its jurisdiction provided it pays for them with own-source taxation. Admittedly, Saskatchewan was in receipt of equalization and other intergovernmental transfers at the time, but the province had no means to transfer the cost of this program onto Ottawa. Its citizens paid via taxes on themselves. This induced within the provincial government a healthy attention to the complex managerial details of running a health insurance agency.

Medicare was a highly controversial social policy initiative.[23] The provincial government was obliged to contend with powerful hostile interest groups. Had jurisdiction over health policy been shared — either with the courts or Ottawa — displeased interest groups would probably have used these avenues in an attempt to block implementation. They might well have succeeded, at least to the extent of delaying implementation beyond the next provincial election. Strict accountability demonstrated its worth. It allowed a government to innovate despite strong interest group opposition, and placed evaluation where it belongs — in a general election among all citizens. The fate of medicare under the successor government in Saskatchewan should give the sceptics of provincial jurisdiction some reassurance. When a social program proves transparently popular, public preferences successfully manifest themselves — even when the government is ideologically ill-disposed.

Case Two: British Columbia and the welfare residency requirement. The Canada Assistance Plan (CAP) began in the 1960s, out of an admirable desire on the part of Ottawa to share the cost of provincial social assistance programs. Under CAP rules, both levels of government became responsible for social assistance. The provinces would undertake on-the-ground administration; Ottawa would establish appropriate national standards. The key national standard that the provinces agreed to respect was that financial need become the sole criterion for welfare eligibility, that is, that the provinces would not impose other requirements based on age, work/training requirements, or length of residency. Provided the provinces respected this national standard, Ottawa would pay one-half of all provincial costs of social assistance.

The availability of 50-cent dollars encouraged provinces with fiscal discretion to be generous. The most dramatic example was Ontario, which more than doubled its normalized caseload between 1983 and 1993. It passed from being the province with the lowest caseload in the early 1980s, to being the province with the highest by the early 1990s.[24] In 1990, Ottawa undertook an ad hoc initiative to constrain the generosity of provincial social assistance programs — Ontario's in particular — by imposing a "cap on CAP" payments to the three "have" provinces (Ontario, British Columbia, and Alberta). Alberta was not bound by the cap because, starting in 1993, it introduced a series of reforms which halved the provincial caseload. In 1995, Ottawa further curtailed its cost-sharing by scrapping CAP (and the Established Program

Financing transfer), substituting a new smaller transfer, the Canada Health and Social Transfer (CHST). This new transfer is a block grant with many fewer conditions attached. The one remaining condition is that provinces not impose a residency requirement on welfare applicants.

When, in 1991, the British Columbia NDP came to power, it launched a program of enhanced welfare generosity with little attention to either the likely effect on welfare use or the impact of the federal "cap on CAP" which prevented the province from shifting half the incremental cost to Ottawa. Between 1991 and 1995, the normalized caseload rose by 30 percent. Simple regression analysis suggests that this increase in welfare use is largely attributable to the NDP's introduction of a relaxed culture of provincial welfare administration. That, however, was an unpalatable conclusion for the NDP to accept.

A more palatable conclusion was to blame a Conservative provincial neighbour and a Liberal federal government. To symbolize this alternate explanation, the provincial government flouted Ottawa's one remaining condition on receipt of CHST funds and, in late 1995, imposed a three-month residency requirement on welfare applicants. Ottawa duly responded by withholding CHST funds and, thereby, the NDP was able to launch a very public partisan squabble. British Columbia would have been willing, provincial politicians claimed, to take Alberta's poor if Ottawa was not "offloading responsibilities and costs onto the provinces."[25] "Why is it okay," asked the provincial social services minister, "according to the Liberal government, that provinces [i.e., Alberta] who slash their welfare rates and cut and cut are allowed to do that, whereas British Columbia, who actually has strengthened their social safety net, is not allowed to have a residency requirement?"[26]

Even if Alberta residents had been migrating to British Columbia welfare rolls in large numbers since 1993, the case for a residency requirement would have been weak. But the provincial government launched its residency requirement with no evidence to suggest Alberta's 1993 reforms had increased out-of-province welfare applications in British Columbia.[27]

And, the accusation of federal "offloading" needs to be placed in context. Between 1990-91, the last full fiscal year under their Social Credit predecessors, and 1995-96, the NDP allowed the provincial welfare budget to increase by $1.3 billion. This increase was nearly three times the magnitude of the cut in federal transfer revenue between 1994-95 and 1996-97. The cut, under $500 million, was equivalent to 2.3 percent of provincial revenue for the 1996-97 fiscal year.[28]

The growth in conditional intergovernmental transfers over the preceding two decades inevitably invited conflicts of this nature, particularly when Ottawa began to address its fiscal problems. Given the culture of fiscal unaccountability bred by large intergovernmental transfers, rancour becomes understandable. Which is not to excuse it. The provincial BC government exploited ambiguities surrounding responsibility for social assistance policy to obfuscate accountability for its conduct of social assistance programs. To be blunt, increasing the normalized social assistance caseload by 30 percent during an economic boom is indicative of a poorly designed program.

None of this discussion implies that welfare residency requirements are good social policy. An important principle in free trade agreements is national treatment, the idea that host governments will not impose laws on foreign firms that are more restrictive than those imposed on domestically owned firms. It is even more important that governments apply this principle to their own citizens within a country. It is legitimate for British Columbia to vary the rules for welfare applicants, provided it does so for all applicants; it is not legitimate to use regulations as a device to impede interprovincial migration by Canadians in search of better opportunities. Had provincial politicians not obfuscated the matter by partisan attacks on Alberta Conservatives and federal Liberals, political discussion over residency requirements might have been more lucid.

Albeit I am loathe to puncture watertight compartments, I accept that residency requirements are odious and that it is important to eliminate them — by intervening on provincial jurisdiction if necessary. This constraint on provincial social assistance policy would probably be better couched in terms of the *Charter* mobility right than a condition attached to the CHST. Conditional grants utilizing national standards are simply too weak an instrument.

MINIMIZE THE MUDDLE IN THE MIDDLE: AVOID JUDGES AND MINIMIZE EXPECTATIONS FROM COMPLEX INTERGOVERNMENTAL COORDINATING MECHANISMS

Some social policy experiments succeed; some fail. A parallel exists between the chutzpah of business entrepreneurs and of political leaders. The former are essential to the success of capitalist economies, the latter to democracy in general and the welfare state in particular. Politicians engaged in persuading citizens to support their ideas with their votes — and to pay the requisite taxes — are not unlike entrepreneurs persuading potential financial supporters to risk their money in building the entrepreneur's better mousetrap. Many times the politicians' new ideas turn out to be less brilliant than originally touted; so too with the better mousetraps. Successful capitalist economies require the freedom of entrepreneurs and investors to make mistakes. Successful welfare states require an analogous autonomy on the part of elected governments.

The competitive process, whereby manufacturers of good mousetraps in the long run drive out bad mousetraps, is a time-consuming and messy one. So too is the electoral process whereby citizens select good social programs over bad. In neither case is there a feasible substitute. This implies we resist the temptation to construct elaborate mechanisms intended to oversee and coordinate social policy decisions of governments.

Unless governments are violating truly fundamental civil liberties — as I would allow was the case with the BC residency requirement — the courts should not intervene in this dynamic. Had the Charter been in existence in 1962, Saskatchewan physicians might well have used it to challenge introduction of a mandatory health insurance plan. The plan obliges physicians to accept payment from a government agency, and to abandon private contracting for payment between themselves and patients. A reasonable legal argument exists to the effect that this violates mobility rights under the Charter, one of which assures Canadians "the right ... to pursue the gaining of a livelihood in any province" (section 6.1.b). The Saskatchewan government, it could be argued, was taking to itself too much power to determine whether physicians could earn a living, and under what conditions. Presented with this argument, a sceptical Supreme Court might well have called upon the Saskatchewan government to come up with a less radical infringement on physicians' freedom to contract with their patients.

Maybe I am guilty of overemphasizing the importance of precise jurisdictions and reliance on electoral accountability. Undoubtedly, Harvey Lazar thinks so. He observes that the federal approach to the social union has, in the last few years, been inching toward some version of "collaborative federalism." From the perspective of provincial administrators, most probably perceive the decade to have begun with "collaborative federalism" (a large muddle in the middle) and to be groping toward the "disentangled federalism" pole of Lazar's Figure 1.[28] Social programming has been "collaborative" over the last decade, in the sense that the provinces perceive themselves as leading on most dossiers in a context of (ambiguous) national standards, declining federal transfers, and complex Ottawa-designed fiscal incentives impinging on both provinces and individuals.

Admittedly, there will always remain elements of social policy that cannot be adequately given over to one or other level of government. For these elements, some form of collaborative federalism must be worked out. How should we organize this "muddle in the middle"? My basic conclusion is to keep such arrangements simple and few. Here is a brief critique of two important attempts to answer the question.

ACCESS

Tom Courchene, in an important paper released in 1996 by the Ontario government, has stated the ideal:

> the provinces must have the flexibility to design and deliver their own vision and version of the socio-economic envelope.... The most cited exemplar here is the experimentation in Saskatchewan which led to Medicare.... The more general

point is that the on-going blossoming of provincial experimentation across a range of fronts is absolutely critical to recreating an efficient and viable social Canada. The policy challenge here is to ensure that this experimentation takes place within a framework of "national" (federal, federal-provincial or interprovincial) norms or principles.[30]

We should add that federal experimentation within its jurisdictions is also critical. Courchene is careful to insist that we cannot have our cake and eat it too: to allow more autonomy necessarily implies less restrictive standards or, to say the same thing another way, there is a price to be paid in terms of forgone experiments if we impose stricter standards. Courchene is sceptical of the ability of Ottawa to administer a set of national standards on the provinces but he is sanguine that, over time, it is feasible to construct an "enforceable interprovincial accord whereby the provinces jointly implement and maintain a framework of principles and standards/equivalences that will guarantee across Canada rights such as mobility and portability."[31]

I am less sanguine on this than is Courchene. Imposing standards on reluctant governments is tough to do, and we should attempt the exercise sparingly. The danger exists that, by overselling standards, we raise false expectations among Canadians about the potential of any coordination mechanism and, subsequently, generate confusion and disappointment when the standards are found not to work.

Second, we must keep clear the distinction between securing the economic union and what is, by analogy, often termed securing the social union. The essence of an economic union is establishing uniform rules over a market regulated by multiple governments. A central principle of any economic union is "national treatment," that governments treat all economic agents similarly, regardless of their state of origin. Having accepted the logic of national treatment in the context of NAFTA, Canadians are currently concerned — via the Interprovincial Trade Agreement, for example — to apply the principle more rigorously with respect to interprovincial trade.[32] However, social policy is much more than setting rules or standards. The second and third dimensions of social policy (discussed earlier) mean it is often akin to running a large corporation. To the extent this is true, seeking appropriate national standards is an exercise in alchemy — one doomed to failure.

Attempting to build national social policy standards "from the bottom up" is often justified by reference to the attempts by members of the European Union to create a workable social charter. While the economic advantages from the European common market are undeniable, the benefits of a social charter remain nebulous. It may impose some very wide margins within which member states operate their social policy, but it will almost certainly remain at the level of the *Canada Health Act*, a statement of goals that provides a vague constraint on the social policy of member states but does not address the ongoing tough trade-offs required to run a successful welfare state. Realistic European administrators do not entertain the illusion that there can be equally generous social programs in low-productivity economies (such as Portugal) as in high-productivity economies (such as Germany). Canadians should not expect that a poor province like New Brunswick be as generous as a rich province like Ontario in setting welfare benefit levels. (Even after the new Conservative government reduced Ontario benefit levels, they remain nearly two times higher than in New Brunswick.)

In a few instances, social policy overlaps economic policy so closely that the distinction between an economic union and social union becomes untenable. For example, all provinces are guilty of a variety of explicit barriers against employment of out-of-province workers. These clearly violate the spirit of an economic union. While nominally a social policy, a residency requirement on a welfare application is also a barrier against out-of-province workers. It has the clear effect of discouraging interprovincial migration among low skilled workers. Accordingly, in this instance, it is appropriate to generalize the concept of national treatment and seek a mechanism — interprovincial agreements, the courts imposing a Charter right, or some other — to constrain provincial welfare policy. By all means, a province should be able to tighten or relax administrative rules covering social assistance. The constraint imposed by "provincial treatment" is that all welfare applicants be treated equally. Whether the applicant originally lived in Fort St. John or across the border in Peace River, Alberta, should not affect his or her welfare eligibility in Vancouver.

Courchene optimistically concludes, "there exist plenty of opportunities for mutual gain [in social policy] arising from enhanced coordination, harmonization or even just from greater information sharing."[33] Although sceptical about the potential for coordination and harmonization, I agree wholeheartedly on the value of information sharing. For the electoral dynamic to function adequately in generating accountable public policy, reliable information is essential. Generating good information about the outcomes of social policies is often expensive, and governments often restrict access to relevant potentially embarrassing information.

REPORT TO THE PREMIERS

Here is a second important attempt to organize the "muddle in the middle."[34] This document, released in late 1995, reflects an attempt at consensus-building among nine provinces (Quebec excepted) to define federal-provincial responsibilities in an age where the provinces are, whether they like it or not, assuming more responsibility:

The Council [representing provinces plus territories] believes the following criteria should be used in clarifying federal-provincial roles and responsibilities in the social sector:

•   federal activity in areas of sole provincial responsibility should occur only after federal/provincial-territorial consultation, and provincial/territorial agreement on how federal spending can be effectively applied;

•   as responsibilities within the federation are clarified and realigned, commensurate resources can also be transferred;

•   areas of joint federal-provincial/territorial responsibility be minimized in those instances in which this would improve the effectiveness of these programs;

•   the use of federal spending power in areas of sole provincial/territorial or joint federal-provincial/territorial responsibility should not allow the federal government to unilaterally dictate program design;

•   the federal government accept full responsibility for all programming for Aboriginal people, both on and off reserve, with a gradual transfer of authority to Aboriginal communities.[35]

Figure 2, drawn from the report, envisions an evolution of social policy from the oval on the left — with a large area of "ad hoc federal/provincial involvement" — to the oval on the right — with larger areas of exclusive federal or provincial responsibility and a much smaller area of "co-operative federal/provincial involvement."

The report displays a certain naïveté in its expectations for restoring the pre-1995 level of intergovernmental transfers from Ottawa. It also underestimates the difficulty of designing good social programs for Aboriginals. Since they are leaving reserves and increasingly living in cities like the rest of us, the potential for separate aboriginal programming is much less than implied here. That said, the report lays out a number of useful pragmatic guidelines. It wants an end to unilateralism in federal use of its spending power (e.g., no more unilateral adjustments in intergovernmental transfers). If Ottawa does spend in an area of provincial jurisdiction, provinces should be able to opt out of the federal program with full fiscal compensation.

Inspired by dispute resolution mechanisms in free trade agreements, the report's authors want an interprovincial mechanism for dispute resolution in matters of social policy. The first stage of such resolution would be provision of relevant accurate information. If that does not allow for a solution, the second stage would be mediation. If necessary, the third and final stage would be arbitration — perhaps via a panel appointed by the concerned senior governments.

Proposition Three: Respect comparative advantage, and celebrate competitive federalism. Ottawa has a comparative advantage in delivery of programs that redistribute income according to relatively straightforward rules, but most

Figure 2: Clarifying Federal-Provincial Responsibilities for Social Programs

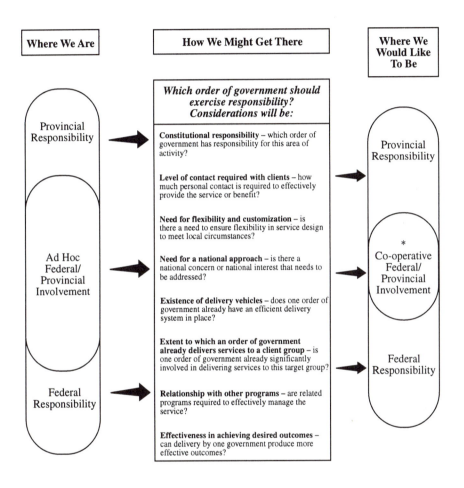

*There will always be areas in which both governments should operate, and the aim should be for a process of effective and respectful cooperation in these areas. Cooperation means that major decisions on program design, financing and delivery should be made through agreement by both orders of government, with delivery of programs by one or the other.

Note: Federal-territorial cooperation should also address the need to clarify responsibilities as proposed in this chart, while reflecting the financial arrangements for the delivery of social programs to aboriginal residents of the territories.

social programs entail complex administration and, in such cases, provincial jurisdiction should unambiguously prevail. Much of the discussion of Proposition Two turned on the value of explicit provincial jurisdiction. That does not deny Ottawa's role in social policy. As stated in the introduction, the comparative advantage of Ottawa is most evident in programs that redistribute income among Canadians according to straightforward rules. Seniors' benefits are an example. If the goal of social policy is to redistribute income from rich to poor, federalism offers few advantages over a unitary state.

On the other hand, the two other dimensions of social policy entail political and administrative discretion. Here, the provinces have a comparative advantage. While the welfare state has the potential to be more efficient than the market in providing certain services and realizing some important collective values, it realizes that potential only if public sector "entrepreneurs" — that is, elected politicians and senior mandarins — actually undertake processes of creative destruction to adapt social progams to changes in society. Understanding the case for decentralized jurisdiction is the political analogue to understanding that decentralized property rights and free markets are a necessary (if far from sufficient) condition for realizing the productive potential of industrial technology.

Decentralization of jurisdiction creates competition within the public sector. At any point in time, different provinces may do things differently within their jurisdictions. The potential benefits should be considered both in terms of long-run innovation and short-term efficiencies. The long-run benefit is to increase experimentation, by enabling entrepreneurial provincial politicians in one province to innovate in social policy independent of the preferences of voters in other provinces. As in the market economy, voters favour some innovations; these are, with a lag, copied in other provinces. Other provincial innovations fail the test of popular support and are dropped. The short-run benefit has three aspects:

- *Reduce managerial scope.* The three most important spending ministries in all provincial governments are health, education, and welfare. Were these functions run out of three Ottawa mega-ministries, they would (as measured by annual revenues) be larger than any publicly traded private company in the country. However well intentioned, mandarins at the centre face more difficulty in assembling relevant information than their provincial equivalents, each responsible for a much smaller domain. Even after decentralizing to the provincial level, these ministries in large provinces manage revenues that place them among the top 20 of Canadian private companies, and they generate some opaque Kafkaesque bureaucracy.

- *Limit the dynamic of concentrated benefits and diffuse costs.* Decentralization is a partial solution to the problem of inefficient interest group lobbying. Not all, but most, social programs are local inasmuch as the benefits accrue primarily to residents within the relevant province. Politicians have a universal tendency to advocate programs that confer concentrated benefits on identifiable local populations, while diffusing the costs over a larger population. Such tendencies encourage the accretion over time of inefficient programs. Decentralization does not eliminate this problem but lessens its severity. When provincial citizens choose by their votes to "buy" new programs, they must more-or-less agree to pay for them via provincial taxes. The per capita cost of any provincial program is larger than the cost of a program of equal absolute cost financed nationally. Hence, public debate of net benefits is likely to be more realistic.

• *Lower the cost to people of indicating their preferences as to what they want in terms of locally supplied public services.* Assembling and distributing information on policy options, and determining public preferences over some set of policy options is a complex social process. The larger the jurisdiction, the more complex and more inaccurate. People usually have more accurate analyses and more precise policy preferences about matters close to home than about matters far away. Decentralization can be seen, accordingly, as a means to lower the information requirements surrounding democratic decisionmaking.

This discussion leads to a simple but powerful insight on public policy: decentralization encourages a more efficient use of scarce resources because it encourages innovation, reduces managerial scope, constrains the ability of politicians and interest groups to shift costs, and lowers the costs of determining public preferences. The World Bank has repeatedly stressed this theme in recent "world development reports." An example cited is the value of decentralization to the quality of roads among 42 developing countries.[37] Centralized agencies come up with a few standardized road specifications, and this often results in overbuilt roads for rural areas. Also, centralized agencies underinvest in the hard-to-monitor activity of road maintenance. In those countries where responsibility for roads was decentralized to subnational governments, the World Bank concluded that the percentage of poorly maintained roads was roughly half that of countries with centralized responsibility. Roads may seem too humble an example from which to generalize. But the World Bank found similar results in its comparative analysis of many other local services — such as sanitary water systems.

In Canada a topical candidate for decentralization is labour market training. Here is a major area of social policy, one in which, given low employment-to-population rates among low-skill workers, there is a lot to do. On the other hand, the optimal set of training programs is far from obvious, and experimentation is highly desirable.[38] Ideally, Ottawa and the provinces will agree to a clean exercise in decentralization. This may take the form of concurrent jurisdiction with provincial paramountcy. The large provinces will take up the jursisdiction; smaller provinces need not do so.

I conclude this section on an optimistic note. Poverty among low-income families with children is a major wound in Canadian society and, until now, social policy to address it has been inadequate. In this domain, at least, Ottawa and the provinces are each recognizing their respective comparative advantage. They are currently developing major, by-and-large sensible, polices.

Operating in pre-electoral mode, the Liberals announced in the 1997 federal budget their intention to enrich the tax benefits available for low-income families with children. Unlike years past, the Liberals did not claim that the federal role was preeminent. Instead, the budget displayed a refreshing humility:

> This approach should assist lower-income families with children by allowing each order of government to focus on what it can do best. The federal government is best positioned to run large-scale programs through the tax system. Provinces and territories are better placed to run programs that include regional variations and that respond quickly to changes in the needs and circumstances of individual families.[39]

Ottawa is restricting its intervention to what it can do well: provide a straightforward transfer of money via the income tax system. It is not presuming to dictate the design of what the provinces "build" on this "platform."

The provinces in turn are building anti-poverty programs reflecting their respective strategies. They are currently designing and implementing programs intended to increase reliance on employment earnings as opposed to transfers, and to supplement the after-tax rewards from low-wage employment. Which province has the best building? Which plans are flawed? At this stage, one could give highly tentative responses based on the various blueprints, but more important is to wait, see the buildings in place and being lived in and, at that stage, undertake some rigourous evaluation.[40]

DECENTRALIZATION HAS ITS LIMITS

The comparative advantage of Ottawa lies in programs that redistribute income among Canadians according to straightforward rules. A related idea is that administrative economies may militate in favour of centralized program administration. For example, the federal child tax benefit is administered at minimum cost by use of the federal income tax system. If left to their own devices, provinces may undersupply services with a positive spillover effect. Provinces may undertake insufficient training because trained workers are mobile, and the benefits of their higher incomes and tax revenues may accrue in provinces other than the one in which training takes place.

Avoidance of inefficient migration, realization of scale economies, and encouraging services where positive externalities exist are, all three, classic arguments on behalf of centralized social policy. By-and-large, in Canada, we have allowed for federal preeminence where these arguments are transparently important. The most problematic are labour training and (un)employment insurance.

Interprovincial labour mobility is an incentive for a province to underinvest in training its own citizens. But, there is little evidence of this. The prime goal at present is to raise the distressingly low employment-to-population rates among certain groups — including Aboriginals and low-skill youth — and many provinces are innovating. Given the inefficiencies embedded in EI(UI) programs over the last quarter century, an argument exists to decentralize it as well. However, Ottawa has unambiguous constitutional responsibility for this program, and has this decade begun the controversial reforms required to restore it to the status of a social insurance program — and eliminate those aspects which made it a supplementary social assistance program for the employable. The Liberals have incurred the political costs (not the least of which was loss of 20 Atlantic MPs in the 1997 election), and deserve some credit. Continuity is desirable here; transferring EI(UI) jurisdiction to the provinces makes little sense at present.

Another set of limitations to decentralization is inherent in the three dimensions of social policy. Decentralization may improve program efficiency but, if a poor province lacks an adequate tax base, it will lack adequate revenue to run a reasonable set of social programs. Hence, a good social policy case exists for equalization transfers that, in the language of the *Constitution Act*, allow provinces to "provide reasonably comparable levels of public services at reasonably comparable levels of taxation" (section 36(2)). Provided a province undertakes the average taxing effort among provinces, equalization transfers bring per capita provincial revenues to the average of the five provinces used as a benchmark. As befits the rationale, equalization in Canada takes the form of an unconditional block grant governed by five-year intergovernmental agreements that assure predictable funding over the medium term.

Beyond equalization, there are no sound policy arguments to make on behalf of major intergovernmental transfers. The CHST is a desirable innovation relative to the *status quo ante*. But it should be perceived as a transitional policy, as a means of phasing out the expensive conditional transfer model of social policy symbolized by CAP and EPF, and moving toward a greater respect for social program accountability and for the comparative social policy advantages of each level of government.

WHAT ABOUT THE CHST?

Phasing out the CHST is not a goal that is unanimously shared. Here is the case for doing so. By reducing the size of intergovernmental cash grants and removing conditions, the 1995 CHST reform implied acceptance by Ottawa of the value of clearer program accountability. Relative to the former regime of intergovernmental transfers, the CHST reduced the ambiguity surrounding responsibility for several major social programs — something much to be desired. It is now clearer than before: responsibility for social assistance and health care resides with the provinces and, if citizens don't like the results, they know whom to blame. But ....

The Liberals promised in their 1997 election campaign to restore some of the cuts in intergovernmental transfers. This promise was delivered in Halifax, in the hope of avoiding electoral losses in the Atlantic region. It was a promise that ran counter to all three of the propositions advanced here. Increasing intergovernmental transfers via the CHST retards realization of a balanced budget; it dilutes the trend toward clear accountability for social programs; it represents incremental federal social policy spending without reference to Ottawa's comparative advantage.

One misleading aspect of the CHST debate is the charge that it represents an immoral exercise in "offloading" program costs to the provinces. The prime piece of evidence in support of this charge is the contrast between the percentage cut in CHST cash transfers (relative to the now-defunct CAP plus EPF) and the percentage cut in all other programs. The former cut is 35 percent (line 4 of Table 1), whereas the latter is only 7 percent (line 15).

This comparison is dubious on several counts. First, the critics engage in highly selective accounting. Ottawa transfers revenues to the provinces via programs other than CHST, and these other transfers are also intended to support provinces in the financing of social programs. Adding together all such transfers, we find that Ottawa is proposing a cut of 23 percent (line 13) — not 35 percent.

A second consideration is that Ottawa directly provides social programs to individuals, the most substantial of which are seniors' benefits, labour market adjustment, and Indian and Inuit programs (line 12).[41] The critics imply that an equitable exercise in fiscal restraint would have cut these programs at the same rate as other items. Given an aging population, the difficulties faced by unemployed Canadians and aboriginal poverty, equiproportionate budget cuts would have been immoral. If we exclude intergovernmental transfers and these major social programs, the projected reduction in all remaining program spending is 18 percent (line 14), a figure not far off that applied to aggregate intergovernmental transfers (line 13).

A final argument needs to be made on all this. An important means of restoring fiscal equilibrium at both the federal and provincial level over the next decade will be to lower the public sector compensation advantage.[42] The provinces spend a much higher share of their program dollars on salaries than does Ottawa. Accordingly, the provinces have a much greater potential than Ottawa to realize savings from better control over the public sector payroll. It is reasonable that Ottawa receive some benefit from provincial payroll savings in order to avoid excessive reductions in the social programs it directly administers. Reducing intergovernmental transfers is a means to do so.

Rather than seeking to placate Atlantic Canada, a preferable policy goal is to phase out the CHST entirely. Over a period of, say, five years, Ottawa could eliminate cash payments and simultaneously lower federal income tax rates by an equivalent amount. The provinces would be obliged to take up this tax room. This increase in provincial taxation would be subject to equalization and, to that extent, Ottawa would find itself engaged in some increase in the one remaining intergovernmental transfer.

Before we conclude, here are three arguments — none of which I find convincing — on behalf of Ottawa continuing to devote over 10 percent of its program spending on cost-sharing of provincial social programs via the CHST:

- *Dubious argument one. Cost-sharing provides Ottawa with a fiscal incentive with which to induce provinces to respect national standards.* We have dealt at length with this argument in the context of Proposition Two. At most, national standards operate on the fringe of social policy; it is very hard for one government to impose standards on another reluctant government.

- *Dubious argument two. Elimination of cost-sharing would aggravate the division between have and have-not provinces.* Probably the reverse is closer to the truth. The rationale for equalization enjoys widespread public support among Canadians. On the other hand, the arbitrary unequal per capita distribution of other intergovernmental transfers that emerged by the 1990s engendered political rancour. The majority living in Ontario and the west have concluded that fiscal federalism is an unfair set of programs that takes from them and gives to Canadians living in Quebec and the Atlantic. This thesis is most vigorously put forward by the Reform Party but, as shown by this selection from a major 1993 Ontario government report (written while the NDP was in office), support for the thesis is widespread:

In the period since 1985, there has been a series of discretionary moves by the federal government that have substantially increased the net burden on Ontario residents, through increased levies and reductions in the relative share of federal expenditures in the province. This redistribution of the fiscal burden has not occurred through programs designed for that purpose (e.g., equalization) but rather through unilateral reductions in federal transfers to the provinces targeted on Ontario and other relatively well-off provinces, and through more subtle changes to spending patterns and transfers to persons.[43]

This widespread public sense of unfairness about fiscal federal arrangements is a far more dangerous threat to the success of the Canadian welfare state than the short-term adjustment pains placed on provinces by elimination of the CAP and EPF, and a phasing out of the CHST.

- *Dubious argument three. Elimination of cost-sharing for social programs would further divide the two solitudes and encourage Quebec separatism.* Perhaps, but the historical evidence is hardly supportive of such an argument. For the last generation, Quebec politicians — operating out of both Ottawa and Quebec City — have negotiated skillfully within the intergovernmental transfer system, and realized for their province above-average per capita transfers. In effect, this has meant buying off Quebec nationalism. There has been no constitutional accommodation of that agenda and, instead, offerings of cash. It is an understatement to note that the cash has not had the desired effect of shifting the loyalty of francophone Quebecers toward the federalist cause.

NOTES

Portions of this chapter will appear in a forthcoming book on social policy, to be published by the C.D. Howe Institute.

1. United States, *Canadian Health Insurance: Lessons for the United States*, GAO/HRD-9190 (Washington, DC: General Accounting Office, 1991).

2. The ratio of insurance overhead costs comes from a 1991 study (United States, *Canadian Health Insurance*, p. 29). The OECD is the source for statistics on health-care costs relative to GDP, cited in Canada, "Striking a Balance: Working Group Synthesis Report," in *Canada Health Action: Building on a Legacy* vol. II (Ottawa: Canada Communication Group, 1997), p.12. The infant mortality and life expectancy statistics are from the World Bank, *The State in a Changing World*, World Development Report 1997 (New York: Oxford University Press, 1997), p. 225.

3. Many feel uncomfortable about government discriminating, in any way, on behalf of some group's values and against those of others. It is, however, in the nature of living together that some such discrimination takes place. The appropriate question is not whether to advance collective values, but to what extent and by what means. In a democracy, the majority can legitimately "impose" on others provided they obtain the sanction of an elected legislature — and provided the courts, as guarantors of fundamental civil liberties, do not object. When the Saskatchewan government first introduced mandatory health insurance, this

social program was — to understate matters — controversial. The majority of the province's doctors declared a strike and withheld services. The doctors did not oppose government subsidy of health insurance for the poor and, at the time, any efficiency savings from a "single-payer" system had yet to be demonstrated. The doctors' core complaint was that government should not impose its "socialist" values on those who preferred alternate insurance arrangements, either as health-care providers or as patients. The government insisted that, in this case, imposing a widely shared value was legitimate.

4. Liberal Party of Canada, *Creating Opportunity: The Liberal Plan for Canada* (Ottawa: Liberal Party of Canada, 1993), p. 17.

5. Ibid., p. 20.

6. Canada, *Government Revenues in Canada. Federal Spending. Canada's Economic Challenges*, White Papers (Ottawa: Department of Finance, 1994).

7. Canada, Department of Finance, *The Budget Plan* (Ottawa: Department of Finance, 1994).

8. Canada, Department of Finance *Improving Social Security in Canada: A Discussion Paper*, Green Paper (Ottawa: Minister of Supply and Services, 1994).

9. Canada, Department of Finance, *Creating a Healthy Fiscal Climate* (Ottawa: Minister of Supply and Services, 1994); and *A New Framework for Economic Policy*, Purple Paper (Ottawa: Department of Finance, 1994).

10. I define social spending to include programs that are transparently redistributive — either to poor individuals or poor provinces – or correct market "failures" in a manner that redistributes. Deciding what programs to include and exclude entails some ambiguous choices. For example, the majority of program spending at the provincial level is for health, education, and welfare programs. Ottawa, in turn, provides equalization payments to "have not" provinces to assure that all can provide reasonably comparable social services at reasonably comparable provincial tax rates. However, not all provincial spending is for social programs and, accordingly, not all equalization should be considered social spending. In this simple exercise I have included equalization. Counted as social spending are $41.5 billion in transfers to persons (elderly benefits, social insurance payments such as UI, veterans' allowances, aid to Aboriginals); $27.2 billion in transfers to other governments; $1.6 billion in aid to farmers and fishers; $2.6 billion in international assistance; and $2.1 billion in housing assistance via CMHC. The sum of these items is $75 billion, 63 percent of estimated total program spending of $118.3 billion for fiscal 1994-95. Canada, *Creating a Healthy Fiscal Climate*, p. 36.

11. Canada, *A New Framework for Economic Policy*, p. 73.

12. Ibid., p. 53.

13. Canada, Department of Finance, *Budget Plan* (Ottawa: Department of Finance, 1995).

14. Canada, Department of Finance, *The Budget 1993* (Ottawa: Department of Finance, 1993).

15. Canada, Department of Finance, *Budget Plan* (Ottawa: Department of Finance, 1997).

16. Ibid., p. 44.

17. Ibid.

18. Thomas Kierans et al., *The Courage to Act: Fixing Canada's Budget and Social Policy Deficits,* Commentary no. 64 (Toronto: C.D. Howe Institute, 1994).

19. The 1997 budget (*Budget Plan*, p. 44) projects a deficit, net of the contingency reserve of $6 billion for 1998-99. Given the Finance Department's overestimate of the federal deficit in recent budgets, this may turn into a modest surplus.

20. Quoted in Peter Russell (ed.), *Leading Constitutional Decisions*, 3d ed. (Ottawa: Carleton University Press, 1982), p. 130.

21. The most recent major example of liberal-inspired social policy reform is the abortive attempt, during President Clinton's first term, to introduce a system of universal health-care insurance. The proposal required Washington bureaucrats to set basic program parameters, to make complex administrative decisions, and to use extensive conditional grants to states. Unlike medicare in Canada, a system in which the provinces are independent "entrepreneurs" owning their respective plans, the Clinton proposal envisioned state governments as constrained "franchise operators." With justification, conservatives derided the proposal as a Rube Goldberg invention, and rhetorically asked: Could Washington bureaucrats specify the organizational structure for one-seventh of the US economy (that portion devoted to health care)? Would it not be a US equivalent of failed Soviet central planning? See A. Hacker, "The Medicine in our Future," *New York Review of Books* XLIV, 10 (1997) for a survey of why Clinton's health reform failed.

22. This discussion of the introduction of medicare to Saskatchewan is not footnoted. The best one-volume historical treatment is to be found in R. Badgley and S. Wolfe, *Doctors' Strike: Medical Care and Conflict in Saskatchewan* (Toronto: Macmillan, 1967).

23. In the 1990s, Canadians are wont to cite universal medicare as one of the criteria by which they distinguish themselves from Americans. In 1962 that was far from true. A footnote to this story is that Douglas resigned as premier to assume leadership of the New Democratic Party. His bid for election to Parliament from Regina in the 1962 election became another referendum on medicare, held this time at the height of the controversy over introduction of the program. Douglas lost, and was obliged to enter Parliament via a by-election in a British Columbia riding.

24. A simple regression using two variables explains most of the increase in the normalized Ontario caseload between 1983 and 1995. The two variables are, first, the unemployment rate and, second, the ratio of welfare benefits relative to a reference level of low-wage earnings. Increases in unemployment and a decline in the reference earnings level each explain a portion of the increase in caseload. The increase in welfare benefits are by far the most important component of the explained increase. A similar regression in the case of British

Columbia explains most of that Province's 30 percent normalized caseload increase between 1991 and 1995. The BC regression used the above two variables plus a third: a dummy variable to capture the effect of relaxation of the administrative culture determining access to social assistance upon election to the NDP. An increase in unemployment explains a small portion of the BC increase. The increase in low-wage reference earnings balanced the increase in welfare benefits and generated no net effect. The relaxation of administrative culture is overwhelmingly the most important among these variables. Regression results are available from the author.

25. British Columbia, *BC Benefits : Renewing Our Social Safety Net* (Victoria: Office of the Premier, 1995), p. 6.

26. Quoted in Edward Greenspon, "B.C. Fails to Sway Ottawa on Welfare," *The Globe and Mail* (Toronto), 8 December 1995.

27. Alberta introduced its welfare reforms in 1993. According to unpublished British Columbia government data, those who arrived in the province within the preceeding 12 months comprised 7.5 percent of the provincial welfare caseload in July 1992, and 8.1 percent in July 1994. The proportion of Alberta-origin welfare applicants among all out-of-province applicants has been roughly three-tenths since the province began collecting these data in 1993. (Data on province of origin do not extend back to 1992, before the Alberta reforms.) Introduction of the three-month residency requirement reduced out-of-province welfare applicants by more than half in 1996 relative to 1995, but had no effect on the proportion originating in Alberta.

28. British Columbia, *BC Budget '94* (Victoria: Ministry of Finance and Corporate Relations, 1994), p. 87; and *Budget '97 Reports* (Victoria: Ministry of Finance and Corporate Relations, 1997), pp. 80-81.

29. Harvey Lazar, "The Federal Role in a New Social Union: Ottawa at a Crossroads," in this volume.

30. Thomas Courchene, "ACCESS: A Convention on the Canadian Economic Systems" (Toronto: Ministry of Intergovernmental Affairs, 1996), pp. 9-10.

31. Ibid., Table 2.

32. Daniel Schwanen, *Drawing on Our Inner Strength: Canada's Economic Citizenship in an Era of Evolving Federalism*, The Canadian Union Papers, Commentary no. 82 (Toronto: C.D. Howe Institute, 1996).

33. Courchene, "ACCESS," p. 22.

34. Discussion of this document is based on the text, plus discussions with several officials responsible for its drafting.

35. Ministerial Council on Social Policy Reform and Renewal, *Report to the Premiers* (Ottawa, 1995).

36. See, in particular, the world development reports for 1994 and 1997, World Bank, *Infrastructure for Development*, World Development Report 1994 (New York: Oxford University Press, 1994); and *The State in a Changing World*.

37. World Bank, *Infrastructure for Development*, p. 73.

38. Some provinces — Saskatchewan is the one with which I am most familiar — are trying to integrate labour training and social assistance much more closely.

39. Canada, *Budget Plan* (1997), p. 106.

40. By restraining from explicit answers to the questions in this paragraph, I do not want to leave the impression that I am neutral. I believe the provinces should render access to social assistance less automatic for able-bodied applicants. My preferred set of policies would integrate social assistance and training more closely, evaluate programs more rigorously, and introduce major employment supplements to low-income families with children.

41. Figure 1 ignores the fact that Ottawa delivers some social programs via tax expenditures (e.g., child benefits).

42. While any particular measure of the wage premium is subject to controversy, the public sector wage premium over comparable private sector workers was probably in the range of 10-20 percent by the early 1990s. This premium is concentrated among low-paid workers; at the upper managerial levels, public sector compensation is often below comparable private sector levels. See D. Brown, "No Sense of Direction," in *Paying Our Way: The Welfare State in Hard Times*, ed. J. Richards and W. Watson (Toronto: C.D. Howe Institute), for a survey of the evidence on this subject.

43. Ontario, "The Distribution of Federal Spending and Revenue by Province: Implications for Ontario and Other Provinces," Report prepared by Informetrica, Ltd. (Toronto: Ministry of Intergovernmental Affairs, 1993), executive summary, p. 3.

4

The Federal Role in a New Social Union: Ottawa at a Crossroads

Harvey Lazar

Ce chapitre discute de l'approche du gouvernement fédéral aux relations provinciales à l'égard d'une union sociale, depuis l'élection des Libéraux sous le mandat de Jean Chrétien en 1993. Il fourni une typologie des régimes fédéral-provinciauxl en se basant sur deux séries de caractéristiques: jusqu'a quel point elles impliquent l'interdépendance ou l'interdépendance entre chaque paliers de gouvernement et jusqu'a quel point les relations entre les gouvernements sont hiérarchiques ou non-hiérarchique. Définissant le fédéralisme-collaborationniste comme une relation basée sur l'interdépendance ou la non-hiérarchie entre gouvernements, le chapitre analyse les développement dans sept secteurs de politique sociale et suggère que Ottawa est devenu plus collaborateurs ces dernières années. Aussi, le chapitre suggère que malgré les influences qui on inciter le gouvernement fédéral d'entreprendre cette ligne de conduite, elles vont peut-être être de longue durées. En particulier, la situation fiscale est en train de changer. Si le progrès est d'avantage atteint par le biais d'une approche collaborationniste, pour les quelques années a venir, alors cette façon de gérer les questions sociales à l'intérieur de la fédération pourrait couler les racines culturelles et le fédéralisme-collaborationniste pourrait devenir le nouveau status quo dans la capitale nationale. Mais, le gouvernement fédéral n'est pas encore là, et les prochaines quelques années, durant lesquelles Ottawa vas probablement agir avec prudence vis-à-vis la fiscalité, vont être cruciales pour déterminer s'il vas un jour être parfaitement confortable avec ce modèle de fédéralisme.

INTRODUCTION

The federal government is nearing a crossroads in its relations with the provinces in respect of the social union. For almost three years now, Ottawa has been inching toward a more collaborative approach to the provinces than had been its practice in previous decades. But whether the Liberal government in its second term will continue in this direction is not yet clear.

The uncertainty surrounding this question is not surprising. The Canadian polity is highly diverse, reflecting a broad range of regional, linguistic, ethnic, socio-economic and ideological interests and perspectives. Any political party that seeks seriously to form the national government has to include within its ranks much of that diversity. The result is that the federal government itself inevitably has to reconcile a wide range of opinion on many issues; and the federal role in the social union is one of those issues where opinion does vary.

This chapter discusses three sets of issues. The first has to do with the shift toward enhanced collaboration. In this regard, the chapter poses two related questions: What influences have prompted the federal government to pursue such a policy and are these influences likely to be long-lasting?

The second issue examined is the extent of the federal movement down the road of collaboration. To do this, the chapter defines collaboration as well as a number of other types of intergovernmental regimes, and offers a framework for mapping the regime changes that have occurred. It then uses that framework to judge the distance that Ottawa has moved in relation to a number of major social policy files since the election of the first Chrétien government.

Third, questions are raised about whether the new directions in federal policy are desirable. The chapter assesses the more collaborative approach to the social union in relation both to federal unilateralism, via the spending power, that has characterized many of the events of recent decades and the alternative of "disentanglement" or what is generally called classical federalism. The three criteria used in making this assessment are similar to those used by Keith Banting in his contribution to this volume. They are the effects on policy goals and outcomes, democratic values, and federalism principles.

Foreshadowing what is to follow, the chapter concludes that modest but significant shifts toward collaboration have occurred in the federal approach to the social union. It also concludes that where the shift toward collaboration replaces a regime that has previously been marked by federal unilateralism, there are likely to be more gains than losses in terms of the three criteria. As to the gains and losses associated with shifts between collaborative and disentangled models, they depend on the specific circumstances associated with the sector or program in question. When policy goals are being achieved with disentangled arrangements, there will be little reason to change; where policy goals are not being achieved, then there is a need for a case-by-case analysis of whether enough can be gained on the policy front through collaboration that will outweigh any losses in relation to the other criteria.

Two further points need to be noted by way of introduction. The first is how the term "social union" is defined here. In this context, the social union is the idea that Canadians have similar social rights and obligations of citizenship, wherever in Canada they may live; and the instruments of the social union are the constitutional provisions, federal government mechanisms (such as the ability to tax, spend, and regulate) and intergovernmental arrangements (such as federal-provincial and interprovincial agreements, including intergovernmental transfers) that breathe life into this idea. As Banting notes in this volume, the extent of Canada's social union in the post-World War II years reflected a balance between the pan-Canadian notion of the welfare state and a series of distinctive provincial welfare states.[1]

The other is to make explicit what this chapter is *not* about. In the main, it is not about provincial strategies relative to Ottawa or the factors that shape them. The purpose here is more confined: understanding and assessing trends in the federal government's relationship to the provinces in respect of the social union.

WHAT INFLUENCES HAVE LED THE FEDERAL GOVERNMENT TO BECOME MORE COLLABORATIVE? WILL THOSE INFLUENCES BE LONG-LASTING?

Five factors appear to lie behind the changes in the federal approach to the social union. One is the federal fiscal situation. When the first Chrétien government was elected, it inherited a string of more than 20 consecutive annual fiscal deficits and the accumulated debt was approaching 70 percent of Gross Domestic Product (GDP) and on a strong upward trend. There were concerns that Ottawa would soon be "hitting the wall" in financial markets. This is a point also emphasized by Richards.[2]

The result was strong federal action to restore its finances. As a part of the overall fiscal restraint program, federal transfers to the provinces were reduced very substantially in relation to previously planned levels, particularly through the introduction of the Canada Health and Social Transfer (CHST) in the 1995 federal budget. One consequence was that the political and moral authority of the federal government to determine unilaterally the terms and conditions under which provinces would receive these transfers was correspondingly reduced.[3]

A second factor that contributed to the change of attitude in Ottawa was the increased support for Quebec separation. In the aftermath of the 1995 referendum, all planned federal actions were reevaluated to give a greater weight to their possible effects on Quebec opinion including policies being advanced through the use of the spending power.

Third, the ongoing and determined demands from the westernmost provinces for a more decentralized federation were also being felt in the national capital. The prospects of ongoing squabbling with the governments of Alberta and British Columbia were a particular problem for a Chrétien government that was determined to show that the federation could reform and renew itself without constitutional amendment. In this context, a failure to improve relations with Alberta and British Columbia would, at one and the same time, fuel on-going western alienation and provide ammunition to both the Parti Québécois and the Bloc Québécois regarding the alleged unworkability of the federal system.

A fourth influence was the high level of representation of two regionally-based parties, the Bloc Québécois and the Reform Party, in the Commons. The structure of the House meant that there were no significant pressures in the opposition benches for centralizing power whereas there was extensive pressure in the opposite direction. For Ottawa, making the federation work by reducing intergovernmental tension was one way of taking the sting out of opposition criticisms.

Finally, the federal government's approach to public management was undergoing change at the same time that these other influences were rising in importance. For some time the federal Public Service had been increasingly interested in the "steering," rather than "rowing," which was becoming part of the new public management literature and, with it, the variety of alternative approaches to program delivery — privatization, decentralization, arm's length agencies, etc. — with the objective of enhanced client service at a lower cost. Especially important in this context was a growing interest in "partnerships," a concept that was highly compatible with a more collaborative approach to federal-provincial relations.

This last factor might not have counted for much had the provinces been uninterested in partnership. Indeed, in the face of the CHST cuts, it would not have been surprising if the provinces had undertaken an aggressive political campaign against Ottawa. In fact, however, their response, in the form of the 21 December 1995 Report of the Ministerial Council on Social Policy Reform and Renewal was both moderate and thoughtful. That report recognized the national dimension in social programming and, in the circumstances of the very unpleasant fiscal medicine that provinces were being required to swallow, it offered a more than reasonable basis for further federal-provincial dialogue.

Given the very considerable weight associated with each of these influences, it is easy to understand what has driven the federal government to approach its relationship to the provinces in the social union in a more conciliatory fashion. On one side, the new environment reduced Ottawa's political room to manoeuvre as the political price of unilateralism rose. On the other, the government had to become more results-oriented and, in some situations, this could be best achieved through partnership arrangements with provinces; and, for their part, the provinces had left the door open to such a possibility. Thus, the Liberal Party's 1997 election platform proclaimed:

> Our philosophy of federalism is that the best way for the various orders of government to meet the needs of Canadians is to work together. We know that is

what Canadians want. We will continue to improve the capacity of governments to collaborate.[4]

In turn, this raises a key question: How long will these influences last? And if not all of them are not long-lasting, will federal policy change as and when the pressures on Ottawa dissipate? Some of these influences do indeed seem likely to endure. The prospects of a large secular decline in support for separatism in Quebec are not, at this juncture, strong. The pressures from the governments of Alberta and British Columbia for a more decentralized federation show no signs of abating. To the contrary, as Sid Noel notes elsewhere in this volume, these two provinces have been joined by the Government of Ontario in seeking a different kind of federation than that which has characterized the post-World War II era. The 1997 federal general election has, if anything, made the new Parliament even more regionalized than the one that was elected in 1993. Finally, the new public management theory is receiving widespread attention across much of the industrialized world, suggesting long-term systemic change in approaches to public management, including in relation to social policy.[5] Accordingly, important pressures will remain on Ottawa not to revert to federal unilateralism through conditional shared-cost programs in areas of provincial jurisdiction in the absence of a wide measure of provincial support.

But the 1997 federal general election also illustrates that the fiscal pressure that has constrained Ottawa is easing rapidly. The Liberals and New Democrats both talked about new shared-cost health programs. The Liberal Party undertook to eliminate more than a billion dollars in its previously announced cutbacks in cash transfers to the provinces under the CHST. By all accounts, the federal government's fiscal room to manoeuvre is likely to improve rapidly in the coming few years. Moreover, notwithstanding the above reference to the Liberal Party election commitment to federal-provincial collaboration, that same document indicated also that, in relation to the *Canada Health Act,* the "federal government must retain its authority ... to enforce these principles," suggesting a less collaborative approach in at least that one politically and socially important sector.[6]

What then can be concluded from this analysis? The first is that most of the influences that have driven the federal government toward greater collaboration appear destined to remain strong for at least the next few years. If, during that time, further substantial progress is made in developing and implementing a more collaborative approach, then a new culture may begin to develop in Ottawa under which federal politicians and public servants become more accustomed to meeting their objectives through a partnership relationship with the provinces. As this approach sinks roots in Ottawa, it will become the new status quo. Later, if and when the influences currently driving Ottawa toward collaboration ease, inertia will work in favour of the new collaboration.

If, on the other hand, there is little progress in the next couple of years on the social union front, or if it is confined to only two or three files, then the political and bureaucratic culture is more likely to change at the margins only. The status quo will be unchanged in its foundations. Hence, the suggestion at the outset of this chapter that Ottawa is at a crucial crossroads in relations with the provinces.

The analysis in this section indicates that Ottawa has been under a range of pressures that have helped steer it toward a more collaborative set of relationships with the provinces. The next section documents the nature and extent of movement.

ASSESSING CHANGES IN FEDERAL POLICY

Borrowing from Biggs, the starting point for the analysis is the idea that there is a continuum of intergovernmental regimes on which federal policy can be located.[7] At one end of the continuum there is a federal approach which relies heavily on the use of the spending power in areas of provincial jurisdiction. At this point, federal transfers to the provinces require provincial acceptance of federal conditions. Although there generally is federal-provincial consultation prior to the establishment of these conditions, possibly extensive consultation, the formal decisions regarding conditions are made by the federal government alone and it is not bound to take account of provincial viewpoints. Although this approach is what Banting calls "cooperative federalism" in his chapter, it is referred to here as "federal unilateralism."

Federal unilateralism is characterized by a high level of interdependence among governments. On the one side, the federal government can only achieve its objectives if the provinces accept Ottawa's conditions and in that sense the federal government has to rely on the provinces. As for the provinces, each is dependent on the federal government for its appropriate share of federal revenue and, to that extent, may have to adjust its spending priorities or its preferred way of doing things to avoid losing financial transfers from Ottawa. This latter consideration points to the second characteristic of federal unilateralism: it implies that the federal government is the more senior government and that, therefore, the central government can effectively impose rules on the provinces, within their jurisdiction, without their approval.

The other end of the continuum is referred to here as disentanglement or "classical federalism" and is suggestive of the classical "watertight compartments." A precondition to successful disentanglement is a clarification of the roles and responsibilities of each level of government in relation to a particular grouping of citizens or a particular subject area. Whereas, under federal unilateralism, there is a high degree of interdependence between the central and the regional governments, under the disentangled model both levels of government have a substantial measure of the *de jure* and *de facto* independence in the exercise of their constitutional powers (i.e., we have mutual unilateralism). A second distinction between these models is that, under disentanglement, neither jurisdiction is *de facto* subordinate to the other, as distinct from the hierarchical relationship implied in federal unilateralism.

In the middle is "collaborative federalism." With collaboration, the interdependence among governments remains but, as with the disentanglement model, there is no hierarchy among governments. Below we identify two kinds of fully collaborative models.

With rules-based collaboration, the intergovernmental arrangements reflect the fact that the constitution authorizes both orders of government to act in a particular subject area. (One example is the Canada Pension Plan, which is based on a constitutional provision, section 94A, that authorizes both federal and provincial legislation but with provincial paramountcy.) Alternatively, the constitution may divide authority between orders of government in a single subject area. (For instance, section 91 authorizes the federal government to legislate criminal law and section 92 authorizes the provinces to administer it.)

Consensual federalism is similar to rules-based collaboration but lacks its constitutional imprimatur. It includes political and administrative agreements among governments on how they intend jointly to deal with matters of public policy or public administration. Such agreements imply freely given political consent as there is no constitutional requirement to act in this way; and to qualify as consensual, one order of government cannot be effectively "forced" to agree to the dictates of the other by virtue of some form of financial or other dependence on the other order.

While by definition, consensual federalism and rules-based collaboration are different in significant respects, for our purposes they are similar in that they require a highly interactive process among governments and entail formal agreement in achieving results. For this reason, these are located at the same place in our diagrams below and are referred to hereafter by the term "collaborative federalism."

These models of federalism are relevant to the way in which broad *policy frameworks* are developed and how such policies are *implemented.* In this context policy implementation is being used in a very broad sense to include a number of different activities, such as program design, interpretation, monitoring and enforcement. Figure 1 below deals with both policy frameworks and policy implementation, thus enabling us to map changes in the federal approach to relations with the provinces in respect of the social union.

One qualification must be added here. It will seldom be possible to capture all aspects of the federal strategy by pinpointing a single location in Figure 1. More often, there will be elements in federal behaviour, in relation to a single subject area (e.g., health care) or a single client group (e.g., persons with

Figure 1: A Framework for Mapping Changes in Federal Strategy in Relation to the Provinces

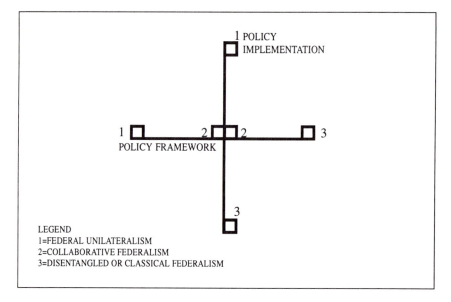

LEGEND
1=FEDERAL UNILATERALISM
2=COLLABORATIVE FEDERALISM
3=DISENTANGLED OR CLASSICAL FEDERALISM

disabilities), that fit on different parts of the diagram. For purposes of this chapter, the focus will be on the larger issues only (e.g., *Canada Health Act*) to avoid adding unnecessary complexity to this analysis.

The above framework can be used in relation to both macrosocial and sectoral policy. Macrosocial policies are considered first. Under macrosocial policy are included those policies that condition a broad range of interventions affecting different groups of citizens (e.g., both children and seniors) and different subject areas (e.g., both labour markets and health care) — sometimes referred to as "horizontal" or cross-cutting policies. Here two examples are pertinent. The first is the provision in the Canada Health and Social Transfer (CHST) to the effect that additional "principles and objectives" (i.e., conditions) surrounding federal fiscal transfers to the provinces under that legislation would be implemented only if "mutual consent" among the provinces and the federal government is achieved. Prior to that enactment, the federal government had reserved to itself alone the power to determine what conditions were to be attached to transfers. For this reason, the CHST provisions entail some shift from the unilateral federal approach in terms of policy frameworks to a less unilateral approach. The elimination of all but one of the conditions associated with the Canada Assistance Plan (CAP) is also suggestive of less federal unilateralism (recognizing that not all of the CAP conditions were onerous).

But when the CHST was enacted, it was the federal government alone that decided to preserve the principles of the *Canada Health Act* (CHA), and the restrictions on the residency requirement for social assistance recipients, as conditions of that transfer. In part for that reason, and in part because the federal government has the exclusive effective authority to amend the provisions to the Canada Health and Social Transfer (including the "mutual consent" provision), although less unilateral than the federal programs it replaced, the intergovernmental regime implied in the CHST legislation is still closer to a federal unilateral than a collaborative model.

To date there has been virtually no change in the level of federal unilateralism associated with the implementation of the CHST. The federal government alone has the legal authority to interpret the five principles of the CHA and to decide whether penalties should be applied. This was illustrated most recently during the federal election campaign when Health Minister Dingwall threatened action against Alberta regarding the planned opening of a private health facility in Calgary.[8] The same is true with respect to the interpretation of the no-residency requirements for social assistance.[9]

In Figure 2 below, the location of EPF (H)/CAP marks our assessment of the degree of unilateralism associated with major federal transfers to the provinces for health and social assistance and services prior to the 1995 Martin

Figure 2: Changes in Federal Strategy Relating to Macrosocial Policy, 1993-1997

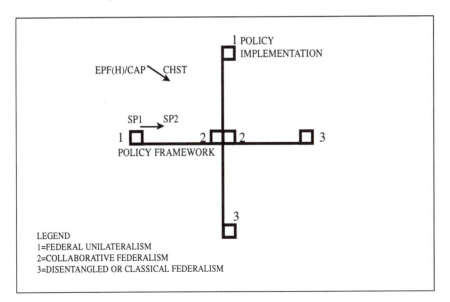

budget. The positioning of CHST is our interpretation of the extent to which the federal government has moved in the direction of collaboration. In terms of policy framework (the horizontal axis), it is suggested that there has been a modest shift in the collaborative direction. But there is only slight evidence of enhanced collaboration regarding the implementation of the CHST (vertical axis).

The second macrosocial policy considered is the commitment in the 1996 federal Speech from the Throne not to use the spending power to create new cost-shared programs in areas of exclusive provincial jurisdiction without the consent of a majority of the provinces, and to compensate any non-participation if it undertakes equivalent or comparable initiatives. Since that announcement, no new federal initiatives have been implemented through the spending power. Further, although the Liberal Party indicated its interest in developing a new shared-cost program with the provinces for medically necessary prescription drugs in its 1997 election platform, the platform also suggested that these actions would not be taken without a significant measure of provincial support.

The line SP1-SP2 in Figure 2 above is our assessment of the extent of the federal government's shift. Since the federal commitment is not embedded constitutionally, or even statutorily binding, the shift is only halfway to the collaborative model.

SECTORAL POLICIES

In this section we consider developments in five sectors since the announcement of the CHST. In three of the five, federal strategy entails increased collaboration, albeit to varying degrees (labour markets, child benefits and disability). In a fourth, child care, the end result of a number of zigs and zags in federal policy entails an approach that is somewhere between disentangled and collaborative. In the case of the CHA, however, there have been no major shifts from a regime that is still largely unilateral. Each of these five files is considered further below

LABOUR MARKETS

During the life of the last Parliament, a new *Employment Insurance Act* (EI) was passed that involved a major restructuring of the provisions of the old *Unemployment Insurance Act*. The scope and depth of these changes qualifies as framework policy. Part I of the new legislation sets out the provisions relating to benefit entitlement. Part II deals with the role of active labour market programs to help the unemployed reintegrate into paid employment. Part II contemplates the possibility that provincial governments may be delegated the role of designing and administering programs that come within its scope.

Unemployment insurance is a federal responsibility under the constitutional division of powers between the federal government and provinces. It is unclear, however, whether active labour market measures are federal or provincial jurisdiction. In any case, a powerful argument can be made that active labour market measures are closely connected to heads of power that fit within both federal and provincial jurisdictions.

The processes leading to the enactment of the *Employment Insurance Act* involved no multilateral consultation between federal and provincial governments. While there was some bilateral consultation between federal and provincial governments, this was largely ad hoc. The governments of the Atlantic provinces were consulted most and made the most determined effort to influence the federal decisionmaking process; and they were major players in an aggressive Atlantic lobby that successfully persuaded the federal government to modify and soften some proposed benefit reductions that would have most affected Atlantic Canada. As to the inclusion of active labour market measures under Part II, with the provision for delegation to the provinces, this was exclusively a federal decision but heavily influenced by Ottawa's recognition that it might be "forced" by pressures from some provinces, especially Quebec, to retreat from labour market training and, perhaps, other active labour market measures.

Given federal jurisdiction for unemployment insurance, it would have been unreasonable to expect provincial governments to be an equal partner in decisionmaking in respect of unemployment insurance reform. But to the extent that federal decisions would have consequences for provincial expenditures on social assistance, more systematic consultation might have been appropriate.[10]

The other key development in the labour market area during the first Chrétien administration was the signing of bilateral labour market agreements between the federal government and eight provinces under which, to varying degrees, provinces have decided to assume greater responsibility for the design of programs under Part II of the EI Act and to deliver those programs to eligible persons (current recipients of benefits under Part I of the EI Act and others who are no longer receiving such benefits but who had such entitlements in the recent past).

Four of the eight agreements — with Alberta, Manitoba, New Brunswick, and Quebec (agreement-in-principle) — involve devolution from the federal government to the provinces. The other arrangements — with British Columbia, Newfoundland, Nova Scotia, and Prince Edward Island — entail co-management. To finance the active programs that the provinces will design and deliver, the four devolution agreements provide that the federal government will transfer an agreed sum of money annually to the provinces for five years. The four provinces have also been delegated the authority to deliver some of the services of the National Employment Service, such as "service needs determination," employment counselling, and labour exchange services. As well, there is some expectation that there will eventually be single window delivery of federal and provincial programs. Around 1,600 federal officials are to be transferred to provincial employment. As for the co-management schemes, they entail federal and provincial governments working in concert in the design and implementation of the active programs, with continued federal delivery.

Overall, this amounts to a large transfer of responsibility from the federal government to the provinces. To the extent that there may have been significant duplication of federal and provincial activity, which was never demonstrated and almost certainly did not exist, it will be reduced. Nonetheless, there is the opportunity for improved client service in the sense that the agreements provide, to take two examples, for combined Canada-Alberta Service Centres and Canada-New Brunswick Human Resource Service Centres where clients can obtain both federal (including Employment Insurance payments) and provincial services (including the services and reemployment measures noted above) at co-located facilities. There are also arrangements for information and data-sharing that may enhance implementation of the programs operated by the two orders of government.[11]

The agreements provide that the provinces will not require minimum periods of residency in their jurisdiction on the part of an individual as a condition of access to provincial benefits under the agreements. Thus, a potential barrier to mobility is proscribed by the agreements. The federal government has also explicitly retained its responsibility for a national system of labour market information and exchange to support interprovincial mobility of labour, for fostering interprovincial sectoral development and for responding to national economic crises.

There is another important signal that the federal government has not removed itself entirely from the promotion of reemployment measures and the strengthening of the national labour market, that is, the federal-provincial agreements on the "primary indicators" for evaluating the results of the program expenditures financed through the Employment Insurance Account that the provincial governments will be delivering.[12]

For those who see federal-provincial relationship as a zero sum competition for power, these agreements represent a victory for the decentralizers at the expense of the supporters of the status quo; and they were hugely influenced by federal concerns to defuse a Quebec-sensitive file and to a lesser extent to improve relations with a number of other provinces.

Although these influences helped to shape federal policy, the impact can be viewed through another lens. In this second perspective, a new partnership is emerging that better reflects the appropriate role of provincial governments in respect of local and regional labour markets and of the federal government in relation to the national and international labour market. This can be a positive development from the viewpoint of clients' interests. First, since individual job seekers, and employers seeking workers, may wish to pursue their search activities on all fronts, from local to international, at the same time, one way for both levels of government to carry out their responsibilities in a client-friendly fashion is through a partnership arrangement along the lines of those that have been negotiated. The agreements also create the prospect that an unemployed person will be able to deal with both orders of government through a single office, and possibly even a single point of contact, even though for purposes of EI Part I they are federal clients and for purposes of EI Part II or social assistance they are provincial clients. In this perspective, the two orders of government have re-ordered their affairs to create a more "client-centred federalism."

Returning to our framework below (Figure 3), LM1 is an assessment of the federal-provincial relationship on labour market matters in the years immediately prior to the EI legislation. There had been little in the way of federal consultation with provinces on earlier unemployment insurance reforms, virtually no provincial-federal consultation on social assistance reforms related to the labour market and modest cooperation on active labour market measures with Ottawa transferring money to the provinces on the basis of a series of bilateral agreements or informal extensions of expired agreements. The relationship surrounding active labour market measures alone can perhaps be characterized as lying somewhere between the federal unilateral and collaborative models, perhaps a bit nearer to the collaborative. But in other and larger respects, on the basis of a number of citizens affected or dollars spent, the labour market, as reflected in the lack of intergovernmental consultation on reforms to unemployment insurance and social assistance, was more disentangled. The Forum of Labour Market Ministers was not meeting regularly and, when it did meet, the big issues were seldom on the agenda. That is, on the larger aspects of the policy framework, the two orders of government were acting independently of one another.

At the implementation level, prior to the introduction of EI legislation, useful federal-provincial cooperation had been started to lower barriers to internal mobility (under the framework of the Agreement on Internal Trade), there had been a long history of collaboration in respect of apprenticeship (the Red Seal program), and a number of interesting federal-provincial co-location experiments were being tried. Importantly, there was a working relationship on such issues as course purchase, for example, Ottawa buying training courses from the provinces for UI recipients. At the same time, the principal elements of federal unemployment insurance and provincial social assistance were disentangled. Thus, on issues of implementation, the model was perhaps halfway between collaborative and disentangled.

**Figure 3: Changes in Federal Strategy Relating to Sectoral Policy,
1993-1997**

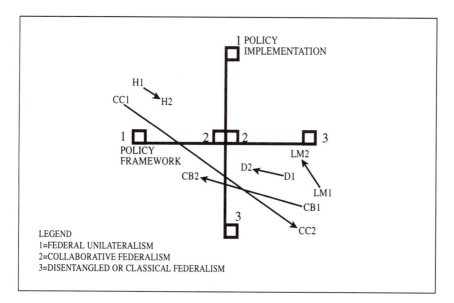

Since the election of 1993, there has been no increase in collaboration at
the policy framework level in relation to income support associated with employment insurance or the main features of social assistance and a modest
increase only in relation to reemployment measures. Therefore, overall, we
show relatively little movement on the horizontal axis over the last couple of
years.[13] But the eight recent bilateral agreements detailed above, which also
allow for collaboration in implementing certain aspects of employment insurance, and the prospects for a single office delivery of federal and provincial
benefits, as well as other examples noted above (including the reduction in
barriers to mobility), suggest a substantial increase in collaboration at the
implementation level.[14] LM2 therefore shows a much more collaborative approach on the vertical axis. If all of the potential benefits of this enhanced
collaboration at the implementation level are to be experienced, however, there
will be need for further improvements and collaboration in policy frameworks
in the years ahead.

CANADA HEALTH ACT

It was noted at the outset that there are ambiguities about the intentions of the
federal government regarding the future of the social union associated with

the inevitable diversity of opinion that is normally contained within any federal Cabinet. This is reflected in the federal government's approach to CHA.[15]

Following the general election of 1993, the Chrétien government created a National Forum on Health. Provincial governments were leery of this federal initiative in an area of clear provincial jurisdiction and, for the most part, stayed well clear of that exercise. The advice Ottawa received from the National Forum on Health included a number of key points that are relevant in the context of this chapter. Declaring the health-care system to be "fundamentally sound," the forum's final report argued that the federal government should preserve and protect the current arrangements, including "public funding for medically necessary services..., the single payer model" support for the five principles of the *Canada Health Act* and, at the same time, strive for a strengthened federal-provincial-territorial partnership.[16] The forum made clear that it believed that an essential element for achieving this end was the maintenance of stable and predictable flow of cash transfers to the provinces as a way of enforcing the Act. The intergovernmental partnership called for by the forum did not, however, extend to joint interpretation and enforcement of the five principles although it did suggest a "more open and transparent process."[17]

The CHA was originally enacted by Parliament in 1984, shortly before the federal election and without the explicit support of the provinces.[18] Nonetheless, perhaps in part because the CHA enjoys widespread support among Canadians, provincial governments have endorsed it. Thus, the Conference of Provincial/Territorial Ministers of Health, in a January 1997 report entitled *A Renewed Vision for Canada's Health System*, stated: "All provinces and territories support the five principles of the Canada Health Act (universality, accessibility, comprehensiveness, portability, public administration) for insured hospital and medical services." Yet the 1996 Annual Premiers' Conference at Jasper also made clear that the provinces were seeking a new consensus with the federal government that would include "a vision document for Canada's evolving health system which would include goals and principles." The premiers also pressed for a clarification of roles and responsibilities between federal and provincial governments.

The Liberal Party's 1997 general election platform, although raising the possibility of new pharmacare and homecare programs, indicates that further extensions to the national health-care system, through the use of the spending power, will require a large measure of support from provincial governments. On the other hand, during the election campaign itself, and consistent with the above discussion, much of the Liberal rhetoric also suggested that Ottawa remains unswerving in its determination that the five principles of the CHA be maintained.[19] Indeed, in commenting on the final report of the National Forum on Health, Prime Minister Chrétien had earlier declared: "Medicare is a cherished legacy that we will never abandon as long as I am Prime Minister." The federal government also holds to the view that the preservation of this legacy requires that only one government can be legally accountable for the interpretation and enforcement of the CHA and that must be Ottawa. Polling data consistently indicate that a high proportion of Canadians want the principles of the CHA to be respected and these data no doubt serve to stiffen Ottawa's political backbone in maintaining its exclusive role, in a formal legal sense, in interpreting and enforcing these provisions. There may also be a federal concern that any opening up of these principles for debate, as provincial premiers have called for (even while supporting them), runs the risk of opening Pandora's box and that the outcome could be an "Americanization" of the system rather than a modernization.[20]

At one level, it may be arguable that the federal unilateralism with regard to the five principles is unimportant since the provinces are on the record as endorsing them. Similarly, Ottawa recognizes that its unilateralism in cutting fiscal transfers to the provinces has been inappropriate, in terms of health-care policy and good intergovernmental relations, and it is seeking to provide greater stability in funding. While Ottawa's good intentions may be of small consolation to provincial administrations currently struggling to cope with reductions in transfers, there is, at least in principle, an awareness that such arbitrariness is wrong. For these reasons, it is suggested here that the policy framework is not entirely unilateral. But it is also much closer to unilateral than fully collaborative.

Perhaps more disturbing to provincial governments than the lack of explicit collaboration on the policy framework is that the federal government alone has the formal authority to interpret the CHA and to determine whether provincial health insurance plans conform with its provisions. Here it is important to observe that under the federal Progressive Conservative governments of Brian Mulroney, there was generally a *laissez-faire* attitude to CHA enforcement. In contrast, the Liberals were relatively quick to address violations when they took office in 1993, including the May 1994 penalties for extra billing by BC physicians.

This does not mean that Ottawa administers the CHA without consulting provinces. Rather, there is a history of the federal and provincial governments working together, including on controversial issues like unregulated private clinics and related facility fees, to reach a common understanding on the interpretation and application of the CHST provisions. Indeed, provinces have been among those "concerned that continued growth in the number of private clinics could lead to the development of a private system of health care in which people who can pay will get faster access."[21]

Notwithstanding this cooperation, provinces would prefer an arrangement under which the legal enforcement authority does not rest exclusively with

Ottawa and they call for a "joint administrative mechanism to interpret the Canada Health Act." To date, however, provinces have been unable to persuade the federal government to cede this formal authority.

Nonetheless, in a press release issued following the federal-provincial-territorial meeting of health ministers on 11 and 12 September 1997, it was announced that the ministers had agreed "to consider and develop a protocol for Federal, Provincial and Territorial governments to discuss issues of concern regarding interpretation of the Canada Health Act." Alan Rock added that "he would like to see a process that formalizes and makes more transparent the steps that should take place with provincial and territorial governments before the federal government makes decisions about violations of the Canada Health Act."[22] Whether predictability and transparency in federal decision-making regarding interpretation and enforcement will be sufficient to satisfy provinces is doubtful. But it is encouraging that both orders of government have agreed to tackle this issue.

The placement of the short line H1-H2 in Figure 3 indicates two things. The first is that at the outset of the life of the first Chrétien government, the kind of federalism being practised in relation to the CHA entailed a significant measure of federal unilateralism, notwithstanding extensive consultation, especially in regard to implementation; and, second, that it changed little over the period.[23] At least for the time being, it appears that there is a fear that policy objectives of one-tier health care would be endangered by a more collaborative model for the CHA.

CHILD BENEFIT SYSTEM

At the sectoral level, perhaps the largest move toward the collaborative approach to the social union has been made in the area of child benefits. For many years, both levels of government delivered substantial programs aimed at supporting families with children. The federal government focused mainly on income support, both through the federal Child Tax Benefit and the cost-sharing of social assistance associated with the Canada Assistance Plan. Provinces helped such families both through their social assistance programs and various services, including child welfare services.

It was long recognized that the overlap, and weak coordination, between federal and provincial governments in the area of income support for families with children was unhelpful in meeting policy objectives related to the reduction of child poverty and the associated aim of improving work incentives for low-income families. For at least much of this period, federal policy was questionable since Ottawa typically exerted political pressure on the provinces to raise welfare rates for families with children whenever the federal government raised tax benefits for children. The result was an immediate improvement in the income of those welfare families but, at the same time, no improvement in the incentive for individuals in such families to search for work or for working families with low labour market earnings to remain at work. Nor were these pressures appreciated by the provinces, since provincial law did not generally anticipate welfare rates being set indirectly by the federal government.

In the early years of the first Chrétien government, Ottawa was reluctant to put additional money into the reduction of child poverty despite a strong lobby that was critical of continuing high levels of child poverty and a growing body of evidence about the high long-term societal costs of such poverty. While federal reluctance to act in this way was, in the main, due to fiscal restraint, Ottawa also shied away from acting because it was open to provincial governments to reduce their social assistance payments, dollar for dollar, to offset the impact of any improvements Ottawa might make with the result effectively being no improvement in the income levels of poor families with children.

At the same time, the two orders of government had for awhile been signalling to one another their interest in a more collaborative approach. At the federal level, Lloyd Axworthy's social security reform process had alerted provinces to the federal interest by raising the integrated child benefit as a policy option and recognizing the issue of work incentives. Even prior to Axworthy's Green Paper, a number of provincial governments had made public their interest in a similar approach (e.g., Ontario and Saskatchewan).[24] Finally, at the June 1996 First Ministers' Meeting, there was an agreement to work together to achieve better integration of income support programs for children through a National Child Benefit System — a system that would replace needs-tested welfare benefits for children with income-tested benefits.

The essence of the agreement was that the federal government would provide a new Canada Child Tax Benefit, an enlarged and simplified child tax benefit, to strengthen the national foundation of income support to all low-income families with children. The initial federal commitment announced in the 1997 federal budget was to increase the more than $5.1 billion being spent annually under the Child Tax Benefit, and a $250 million increase that had been undertaken in the 1996 budget, into a $6 billion commitment beginning in July 1998. Provinces would be free to reduce their social assistance payments on behalf of children by the amount of the increase in the federal child benefit and to reinvest the savings from their welfare budgets into complementary programs targeted at improving work incentives, benefits, and services for low-income families with children.[25]

To fulfill the mandate of the first ministers, federal, provincial, and territorial ministers of social service have met on a number of occasions. Work has proceeded regarding ways of ensuring that increased federal income support would be reinvested, including the development of national reinvestment framework that would "flexibly guide" such reinvestments.[26] In September 1997, the ministers released a paper committing themselves to identify "performance measures that will measure the National Child Benefit's success in achieving its objectives" and incorporating those outcomes into public reports to ensure public accountability.[27]

Not all provinces waited for the intergovernmental negotiations to be completed prior to action. In 1996, for example, British Columbia replaced its existing welfare-based system of child benefits with a BC Family Bonus for "all low and modest income families — not just those on welfare."[28] Quebec, which has remained apart from the formal intergovernmental process, has also introduced a new integrated child allowance to cover the needs of children of low-income families and, in the process, also removed the benefits for children from its welfare programs.[29]

Thus, the new intergovernmental arrangements for child benefits offer the prospects of significantly improved policy outcomes. They also entail a shift in intergovernmental regime — from one that was largely disentangled in terms of policy frameworks to one that is more collaborative. In this case, the collaboration has resulted in agreed policy objectives and a clarification of roles and responsibilities in relation to those objectives. Within that framework, provincial governments retain wide latitude to determine their reinvestment priorities and to design and deliver their own programs in relation to those priorities. At the implementation level, therefore, we have considerable disentanglement.[30]

The line CB1-CB2 in Figure 3 reflects the shift from a somewhat disentangled system in relation to both policy framework and policy implementation — one that was falling short of agreed policy goals — toward a more collaborative policy framework. The overall result will be greater levels of income and other supports for families with children while, at the same time, improving incentives to work and facilitating welfare-to-work transitions. Moreover, it appears that this enhanced collaboration is only a first step. The provinces and Ottawa have also begun discussions regarding a wider National Children's Agenda — one that would involve provincial and federal health and justice ministries as well as departments concerned with social services and income support.

CHILD CARE

Child care is a provincial jurisdiction. In the period prior to the enactment of the CHST, the federal government influenced child-care policy principally through two instruments. It provided tax support to families that expended money on child care; and some provincial expenses on child care were eligible for federal cost-sharing under the provisions of the Canada Assistance Plan (CAP). With the termination of CAP, and its replacement by the CHST, the federal government ceased to share directly in child-care expenses. In this sense, the interdependence of the two levels of government in relation to child care was reduced. But federal transfers under CHST were reduced sharply relative to previously planned levels under the combined CAP and Established Programs Financing and the arbitrariness of the action was suggestive of the old unilateralism. That is, there were contradictory messages for the provinces in relation to child care: federal action had components of both unilateralism and disentanglement.

There was less ambiguity, however, about the federal proposal to the provinces in December 1995 to create a new conditional shared-cost program for child care. Under that proposal, based on a 1993 Liberal *Red Book* commitment, the federal government would have cost-shared an expansion of child-care spaces. The proposal required provincial agreement. Whatever the intrinsic policy merit in the approach, it amounted to a federal effort to establish provincial spending priorities in an area of provincial jurisdiction. While several provinces appeared ready to discuss bilateral agreements with the federal government, the timing was awkward in that provincial social service ministries were under severe budgetary constraints; and soon after Doug Young replaced Lloyd Axworthy as federal minister, the initiative withered swiftly. A few months later, as noted above, the federal Throne Speech committed Ottawa to no further use of the spending power in areas of exclusive provincial jurisdiction without the support of a majority of the provinces.

More recently, child care has reemerged indirectly in the context of federal-provincial discussions of child benefits, as discussed above, under which enhanced provincial spending on child care can be, but is not required to be, part of the provincial *quid pro quo* for an enlarged federal income support to low-income families which children.[31]

It is too complicated to trace this checkered history. Instead only the start and end points are shown in Figure 3. Since provincial child-care systems were constrained by the cost-sharing rules of CAP, and these were determined formally by the federal government alone, the starting point for the intergovernmental aspect of the child-care system is reflected at CC1 (heavily unilateral) in that figure. CC2 reflects the new relationship that now appears to be emerging within the framework of the National Child Benefit System. In between, federal strategy on child care, in relation to the provinces, zigzagged. The current position is, however, much less unilateral than was the case at different points in the recent past.

There is one last observation that is relevant here. It is that the change in federal policy on child care relative to the provinces appears to have had less to do with a consideration of the policy merits or demerits of further federal encouragement for the expansion of child-care spaces and more to do with the kind of federalism Ottawa wished to practise in a period of restraint. Since the 1997 Liberal election campaign was also silent on child care, per se, it appears that child care has indeed been dropped by the federal government as a major "stand-alone" social issue (although it may eventually re-surface in the context of the National Children's Agenda referred to earlier). This suggests that the intergovernmental regime in this area is now closer to disentangled than collaborative.

DISABILITY

As compared to child benefits, progress in better integrating federal and provincial support to persons with disabilities has been modest. The challenge here is huge. The federal government operates three large programs for persons with disabilities (the disability provisions of the Canada Pension Plan, the sickness provision of the *Employment Insurance Act,* and tax support under the *Income Tax Act*) and a number of smaller programs (e.g., the Vocational Rehabilitation of Disabled Persons Program). Provincial governments provide a wide range of services to disabled persons, income support through social assistance as well as the Workers' Compensation programs and, in some cases, automobile insurance. The overall package is poorly coordinated, at best. The result is very uneven levels of support for disabled persons, with some faring well financially and others poorly; and the coordination across governments concerning the weight to be attached to income support relative to services is also inadequately developed.

Provincial premiers decided at Jasper in August 1996 that priority should be given to overcoming the lack of coherence in federal, provincial, and territorial programs for people with disabilities and work has now been undertaken jointly by federal and provincial ministers of social services. A Federal/ Provincial Working Group on Disability Income and Supports has been established and work is proceeding to "develop a shared vision and common agenda" to help Canadians with disabilities. Importantly, in this context, ministers have decided that their work will include the services that will enable people with disabilities to participate more fully in labour markets as well as income support.

Achieving substantial progress in this area will almost certainly take much longer than is the case for child benefits. For one thing, the two earnings replacement programs — Workers' Compensation and Canada Pension Plan — are financed either by employer, or combined employer-employee, contributions — and therefore any effort to integrate all of the income support programs into a single guaranteed income for persons with disabilities would inevitably be far more complicated than is the case in relation to child benefits (where only the general revenues of the federal and provincial governments need to be considered). Furthermore, there are substantial differences in purpose between the different categories of income programs. For these reasons, it is more likely efforts will be made to harmonize disability income programs, perhaps by acting jointly to reduce work disincentives, improve information-sharing and encourage some joint activity (e.g., assessment of disability) rather than attempting a "big-bang" single integrated program.

Nonetheless, both orders of government have decided that a more collaborative approach is preferable to the current mutual unilateralism. The beginnings of progress in this area are reflected in the D1-D2 line. Whether these beginnings will generate concrete outcomes is still an open question. To date there is no high visibility initiative that parallels what has happened in child benefits or labour markets.

It is also arguable that there is a clear case for more collaboration in policy implementation in this area. The absence of a coordinated approach to large benefit programs (e.g., CPP Disability and Workers' Compensation) leads to efforts from one order of government to pass costs on to the other. This may be confusing for clients and costly for administration. Accordingly, it will be important to not only focus more on a collaborative approach to policymaking but also to get a greater coherence in program implementation.

SECTORAL CONCLUSIONS

In three of the five sectors noted, there is a move toward more collaboration either in policy framework, policy implementation or both. In two of the three — labour markets (implementation) and child benefits (framework policy and to a much lesser degree implementation) — the shift toward collaboration on the part of the federal government is significant. In the case of disability provisions, the direction appears similar, but it is premature to assess how much progress will be made in achieving improved policy outcomes. Given the technical complexity of the area, a strong political commitment will be required to advance the agenda in a large way although modest gains are a plausible outcome.

In the case of health care, the federal government is torn between a more collaborative approach and its interpretation of a public mood which appears to want Ottawa to continue to play a "strong" role to maintain one-tier health. What remains to be seen is whether it is possible for Ottawa to sustain a strong role while moving toward a more collaborative approach.

What has happened in child care is less the product of a conscious child-care strategy by Ottawa and more the outcome of the child-care file being swamped by concerns about the working of the federation and fiscal restraint. Nonetheless, the result is a shift away from a regime that had significant elements of federal unilateralism to one that is part-way between disentangled and collaborative but closer to disentangled.

IS MORE COLLABORATION DESIRABLE?

The analysis to this point suggests that, owing to changing circumstance, the federal government has been moving toward a more collaborative approach to the social union. In cases where there has been disentanglement between Ottawa and the provinces, as with child benefits, disability, and major labour market programs, there is a trend toward more collaboration. Where there has been federal unilateralism in macrosocial policy, it is being reduced, for example, restraint of the spending power and the reduction of conditions associated with social assistance. At least for the moment, something has changed. Ottawa appears to be taking the view that interdependence is a fact of life and that it needs to be managed. The reasons for this change were noted earlier. In this section we shift from the positive to the normative and ask two questions. Where we now have federal unilateralism, through the spending power, is collaboration to be preferred? Where we have had disentanglement, is collaboration better? Answering these questions involves a consideration of the effects of these alternative intergovernmental regimes on policy goals and outcomes, democratic values and federalism principles.

In relation to federal unilateralism, the three cases discussed above (child care, the *Canada Health Act,* and the elimination of most of the CAP conditions under the new CHST) do not allow any generalizations regarding any presumed benefits in terms of better social policy that might be seen as large enough to offset any costs such unilateralism might impose in terms of respect for federalism principles. In the child-care example, all that could be concluded was that policy objectives could not be achieved in the face of provincial irritations and fiscal shortfalls at both the federal and provincial levels. In effect, Ottawa's child-care policy has now been subordinated to the federalism and fiscal agendas.

As for the unilateralism associated with CAP, it is generally acknowledged that whatever benefits CAP provided in terms of common social citizenship (and these were relatively few), it discouraged provincial innovation. The current federal position on social assistance, as implied by both the virtual elimination of CHST conditions for social assistance and the new federal-provincial arrangements on child benefits, suggests that Ottawa too has come to recognize that any social policy gains associated with CAP were insufficient to offset the adverse effects on federalism principles (such as the respect for diversity that is implied in the division of powers).

As for the continued federal unilateralism associated with the CHA, it is difficult to form a definitive view since there is ambiguity around the counterfactual, that is, is it a two-tier Americanized system of health care or a modernized collaborative CHA?

The controversy surrounding the interpretation of the CHA is worth dwelling on because it highlights the different values that Ottawa has to weigh

— the trade-offs — in determining its position on the future course for the social union. If the Chrétien government were to follow the words of its own 1997 *Red Book* regarding the importance of collaboration, it would shift to a joint federal-provincial mechanism for interpretation and enforcement of the CHA. The rub here is that Ottawa is almost certainly convinced that this would increase the probability of a two-tier health-care system; and the Liberals also promised to safeguard the current set of CHA principles.

Alternatively, if interpretation of the CHA were assigned to an arm's length party, there is a concern that democratic values would be jeopardized since any such arm's length arbiter would not be directly accountable to voters. If such an arbiter functioned in a predictable and transparent fashion, then some of the potential criticism about its legitimacy might be softened; and if its interpretations drifted too far from federal commitments, it would be feasible for Ottawa to amend the CHA to better achieve the desired outcome. Such amendments could, however, offend some provinces who were supportive of the interpretations being given by the arm's length referees, re-igniting the concern about federal unilateralism. In short, there is no easy answer to the issue of CHA interpretation and enforcement that is a "winner" on all three fronts: achievement of policy goals, maintenance of democratic values and respect for federalism principles. The most recent federal-provincial-territorial initiative (announced in the September 1997 Conference of Ministers of Health) can be viewed, however, as an effort to seek out the optimal point in relation to these three criteria.

The CHA aside, there appears to be a significant measure of agreement concerning the potential benefits of federal-provincial collaboration relative to federal unilateralism. This is suggested by the position of all the provinces except Quebec. The message from the nine provincial premiers at Jasper in August 1996 indicates that provincial governments of all political shapes — from NDP to very conservative Progressive Conservatives — and provinces of varying wealth — from the richest to the poorest — are unanimous in their belief that the federal spending must be subject to some measures of provincial control. As for the current Quebec government, so long as Canada survives, it would scrap the federal spending power entirely and move to a fully disentangled model, with a minimal federal role in social matters. The necessity of enhanced provincial control of the federal spending power has also been acknowledged by recent federal governments including the Progressive Conservatives in the Charlottetown Accord and the Liberals, as noted earlier, in the 1996 Throne Speech. Indeed, it is difficult to find any commentators who would preserve the unfettered right of Ottawa to use the spending power.

The bottom line on federal unilateralism, even if preceded by extensive intergovernmental consultation, is that it entails a view about federalism that presumes that Ottawa is the senior order of government and that it knows more about areas of provincial jurisdiction than do the provinces. The fact that there is a consensus to limit the spending power, as noted above, is an indication that federal unilateralism is increasingly seen as unacceptable in today's Canada. This suggests that the remaining controversy regarding the CHA may be an exception to the general rule.

It is more difficult to reach a conclusion about the merits of collaboration relative to disentanglement or classical federalism. Yet the factors leading to enhanced collaboration in the cases of child benefits and disability are suggestive of the kind of situation where collaboration may be desirable. That is, it may be desirable in cases where both levels of government have legal authority to act in respect of a particular group of citizens, or a particular subject area, and where there is dissatisfaction with policy outcomes.

There are risks in collaboration. As John Richards argues in this volume,[32] collaboration, or what he dubs the "muddle in the middle," complicates political accountability, enabling federal and provincial governments to blame one another when programs are ineffective with the voter unsure about which order of government to hold accountable. Classical federalism avoids concerns about political accountability, eliminates the transaction costs of collaboration and respects federalism principles. Accordingly, in cases where the classical model generates satisfactory policy outcomes, it will be preferable to collaborative models.

In practice, however, both levels of government are legitimately involved in many areas of social policy. Several factors explain this overlap. One is the concurrent constitutional jurisdiction in relation to immigration and benefits for seniors. A second and more important factor is the role of the federal personal income tax system. It plays a key role in determining income distribution and therefore it inevitably impacts on many provincial programs, including those that are directly or indirectly concerned with income distribution. The income tax law also encourages some activities more than others (e.g., deductions or credits for postsecondary education) and these decisions also have implications for provincial programming. Moreover, there appears to be a view that the income tax system is an efficient instrument for delivering certain types of income support programs. Therefore, the role of the income tax system as an instrument of social policy may increase in the years ahead; and the fact that the federal government is planning to proceed with a Canadian Revenue Agency may increase the openness of provinces to use the tax collection system as a vehicle for implementing some of their programs. Finally, there are important interactions between provincial and federal legislative and spending decisions even when each government is acting in its own jurisdiction. For example, as noted above, federal EI decisions may affect provincial social assistance; and provincial decisions on Workers' Compensation may affect the costs of CPP Disability.

Policy collaboration involves costs. It requires financial and staff resources. It makes the task of any single government more complicated than would otherwise be the case. The habit of policy collaboration is a constraint on any government's freedom of action. It can certainly slow decisionmaking. Pushed to an extreme, collaboration can be an excuse for inaction or lead to policies that constantly involve the "lowest common denominator" in policy. It can also complicate democratic accountability.

Yet the challenges to social policy in Canada are not mainly about difficulties associated within collaboration. For one thing, much of Canadian social policy is disentangled. Provinces and territories run the primary and secondary systems without any federal involvement (except on reserves). In the case of postsecondary education, the federal role is confined to facilitating access, through tax incentives, student loans, and support for research. As for the actual running of the hospital system, and practitioner-patient relationships, this too is largely disentangled. The CHA is mainly about insuring equal access to comprehensive services regardless of income. The provinces also design and deliver virtually all social services without any federal involvement. Conversely, the government has played the principal role in designing and delivering income support for seniors (recognizing that the QPP is separate).

Thus, in recent years, the difficulty in the ongoing interaction among federal and provincial ministers and officials has been less the so-called "democratic deficit," or the perception of such a deficit, that can exist with intergovernmentalism than the absence of an intergovernmentalism that has focused on solving concrete problems.[33] The evidence for this is in the fuss governments give to occasional efforts at collaboration (as has been the case recently regarding children). But if collaboration were normal in situations of significant overlap, there would be less need for fussing and, with more maturity, less bickering. Interestingly, ongoing work by Ekos Research indicates a desire among the Canadian public for both federal and provincial governments to be present in many areas of the social union, with a "desire for greater cooperation among governments."[34] For those who want to minimize disagreement among governments, of course, the obvious palliative is to minimize the intergovernmental process. But such an approach suggests that the role of government is to convenience itself, not to serve citizens.

It is by no means implicit in the above that more collaboration is always better: that on all files, the public interest is best served by gravitating to the centrepoint in the figures above. Where there is disentanglement and satisfactory policy outcomes, as already noted, the status quo may well be best. But where there are poor policy outcomes and significant overlaps exist, collaboration may be better. In cases where governments consider moving from a disentangled position to one of more collaboration, it will always be necessary to weigh the potential benefits in terms of policy coherence on a particular issue against the possible costs noted above — transaction costs, reduced political accountability, lowest common denominator, etc.; and there will certainly be a need to wrestle with ways of minimizing reductions in accountability where collaborative models do emerge. In some cases, halfway to collaboration may be far enough or even too far; and that half-way point may be collaboration on the policy framework, as with child benefits, with both levels of government then free to design and deliver their programs with that framework on a disentangled basis. Interestingly, such an approach fits well with John Richards' proposition that provinces concentrate on services and the federal government on income.

CONCLUSION

The evidence from recent history suggests that the federal approach to the social union is becoming more collaborative. Ottawa is less inclined to use the spending power to provide conditional transfers to the provinces in areas of exclusive provincial jurisdiction without a wide measure of provincial concurrence. There is also less inclination on the part of the federal government to use the spending to transfer money to individuals without coordinating its activities with provinces if the provinces are also providing services or income support to the same target groups. In the first case, the limits on the spending power reflect a concern that federal action, while constitutional, runs counter to the broad political principles of federalism in Canada and creates too much tension in federal-provincial relations. In the second case, the readiness to coordinate reflects a belief that, in modern systems of government, it is impractical to build genuinely watertight compartments everywhere; and where such compartments are impractical, better policy may result from a serious effort at joint problem-solving.

Yet, it is by no means certain that this movement toward collaboration will continue. As federal finances improve, the temptation to "go it alone" could return. Going it alone is unlikely to involve further use of the spending power to create shared-cost programs with the provinces in areas of exclusive provincial jurisdiction without a substantial measure of provincial concurrence. The Chrétien Liberals have committed themselves too unequivocally against such actions to travel further down this road. Rather, if it does occur, going it alone is more likely to entail direct transfers to individuals, whether in the forms of cash, refundable tax credits, loans, or loan guarantees in situations where there are overlapping federal and provincial interests.

With the important exception of Quebec, which disputes the legitimacy of the spending power and prefers a classical model of federalism, the provinces have recently re-affirmed their commitment to collaboration. At their August 1997 annual conference, "premiers expressed their desire to strengthen the role of the Federal/Provincial/Territorial Council on Social Policy Renewal in coordinating and monitoring ... work on social policy renewal." The premiers also called for provincial negotiations with Ottawa on a "broad framework agreement" that would add cross-sectoral issues like common principles, the use of the federal spending power and dispute resolution to the already large sectoral agenda that is being tackled by the council. In other words, Quebec excepted, it appears that there is a willing set of provincial partners if the federal government wishes to continue dancing. This openness of the provinces to collaboration should thus reduce the incentives of the federal government to act on its own.

The ability of Ottawa to stay the course on the collaborative model may also have implications for political reconciliation within Canada. Here, it is not necessary to be an insider to know the kinds of considerations that must be in the minds of federal Cabinet ministers. On the one side there will be concerns that in ongoing political battles regarding the future of Quebec, any new federal spending (or adjustments to existing spending) in social areas where the province is already active, or is even planning to be active, will be portrayed by the PQ and BQ as an "invasion" of presumed provincial jurisdiction. On the other side there will be concerns that if the federal government does not have some significant direct relationship with individual Quebecers, other than as a tax collector, it will make itself irrelevant to them. The former concerns speak to the desirability of the classical model, with Ottawa's watertight compartment within the social union being very small; the latter concerns presume the need for collaboration. In this regard, to the extent that the federal government is able to reach agreement with the provinces other than Quebec on social union issues, on a basis of genuine partnership and mutual respect, it may serve to strengthen the belief among federal ministers that they should be willing to continue making direct transfers to individuals, including in Quebec. In that perspective, such transfers might be seen as a win-win scenario, strengthening both the efficacy of the social union and the benefits to individual Quebecers in remaining part of a wider Canadian polity.

The social union reform agenda remains large. There are any number of issues on which the possibility of collaboration, at least at the level of policy frameworks, offers the prospects of improved policy outputs; and with a few more successful negotiations to accompany what has been achieved on child benefits and labour market training and development, the more likely it is that the habit of collaboration could become the new status quo in Ottawa. But the federal government is not there yet. Rather, we are at a crossroads in the working of the federation; and the next few years will be crucial in the direction that is taken.

One final observation: to the extent federal and provincial governments continue on the collaborative model, there is the risk of insufficient transparency and uncertain lines of accountability in the new social union. The greater the reliance on collaborative models, therefore, the more the two levels of government will have to address simultaneously issues of openness and democratic accountability.

NOTES

1. For a detailed discussion of alternative definitions of what is included in the social union, see unpublished conclusion from the Canadian Policy Research Networks' 24 March roundtable, Kathy O'Hara, "A Framework of Principles and Objectives for the Social Union"(Ottawa: Canadian Policy Research Networks, 1997), pp. 1-3. The definition used here is narrower than that in Margaret Biggs, *Building Blocks for Canada's New Social Union*, Working Paper no. F-02 (Ottawa: Canadian Policy Research Networks, 1996).

2. John Richards, "Reducing the Muddle in the Middle: Three Propositions for Running the Welfare State," in this volume.

3. According to *The Globe and Mail*, 31 May 1997, p. A4, Premier Clark of British Columbia stated at the end of the Western Premiers' Conference that the "federal government has been the principal cause in undermining medicare and so has lost its moral authority to tell the provinces what to do." The formal communiqué of the conference was almost equally blunt: "the federal government should be challenged to match its stated commitment to *Canada Health Act* principles with the financial commitment to support those principles in the delivery of health services" (p. 9).

4. Liberal Party of Canada, *Securing Our Future Together* - The Liberal Plan (Ottawa: The Liberal Party of Canada, 1997), p. 19. The Liberal Party's assertion that it knows that collaboration is what Canadians want is consistent with the Ottawa-based EKOS Research findings during ongoing public opinion surveys on this issue. The prime minister's speech of 25 March 1997 to the Laval Chamber of Commerce uses very similar language: "Our philosophy of federalism is that collaboration among the various orders of government in Canada is necessary to best meet the needs of Canadians."

5. Leslie A. Pal, "Alternative Instruments of Governance: Models, Trends and Implications for Income Security Policy," submitted to the federal government project on Governance Implication of Labour Market and Income Polarization (Ottawa: Statistics Canada and Human Resources Development Canada, 1997).

6. Liberal Party, *Securing Our Future Together*, p. 15.

7. Biggs, *Building Blocks for Canada's New Social Union*.

8. The premier of Alberta wrote to the prime minister on 16 May 1997 complaining about David Dingwall's "arbitrary and ill-informed deduction." Tabled in the Alberta Legislature, 20 May 1997.

9. There will be a fuller discussion of the CHA per se, in the sectoral analysis below.

10. It is also true that provinces do not discuss major amendments to social assistance law with the federal government, but there is no parallel uploading of costs to Ottawa when provinces restrict their social assistance programs.

11. Thus, the agreements require the provinces to undertake their activities relating to labour exchange services in a fashion that is "methodologically consistent" with the operation of the National Labour Exchange System. There is also

provision for a joint strategy in the gathering, production, and dissemination of local and provincial labour market information to be carried out in a way that is consistent with the National Labour Market Information System.

12. These primary indicators include the number of "active EI claimants" (a term that has a precise meaning under the agreements) that have access to provincial benefits and measures, the proportion of clients who are successfully reemployed, and the consequential savings to the EI account (e.g., section 7.1 of the Canada-Alberta Agreement). Targets have been agreed to and published by the two levels of government and provision is made for establishing mechanisms for jointly setting future targets and for jointly reviewing and assessing achievements. There is also provision that the measurement of primary indicators will be based on a methodology established by the federal government to allow for national results to be reported to Parliament. In addition, there is provision for a joint evaluation of results.

     There are a number of good questions that can be asked about the accountability framework that the two governments have established for themselves (e.g., how can program effectiveness be judged when it is unclear whether the EI clients who will receive reemployment assistance from a province are those closest to or furthest from being "job ready?" What is the historical record that lies behind the current targets?). These questions should be pursued in public debate — by committees of the federal and provincial legislatures.

13. Note that this assessment understates, in one important respect, the increased collaboration relative to the policy framework. The new federal-provincial Child Benefit System, discussed below, helps improve labour market incentives.

14. As this chapter was being completed, there were still no signs of a federal-Ontario Labour Market Agreement. The principal obstacle is that the amount of money that the federal government is prepared to transfer to Ontario is substantially less than the amount considered fair by the Ontario authorities.

15. The CHA is, of course, only one element of Canada's health-care system(s). It bears noting that many other elements of the system(s) entail intergovernmental arrangements that are more collaborative or more disentangled than is true of the CHA.

16. National Forum on Health, *Canada Health Action: Building on the Legacy*, vol. I (Ottawa: Canada Communication Group, 1997), p. 21.

17. Ibid.

18. The principles can be traced back to the cost-sharing associated with the *Hospital Insurance and Diagnostic Services Act* (1957), the *National Medical Care Act* (1966), and their replacement through block funding, in 1977, via the Established Programs Financing legislation.

19. See, for example, the press release by Prime Minister Chrétien dated 4 February 1997. See also Liberal Party, *Securing Our Future Together*, p. 15, which states: "The federal government must retain its authority under the Canada Health Act to enforce these principles."

20. This possibility is hinted at in the final report of the National Forum on Health. As already noted, the starting point for the forum is its belief that the health-care system in Canada is "fundamentally sound" (*Canada Health Action* Vol. I, p. 11) and that this soundness is linked to the five principles. It rejects the practicability of relying on the "collective will of the provinces to develop and maintain a set of national principles" (*Canada Health Action* Vol. II, p. 28), and declares that there is "no viable alternative to federal-provincial transfers if we are truly serious about maintaining national health care principles as we know them."

21. Federal/provincial/territorial ministers of health, press release of meeting, dated 15 September 1994. Quebec and the Northwest Territories ministers were not present. Practices in four provinces — Nova Scotia, Newfoundland, Manitoba, and Alberta — have all been found, to one degree or other, to be non-conforming. The first three situations are still not resolved and remain subject to very small withholdings.

22. Press release, 12 September 1997.

23. It is recognized that huge changes are being implemented by the provinces in relation to the design and delivery of many health services. Almost all of these changes raise no issues concerning the five principles of the CHA. In that sense, much, but by no means all, of the health-care system can be seen as a disentangled model. The discussion here has been confined to the CHA.

24. In fact, the antecedents of this approach date back to the 1970s and even earlier (e.g., the 1943 Marsh Report, the system of federal Family Allowances that followed, the 1970 federal Family Income Support Plan proposal, Quebec's 1971 Castonguay-Nepveu Report, etc.).

25. See, for example, the communiqué from the 37th Annual Premiers' Conference, Jasper, 21 August 1996; and Canada, Department of Finance, *Working Together Towards a National Child Benefit System* (Ottawa: Minister of Supply and Services, 1997).

26. Federal/Provincial/Territorial Ministers Responsible for Social Services, press release, 19 February 1997.

27. Federal/Provincial/Territorial Ministers Responsible for Social Services, *The National Child Benefit: Building a Better Future for Canadian Children* (Ottawa: Minister of Supply and Services, 1997).

28. British Columbia, *British Columbia's Proposal for a National Child Benefit* (Victoria: Government of British Columbia, 1997).

29. Other premiers have also indicated planned actions, including an Alberta Family Employment Tax Credit, a Saskatchewan plan to create both an income-tested child benefit and an earnings supplement for the working poor, and an Ontario Child Care Tax Credit. New Brunswick is also starting a modest income-tested child benefit and working income supplement.

30. Even this conclusion is qualified in that one province, British Columbia, has asked Revenue Canada to deliver its BC Family Bonus.

31. The 1997 Ontario budget indicates that Ontario will implement a new child-care tax credit as a part of its commitment to the new intergovernmental agreements.

32. Richards, "Reducing the Muddle in the Middle."

33. See Robert Williams, "Without Mysteries or Miracles: Conducting Cultural Policy in the Canadian Federal System," in *Canada: The State of the Federation 1996*, ed. Patrick C. Fafard and Douglas M. Brown (Kingston: Institute of Inter-governmental Relations, Queen's University, 1996), pp. 189-212.

34. EKOS Research Associates Inc., *Rethinking Government* (Ottawa: EKOS Research Associates, 1996).

5

Economic Integration in Canada through the Agreement on Internal Trade

Robert H. Knox

L'Entente d'échange interne a deux ans. Cet article révise ce que l'Entente a contribué à l'ouverture du marché domestique canadien et à l'amélioration de son efficacité. Il considère aussi comment l'Entente a fonctionné comme un arrangement qui a permis aux gouvernements canadiens de continuer à travailler de façon coopérative pour améliorer l'intégration économique dans le marché domestique.

L'article conclut que l'Entente a déjà contribué à améliorer l'intégration économique dans le marché domestique mais que cela est toujours en progrès. Le gouvernement fédéral et les provinces doivent continuer d'enlever les barrières à l'activité commerciale domestique et à améliorer la structure d'exploitation de l'Entente, notamment les procédés de prise de décision qui nécessitent le consensus et le système de résolution de conflit pour le rendre plus accessible, vite et transparent. Si les gouvernements sont en mesure d'utiliser les structures établies par l'Entente pour continuer un procédé d'intégration économique domestique coopératif, cela sera un accomplissement important dans la réforme non constitutionnelle.

The heart of the problem lies in the fact that the simplest requirements of provincial autonomy ... involve the use of powers which are capable of abuse ... the problem is to preclude or restrict abuses without interfering with legitimate and even necessary powers.

Rowell-Sirois Commission, 1940

Federalism justifies variation among provinces in response to local preferences ... the need to accommodate diversity ... must be balanced against the objective of gains from trade ...

Macdonald Commission, 1985

The Agreement on Internal Trade is now just two years old, yet it is a key avenue for tangible reform of the federation by "non-constitutional means." It is a complex and technically diverse intergovernmental agreement, attempting to deal with an ambitious range of issues affecting the integrity of the Canadian economic union.

Coming as it did in the immediate aftermath of failed attempts at constitutional reform (including reform to change constitutional provisions affecting internal trade), the agreement is among the more prominent examples of the kind of reform to which this volume is devoted. For this reason the agreement has come under considerable scrutiny — even though, as noted below, its potential for change is not yet realized and it has not been well understood or promoted among the community (i.e., Canadian citizens and businesses) it was meant to serve.

There is already a substantial body of analysis on what the agreement says. The purpose of this chapter is to document the extent and nature of the reduction of barriers to internal trade that have occurred since it was signed. By placing the agreement in its broader context and providing insight into its actual operations, more light can be shed on the pitfalls and promise of this area of ongoing reform of the federal system.

This essay argues that the Agreement on Internal Trade deals with two problems that Canadian governments had been unable to solve despite 15 years of trying. It allows provinces to adjust and develop policies and practices to improve national economic integration without compromising their policy capacity in other areas. Furthermore, it commits Canadian governments to an agenda and an operating structure to improve domestic economic integration progressively and cooperatively. The Agreement on Internal Trade has improved economic integration in the two years that it has been in place, but, as will be shown below, governments are not applying the Agreement to its full potential.

INTRODUCTION

Internal trade barriers and discriminatory commercial policies and practices are normal in any federation. Canada is no exception. Within the limits established by the constitution, provincial governments use their legislative authority to serve the interests of their constituents. This includes protecting and discriminating in favour of local businesses and using policies and practices to provide advantages to the provincial economy.

It is also in the interest of provinces to maintain the effectiveness and the integrity of the economic union. The advantages of this are less obvious and tangible. It is also difficult to accomplish this objective in the ambiguous Canadian constitutional framework that supports diversity and divides responsibility for economic policy between the provincial and the federal governments. In Canada the rules for domestic trade derive from section 121 of the *Constitution Act, 1867* which says that articles of growth, produce, or manufacture of any province shall be admitted free into other provinces; and section 91(2) which establishes the authority of Parliament for regulating trade and commerce, including trade between provinces.

Generally section 121 has been interpreted as applying to goods and to tariffs and taxes, but not necessarily to non-tariff barriers and/or to the movement of people and investment and trade in services. Section 6(2) of the *Canadian Charter of Rights and Freedoms* now guarantees mobility rights and some recent judicial decisions have interpreted section 121 more broadly than before but the legal character of Canada's economic union remains unclear.[1] The federal government has not used section 91(2) to establish general rules and a regime for managing interprovincial trade and commerce. At this stage in the evolution of the Canadian constitution, it is uncertain whether the federal government could take this step without provincial consent and without changing the constitutional balance between federal and provincial jurisdiction.

Barriers to interprovincial trade and commercial activity were not a major issue until about 1980 when businesses, through their associations, began to focus on them as a factor that was having a negative impact on their efficiency, competitiveness, and growth potential.

Canada's economy expanded rapidly in the years following World War II, but trade was still largely resource-based internationally and the domestic market was still relatively protected and isolated. There was a national consensus regarding the value of markets and freer trade as an essential ingredient of economic growth, but this was understood to be an international not a domestic issue. Canada participated in successive rounds of trade liberalization under the General Agreement on Tariffs and Trade (GATT) starting with a tariff reduction on goods and expanding to include non-tariff barriers and, eventually, services and investment as part of the Uruguay Round in the 1980s.

As a result of the 1985 Canada-US Free Trade Agreement, (CUSFTA) later expanded to include Mexico as the North American Free Trade Agreement, Canada became part of a more or less open continental market by the early 1990s. The North American Free Trade Agreement (NAFTA) also produced a potential political problem. In effect, the availability of markets in the United States that were more accessible to Canadian exporters than their own domestic markets could eventually sap the integrity of Canada's economic union.

While all this was going on internationally, nothing much had happened to develop an open and efficient domestic market since the Rowell-Sirois Commission (the Royal Commission on Dominion-Provincial Relations) identified interprovincial trade barriers as a potential issue. For most of the period after World War II, Canadian businesses and most professional and skilled trade groups generally accepted and even encouraged protectionist practices that gave them a local competitive advantage.

But in the face of more open international trade, and the development of new technologies and rapid economic globalization, it was increasingly difficult to ignore or justify local protectionist practices. This was particularly the case if these practices reduced the efficiency and competitiveness of Canadian business, limited the development of a productive and appropriately skilled workforce and constrained domestic employment growth and investment.

By 1980 the Canadian economy was less isolated, more diverse, and was beginning to anticipate the pressures of a more open and competitive global economy. Canadian business identified two particular problems in the domestic market. First were government policies and practices that discriminated against workers, goods, services, and investment from other jurisdictions. Second were the different regulations and standards and similar measures that made doing business in other provinces complicated and expensive.

Canadian business began to press governments to remove these barriers and to reduce regulatory burden and complexity. But, while there was an established apparatus and consensus for dealing with international trade issues, there was no similar system to manage domestic trade.

This chapter outlines the current status of the Agreement on Internal Trade reached in July 1994 and that came into force in July 1995. The second section provides a brief discussion of the protracted intergovernmental process leading up to the agreement. Section three provides an overview of the main principles and scope of the agreement. The fourth section discusses the implementation of the sectoral aspects of the agreement (ch. 4-15), while section five covers the implementation of the operating structure and institutions, including the dispute resolution process (ch. 16 and 17). The conclusion draws together comments on the extent and nature of the reform which the agreement represents.

THE INTERGOVERNMENTAL PROCESS ON THE WAY TO THE AGREEMENT ON INTERNAL TRADE

In 1980, the federal government proposed a reformulation of section 121 of the *Constitution Act, 1867* as part of the repatriation round. The proposed wording said that no Canadian government could discriminate on the basis of residence "in a manner that unduly impedes the operation of the economic union." Other parts of the proposal protected measures that might be inconsistent with this provision but were "in the interests of public safety, order, health or morals." Parliament (but not provincial legislatures) would also be allowed to continue policies for equalization and regional development.

This proposal was rejected by nine of ten provinces because it placed unacceptable constraints on provincial powers and extended federal authority and reserved regional development to the federal government. Consideration of this proposal was brief and not substantial.[2] This was nonetheless the start of a 14-year process that would lead to the *Agreement on Internal Trade* signed by all Canadian provinces and territories and the federal government in July 1994. During this time, a consensus on the importance of an open and efficient domestic market developed along with a commitment to make the necessary changes to accomplish this goal. Still, almost nothing of substance happened until 1993.

The fundamental problem remained the same through all the discussions and negotiations over this period. There remained a pervading concern by provincial governments that to remove barriers to domestic trade and to eliminate or harmonize other measures that make the economic union less efficient would reduce their economic jurisdiction and limit their policy and legislative flexibility and authority in other areas. Notwithstanding regular First Ministers' Conferences (FMCs) and meetings of committees of ministers, there was no formally mandated, cooperative process by which Canadian governments could jointly manage the domestic market in a way that would support continuing economic integration and respond to rapidly changing global economic conditions. All governments, the federal as well as provincial, tended to see the problem in "zero-sum" terms — any reduction in provincial authority would increase the federal government's jurisdiction and any formal cooperative arrangement for managing the domestic market would allow the national government to intervene in provincial affairs.

After 1980 there were a number of proposals and intergovernmental initiatives to resolve domestic trade issues. The issue remained prominent, sometimes near the top of the intergovernmental agenda and never far beneath the surface. The "Macdonald" Royal Commission on the Economic Union and Development Prospects for Canada was set up in 1982 by the government of Prime Minister Pierre Trudeau specifically to deal with economic integration. But while the Macdonald Report made recommendations for mechanisms to reduce internal trade barriers,[3] its more prominent recommendations dealt with the need for a free trade agreement with the United States.

Over the subsequent period from 1985 to 1992, two issues eclipsed direct intergovernmental attention to internal trade as such. First, the negotiations with the United States over the (CUSFTA) and subsequently with the United States and Mexico over the NAFTA had priority over internal trade negotiations, although in many respects they subsumed them. Some barriers to internal trade also constitute international trade barriers, and some provisions of the *CUSFTA* and *NAFTA* eliminate barriers to internal trade or change the context of the regulation of the domestic market.

Second, from the first agreement at Meech Lake, federal-provincial relations were dominated for the next five years by attempts at constitutional reform. The economic union issue in general became a prominent part of the post-Meech, "Canada" round. Constitutional solutions to improving the economic union took a variety of forms, including a statement of general principles (e.g., the "Canada Clause" in the Charlottetown Accord); an improved section 121 (e.g., Government of Canada proposals, September 1991, and the "Charest" report of March 1992); and a new federal legislative power over the economy (the federal government's 1991 proposals for a new section 95A).

While the broader free trade and constitutional issues dominated, the federal and provincial and territorial governments pursued internal trade issues, first, through the Committee of Regional Economic Development Ministers starting in 1985, and then through the Committee of Ministers on Internal Trade (CMIT) starting in 1987. Successive Annual Premiers' Conferences (APCs), starting in 1986, and First Ministers' Conferences on the economy, starting in 1987, also discussed internal trade issues.

This process tried various options including voluntary "standstills" on new barriers to trade that failed almost as soon as they were accepted and negotiation of agreements on specific issues such as government procurement and liquor board marketing practices. Little of substance was accomplished.

By late 1992, with the failure to ratify the Charlottetown Accord, Canadian governments faced an internal trade agenda that was more urgent than ever. In trade policy terms, the differences between 1980 and 1992 were significant.

Economic globalization was now a reality. North American free trade was in place and the World Trade Organization was about to emerge from the GATT Uruguay Round along with further international trade liberalizing measures. Through extensive intergovernmental consultations with Ottawa over those international trade negotiations, most provinces now had knowledge of and experience with international trade policy. Similarly, major Canadian business associations had made the reduction or elimination of internal trade barriers a policy priority.

Although some provinces were more wary than others, making the domestic market more open and competitive was a priority and an objective for all Canadian governments, if they could find an acceptable way to do it. The years of work on domestic trade issues, particularly the recent constitutional discussions, had clarified the essentials of the problem and developed a cadre of informed and knowledgeable ministers and officials with clear negotiating positions.

In March 1992, at a conference on the economy, the first ministers agreed to accelerate the process to reduce internal trade barriers, to strengthen domestic trade linkages and to find ways to minimize competition for investment. They set a deadline of March 1995 for the Committee of Ministers on Internal Trade to achieve this objective. In May 1992, the Committee of Ministers on

Internal Trade approved three *Principles to Enhance Internal Trade in Canada* and a moratorium on new barriers.

By December 1992, as noted, the constitutional route had failed completely with the negative response to the referendum on the Charlottetown Accord. However, this result seemed to reinvigorate the non-constitutional process of internal trade negotiations, perhaps because public opposition to the Charlottetown Accord did not appear to be related to the issues of economic union or internal trade.

Michael Wilson, the federal minister of industry, tabled a proposed Statement on Canada's Internal Trade at a meeting of the Committee of Ministers on Internal Trade. The statement committed Canadian governments to negotiate a comprehensive agreement "to remove barriers and reconcile regulations, standards and administrative practices in all of the economic sectors and subject areas agreed to by governments." The negotiations would begin by July 1993. The agreement would be completed by 30 June 1994 and ratified by 30 June 1995. To the surprise of many officials, ministers agreed. They would recommend to their governments that they proceed as set out in the statement.

On behalf of their governments, ministers formally agreed to the process at their meeting in Montreal on 18 March 1993.[4] The negotiations got underway in July 1993. A year later, at a conference in Ottawa on 18 July 1994, first ministers signed the Agreement on Internal Trade (AIT). It came into force on 1 July 1995.

THE AGREEMENT ON INTERNAL TRADE: OVERVIEW

The Agreement on Internal Trade has four components.[5] First, it sets out objectives and general trade rules for domestic trade (Parts I, II, and III). Second, it contains chapters for each of the economic sectors covered by the agreement (Part IV). Third, there are Chapters defining an operating structure and dispute resolution procedures (Part V). Finally, it contains provisions of general application (Part VI).

The first component of the agreement sets out general objectives and, in Part III – General Rules, establishes operating principles for Canada's domestic market. These rules provide for non-discrimination,[6] the right of entry and exit[7] and a prohibition on measures that create obstacles to domestic trade.[8] Other rules provide for the reconciliation of standards and regulations[9] and require governments to ensure that measures and procedures relating to matters covered by the agreement are accessible.[10] Effectively these last two rules establish a basis for positive economic integration through the agreement while the first three rules establish limits on government authority in relation to domestic trade.

Governments deal with the limits that broad trade rules might have on their capacity to act in other policy areas by applying the concept of "legitimate objective." Governments have further ensured the flexible application of the broad trade principles by limiting their application to matters covered in the specific economic sector chapters in Part IV.[11] To add suspenders to the belt, an article in Chapter Three[12] confirms that the agreement does not alter the legislative or other authority of Parliament or of the provincial legislatures or any other authority established by the constitution. Together these measures deal with one of the concerns that prevented agreement on internal trade after 1980. The question is do they make the principles for domestic trade contained in Chapter Four ineffective? In my view they do not.

Governments have undertaken to apply the agreement.[13] If they respect the intent, spirit and substance of the agreement, they will use the principles in Chapter Four – General Rules, to guide the development and application of their policies and practices. The rules in Chapter Four apply to the specific sector chapters (in Part IV – Specific Rules) in one form or another. This allows for flexibility and restructuring to make the rules more effective and appropriate.

Part IV includes ten chapters on specific economic sectors that are covered by the agreement. Some of these chapters, such as those on government procurement, investment, labour mobility, and consumer protection, break new ground and should produce significant integration in Canada's domestic economy. Others, such as those covering transportation, communications, and environmental protection, reinforce and support economic integration processes already underway. Still others such as the one for agricultural and food products and, to an extent, the one for alcoholic beverages establish a schedule and a process for dealing with issues in the future.

Most chapters include a form of institutional structure and provisions for continuing consultation and review that are intended to promote continuing positive economic integration through the reconciliation and harmonization of policies and practices.

The details of the sectoral chapters (5-15) and the operating structure (16-17) are provided in subsequent sections of this chapter.

However, Chapter Eighteen – Final Provisions, includes articles that qualify the rest of the agreement by including a number of general exceptions. First, programs for regional economic development are exempted.[14] (These exceptions are subject to constraints and reporting requirements. There are no reports yet on how much regional economic development exceptions have been used.) Also exempt are policies and programs for Aboriginal Peoples[15] and measures to support culture or cultural industries.[16] In addition, financial institutions and services are excluded.[17] (The issue for governments was securities regulation, which was being negotiated separately.)

The final chapter also includes several other important provisions, including: a "standstill" on any new measures or amendments inconsistent with the agreement, or which decrease conformity with the agreement.[18] It also contains a provision that requires an annual review of the scope and coverage of the agreement, that is effectively a commitment by governments to extend and expand the agreement.[19] Finally there is a commitment to complete negotiation of the energy chapter.[20]

THE SECTOR CHAPTERS AND THEIR IMPLEMENTATION

In assessing the results of the negotiation for the agreement and, more especially, its implementation, a few basic questions have been posed: What is the principal barrier to be removed by each part of the agreement, and how effective are the provisions in the agreement covering that barrier? Based on available evidence in the first two years, how has each part of the agreement been implemented and is it reaching its potential for improved economic integration in Canada? Are the operating structures and processes, including dispute resolution, adequate to the task of fulfilling the broader objectives of the agreement? To answer these questions, the following section summarizes the agreement, and its implementation thus far, particularly in the following areas: procurement, investment and business access (including incentives), labour mobility, and consumer protection.

PROCUREMENT

The Agreement on Internal Trade, through Chapter Five on Procurement, establishes a national open market for public sector procurement by establishing non-discriminatory rules and procedures for public sector procurement and developing a national electronic tendering system available to all governments and government agencies. Ultimately the terms of the procurement chapter will be extended to the broader public sector (municipalities, municipal organizations, school boards and publicly-funded academic health and social service entities, the so-called MASH sector as in municipalities, academic institutions, schools, and hospitals).

To date, a common electronic tendering system has been developed by an intergovernmental technical working group that was set up as part of the agreement.[21] This working group has selected a supplier to provide a system that should be operational within the next two years. Eventually suppliers anywhere in Canada will be able to access most public sector tenders on this single system. As this chapter was being completed in September 1997, negotiations to extend the provisions of the procurement chapter to the broader public sector (the MASH sector) were incomplete.

The agreement called for negotiations on arrangements to include the MASH sector to be completed by 30 June 1995[22] and to come into force on 30 June 1996.[23] These negotiations were nowhere near complete by either of these dates. Initially the main issue was concern by the groups and governments affected that they would be burdened with a complex, rigid, and expensive system. The health sector was particularly concerned that, if the procurement chapter applied to them, they would be unable to use strategic purchasing that allows them to engage their suppliers in hospital operations to reduce costs.

Most of the issues have been resolved in most jurisdictions. There is now a draft text that is acceptable to all provinces except British Columbia which, apparently, continues to believe that the provisions in the current procurement chapter are too complicated. The BC government is not prepared to require their MASH entities to apply them. They proposed another option based on a "best efforts" application of the open tendering principles in the agreement. Other governments believe this approach is unworkable.

Provincial governments (the federal government is not part of this negotiation because they do not have MASH entities within their jurisdiction) have been at a stand-off on this matter for more than a year. The agreement[24] requires that decisions be made by consensus. Since the Government of British Columbia has said that it will not accept what other provinces wish to accept there is an effective veto by BC and an impasse.

At their annual conference in August 1997, premiers directed internal trade ministers to meet as soon as possible and conclude "an arrangement to include open tendering provisions for MASH sector procurement, in a manner acceptable to all jurisdictions if possible."

Since BC is unlikely to agree, apparently other provinces are, reluctantly, prepared to proceed without that province. Excluding one jurisdiction is inconsistent with the economic integration objectives of the agreement. It could establish a precedent, which, if broadly applied in the future, would "fragment" rather than integrate the domestic market. Nevertheless, if used occasionally, it is an effective and flexible means to promote transition toward economic integration.

Critics believe that exclusions in the procurement chapter mean that it is less than comprehensive.

For example the agreement applies to purchases of goods $25,000 and over and to services and construction contracts $100,000 and over.[25] A number of government agencies and Crown corporations are excluded[26] as well as some services.[27] Procurement contracts can be excluded to support regional and economic development but only under certain conditions[28] and procurement procedures allow exclusions for such things as urgency or where issues such as confidentiality and public health and safety are involved.[29]

Some of these exclusions are necessary to provide for efficient procurement. For example, the cost of the tendering process makes purchasing goods by tender below $25,000 inefficient. Other exclusions are currently under review as required by the agreement.[30] Reports are that governments are making progress in reducing the number of entities excluded, but have failed to come to terms on the services excluded.

So far there has been no move to change threshold levels, but, based on experience since negotiations on procurement started in 1988, further liberalization will begin once governments have an opportunity to adjust to the new environment and have a better understanding of how the agreement works.

Critics also believe that the procurement chapter must have an accessible, quick and transparent "bid-protest" system to be effective and that current procedures[31] do not meet these criteria. Like most systems for dispute resolution in the agreement (and for that matter those proposed during the 1992 "Canada round" of Constitutional discussions) the bid-protest procedures for provinces (procedures for the federal government are different) are designed to be non-adversarial and to resolve issues through discussion and mediation. It is also, fundamentally, a government-to-government system and depends on the interest and energies of officials.

The federal government uses the International Trade Tribunal (ITT), which also handles procurement issues under NAFTA, to deal with bid protests. The virtue of this system is that ITT is a third party with quasi-judicial procedures dedicated to dealing with disputes. It also has the power to halt procurement proceedings and to reverse decisions as well as to recommend compensation. As an agency with a specific mandate to resolve disputes it is probably more accessible than provincial systems.

On the face of it, the best arrangement to deal with bid protests would be a single national system with the authority to intervene in procurement processes if necessary. But this was further than provinces were willing to go during negotiations.

As it stands, the provincial bid-protest system needs improvement in a number of areas. Unless provinces have taken the trouble to describe the bid-protest process and identify contact points in tender documents the process may not be particularly accessible. There is no capacity for the provincial contact point to intervene in the procurement process and no clear remedy for the complaining supplier unless provinces have defined one in their own procedures. As a result, a supplier is dependent upon the capacity of the "contact point," an official who usually has other responsibilities. There is no mandated third-party oversight of the process or the players. Furthermore, there is no formal public reporting of suppliers' complaints that have been resolved or dealt with in some other way. As a result it is almost impossible to tell if the process is working. Changes are possible. The chapter[32] requires a review of the bid-protest system in 1998. Probably it is too soon for substantive changes.

The Internal Trade Secretariat recently started tracking complaints. Thirteen bid protests have been listed since 1995. Eight of these are through the federal government system. Four of the protests were resolved or upheld, seven were denied or dropped and two are pending. It is hard to tell if this is a complete list or if a significant number of potential protests were never made because suppliers were unaware of the process or because they did not believe it would be worthwhile to use it.

Has the procurement chapter improved economic integration in Canada's domestic market? No doubt it has. Government procurement at the federal and provincial level is more open and accessible across the country and, imperfect as it may be, Canada has an undertaking in place for a national public sector procurement market that was not there before. Has the procurement chapter realized its full potential? The answer is no. It is disappointing, but not terminal, that governments are unable to meet negotiating deadlines and implement other obligations such as the reduction of excluded entities and services and that the review of the chapter, including the appropriateness of the existing thresholds, has not been done.

IMPROVING BUSINESS ACCESS

One of the issues for domestic commerce is the difficulty and the potential extra costs involved in doing business in other provinces. Each province has the power to regulate and set standards for business activities in its own region. There are two aspects of this issue examined below. First are the measures and practices that treat businesses from outside the province differently from those located inside. Second are the regulations, standards and other measures that are different from jurisdiction to jurisdiction even though they are intended for the same purpose. An example is the different corporate reporting and registration requirements that are in place in each province.

In some cases, the objective of discriminatory provisions and different regulations may be to exclude businesses from other provinces or at least to give an advantage to local business. In most cases, however, the problem is one of omission, or at least the absence of a compelling reason for change, and the want of a mechanism for resolving differences in practices and regulation.

The agreement deals with these issues in two ways. First, it seeks to resolve differences in standards and regulatory measures that create barriers to trade.[33] Most chapters — but most importantly those on investment, labour mobility, consumer protection, transportation, environmental protection, and natural resources — include specific obligations to reconcile these differences and require regular reviews to identify issues not already covered by the agreement. Second, it attempts to eliminate discriminatory practices altogether.

Chapter Six on Investment provides for non-discriminatory treatment of Canadian businesses regardless of where the head office is located, where the firm is incorporated or where the owners live. It also eliminates local presence and residency requirements as a condition for carrying on business or making an investment[34] and restricts the use of local purchasing and local sourcing requirements.[35] Chapter Eight – Consumer Related Measures and Standards, prevents governments from requiring individuals to live in a province or territory as a condition of licensing, registration or certification as a supplier and allows local presence and residency requirements for businesses only where necessary for consumer protection.[36] It also eliminates any discriminatory fees or other requirements for the licensing, registering or certification of suppliers.[37]

Within the next year, implementation of another provision in the investment chapter will ease the compliance burdens for firms conducting business in more than one jurisdiction. In the agreement, governments undertook to reconcile corporate registration and reporting requirements and agreed to produce an implementation plan by 15 July 1995.[38] They missed the deadline but last year, ministers approved an implementation plan that is now being applied.

In summary, these measures will undoubtedly improve domestic economic integration. However, Canadian governments have not yet come to terms with the need to reconcile different standards and regulations even though the agreement provides the structure and the obligation. Probably the problem is a lack of specificity to provide focus. Either businesses and associations, in cooperation with government, will have to develop a menu of issues to be resolved or governments will have to look to new mechanisms, such as cooperative national institutions for standard setting, for regulation, and for inspection. This approach is being implemented in the securities industry and in agriculture, and it will probably happen elsewhere if and when the need becomes acute.

THE CODE OF CONDUCT ON INCENTIVES

In the initial discussions of barriers to interprovincial trade in 1985, competition for investment among provinces became a collateral issue. Its main proponent was British Columbia. They were concerned that neighbouring provinces, particularly Alberta, were enticing operating companies away from BC with subsidies and other incentives. In other words, provinces were "poaching" businesses with jobs that would not have relocated otherwise.

There was also the situation in which companies that were interested in moving or investing would "subsidy hunt" or auction their investment to the highest bidder. For the larger provinces — Ontario, Quebec and British Columbia — the competition was with American states that could offer attractive packages of municipal and state tax relief and infrastructure incentives as well as subsidies. These provinces were not anxious to change their practices. Smaller provinces, on the other hand, frequently found themselves competing against one another for the same investment.

The Agreement on Internal Trade includes a Code of Conduct on Incentives in the investment chapter as an annex.[39] It prevents governments from giving incentives or subsidies, of any kind, to businesses to lure them away from other Canadian jurisdictions and rules out incentives that would allow an enterprise to undercut a competitor from another province for a specific contract.[40]

The code commits governments to use their best efforts to avoid incentives that sustain uneconomic operations, that increase capacity that is not warranted by market conditions or that is excessive and to avoid bidding wars.[41] The annex also requires an annual report on incentives that will describe the incentive programs offered by governments, the amounts of incentives paid by type and amount of individual grants over $500,000 and loans or loan guarantees and equity over $1 million. So far this report has not been produced by the Working Group on Investment that is responsible for it. The working group itself only started meeting regularly in 1996.

The Code of Conduct on Incentives has already been tested twice but inconclusively. In the spring of 1995, about four months before the agreement came into effect, United Parcel Services (UPS) announced that it would consolidate its administrative and call centre operations in Moncton, New Brunswick. The consolidation involved 900 jobs including about 300 from British Columbia. British Columbia protested that New Brunswick used subsidies to attract UPS. They said that these kinds of subsidies were prohibited by the Code of Conduct on Incentives and that, according to Article 1807, New Brunswick was committed to a standstill on measures or actions that were inconsistent with the agreement after it was signed by the first ministers in July 1994.

New Brunswick's position was that UPS had already decided to consolidate its administrative activities somewhere in North American and decided on New Brunswick and that the commitment was made, but for the details, before the agreement was signed in July 1994. Therefore, any incentives provided were consistent with the agreement. New Brunswick also maintains the Code of Conduct on Incentives is incomplete. Before the agreement was signed the parties had agreed to clarify how incentives would apply in cases where a business was consolidating its activities. This had not been done.

The agreement provides for consultation among parties who disagree. Although BC and New Brunswick took their positions to the media first, there was eventually consultation under the terms of the agreement. These went on for about 18 months during which British Columbia asked for information and New Brunswick provided some information but withheld some to protect commercial interests. Ministers were consulted twice but were unable to resolve the issue.

Finally, in September 1996 *The Globe and Mail* reported that: "New Brunswick will not submit to the scrutiny of a new interprovincial trade tribunal looking into the province's acquisition of 900 United Postal Service jobs last year." *The Financial Post* reported that: "[The] B.C. Industry Minister [said] that he will recommend repudiation of the [internal] trade deal to his cabinet colleagues ... B.C. charges that New Brunswick is unwilling to participate in the formal dispute settlement process under the terms of the *Agreement*." There it stands. Both British Columbia or New Brunswick could ask for a panel but neither has.

Meanwhile, around the same time it was reported that in May 1995, nine months after they signed the Agreement on Internal Trade, Saskatchewan decided to provide a $5 million forgivable loan to a BC meat packer to consolidate its operations in Saskatchewan. It appears from these reports that the Saskatchewan government knew that its decision was inconsistent with the agreement but decided to go ahead anyway. BC has not protested this issue.

Probably both New Brunswick and Saskatchewan legitimately thought their initiatives to attract business were not yet covered by the agreement. It is at least arguable. British Columbia, for its part, has a right to feel frustrated. For the BC government, the Code of Conduct on Incentives was an essential part of the agreement and one of the main reasons it could support it. It made this clear during negotiations. Now it appears that the code is ineffective.[42]

It is likely that the problem lies with the dispute resolution process that cannot resolve issues quickly and with some kind of satisfaction for the protagonists (dispute resolution is covered in more detail below). On the other hand, the agreement's dispute resolution process may be more effective than it appears. It is based on the premise that, generally, governments will avoid doing things that require them to publicly defend policies that are inconsistent with the agreement and that might be politically embarrassing. Maybe governments will ensure that their programs are consistent with the Code of Conduct on Incentives in the future.

LABOUR MOBILITY

Provinces have the constitutional responsibility for regulating the workplace and determining occupational standards and qualifications in their jurisdiction. In most provinces much of the administration of professional standards has been delegated by legislation to professional associations. Effectively there are different occupational and professional licensing bodies in every province. Over time this has resulted in different provincial requirements to qualify or to be certified, some tending to protect a profession or trade, but most to meet what are understood to be local conditions and to meet their statutory obligation to protect standards and ensure adequate qualifications for practitioners or workers.

Now, because of increased mobility and improved communication, the practical differences in occupational and professional training and competence across Canada have been reduced. However, the fragmented structure for developing and applying standards and qualifications remains. Mobility for Canadians is guaranteed by section 6 of the *Canadian Charter of Rights and Freedoms*. This means that Canadians cannot be refused entry or work or the right to practise their trade or profession because they have come from another province. This has been confirmed by the Supreme Court in a ruling on a case of a lawyer qualified to practise in Alberta who was refused the right to practise because he was not associated with a firm of practising in Alberta.

Section 6 of the Charter does not override the requirement to be qualified so that, even though Canadians have the right to move to and work in other jurisdictions, the problem of different and sometimes onerous and restrictive occupational standards and licensing practices still exist.

Chapter Seven of the agreement is intended to reduce these practical barriers to mobility and incudes three measures to accomplish this objective. First, it removes residency as a condition for access to employment opportunities, for licensing, certification or registration or for eligibility for an occupation.[43] Second, it establishes that requirements for licensing, certification or registration of workers must relate principally to competence, must be published and must not result in unnecessary delays or burdensome costs.[44] Third, the agreement requires that qualifications of workers from other jurisdictions must be recognized and differences in occupational standards reconciled.[45]

The key requirement is the commitment to reconcile occupational standards and recognize qualifications. Accomplishing this objective has eluded Canadian governments for years. The main problem is the number of professions and skilled trades and the number of organizations involved in setting and administering standards for them. For example, the Labour Market Coordinating Group, the officials responsible for implementing the chapter, has identified and contacted more than 400 non-governmental trade and professional groups who are required to change their policies and practices to be consistent with the agreement.

An annex to the chapter[46] requires provinces to begin this process within 12 months after the agreement came into force. Governments met this deadline and work is now underway to mutually recognize qualifications and reconcile standards. The problem is that there is no deadline for completing this process.[47] Even though governments have taken steps to notify the 400 or more non-governmental occupational licensing bodies of their obligations and to set out procedures, little has changed. Premiers acknowledged this at their annual conference in August 1997.[48]

In February 1997, the federal government announced a program to provide funding to consortia of provincial occupational groups to help them develop harmonized standards and qualifications. Four groups have been funded and 12 applications are being considered. This program is likely to produce results but it is possible that governments will have to consider ways to bring closure to the process for occupational groups and to speed up the process of harmonizing occupational standards for trades. They plan to do this in the spring of 1998.

In the meantime, governments are using the procedures for consultation in the chapter[49] to identify and resolve issues while the process of reconciliation is underway. Some of the issues raised through this process are illustrated in the examples that follow:

- An Emergency Medical Technician from Alberta found that his quali-fications were not recognized in Ontario and that he would have to go through the Emergency Medical Care Assistant Challenge Eligibility process at Humber College to assess his prior training, knowledge, and skills against the current program curriculum. He believes that Ontario is violating the agreement by not recognizing the equivalency of his Alberta qualifications. Ultimately the technician was success-fully qualified in Ontario and Ontario has said that it is reviewing its procedures. The case remains open because the professional associa-tion in Alberta remains concerned that the Ontario Eligibility Challenge process violates the agreement.

- Many residents of Sparwood, British Columbia work in Crowsnest Pass, Alberta. They were being charged higher fees for various work and business permits. BC complained, citing Article 707: Licensing, Certification and Registration of Workers. The issue was resolved when Crowsnest Pass passed a by-law expanding the area of residency for workers and business, but the discriminatory practices have not changed.

- The owner and operator of a funeral chapel on the Alberta side of Lloydminster wanted to open a chapel on the Saskatchewan side of the city. He was trained in Saskatchewan but only licensed in Alberta. The Saskatchewan Funeral Services Association requires all out-of-province licensed embalmers to take a one-year internship program under a Saskatchewan licensed embalmer to be accredited. Although he was trained in Saskatchewan, the Saskatchewan Funeral Services Association would not waive the internship requirement. The issue has not yet been resolved.

- A graduate in Occupational Therapy from McGill University worked in occupational therapy in Ontario for 13 years before moving to Al-berta in 1996 and applying to practise there. The Alberta Association of Registered Occupational Therapists requires applicants to write the Canadian Association of Occupational Therapist (CAOT) certification exam. Following a complaint, the Alberta Professional Examination Board in Occupational Therapy agreed that, based on her education and currency in practice, she qualified to be licensed under a "grandparenting" clause in the Alberta Occupational Therapy act.

These examples demonstrate the effective use of the consultation process in the labour mobility chapter in the agreement. It is interesting to note that the complaints, though sometimes successful, do not necessarily lead to changes in policy or practice. Nor does the chapter solve all outstanding labour mobility issues.

For example, it is not clear how the agreement would resolve the hiring hall and licensing practices of Quebec construction unions that, by legislation, are allowed to grant permits only to workers in specific regions of Quebec. This generally excludes qualified workers from outside Quebec as well. The agreement also may not resolve the long-standing problem of Certified General Accountants (CGAs) who are allowed to sign financial statements in some provinces but not in others. This issue might be resolved when provinces go through the process leading to the mutual recognition of qualifications and the reconciliation of standards.

In summary, the labour mobility chapter is clearly promoting domestic economic integration in an area that has been a problem for Canadian governments for some time. It is also an example of how the agreement and, potentially, any other domestic intergovernmental agreement, can be used to implement and reinforce constitutional provisions and principles. In this case, section 6 of the *Charter of Rights and Freedoms* guarantees mobility for Canadians. Chapter Seven: Labour Mobility, extends the effectiveness of the mobility principle in the Charter by reconciling occupational standards, qualifications, and regulations.

CONSUMER-RELATED ISSUES

All Canadian governments have measures to protect consumers. The federal government's interest is with goods and services that are traded interprovincially. Therefore, the federal government has labeling and packaging regulations and is responsible for such things as weights and measures (legal metrology). Provinces are responsible for protecting consumers in relation to commercial activities that happen within their jurisdiction and in areas of provincial responsibility.

Chapter Eight deals specifically with commercial activities. Since all provincial governments occupy the same legislative and policy space there is significant overlap, duplication, and inconsistency in consumer measures. The scope of the chapter is broad. It establishes that the chapter applies to all "consumer related measures and standards adopted or maintained by a party."[50] It also eliminates discriminatory fees for licensing, registration, and certification.[51] And it removes residency or local presence as a requirement for licensing, registration or certification except measures to establish a legal presence for consumer protection.[52]

Beyond that, governments have chosen to deal sequentially with a number of specific measures. Three specific issues were identified to be reconciled immediately.[53] With respect to *Direct Sellers Harmonization,* governments agreed to harmonize cancellation rights and contract content requirements that will apply to direct sellers and provide the same consumer protection across Canada by June 1996. In the area of Cost of Credit Disclosure, governments agreed to standardize minimum disclosure requirements and the methods by which cost of credit is calculated and reported. A legislative "template" has been drafted to assist governments in preparing legislation that is expected to be passed in all jurisdictions by July 1998. Measures concerning *Upholstered and stuff articles* have been harmonized in the remaining jurisdictions that regulate these matters.

The chapter also specifies a second tranche of measures to be assessed and reconciled as appropriate after July 1997, including: reciprocal investigative powers, enforcement of revocation rights, financial compensation for consumers, and enforcement of judgements.[54]

In summary, the consumer-related measures chapter is an example of a step-by-step approach to economic integration that is appropriate to the diverse nature of the issues involved. As is the case with other obligations in the agreement, governments have had problems meeting the deadlines specified in this chapter. Nevertheless, even 12 to 18 months behind schedule, harmonizing direct selling measures and introducing legislation to standardize the disclosure of the cost of credit in Canada are significant for domestic economic integration.

OTHER SECTORS

Other sector chapters also support economic integration to a greater or lesser degree depending on the policy issues. Without exception, however, they all include a commitment to the objectives and general principles of the agreement and a structure and a program to identify and resolve issues to increase domestic economic integration.

The agriculture and food sector probably is more regulated and government managed than any other in Canada. Much of it is for health, safety, and environmental reasons. But much of it, including supply management, is also intended to protect national and local producers and processors.

Chapter Nine on Agriculture and Food consists of commitments to study and to a rigorous work program. These include a commitment to review supply management, the *Western Grain Transportation Act* and the "agricultural safety net programs"[55] and to a review of the scope and coverage of the chapter by 1 September 1997 to "achieve the broadest possible coverage and further (liberalize) internal trade in agriculture and food goods."[56]

Agriculture ministers have postponed this last obligation until December 1998. They will develop a revised chapter based on stakeholder consultations to be completed by July 1998. The chapter will be based on "principles" which means that they will devise a set of rules, probably similar to the General Rules in the agreement, that will apply to all aspects of the agriculture and food sector.

Still, there are small changes in the agricultural sector and signs that the industry is beginning to prepare for greater changes to come. An example is the dairy industry. To start with, dated and unnecessary colouring restrictions for margarine have disappeared in most of Canada and the remaining regulations in Quebec are now subject to the general rules of the agreement.

The industry is changing rapidly, partly as a result of international trade agreements but also in anticipation of an open domestic market in dairy products. Specifically: licensing of fluid milk distribution has disappeared in western Canada; Ontario is reviewing similar regional regulations; there is substantial consolidation among domestic milk processors particularly in Quebec and Ontario and large international processors have acquired domestic companies; milk producers from Manitoba east have established a common market in fluid milk; and milk distribution regulations in the Atlantic region are under pressure as at least one company, Farmers Cooperative Dairy, seeks to improve its competitiveness by establishing an integrated regional operation.

In effect, the agreement has, in some cases, stimulated economic integration even though the issues are not directly covered. For example, liquor regulation and Liquor Board marketing practices have been recognized for a long time as a source of barriers to interprovincial trade. In the 1980s the main issue was rules that required a beer to be brewed in most provinces where it was sold. Most, but not all, of the barriers to interprovincial trade in beer disappeared in 1992. Chapter Ten on Alcoholic Beverages will complete the process of integration over the next few years. The sector will remain highly regulated and some provinces, like Newfoundland, will continue to protect their industry as long as possible.

Chapter Eleven on Natural Resources is intended to deal with measures that require natural resources to be processed in the province where they are produced. Some measures remain but there are provisions for consultations to resolve these issues over time.

The communications industry is probably one of Canada's most technologically advanced and competitive sectors. The industry has also been integrated on a national basis for some time. Chapter Thirteen – Communications, confirms this open domestic market and establishes a process to monitor the sector and deal with practices that may be inconsistent with the agreement should they arise in the future.

In the motor vehicle transportation sector, intergovernmental committees of ministers, officials, and technical experts have been in place for more than

20 years, integrating the industry in Canada. The industry has been deregulating for about ten years, since the federal *Motor Vehicle Transportation Act* was revised in 1987. The object of this process has been to develop harmonized standards and to mutually recognize and harmonize licensing and inspection. Chapter Fourteen on Transportation commits governments to continue this process of integration and establishes a tighter time table and more specific commitments and allows for complaints to provide discipline.

The process to harmonize environmental measures that may limit trade and increase business costs unnecessarily was in place before the Agreement on Internal Trade was negotiated. The Canadian Council of Ministers of the Environment (CCME) has the responsibility to manage this process. Chapter Fifteen on Environmental Protection confirms this process to resolve trade issues that result from environmental regulation and puts it in the context of the principles of the agreement.

THE OPERATING STRUCTURE

Chapter Sixteen establishes a Committee on Internal Trade to implement and operate the agreement and to assist in resolving disputes.[57] The terms, scope and coverage of the agreement defines the mandate of the committee. The committee is also required, annually, to review scope and coverage and to make recommendations to expand the agreement*.*[58] The committee is to be composed of "cabinet-level representatives ... or their designates."[59] Alberta and Saskatchewan are represented by ministers of intergovernmental affairs. Other governments are represented by ministers responsible for industry and economic development. In other words the committee can consider any issue related to the domestic market and should be an effective vehicle to oversee and promote economic integration in Canada.

Some of the architects of the agreement thought that the Committee on Internal Trade would operate like the GATT or WTO governing council. In this view, the committee would become the central forum for negotiating and resolving all domestic market issues across all economic sectors. Normally governments would be represented by a minister with broad responsibility for domestic trade and intergovernmental issues related to the domestic market. On specific matters, governments would be represented by the minister with the appropriate responsibility for the issue being discussed. All negotiating or work groups would report to and through the Committee on Internal Trade.

The Committee on Internal Trade has not functioned this way and is unlikely to do so. This is because of the competing jurisdiction of a network of ministerial level intergovernmental committees that has evolved in Canada since the 1960s. These committees are in place for almost every chapter/sector in the agreement (Labour Mobility, Consumer Affairs, Transport, Natural

Resources, Agriculture, Environment, Communications) and will continue to operate independently of the Committee on Internal Trade. The internal trade related issues in these portfolios will probably not be considered directly by internal trade ministers. As a result, many issues, and therefore a large part of the internal trade and economic integration agenda, will remain outside the agreement's institutional structure. In effect, an intergovernmental mechanism with a broad responsibility for promoting economic integration in the domestic market has not evolved yet in Canada, although the mandate and structure exist in the Agreement on Internal Trade.

The agreement establishes that the chair of the Committee on Internal Trade will rotate annually among governments.[60] In fact, the joint federal/provincial sharing of the chair that started in 1987, when the Committee of Ministers on Internal Trade was first established, remains in place. Furthermore, the province sharing the chair, Manitoba, has not changed since 1990.

There are probably practical reasons for continuing the arrangement of federal/provincial co-chairs. First the federal government's interest is national in scope. The federal priority and responsibility is to promote an open and efficient domestic market. The federal minister is, therefore, able to focus resources and time, as well as a national perspective, on the public policy issues involved in the proper functioning of the domestic market and of the agreement. Second, continuity has been an important factor in starting up the agreement. Having the same ministers in the chair through the negotiation and during the first years of operation probably has improved the odds that the agreement will get off the ground.

Finally, rotating the chair annually requires a strong and experienced secretariat with sufficient staff and resources. To provide continuity and consistency in the operation of the agreement, the executive director of the secretariat should have a clear and accepted mandate to provide technical and policy advice to the chair on national domestic trade issues as well as on the effective functioning of the agreement. The Internal Trade Secretariat is in place but still evolving. It is not clear that it has these attributes yet or that all governments accept its policy function in relation to the chair of the Committee on Internal Trade. An annually rotating chair is probably the most effective and appropriate arrangement in the long run but, until the agreement is understood and accepted by both governments and the private sector and is operating effectively, a shared federal/provincial chair with tenure of three to four years is probably the most effective arrangement.

Chapter Sixteen establishes that the committee's decisions will be taken by consensus.[61] There was no consideration of alternatives during negotiations. Decision by consensus now seems to be a problem for the committee in implementing and operating the agreement. Since concluding the agreement in July 1994, the Committee on Internal Trade has met about every six months, sometimes more frequently. During this time the committee has been preoccupied with the extension of the procurement chapter to the MASH sector and this has been delayed because provinces have been unable to find an approach acceptable to all.

During this period the committee also dealt with a number of other issues including the dispute between British Columbia and New Brunswick concerning the relocation of UPS. The committee was unable to mediate this dispute successfully. The work program set up under the agreement is behind schedule in almost every respect. Work has not started on obligations such as the review of the scope and coverage of the agreement except in a cursory way. Simple administrative matters like producing the first annual report are behind schedule. A draft of the annual report for the period to the end of March 1996 has been on the table since March 1997. It is still under discussion. As well, reporting requirements under most articles and chapters have not been honoured.

The problem in maintaining momentum on the agreement's work program is partly the result of the requirement for consensus on even straight forward issues. It is also partly that internal trade ministers do not control the full agenda and rely on other ministers, and the officials reporting to them, to meet the obligations of the agreement. These groups have the same problem of motivation, resources, and consensus as internal trade ministers and their officials.

The third problem is the organization of the committee of officials — Internal Trade Representatives (ITRs) — that supports the committee of ministers, and the role and resources of the Internal Trade Secretariat. The agreement establishes a national Internal Trade Secretariat to support the Committee on Internal Trade.[62] It is located in Winnipeg. The Executive Director of the Secretariat is the senior official and reports to the co-chairs of the committee of ministers and takes directions from the committee.

The executive director is also, effectively if not officially, the chair of the committee of Internal Trade Representatives (ITRs) from each government. Internal Trade Representatives are informally responsible for making the agreement work. Although the ITRs committee has no formal standing in the agreement and no specific terms of reference, they work with the executive director of the Internal Trade Secretariat to carry out the directions of the Committee on Internal Trade, to negotiate and resolve issues, and to monitor and oversee the agreement.

The original idea was that ITRs would take responsibility for specific issues such as liaison with specific sectors or the operation of specific chapters, chair working groups, and provide resources to carry out specific projects. The reality is that most Internal Trade Representatives have other jobs and most governments have not provided specific resources to support the internal trade process (only Alberta and the federal government have officials working full time on the internal trade file).

The Internal Trade Secretariat has a restricted budget. During negotiations, some governments were clear that they would provide only limited resources to a national secretariat. One issue was a desire not to be seen to be expanding public administration when there was a concern about the size of government and most governments were cutting back. An unspoken issue may be the concern on the part of some governments that a strong national internal trade bureaucracy would reduce governments' control over the internal trade agenda and the functioning of the agreement.

The operating structure and processes supporting the agreement are changing gradually as those involved develop greater mutual trust and a better understanding of the problems in its implementation and operation. In the meantime, it is difficult to maintain the agreement's work program on schedule, to maintain effective links with sector groups, to communicate and consult with the private sector, and to carry out the operational tasks and research necessary to make the agreement effective.

In summary, The agreement notionally provides a standing intergovernmental process with the operating infrastructure that Canadian governments need to integrate the domestic market: the Canadian version of the GATT Secretariat or the European Community Commission. But the Committee on Internal Trade and the Internal Trade Secretariat are still evolving. The committee needs to reconcile the requirement for consensus with the need for a more effective decisionmaking process. It also needs to consolidate the internal trade issues in all economic sectors into a concerted process to improve domestic economic integration; and finally, it must provide adequate resources to meet the provisions of the agreement and develop a responsive organization to support its activities.

DISPUTE RESOLUTION

Resolving disputes and enforcing commitments is an issue in all trade agreements. Generally speaking, international trade agreements rely on government-to-government consultations, mediation and panels to resolve disputes, and the withdrawal of benefits or retaliation to enforce decisions and the agreement generally.

The situation within a national structure, dealing with non-tariff barriers that arise from day-to-day government operations is different. First, disputes often result from specific problems for specific companies or individuals that require immediate solutions rather than extensive changes to government policy or protracted government-to-government discussion. Second, retaliation in relation to non-tariff barriers within a federation governed by a constitution is difficult and destructive to the domestic market and the economic union. Finally, in a national structure, the justice system is the usual means of dealing with disputes and fines or financial compensation are the normal remedy to satisfy civil issues. Courts can also force changes to government measures if they do not conform to laws or the constitution. Still, the justice system is not really a satisfactory way to promote economic integration.

Although Canadian governments can apply the normal trade policy model to dispute resolution, they need to find creative ways to make it work effectively in a domestic context. The private sector, which was pressing for an agreement on internal trade, wants an accessible, transparent, inexpensive, non-adversarial process that is enforceable and would resolve its problems quickly and practically and eliminate the offending policy or practice in the future. Most provincial governments want a system that is inexpensive and allows them some control over the issues to be considered and that does not allow third parties, namely the courts, to define policy. The federal government prefers a system that the private sector, as well as governments, could use, ideally a single, third-party system such as a national commission or tribunal whose decisions could be enforced by the courts.

The system in the agreement emphasizes consultation and encourages dispute avoidance at a number of levels. Most sector chapters (Part IV) provide for consultation and reference to the ministers responsible for that chapter before resort to the agreement's general system set out in Chapter Seventeen – Dispute Resolution Procedures. The general process in Chapter Seventeen allows parties to proceed through further consultations or, by agreement, to refer the matter immediately to the Committee on Internal Trade or to a panel for consideration.

In addition, a person or a company can make a complaint if a government declines to act on their behalf, and if a neutral "screener" appointed by each government agrees that the complaint is legitimate. After that, the process includes consultation, reference to the Committee on Internal Trade and eventually a panel if the issue cannot be resolved at an earlier stage. Governments have agreed to implement the recommendations of panels.[63] If governments do not comply the panel report is published and referred back to the Committee on Internal Trade for action; including, in the case of complaints by governments, retaliation. If the system is effective in dealing with complaints through consultations there will be few panels. There may also be little policy integration resulting from a process that does record or follow-up issues with policy change.

According to information gathered by the Internal Trade Secretariat, which may be incomplete given the informal and dispersed character of the first consultation stage of the dispute resolution process, 36 complaints have been made since the agreement came into effect on 1 July 1995. Of these, seven were dropped, seven were denied, six were resolved or the complaint upheld, five were cases where there was no basis for the complaint, and eleven are pending. The average length of time for dealing with the complaints that have been concluded one way or another is seven months. But the average in the second year of operation, 1996-97, was three months. Performance may improve with time.

Although the main dispute resolution processes in Chapter Seventeen have not been used the first issue may now be pending. Early in 1997 the federal government passed legislation to ban the use of the gas additive MMT by banning interprovincial trade in the product. The basis for this policy was technical evidence that MMT contributes to pollution. It has been banned in the United States for this reason. The refining industry disputes the technical evidence and contends that the ban is not justified.

In April 1997, Alberta and Saskatchewan, with Nova Scotia and Quebec as intervenors, launched a complaint under the agreement.[64] Presumably the basis for the complaint is that the federal government, even though it has the constitutional authority to regulate interprovincial trade, cannot, under the terms of the Agreement on Internal Trade, use this authority to create an unjustified barrier to interprovincial trade.

The federal government will probably argue that it passed the legislation to meet a "legitimate objective" as defined by the agreement and will refer to the article in the environment chapter that says "an environmental measure shall not be considered to be inconsistent with this agreement by reason solely of the lack of full scientific certainty regarding the need for the measure."[65]

It may be difficult for either party to back away from this dispute so that consideration by a panel may be the only way to resolve the issue. It is now going through the consultation process prescribed by the dispute-resolution chapter and that, depending on the wishes of the parties, can be a protracted process.

Effective issue identification and dispute-resolution procedures are as important as anything else to promoting economic integration. Governments tend to be blind to weaknesses in their policies and practices and naturally, and correctly, disinclined to change without reason. An arrangement that encourages those affected by government measures to raise issues is essential to a process of continuing and relevant change and improvement and an effective process for this purpose is one that is accessible, responsive and not arbitrary.

Those who negotiated the agreement were aware of these considerations and developed a system for dealing with complaints based on consultation and mediation rather than on an adversarial approach.

Unfortunately the result for an outsider, however, is like dealing with a black box and it is not clear that the process even serves the interests of governments. First, the agreement has not been well publicized so only the well informed or those with time and money will know how to raise an issue under the agreement, who to contact and under what conditions. Second, for most people making complaints, the best solution to a problem is a quick, clear answer either way so that they can get on with their business. The procedures set out in the agreement process takes time, as long as 18 months if there is any difference of view and probably a minimum of two or three months even for simple issues. Third, the dispute resolution should lead to changes in policies and practices. Identifying issues, keeping records and following up on the policy implications of issues raised through complaints is essential for continuing policy change and improvement. It is not certain that this kind of process is in place.

For the Internal Trade Agreement, the best dispute-resolution process is likely to be a well-publicized, single national system, accessible from anywhere in the country, with people dedicated to resolving issues using techniques similar to those used by ombudsmen and with panels available to deal with complex disputes or those that cannot be resolved through normal mediation processes. No complaint process should take longer than 90 days. This arrangement would also provide a database of issues and problems that would help to adjust the agreement and improve domestic market integration.

CONCLUSION

The Agreement on Internal Trade solves the problems that prevented Canadian governments from dealing with domestic trade issues through 12 years of constitutional and other types of negotiation after 1980:

- it allows provinces to change their policies and practices to remove barriers to trade and increase national economic integration without compromising their policy capacity in other areas;

- it provides an intergovernmental operating structure that allows Canadian governments to identify issues and adjust policies and practices cooperatively and responsively.

The question is: Does the Agreement on Internal Trade accomplish real economic integration? Critics say no. They say the agreement is too complex, that it has substantial exceptions that confirm, rather than remove, trade barriers, that it defers issues and is unenforceable with an inaccessible, opaque and toothless dispute-resolution process.

The other view is that the Agreement on Internal Trade has helped, and is helping, to integrate the Canadian economy.

- The General Rules in the agreement, accepted by all Canadian governments, are now the benchmark for trade and economic relations between provinces and territories.

- Through a range of initial measures, the agreement has improved economic integration by establishing a national public sector procurement market, resolving labour mobility issues, establishing rules for subsidies and incentives and dealing with long-standing consumer issues.

- There is a program and a process to deal with outstanding issues, to reduce and remove exceptions and to expand the coverage and improve the functioning of the agreement. Even if the process is slow and erratic it is probably also irresistible and change will inevitably happen at a time and in a way that reflects the interests of all Canadians.

- There is an institutional structure — the Committee of Ministers on Internal Trade, the Internal Trade Secretariat, and the compliance and dispute-resolution processes — that Canadian governments can use to manage, cooperatively, trade and economic relations. If these institutions are not fully effective yet, the potential for use exists for governments.

The agreement is not perfect and some of these imperfections in its substance and its implementation could be terminal. Most could be fixed with sufficient interest, goodwill, and ingenuity.

In summary, the parties to the agreement need to go the extra distance to reach its potential as a major breakthrough to an effective Canadian economic union. Specifically:

- Governments have to give the agreement profile. Unless individuals and businesses use the agreement to deal with domestic trade issues that affect their business and governments are seen to be using it to improve economic integration, the agreement could disappear without a trace. It is not clear that there is an alternative to the agreement;

- Governments need to consider an alternative to the requirement for consensus as the basis for all decisionmaking;

- The Committee on Internal Trade should be responsible for managing economic integration in the domestic market;

- Consultation and dispute-resolution processes have to be more accessible, effective, and quick and contribute to changing and improving the agreement.

In conclusion, governments and critics should remember that the agreement does what could not be done by other means, including constitutional reform. Indeed as one of the more prominent of attempts by Canadian governments to reform the federal system without constitutional amendment, the Agreement on Internal Trade deserves special scrutiny. It achieves its results through a complex intergovernmental agreement that is still stymied by the consensus-only decisionmaking of Canadian intergovernmental relations. Yet it also achieves its results with diversity and flexibility and in a way that does not appear to interfere with the sovereignty of the federal and provincial legislatures, which is the federal balance in Canada.

The agreement is also a work-in-progress with an important amount of unfinished business as governments negotiate workable rules affecting procurement, agriculture, and energy among other areas. Thus there is much continuing opportunity for governments to improve upon and extend the Agreement on Internal Trade. The framing of an effective ongoing process may be the important achievement of such non-constitutional reform.

NOTES

1. Among the judgements usually cited are La Forest J.'s comments in the *Law Society of Alberta v. Black et al.* This case was a Charter challenge based on mobility rights guaranteed by section 6(2) of the *Canadian Charter of Rights and Freedoms* and *Morguard Investments Ltd. v. De Savoye* and the tests used by Dickson C.J. in *City National Leasing, supra.*

2. See Robert Howse, *Economic Union, Social Justice and Constitutional Reform: Towards a High But Level Playing Field* (Toronto: York University Centre for Public Law and Public, 1992), pp. 61-72.

3. Royal Commission on the Economic Union and Development Prospects for Canada *Report*, Vol. III (Ottawa: Minister of Supply and Services, 1985), pp. 135-40.

4. Meeting of Ministers of Internal Trade, *Communiqué*, Montreal, 18 March 1993.

5. The *Agreement on Internal Trade* is available on the Internet at the Internal Trade Secretariat web site (www.intrasec.mb.ca/) or the Industry Canada web site (strategis.ic.gc.ca/IPTrade). Detailed commentary on the provision of the agreement is provided in Michael J. Trebilcock and Daniel Schwanen (eds.), *Getting There: An Assessment of the Agreement on the Internal Trade* (Toronto: C.D. Howe Institute, 1995); see also Bryan Schwartz, "Assessing the Agreement on Internal Trade: The Case for a 'More Perfect' Union," in *Canada: The State of the Federation 1995*, ed. D.M. Brown and J.W. Rose (Kingston: Institute of Intergovernmental Relations, Queen's University, 1995).

6. Article 401.

7. Article 402.

8. Article 403.

9. Article 405.

10. Article 406: Transparency.

11. Article 400: Application.

12. Article 300: Reaffirmation of Constitutional Powers and Responsibilities.

13. Article 101: Mutually Agreed Principles.

14. Article 1801: Regional Economic Development.

15. Articles 1802: Aboriginal Peoples.

16. Article 1803: Culture.

17. Article 1806: Financial Sector.

18. Article 1807: Measures Subject to Transitional Provisions; and 1808: Non-Conforming Measures.

19. Article 1810(4).

20. Article 1810(2) & (3). Negotiations of the Energy Chapter are not complete. The problem has been to define an acceptable commitment on the transmission of electricity across the territory of another province and how to open provincial markets to competition in electric power given the heavy debt obligations of Crown producers and monopolies. The sector is changing rapidly, however, particularly in Ontario, which is now considering unbundling the production, transmission, and retailing of electricity, and privatizing some elements of the industry. A recent ruling by a US energy regulating agency has closed off exports to the US unless exporting provinces reciprocate by opening their markets to imports. Apparently agreement on an energy chapter is now close and premiers, at their annual meeting in August 1997, agreed to complete these negotiations within the next 12 months.

21. Article 516(3).

22. Article 517(1).

23. Article 502(4).

24. Article 1601(5).

25. Article 502: Scope and Coverage.

26. Annexes 502.2A and 502.2B

27. Annex 502.1B

28. Article 508: Regional and Economic Development.

29. Article 506(11) and Article 507: Non-Application.

30. Articles 516: Future Reviews; Article 517: Future Negotiations.

31. Articles 513 and 514.

32. Article 516(4).

33. See Article 405: Reconciliation; and Annexes 405.1 and 405.2.

34. Article 604: Local Presence and Residency Requirements.

35. Article 607: Performance Requirements.

36. Article 806: Residence and Local Presence Requirements.

37. Article 805: Licensing, Registration and Certification Fees.

38. Article 606: Corporate Registration and Reporting Requirements.

39. Annex 608.3.

40. Annex 608.3, paragraphs 4-7.

41. Ibid., paragraphs 4-7.

42. In the news release on internal trade issued at their annual conference in August 1997, premiers directed internal trade ministers to "examine, as a major priority, potential clarifications and improvements to the *Agreement's* Code of Conduct on Investment Incentives."

43. Article 706: Residency Requirements.

44. Article 707: Licensing, Certification and Registration of Workers.

45. Article 708: Recognition of Occupational Qualifications and Reconciliation of Operational Standards; and Annex 708 that establishes the process for implementing the terms of Article 708.

46. Annex 708, paragraph 10.

47. Governments are obligated to complete this process "within a reasonable period of time." Ministers responsible for this chapter, the Forum of Labour Market Ministers (FLMM), recognize that this obligation is too broad and, in the next few months, will recommend to internal trade ministers a more specific commitment.

48. The Annual Premiers' Conference news release on the *Agreement on Internal Trade* identified "compliance of regulatory bodies with labour mobility provisions" as one of the agreement's outstanding issues that they directed their internal trade ministers to resolve.

49. Article 711: Consultations.

50. Article 801: Scope and Coverage.

51. Article 805.

52. Article 806.

53. Annex 807.1.

54. Article 808: Cooperation on Consumer-Related Measures and Standards.

55. Article 903.

56. Article 902(4).

57. Article 1600: Committee on Internal Trade.

58. Article 1810(4).

59. Article 1601(1).

60. Article 1601(4).

61. Article 1601(5).

62. Article 1603: Secretariat.

63. Articles 1708 and 1719.

64. Chapter 15: Environmental Protection.

65. Article 1505(8).

6

Canadian Regardless of Origin: "Negative Integration" and the Agreement on Internal Trade

Daniel Schwanen

Dans cet article, Daniel Schwanen passe en revue les dispositions de l'Accord sur le commerce intérieur qui ont pour but d'éliminer les mesures qui font discrimination sur la base de l'origine provinciale des biens, services, personnes ou entreprises. L'auteur a trouvé que, malgré un progrès réel dans certains domaines, plusieurs étapes concrètes prévues par l'ACI et dont le but était de rendre ces dispositions effectives, n'ont pas été franchies. De plus, il estime que le mécanisme de règlement des différends de l'Accord n'a pas été pleinement utilisé. L'auteur discute des raisons possibles de cette mise en oeuvre incomplète de l'Accord, et propose nombre de mesures qui pourraient en accélérer le processus et en réaliser les promesses.

INTRODUCTION

In this chapter, I will examine some of the progress accomplished so far under the Agreement on Internal Trade (AIT), signed in 1994 between the Canadian provinces and territories and the federal government. Specifically, I will be concerned here with whether the commitment made in the AIT to remove laws, regulations, or practices in effect in one province (or territory) that discriminate against out-of-province persons or businesses, has been fulfilled.[1]

Attempts at removing discriminatory barriers often come under the rubric "negative integration," because getting rid of the barriers in these cases usually involve banning an offending set of behaviours. However, to give practical effect to negative integration, it is not enough just to agree to refrain from certain practices. Specific steps must also be taken, such as, in the AIT, the disclosure of information necessary to ensure transparency in the treatment of out-of-province entities, the publication of reports monitoring compliance with the agreement, and the creation and operation of mechanisms, such as the one governing dispute settlement, necessary to enforce the commitments.

Much of this chapter will be concerned with whether such actual steps as Canadian governments promised to do under the AIT in order to remove inter-provincial discrimination have been fulfilled. But first, I will briefly review the purpose of negative integration and the various tools which can be used to secure the non-discriminatory behaviour which it entails. Following this, I will review the commitments made in the AIT, both in general and in specific sectors, and assess whether the steps that were to have been taken under the agreement have in fact been taken. I will then look at whether and how the dispute settlement process has been used to ensure that the parties to the agreement[2] stick to their obligations not to discriminate. Some thoughts will then follow on what is left to be desired in the process of negative integration undertaken with the AIT, and on what can be done to improve it.

My conclusion regarding the achievement of the goal of non-discrimination under the AIT is that significant progress has been made toward it, but not always at the pace that signatories were pledged to follow under the agreement. The continued elimination and avoidance of discriminatory barriers would be greatly helped by governments making at least as much information public as they had promised to do when they signed the AIT, including on the progress of trade disputes. In addition to giving greater public profile to the agreement, I would favour strengthening the AIT's institutional structure, in order to accelerate the pace of outstanding negotiations, and would urge governments to implement legislation that would steep their day-to-day operations in the principles of the agreement, in order to enshrine the latter's status as a fundamental tool of the common citizenship of Canadians. Finally, the federal government should contemplate a more interventionist role in areas where implementing the agreement is meeting serious stumbling blocks.

PURPOSE AND TOOLS OF NON-DISCRIMINATION OR NEGATIVE INTEGRATION

The benefits of an integrated economic area can initially be understood in terms of a more efficient allocation of resources within the area, with individuals and regions being allowed, through their participation in a wider market, to specialize in what they are relatively better than others at producing, and thus generating higher incomes. In order to achieve this better allocation, it is necessary that goods and services providers, and people and capital, be able to seek business or employment across regions. Non-discrimination on the basis of origin, or negative integration, is in turn essential to such dynamics being allowed to take place.

For Canada, evaluations of the dollar amount of additional national income that would result from a more efficient allocation of production, compared with the pre-AIT situation, have indicated that these gains would be significant, although not overwhelming since the Canadian market was already well-integrated in many sectors even before the agreement came into effect.

But the gains from a more open market exceed those which can be evaluated simply by looking at how production across the country might be reallocated on the basis of comparative advantages, once the removal of remaining barriers allowed firms and individuals to do so. Many economists have pointed out that the benefits from a more completely integrated market also include higher economies of scale (with a larger sized market lowering the average cost of output), the dynamic effects of increased competition (due to the incentive to adopt the best processes and technologies), and the reduced deadweight cost of lobbying for protection.[3]

In any of the above senses, the rationale for integration is not different than that existing for entering into larger free trade areas (and some of the same caveats, such as the danger of diverting trade away from other, potentially lesser-cost trade partners, exist as well). Indeed, on all of the above counts, free trade with the United States since 1989 would have generally reduced the relative advantage of a more integrated Canadian market. However, while access to the US market has become much easier for many Canadian firms, it remains strewn with barriers in a number of sectors, particularly in agriculture, in most services, in construction, for firms bidding on public sector contracts, as well as for small- and medium-sized businesses in virtually all sectors, because of the administrative costs of qualifying for tariff-free status and the risk of attracting trade "remedy" action across the border.[4] For these firms among others, maintaining or increasing access to the Canadian market constitutes an important, even vital, underpinning to their growth and investment strategies.

Another benefit of an integrated market is that, apart from its positive effect on national and individual incomes, it also reduces individual and corporate risk through the creation of a reciprocal economic citizenship, in that it requires people and firms to be treated, if not always the same everywhere (a matter of "positive integration"), then certainly to be treated everywhere as a citizen (the essence of "negative integration"). Thus, tools that ensure negative integration across a wide area reduce the risk from having to operate within the confines of smaller, more specialized economies, and this benefit accrues even to those who never actually take advantage of opportunities to expand or move beyond provincial borders.[5]

Within a political union, negative integration is all the more valuable in that it allows the benefits of both income gains and reduced risk to take place within an institutional structure that all regions hold in common. As a result, the economic gains from integration need not occur at the cost of having to adopt a foreign institutional (e.g., legal) structure, or of people having to move to a foreign country and lose the benefits of citizenship (e.g., public pensions) if, for example, their skills are not easily marketable in their province of origin. The advantages of an economically integrated political union can also extend to international bargaining, since when representatives of the union "speak with one voice" on issues of common interest (or support each other's position on a reciprocal basis), each constituent unit can leverage its bargaining power to that of the whole.

Of course, any of these benefits will obtain within the union provided that the political compromises involved in maintaining the economic union — especially with respect to basic reciprocal rights and obligations, and to who is responsible for making decisions for the whole — can be struck and adhered to by the members of the union.

In Canada, attempts to remedy shortcomings with respect to the legal and institutional basis of economic union led to the creation of an intergovernmental Committee of Ministers on Internal Trade (CMIT) in 1987, produced some regional and sectoral trade agreements in the late 1980s and early 1990s,[6] and culminated in 1994 in the more comprehensive AIT.

Although the federal government is a signatory to the AIT on par with the provinces, it is important to note that this does not mean that it has let go of any of its other options for removing discriminatory practices or otherwise strengthening the Canadian economic union. This is important to note, because unlike the European model, the AIT itself has little or no judicial "backstops," available to citizens, businesses or governments, should a signatory decide to ignore some of its provisions. The AIT does have a dispute settlement mechanism (DSM) which is admittedly more open to citizens than equivalent international procedures, but there is little that can be practically done if governments decide not to comply with them. Legislations implementing the agreement, introduced in some provinces and at the federal level, fail to make the AIT directly applicable in law.[7] It has little non-political supporting structure, save for a Secretariat established to provide administrative and operational support and "such other support" as the Cabinet-level Committee on Internal Trade (CIT), which replaced the CMIT and which ultimately supervises the implementation of the agreement, "may direct" (article 1603). Given the current terms of the AIT, all that can be done to ensure its implementation, apart from appealing to the DSM or applying direct political pressure on the signatory governments, is to expose any violation or lack of progress, and suggest ways of improving the process in order to make it easier to achieve its promises, as I will attempt below.

NON-DISCRIMINATION IN THE AIT: COMMITMENTS AND RECORD TO DATE

In this section of the chapter, I will review two kinds of promises made by governments in the AIT to eliminate discriminatory barriers to the Canadian economic union. It should be noted that the practices targeted by this promise need not only be provincial: federal measures that discriminate against the movement of goods, services, people, and investment between provinces[8] are considered equally reprehensible under the AIT, as indeed they should be.

The first type of promise concerns agreements to adopt on an ongoing basis a certain behaviour, for example, non-discrimination toward another province's suppliers, or to follow transparent procedures. It is difficult to judge on the face of it whether actual behaviour has conformed to these promises, especially since, as we have seen, the implementing legislation in the provinces and federal jurisdictions involved mostly housekeeping items, and hence did not result in the AIT becoming directly applicable in law. The best indicator of whether the agreement is being followed on this general "good behaviour" score may lie in the record of the complaints that have been brought under its dispute avoidance or dispute settlement mechanisms. I will leave an examination of this record for the next section of the chapter.

The second type of promise made in the AIT concerns specific steps that governments promised to take, often within a stated deadline, to deliver on a certain administrative procedure, to make recommendations, or even conclude negotiations on certain specified issues in order to complete the coverage of the agreement. These are commitments to act and to deliver a product, even if it is only a report, the progress of which is relatively easy to track. In this section of the paper, I will review the status of these specific commitments to act, listed according to the sector or activity to which they apply. First, however, a short review of the AIT's general principles and rules as enunciated by the signatory governments is in order.

GENERAL PRINCIPLES AND RULES

Apart from the general undertaking enunciated in the AIT to reduce and eliminate barriers to the extent possible, the parties to the agreement have also agreed, under the heading of "mutually agreed principles" (article 101), to be guided by two broad rules of behaviour that speak most directly to the question of eliminating interprovincial discrimination, namely that of not establishing new barriers to internal trade, and that of treating persons, goods, services, and investments all equally, irrespective of where they originate in Canada.

The "reciprocal non-discrimination" principle is in turn made operational by the rule on reciprocal non-discrimination (article 401). Under this rule, governments (including the federal government) agree to grant out-of-province goods, persons, services, and investments of another province at least the best treatment they accord to those originating within a particular province ("provincial treatment," akin to national treatment in international trade agreements), and also, at a minimum, the best treatment it accords goods coming from another province or country (equivalent to a "most-favoured-nation" clause). The rule is meant to apply to goods that are "like, directly competitive or substitutable" and to the treatment of persons, services, and investments "in like circumstances."

There can be exceptions to the above rule, and these exceptions are defined in such a way as to provide a balance between the principle of non-discrimination, and "legitimate" public objectives that may require the existence of measures that are on their face, or could be construed as, discriminatory. Contrary to previous attempts at entrenching exceptions in rules governing trade within Canada, however, (notably those contained in the early drafts of what became the Charlottetown Accord) a discriminatory measure must pass a severe test before it can be considered admissible under the agreement (article 404 -see below).

Box 1: General Acceptability Test for Discriminatory Measures

Even if it discriminates on the basis of provincial residence, a measure is still acceptable under the terms of the Agreement on Internal Trade if:

a) Its purpose is to achieve a legitimate objective, defined as either:
   - Public security and safety
   - Public order
   - Protection of human, animal or plant life or health
   - Protection of the environment
   - Consumer protection
   - Protection of the health, safety and well-being of workers
   - Affirmative action programs for disadvantaged groups

b) If goods, services or investments meet the legitimate objective of a measure, then the measure must not operate so as to unduly impair their access to the jurisdiction imposing the measure.

c) The measure is not more trade restrictive than necessary to achieve the legitimate objective.

d) The measure does not create a disguised restriction on trade.

The AIT also contains transparency provisions, which are very much complementary to the non-discrimination requirements, because they allow verification of whether specific practices actually conform to them. Among specific undertakings concerning transparency, governments must ensure that relevant information, ranging from laws to guidelines to administrative rulings, are made readily accessible; that parties to the agreement notify the other parties in advance of any measure they are proposing to adopt that may affect the operation of the agreement; and that they maintain enquiry points to answer enquiries and provide information required under the agreement (article 406).

Certain provisions in Annex 405.1 of the agreement directly relate to the objective of ensuring non-discrimination in how standards and standards-related measures are set or implemented (in addition to those aimed at reconciling a number of standards and standards-related measures across Canada, the scope of which falls under "positive integration" rubric). These provisions require that the parties "shall" specify their standards in terms of performance or competence, "shall" ensure that procedures to assess the conformity of goods to their standards are non-discriminatory and expeditious, and with respect to persons, services and investments "of all other Parties," "shall endeavour to ensure such non-discriminatory and expeditious treatment."

If these rules had been governing trade within Canada from the time the accord officially came into effect; if, for example, they had been entrenched in the constitution or otherwise made enforceable before the courts and any derogation been transparent, it is fair to say that today individuals and businesses would be facing no discriminatory barriers between different parts of the country. However, despite or perhaps because of the clarity of the general rules, *almost all* of the AIT's sectoral chapters begin with an article stating that the general rules apply only to the extent specifically allowed by the chapter! This means that, in effect, it is left to the specific chapters not only to expand on or, conversely, circumscribe the application of the general principles, but even in some cases to start from scratch in the application of those general principles to the sector. Thus, the reach of the agreement cannot be understood without reference to its sectoral chapters, to which I now turn.

SECTORAL COMMITMENTS

The very idea of sectoral exceptions opens the door to serious gaps between the general rules and their practical application to specific sectors. I will now detail both how the rules are to be applied and what the key exceptions are in six of the sectors covered by the AIT, and the extent to which governments are meeting specific sectoral steps as agreed to in the AIT. With respect to the latter, I have attempted to give an idea of progress accomplished under the agreement in a series of tables. For each sector or group of sectors, the tables show, in summary form, the specific steps undertaken by governments toward removing discriminatory barriers, and the status of these commitments according to whether they have been acted upon, tangible progress has been made toward them, or conversely nothing of substance has been achieved.

Public Sector Procurement

As with many of the other chapters of the agreement, chapter five on public sector procurement begins by stating that the "general rules" of reciprocal non-discrimination and of transparency do not apply in this case. However, this is redeemed by article 504, also titled reciprocal non-discrimination, which states that non-discriminatory treatment is to be given in any province to goods and services and suppliers from another province. This provision also applies to the federal government, that is, it cannot discriminate between goods, services or suppliers of a particular province and those of another. There are also detailed provisions respecting the valuation of procurement and the procedures for procurement, including the use of source lists, which together are meant to ensure a very transparent system for both suppliers and governments (articles 505 and 506). As part of these measures, all governments were to have designated, by 1 January 1995, an electronic tendering system or newspaper(s) accessible to all Canadians in which it will issue its calls for tenders. As well, a working group on electronic tendering was formed, with the objective of developing a common, or at least fully compatible, electronic tendering system between the parties.

The agreement not to discriminate means specifically, but not exclusively, that practices such as inviting only local suppliers to bid on contracts, the biasing of technical specifications in favour of local suppliers, or the use of preferential margins in order to favour particular suppliers, are generally forbidden for the type of contracts covered under the agreement. The contracts covered by the commitment are those above a certain threshold ($25,000 for goods, $100,000 for services and construction), and only those issued by certain entities listed in Annex 502.1A, which includes government departments as well as a large number of public boards, agencies, commissions, councils, offices, centres, foundations, cultural institutions, tribunals, etc. of the public service. Only a few provincially-owned commercial enterprises are listed in this annex. Even then, however, many types of services are excluded from the AIT regardless of the procurement entity, including the purchase of many professional services and of advertising and public relations services.

Other publicly-owned entities, listed in Annexes 502.2A and 502.2B, are at least temporarily excluded from the AIT's procurement chapter. The first of these annexes lists a number of "entities that are not accountable to executive branches of governments of the Parties, entities whose object is national security, businesses of a commercial nature or in competition with the private sector, and state monopolies involved in the transformation and distribution of goods and services," in particular a number of publicly-owned electric utilities and liquor boards. With respect to these entities, negotiations are to be completed by 30 June 1996 that would list them definitely into 502.1A (i.e. covered by the non-discrimination provisions of the chapter), or in 502.2B. The latter annex lists entities covered by non-intervention commitment, that is certain "entities that are businesses of a commercial nature or in competition with the private sector, and state monopolies involved in the transformation and distribution of goods and services" for which we are pleased to learn that governments "shall not direct those entities to discriminate" against out-of-province suppliers, "including those related to construction."

In the meantime, governments may not direct the procurement of those entities remaining in 502.2A, except in accordance with the provisions of the chapter concerning regional and economic development. These state that a government may "under exceptional circumstances" exclude a procurement from the applicable provisions of the AIT for regional and economic development purposes, although notice must be given of the exceptional circumstances. Governments may challenge the extent or effect of the use of this exception by another government (article 508).

Annex 508.3 contains a list of regional and economic development policies and programs at the federal level and in BC, the two territories, PEI and Newfoundland, that will be allowed to continue even though they would otherwise not conform with the procurement chapter. But provinces maintaining such policies or programs must prepare an annual written report on them, and must submit these to review by 1 January 1998 "to ensure that they meet their regional and economic objectives" (article 508.4). In general, each government must report annually on the number and aggregate value of procurements equalling or exceeding the above-mentioned threshold values, as well as an estimated total value of procurements falling below the threshold for the three broad categories of goods, services, and construction (article 511.1). As well, governments must report on the value of procurement above the threshold but excluded from the provisions of the chapter for various reasons (including regional and economic development).

Each party must also provide, annually, basic information on its procurement procedures, such as names of contact points that each party must designate under the agreement and how to register on a source list. The Secretariat is to compile this information into similar format for each government, and this information is then to be published as an annual advertisement (article 511.6).

As well, before July 1996 and each March thereafter, the parties are to review whether the procurement chapter is meeting its objectives, assess and if necessary adjust threshold levels, and otherwise review the chapter and assess opportunities to include procurements that it does not cover. These findings and any recommendations are to be presented to the CIT for inclusion in the agreement's annual report (article 516.1).

The provinces also agreed to extend coverage of the AIT's procurement chapter to municipalities and municipal organizations, schools and publicly-funded academic, health, and social service entities by 30 June 1996, with negotiations to be completed by June 1995 (article 517).

Finally, the procurement chapter also contains a bid protest procedure, which will be reviewed below in the discussion on dispute settlement. However, I will note here that the bid protest procedures will initially be different for provincial and federal contracts, and that the parties committed themselves to issue recommendations toward harmonizing or reconciling these procedures "no later than three years" after the AIT came into effect, that is, by July 1998 (article 516.4).

As Table 1 indicates, some progress has been made on the AIT's procurement undertakings, particularly with respect to establishing a national, electronic contract tendering system. Regarding the incorporation of the MASH sector into the agreement, the deadline originally envisaged has come and gone, although we can be encouraged by the fact that a draft proposal to this effect is circulating. Governments obviously do not agree on this draft proposal, and it would probably be valuable to circulate it or a summary of the issues outstanding, so that the process in this instance may be spurred by public debate. A more bothersome issue to me, although less immediately important in terms of potential economic benefits, is that some of the key reports mandated by the agreement with the goal of fostering the emergence of non-discriminatory and transparent procurement practices, have either been issued sporadically, or have not yet been approved for public consumption. This is difficult to understand, because these undertakings do not involve negotiations between provinces, where deadlines may be missed because of disagreements among governments, but only require each to report on their current procurement practices. If the time or funds allocated toward the release of these reports are not realistic, then they should be reappraised, but it is vital for the success of the procurement portion of the agreement — which relies a lot on accurate and transparent information — that the information which was to be issued be produced and made public.

Table 1: **Non-Discrimination in Public Sector Procurement,**
Status of Steps to be Taken under AIT

Measure	Completed	Progress/ Partial	Not Done
Designate contact points for complaints by suppliers and other governments	Yes		
Establish working group on electronic tendering	Yes		
Designate common electronic or newspaper tendering system by January 1995	Yes, late		
Annual report on value of procurement		1995/96 done, but not approved by ministers	
Annual written report of non-conforming regional development policies and programs		1995/96 done, but not approved by ministers	
Review of non-conforming regional development programs by January 1998			Still within deadline
Information on basic procurement procedures to be advertised annually			X
Annual report to CIT on the operation of the chapter and recommended changes		Only one report issued	
Extend to MASH by June 1996		Draft proposal only	
Definite listing of certain entities as covered or not		Proposals have been submitted	
Recommendations to reconcile provincial and federal bid protest procedures by July 1998			Still within deadline

Investment

The general non-discrimination principles of the AIT are being superseded, in chapter 6 on investment, by a slightly differently worded article which states that an investor from across Canada will, in any province, receive at least the best treatment given to any other Canadian investor in that province (article 603), although measures inconsistent with this undertaking are still permissible if they meet a "legitimate objective" test which is also worded slightly differently than the general test described above (essentially making it more consistent with investment instead of trade issues). Article 603 also specifies that there will be no difference in the treatment accorded, in "like circumstances," to out-of-province firms established and carrying their activity in that province relative to that accorded to local firms. Furthermore, under article 604, governments cannot impose local presence or residency requirements as a condition of establishment, acquisition or carrying on business in a province.

The investment chapter's commitments regarding local presence and residency requirements did not, however, apply immediately to measures contravening them at the time the agreement was implemented. Respecting these, governments were to have listed by 31 December 1995 any existing measure inconsistent with the agreement, and governments were to have made recommendations to the committee regarding the appropriateness of retaining, removing or replacing these measures by 31 December 1996.

Other parts of the chapter forbid governments to condition the receipt of an incentive (e.g., a subsidy) on the recipient achieving a certain level of local content or on purchasing goods and services locally, and forbid discrimination in the receipt of incentives based on ownership or location of head office (within Canada) in the availability of incentives. Article 612 also builds on the AIT's general transparency provisions, by requiring the parties to promptly make relevant measures available, to simplify any reporting requirements, and to facilitate the development of electronic databases on investment-related programs and measures.

An important annex (608.3) contains a code of conduct on incentives (ranging from cash grants to price support, but excluding general investment promotion activities such as market information) adopted as part of the AIT negotiations. Under the code, the parties promise not to use such incentives to induce the relocation of an enterprise's existing Canadian operation from one province to another, or to undercut a Canadian competitor in obtaining a specific contract within Canada, and in general to agree that they will try to avoid incentives that "harm the economic interests of other Parties," such as sustaining non-economically viable operations in one province that compete with facilities in another province.

Finally, in order to carry out the obligations of the chapter such as the listing of incompatible existing measures and helping parties through consultation procedures in the event of disputes, the parties have established a Working Group on Investment. The WGI must also prepare an annual report on incentives for submission to the committee, including a report on any matters that have given rise to consultation between the parties.

As indicated in Table 2, partial progress has been accomplished on a few steps agreed to in the AIT's investment chapter which concern negative integration, but the key outcomes, the elimination of local presence and residency requirements and the publication of an annual report on incentives, have not yet been achieved, and are clearly past their deadlines. Particularly as some disputes have erupted with respect to the code of conduct on incentives (see below), the absence of an authoritative report on such incentives is an impediment to the well-functioning of the agreement.

Table 2:   ***Non-Discrimination in the Treatment of Investors, Status of Steps to be Taken under AIT***

Measure	Completed	Progress/Partial	Not Done
Set up Working Group on Investment	Yes		
List existing presence and residency requirements by December 1995	Yes, list awaits CIT approval		
Recommend steps re: presence and residency requirements by December 1996		Awaiting approval of ministers	
Annual report on incentives		1995/96 reports submitted. Await ministers' approval	

Labour Mobility

As with many other chapters of the AIT, chapter 7 on labour mobility begins by stating that the *general* rule of reciprocal non-discrimination is not applicable to this specific chapter, although the general rule on transparency applies. Instead, as I will detail here, there are specific commitments not to discriminate in certain key practices affecting labour mobility.

The chapter's obligations apply to measures such as occupational standards, licensing, certification, registration and residency requirements of
workers,[9] which create barriers to labour mobility (article 702). Governments
are also committed to seek compliance "within a reasonable period of time"
with the obligations of this chapter with other public sector and non-
government bodies (such as professional corporations, regulatory bodies, trade
unions or industrial associations) falling under their jurisdiction and exercis-
ing an authority delegated by government over the establishment, assessment
and recognition of standards related to licensing, certification or registration.

Much of the AIT's labour mobility provisions concern the mutual recognition and reconciliation of standards (on this, see article by Robert Knox in
this volume), but as I have said the chapter also makes explicit commitments
not to discriminate. Under article 706, governments cannot impose residency
requirements as a condition for access to employment opportunities, licensing, certification or registration of workers, or eligibility for a worker's
occupation. More broadly, workers from across the country are to be accorded
in any province a treatment at least as favourable as that awarded to that province's own workers. Article 707 contains some detailed commitments that have
the effect of strengthening the non-discrimination provision with respect to
licensing, certification, and registration measures. These include an understanding that they will relate principally to competence, that there will be no
unjustified delays or cost differentials for out-of-province workers and, regarding transparency, that these measures be "published or otherwise
accessible."

In keeping with the agreement's general philosophy, measures that do not
conform with these non-discriminatory provisions are still permitted, where
the purpose of the measure is to achieve "a legitimate objective," and meet
certain tests ensuring, notably, that it is not more trade-restrictive than necessary and does not create a disguised restriction to mobility (article 709.1).
However, the definition of "legitimate objective" specifically as it applies to
the labour mobility chapter is broader than that generally in effect through the
agreement. It includes "provision of adequate social and health services to all
geographic regions" of a province, and the more nebulous category of "labour
market development."

Under the AIT, the Forum of Labour Market Ministers ("the forum," which
predates the AIT) is responsible for developing a framework permitting
governments to "establish and review annually" a list of discriminatory measures falling under the "legitimate objective" rubric and meeting the tests just
mentioned, that is, a list of permissible discriminatory measures. Governments
are to participate in this exercise by giving written notice of all discriminatory measures adopted or maintained under the "legitimate objective"
exemption. The notice "shall indicate the Party's justification for the measure
and the anticipated duration of the measure" (articles 709.2 and 709.3). In

addition, compliance with the AIT may be suspended for a period of six months (renewable), but only under exceptional and tightly controlled (by the other parties) circumstances. A contact person is to be designated by each party to receive complaints from other governments concerning the interpretation or application of the labour mobility chapter, and complaints from persons (workers, employers, etc.) regarding a party's actual or proposed measure (article 711). The forum also established a Labour Mobility Coordinating Group (LMCG), composed of the contact points, in order to coordinate the chapter's implementation on the FLMM's behalf.

In addition to these specific steps, the AIT also requires the forum to "develop a workplan for the implementation" of governments' obligations under the labour mobility chapter, and to "produce an annual report on the operation" of the chapter. The annual report is specifically to include (under article 712) an assessment of the chapter's effectiveness — and recommendations to remedy any concerns with respect to the effectiveness — as well as a report on any disputes on the interpretation and application of the chapter, and on steps to resolve them. Governments are to report on such compliance through assessments and the annual report prepared by the forum.

The status of specific steps to be taken under the AIT's labour mobility chapter toward the removal of discriminatory barriers is shown in Table 3.

As explained above, the ability for individuals to move where they perceive their best earnings opportunities to be, without sacrificing certain basic tenets and advantages of Canadian citizenship, is one of the principal advantages for Canadians of the economic union. Even if they did not move in search of opportunities across the country, the ability to do so is still worth something to each individual, in that it reduces his or her economic risk of engaging in a particular occupation. In the event, hundreds of thousands of Canadians move across the country every year, with every province experiencing significant two-way population flows.

In that light, it is gratifying that some significant progress on removing discriminatory barriers has been accomplished under the labour mobility chapter of the AIT. In fact, the LMCG has initiated some key measures not expressly called for under the "priority for action" guidelines for developing the workplan (outlined in Annex 712.2). These include notably a survey of practices (which was answered by 300 of the 400 occupational regulatory bodies asked to participate), guidelines to assist regulatory bodies to comply with the chapter, and a communications strategy designed to implement the chapter. In addition, the federal government is offering financial support to help regulatory bodies comply with their obligations.[10]

Clearly, section 6 of the Charter will remain the cornerstone of individual mobility rights across Canada, but actions taken under chapter 7 of the AIT have also advanced the cause of mobility in a proactive fashion, as it relates to skilled workers and regulatory bodies by bringing most relevant non-

Table 3: **Non-Discrimination in Occupational Standards and Requirements, Status of Steps to be Taken under AIT**

Measure	Completed	Progress/Partial	Not Done
Framework to list and review all discriminatory measures	Framework in place		
Governments give notice of all discriminatory measures, justification, and anticipated duration		No measures to be listed	
Annual review of discriminatory measures		Ongoing – part of annual report	
Develop workplan to implement chapter	Yes, initial workplan and subsequent workplan (1996/97)		
Seek compliance with wide public sector and non-government bodies		Four hundred regulatory bodies invited to comply on 1 July 1996	
Parties to designate contact points to receive complaints	Yes (turned into Labour Mobility Coordinating Group)		
Annual report by Forum of Labour Market Ministers		1995/96 Report has been published	

government bodies into a process similar for all, and where all are working under the same guidelines and toward clearly established objectives. The caveats here are that such work is still very much in progress, and that, when the provinces feel they have the power to threaten another with retaliation for measures to which they object, they will do so, as demonstrated in the case of the dispute over the right of Ontario construction workers to work in Quebec, which flared up again shortly after the entry into force of the AIT. Nevertheless, in the latter case, the dispute was resolved along lines compatible with the obligations of the labour mobility chapter, and recourse to the dispute settlement mechanism would clearly have been available in the event a similar dispute involved a complaining province which did not have the economic clout necessary to retaliate.

Consumer-Related Measures and Standards

With respect to consumer-related measures and standards (chapter 8 of the AIT), the agreement's general rules of non-discrimination and transparency are meant to apply in their integrity. Much of this chapter is concerned with the harmonization of standards (i.e., positive integration) in three specific areas. Provisions related to negative integration include the elimination of differences in licensing, registration, and certification fees in any province between suppliers based in that province and others in Canada, except to the extent that the difference reflects actual costs (article 805, taking effect on 1 July 1996). The AIT also forbids requiring residency as a condition for awarding licensing, registration, or certification in a province (article 806). Likewise, any requirement imposed on suppliers as a condition of licensing, registration, or certification, (such as maintaining a place of business or an address for service, post a bond, etc.) is only allowed to the extent necessary to achieve a legitimate objective.

As with the labour mobility chapters, the definition of "legitimate objective" differs from the one given under the agreement's "general" principles, but in this case seems more restricted, focusing on the right of parties to establish the level of consumer protection it considers "appropriate," when this is done to achieve "the protection of the personal safety of consumers or the economic interests of consumers [including contractual fairness, protection of privacy, etc. as defined in the agreement]" (articles 803, 804 and 810).

In addition, article 809 requires the establishment of a Consumer Measures Committee, which is enjoined, under article 808, to report, "no later than 1 July 1997" on agreements concluded by governments on mutual enforcement of standards (e.g., reciprocal investigative powers and enforcement of judgements), and under article 810 to develop dispute resolution mechanisms specific to the chapter (to be used, as with all chapter-specific dispute resolution procedures, before a dispute can proceed to the overall agreement's dispute settlement mechanism, see below).

The status of steps to be taken under the AIT's chapter on consumer-related measures and standards is shown in Table 4 below. The table shows that, even with these straightforward requirements not to discriminate, and the relatively narrow range of harmonization measures contemplated under the chapter, it appears that certain steps required under the agreement are still posing some difficulty, although progress has been made in all areas.

Table 4:   **Non-Discrimination in Consumer-Related Measures and Standards, Status of Steps to be Taken under AIT**

Measure	Completed	Progress/Partial	Not Done
Establish committee on consumer-related measures and standards		Yes	
Develop appropriate DSM before July 1995		Approved by ministers, but not yet adopted	
Eliminate discriminatory fees by July 1996	Yes		
Report on cooperation and mutual enforcement by July 1997		Preliminary report out	
Submit annual reports for transmittal to committee	Yes		

Agricultural and Food Goods [11]

General rules of non-discrimination and transparency apply to this chapter of the agreement (chapter 9). However, because the chapter explicitly applies to measures identified as "technical barriers to trade" by the federal-provincial Agri-Food Inspection Committee (the "inspection committee"), the reach of the chapter is determined in practice by the various agriculture ministries represented on the committee. By "technical barriers," it is meant such things as differences in product, process or packaging standards or transport regulations, and not policies such as supply management and financial assistance programs (many of which are contentious but, according to an annex to the chapter, are currently being addressed through the Agri-food Policy Review).

Few provisions of this chapter deal with specific discriminatory barriers. There is a prohibition on "arbitrarily or unjustifiably" discriminating in the application of sanitary and phytosanitary measures (article 904). With respect to other measures, the signatories agree more generally not to amend an existing measure, or adopt a new one, so as to restrict trade in an agricultural or food good (article 905), that is, a standstill provision.

Under article 902, the inspection committee provided the CIT, before the entry into force of the AIT, with a written notice of measures identified as

Table 5: ***Non-Discrimination in Agricultural and Food Goods, Status of Steps to be Taken under AIT***

Measure	Completed	Progress/Partial	Not Done
Inspection committee to list technical barriers to trade before July 1995.	Yes		
Include barriers "with policy implications" in the coverage of the AIT by September 1997	Yes		
Ministers to review chapter coverage by September 1997		Delay requested by ministers	
Public notice of all new measures and amendments ahead of implementation	Yes		

technical barriers, following which specific measures to remove those "with policy implications" were in the "scope and coverage" of the agriculture chapter. Some clearly discriminatory measures have fallen under this provision of the AIT, including Ontario, Quebec, and Prince Edward Island regulations on coloured margarine designed to keep out-of-province producers from the domestic market. By 1 September 1997, the agriculture ministers were also to have reviewed the chapter and any recommendations for change, with a view to achieving "the broadest possible coverage" under the chapter, but this deadline was extended at their request.

It is striking that, unlike other sectors covered by the AIT, the obligation of agriculture ministers to report to the CIT is minimal in the case of agriculture. Along with other provisions of this chapter, this suggests that the process is to be squarely controlled by the various departments of agriculture.[12] Furthermore, no periodic report on any of the operation of this chapter seems to be required. On the plus side from the point of view of eliminating discriminatory practices, the chapter does build quite a bit on the AIT's general transparency provisions with respect to new measures or amendments to existing measures that may affect trade in agricultural or food goods. These changes are to be published and submitted to other agricultural ministers at least 20 days prior to the adoption or amendment of the measures, and other governments and any interested persons are entitled to have their comments on the measures taken into consideration (article 907).

Included as a barrier with "policy implications" in the AIT's coverage has been Quebec's regulation prohibiting margarine sold in the province to be coloured like butter. However, it seems clear that the province, despite initial promises to act on this matter under the AIT's agricultural chapter, will not comply in this case, which, while not imposing huge costs on other provinces as a whole, is a major irritant for the (mostly Ontario-based) margarine producers involved.[13] It appears that this particular trade restriction will be challenged under the DSM provisions of the AIT, which would be a major step in removing discriminatory barriers in the agri-food sector in Canada.

Alcoholic Beverages

The general rules of reciprocal non-discrimination and transparency, as well as the general definition of legitimate objective, are said to apply to the AIT's chapter on alcoholic beverages (chapter 10), in particular with respect to listing, pricing, access to points of sale, distribution, merchandising, and cost of service fees and other charges (article 1004) levied by the competent authorities overseeing the alcoholic beverage market in each province.

In practice, however, many provinces have reserved the right to continue certain measures that do not conform with these general rules. The hope for improvement here results from promises made in the AIT that all these measures will be reviewed before a certain date, namely 1 July 1996 for differential floor pricing mechanisms for beer maintained by Nova Scotia, the differential cost of service or other charges maintained for beer by New Brunswick and Quebec, and Ontario's application of its Canadian grape content requirement; and 1 December 1999 for Newfoundland's measures denying access for out-of-province beer to its outlets of brewers' agents. However, governments will still be able to apply certain measures specifically authorized by international trade agreements, such as measures in Ontario and British Columbia requiring private wine store outlets to discriminate — to an extent — in favour of provincial wines, and measures in Quebec requiring any wine sold in grocery stores to be bottled in Quebec (although the province must open other outlets to wine bottled outside the province). In this light, however, British Columbia and Quebec have agreed to negotiate reciprocal equivalent access for wine and wine products by 1 July 1996. Table 6 shows that progress on these promises to review or remove even partially the remaining discriminatory barriers to trade in alcoholic beverages has been slow, or has not lead to the hoped-for result.

Governments also agree to report annually to the CIT on whether there have been any complaints made under the chapter's dispute settlement procedures, on whether there are any changes proposed to the chapter, and on any "arrangement proposed or entered into under article 1800 (Trade Enhancement Arrangements) relating to trade in beverage alcohol products."

Table 6: Non-Discrimination in Alcoholic Beverages, Status of Steps to be Taken under AIT

Measure	Completed	Progress/Partial	Not Done
Review Nova Scotia differential floor pricing for beer by July 1996		Review done, but no change	
Review New Brunswick and Quebec differential cost of service and other charges by July 1996, where other parties also effectively maintain higher charges		Ontario still working on its charges; NB said it will not remove its charges	
Ontario Canadian grape content requirement to be reviewed by July 1996	Ontario will meet 1999 removal deadline		
Quebec and BC to negotiate equivalent access for wine by July 1996		Still at discussion stage	
Newfoundland's measures denying access to its brewers' agents outlets to be reviewed before December 1999			Still within deadline
Parties to report annually to the committee		First draft of 1996/97 report	

DISPUTE SETTLEMENT: THE PROOF OF THE PUDDING

ROLE AND COVERAGE OF THE AIT'S DISPUTE SETTLEMENT PROCEDURES

As we have discussed, the observance of many of the commitments entered into by governments in the AIT with respect to "negative integration" involves not specific actions or steps, but rather refraining from acting in a non-discriminatory way. It is difficult for an outside observer to judge whether this last commitment is being honoured on an ongoing basis. However, governments can be taken to task, through the agreement's dispute settlement process, by those (governments or persons) who feel that existing or proposed measures discriminates against them on the basis of provincial residence or place of business, and are therefore contrary to undertakings made in the agreement.

Although other institutions set up under the AIT, either at the ministerial decisionmaking level (e.g., the Committee on Internal Trade) or at the technical level (the Secretariat), allow for ongoing informal discussions of potentially contravening measures, the AIT's dispute settlement mechanism (DSM), set out in chapter 17, is the only available venue for formal testing of a particular measure by a government against the promise it has made not to discriminate. In particular, it is the only available forum in which the "legitimate objective" defence, which governments can raise in order to justify an otherwise discriminatory measure, can be formally tested.

Indeed, the dispute settlement mechanism of the AIT is focused almost entirely on enforcing the negative integration or non-discrimination aspects of the agreement. The agreement's DSM cannot, in general, be invoked in cases where governments allegedly fail to comply with their "positive" obligations or undertakings under the agreement, such as commitments to harmonize standards in a number of areas. And even this enforcement ultimately relies not on a legal obligation to remove an offending measure — since the agreement is not a legal document — but in large part on the willingness of governments to heed the decisions of the independent panels, which are the last possible stage of adjudicating a dispute under the AIT (the agreement also contains provisions for applying various degrees of moral suasion and even retaliation on governments not conforming with panel decisions, but retaliation is not likely to be an effective weapon in most cases, mostly because the type of simple retaliatory measures available between countries would, happily, be unconstitutional within Canada, while other types of retaliatory action authorized under the AIT might be more administrative trouble than they are worth).[14]

Within these limitations, there are two types of general dispute settlement procedures under the AIT. One concerns disputes brought by governments against other parties to the agreement, including on behalf of citizens or businesses having a "substantial and direct connection" with it (such as a place of business or residence). The other concerns disputes brought up by citizens against any government. The main difference between the two is that citizens can only bring up cases which their own government is unwilling to take up, and are obliged to go through an independent "screener," a type of ombudsman who will make sure there is some substantial basis to the case, before a complaint can proceed to the DSM.

There is considerable emphasis in the AIT, as indeed increasingly in international agreements, on dispute "avoidance" mechanisms, in the sense of requiring the complainant and the party complained against to endeavour, within a certain period, to settle a question amicably, and if needed, to seek expert advice before taking more confrontational steps. Thus, in the AIT, complaining provinces are expected to make use of the specific procedures for consultation, mediation, and conciliation contained in sectoral chapters and in chapter 17 itself, before moving to intervention by trade ministers in the dispute, and ultimately, to public adjudication of a dispute by an impartial panel (private complainants are expected to follow a similar route after receiving approval from the screener, and may be awarded costs if successful, but not damages or injunctive relief).[15] However, even the consultation step can be considered part of the dispute settlement process from the moment it is invoked, and parties are to notify the Secretariat of their use of this and other successive steps involved in the DSM.

As is the case with international agreements such as the NAFTA, the government procurement provisions of the AIT are subject to a "bid protest" procedure separate from the agreement's overall DSM. Under this procedure, bidders may enlist their provincial government to challenge the way contracts have been awarded in another province, and their complaint may ultimately be examined by a bi-provincial review panel, which will assess whether the procurement practices conformed with the AIT (article 513). In the case of federal procurement, suppliers may lodge a protest directly with an independent reviewing authority (article 514). However, when a supplier's government is unwilling to take up its case against another province's entity, the supplier may use the chapter 17 procedures for person-to-government complaints. A provincial government may also use the government-to-government dispute settlement procedures in chapter 17 when it takes up a complaint against a federal government entity on behalf of one of its residents.

To give effect to the DSM, governments agreed to take a number of steps, including naming contact points for receiving complaints under certain chapters (article 512 for procurement, article 711 for labour mobility), naming rosters of panelists to sit on procurement disputes "before the entry into force of this agreement" and deliver notice of the roster to the other parties (article 513.7), and, with respect to the general dispute settlement, maintain a roster of panellists (article 1705) and establish "before the date of entry into force of this Agreement," model rules of procedures for the panels (article 1706). The seriousness with which governments view the prospect of any measure being overturned by an independent panel can be gauged by the fact that many of these panelists are well-known Canadians whose decisions in these matters would, if they were asked to pronounce on an internal trade issue, likely be respected by the public at large.

THE EXPERIENCE WITH DISPUTE SETTLEMENT TO DATE

The exact number of recourses to the AIT's dispute settlement process and current status of complaints has not been published, unlike what is available, for instance, through the WTO or the NAFTA for disputes pertaining to these agreements. Therefore, the numbers I will cite below result from a compilation based on data which are possibly incomplete or subject to revision. I have not been able to distinguish between those complaints that concern discriminatory measures, and others concerning a failure to harmonize. But as noted above it is almost impossible to lodge a complaint against a government for not fulfilling a promise to harmonize ("positive integration"), whereas they can be taken to task for instances of discrimination as defined by the agreement.

Some analysts have described the AIT's DSM as "dormant,"[16] and headlines concerning the few disputes that have made a public impact have on occasion suggested that the process was easily stalled, in turn putting the entire agreement in jeopardy.[17] In fact, while it is true that no dispute has yet reached the crucial stage of being adjudicated by a panel, if one considers that any complaint passes through an obligatory stage of consultation as part of the DSM, it appears that both governments and private agents have made substantial use of the dispute provisions of the agreement. In the first two years since the coming into effect of the AIT:

- There have been close to 40 complaints made under the agreement's provisions, of which a dozen or so were entered into by governments against other governments, and the rest were entered into by private parties against governments.

- The party complained against most often under the provisions of the AIT has been the federal government (all but one of these complaints has come under the procurement chapter), followed at a distance by Ontario and Saskatchewan, then British Columbia, Quebec, New Brunswick, and Alberta. Only Nova Scotia and the Yukon have never been complained against under the agreement.

- Complaints have arisen most often under the labour mobility and procurement chapters, followed as a distant third by the investment chapter. Together, complaints arising under these chapters have made up about 80 percent of the cases. There have also been complaints under the alcoholic beverages, transportation, and environment chapters.

- An important indicator in my view is that most provinces have intervened at one time or another in the government-to-government dispute settlement process. This is important, because, once a province begins to rely on the DSM to secure compliance with the AIT by others, it can hardly deny other provinces or individuals the use of the same mechanism with respect to its own policies.

However, there are also troublesome facts regarding the use of the DSM, which probably account for its reputation of ineffectiveness:

- Few of the complaints have actually been resolved by changes in the practice complained against. Partly, this is because a significant number of complaints (about a third) were found at an early stage to be without foundation, either because they were not falling under the purview of the AIT, because the complainant lacked standing, or because the measure complained against had already expired. But most of these cases occurred in the first year of operation of the agreement, suggesting that perhaps a learning curve was involved. In fact, the 25 percent or so drop in the total number of cases between 1995-96 and 1996-97 is entirely due to the drop in the number of such "non-starter" complaints, and a plausible explanation for this is that complainants have started "picking" their cases better.

- More worrisome is that many complaints identified as legitimate rarely seem to be resolved quickly. Another third or so of the complaints, some dating back almost two years, seem to be stuck at the "chapter consultation" stage, or such other low intergovernmental stage of the DSM. In fact, over the entire history of the DSM, only one dispute has ever required consultation among CIT ministers, the last possible stage before adjudication by a dispute settlement panel. That complaint (by British Columbia against New Brunswick against incentives provided to UPS to expand its New Brunswick operations) was eventually dropped. The fact that more complaints have not reached higher levels of confrontation is not an indication of ineffectiveness per se of the DSM, since some complaints actually have been resolved at the lesser ("chapter") levels or, in the case of complaints against federal procurement practices, by an independent reviewer. But the number of complaints still pending and the lack of use of either the CIT or panels to resolve them also suggest the possibility that parties may try to avoid an impartial adjudication of the disputes altogether.

- Of the other third or so complaints that were allowed to proceed and that have come to a conclusion, almost as many have been dropped by the complainant as have resulted in corrective action. Although this may well mean that the party complained against was able to justify its measures vis-à-vis the complainant without having to go to a dispute settlement panel, which in principle is the more advisable route if indeed the measure did not contravene the AIT, it also means that the DSM has been pretty limited as a force of actual change in government practices.

Thus, while it cannot be concluded that the AIT's dispute settlement provisions have been ineffective — too many cases remain pending to form such a judgement yet — they certainly have had a very limited impact on reforming measures affecting internal trade. The fact that disputes involving the provinces have usually ended at some low level of intergovernmental consultation suggests either that problems can genuinely be solved at these levels, or that governments are reluctant to bring impartial advice to bear in complaints against them, an interpretation that seems bolstered by the large number of yet unresolved disputes.

CAUSES OF SHORTCOMINGS AND OPTIONS FOR IMPROVEMENTS

WHY CERTAIN UNDERTAKINGS WERE NOT MET

Shortly after the AIT was signed, severe criticisms were published of the very idea of relying on such an intergovernmental agreement to promote a more open and integrated internal market in Canada.[18] Since then, unflattering comments have appeared from both critics and supporters-in-principle of the AIT, regarding progress accomplished so far under its auspices, as measured against the agreement's own promises to remove barriers. For example, the authors of a study published last year by the Organization for Western Economic Cooperation wrote that the AIT "held the potential to move towards a Canadian common market, but has seen only limited success." The Canadian Chamber recently issued a report which said that the AIT required "political will" in order to be "transformed into an effective instrument to seize the opportunities for enhanced internal trade."[19] And by the AIT's Secretariat own admission, "A number of administrative matters, required by the Agreement, remain to be completed [as of 31 March 1997], including rosters of potential panellists, lists of contact points and some information reports." The Secretariat adds that "Governments are committed to dealing with these matters during the next year or reconsidering their function within the Agreement."

As we have seen, the implementation of the provisions of the AIT has indeed been slow, relative to the pace which the signatories had set for themselves at the time the accord was signed. In addition, implementation has not been as transparent as one might have hoped based on promises to release reports on the implementation of various chapters and on remaining barriers.

Abundant speculation, as well as logic, suggest what the reasons for these delays and lack of transparency might be, although little discussion of them can be found in the sparse literature on the topic. Before recommending avenues for improvement, it is worth listing these possible causes. They are:

- *Costs of money and time.* It is conceivable that certain promises made under the accord were unrealistic in terms of the budgets of people and money which governments were willing to lend to the project.

Part of this may be due to the large differences in population and economic size between the partners, the smaller partner tending to have a difficult time finding the resources to issue, or respond to, challenges under the agreement and fulfil their reporting and other obligations. The fact that, according to the Secretariat, governments may "reconsider" the function of some of the agreement's undertakings suggests that for some, the benefits are not worth the costs involved.

- *The political calendar.* Another reason may be that, following the major negotiating exercises of 1993-94, which preceded the agreement, governments considered the main job done and devoted attention to other priorities. The AIT was signed in July 1994, and although both the Conservative government defeated in 1993 and the succeeding Liberals were equally supportive of the agreement, the period since its signature was rich in changes to the Canadian political landscape, ranging from politically absorbing fiscal and social reforms in many provinces to the events related to the close Quebec sovereignty referendum, which may have left the single Canadian market far behind in terms of priorities.

- *Lack of political pressure.* A more serious problem than the political calendar itself may be the lack of pressure on the part of business people, professionals, tradespeople, and others potentially affected by the barriers existing within the Canadian market. It is true that large business organizations and some professional groups, as well as economic think tanks and many individual academics, have periodically voiced their concerns that unnecessary barriers — including most existing discriminatory barriers — were impeding the well-functioning of the Canadian economic union and denying fundamental rights of citizenship. These accumulated concerns were probably the main intellectual force behind the AIT negotiations. However, governments would implement the agreement far more vigorously if they were submitted to ongoing political pressures to do so: if, for example, they were faced with a steady stream of delegations of firms and individuals urging that this be done. But clearly they are not. A possible reason for this, in my view, includes lack of knowledge of the opportunities and reduced economic risks which a truly well-functioning agreement would confer on many Canadian firms and individuals, perhaps combined with a general impression, engendered by the very existence of an agreement, that the issue is already being dealt with.

- *A flawed bargaining mechanism.* An even more serious obstacle to the implementation of the AIT may arise from flaws in the agreement itself, in particular in its decisionmaking structure. Instead of adopting the model used to complete the Single European market, that is, use a qualified majority voting procedure to decide on specific technical measures to implement the goals *which have already been unanimously agreed upon*, the principle of consensus is carried into each minute, technical negotiations, which gives an extraordinary leverage to a single province wishing to hold onto a particularly sensitive barrier. The latter can just say no, as seems to have happened in a number of cases already. This flaw is exacerbated by the fact that there are no independent experts or body (as with the EU's Commission) recommending technical measures to be adopted to fulfil the AIT's obligations. This means that in many cases it is left entirely to the very officials previously in charge of maintaining the barriers to propose ways to remove them, or to explain why it cannot or should not be done, a process that clearly runs the risk of generating only minimal progress.

• *Fear of legitimizing the AIT.* Finally, and not unrelated to the previous point, it is not inconceivable that governments fear legitimizing the agreement by aggressively demanding that other provinces or the federal government submit to their AIT obligations, or by pursuing disputes through the AIT's settlement mechanism, even if they had a legitimate trade complaint against another government. Clearly, if one signatory begins to do so, its own policies will likely come under closer scrutiny by others and members of the public, a situation that governments may not want to face. In this respect, it will be interesting to see whether the Government of Ontario takes up the case of its margarine producers against Quebec restrictions on margarine colouring by using the government-to-government provisions of the DSM, or whether it will prefer that the producers involved take up the person-to-government dispute route available under the AIT.

Keeping these possible obstacles in mind, I will now turn to options for improving the pace of implementation of the accord.

OPTIONS FOR IMPROVEMENT

Because of the genuine, if very slow, progress accomplished so far, and the number of issues reportedly at the "progress" stage and disputes at the "consultation" stage, it seems way too early to call the AIT a failure. There is, however, a danger that the agreement, which became possible because it was a comprehensive, carefully balanced package, will unravel if all of its parts are not made to function properly and promptly. I will discuss here some options which have been put forward for giving a new impetus to the AIT itself, and to the process of removing barriers to trade more generally using the AIT as a centrepiece.

Increased Public and Business Awareness and Participation

It is difficult to judge what awareness of the AIT and of its market-opening provisions the public and individual businesses have in general. Perhaps nothing short of a publicity campaign, explaining rights under the agreement, focusing on specific real-life examples, and listing provincial contact points as well as supporting business and professional associations, would drive home the point. In the meantime, it seems absolutely crucial that documents registering both the pace of progress under the AIT and the road left to fulfil the agreement, be published and receive widespread circulation and discussion, as did the annual European Commission review of progress on the White Paper agenda.

It would be well within the mandate of the Secretariat to issue an annual report on the implementation of the AIT's various chapters, including an evaluation of the reasons for missed deadlines and an assessment of outstanding issues. This report should subsume or summarize all other reports which governments are committed to provide under the terms of the AIT, including those on progress toward harmonizing labour standards and on the operation of their regional development programs. In sum, it seems to me that the Secretariat should be given sufficient resources for a one-time campaign of information on the agreement, and commanded directly to get on with the business of producing an overall report on the progress — and failings, including failures to file required reports — under the agreement. Governments should be able to see and comment ahead of time on this document, but not to veto it.

Strengthening the Agreement's Institutions

The federal government should convene a "three-year summit" in June of 1998, to review the functioning of AIT's institutions. In my view, proposals being discussed at the summit should include a clarification and strengthening of the Secretariat's mandate, along the lines of a mini-European Commission (that is, not a decisionmaking body, but with strengthened policy advice and reporting role), and a temporary one at that, focused only on the task of ensuring that all commitments under the agreement are fulfilled.

Specifically, the Secretariat should be able to play a much greater role in monitoring and reporting on obstacles to implementation of the agreement, as well as seeking expert advice in proposing solutions. It could translate this advice into proposals for specific measures. A key reform would be that the CIT should have to formally vote on measures proposed by the Secretariat (or by other governments) to ensure completion of the AIT, with the votes being publicly recorded.

In addition, governments should consider adopting a rule of qualified majority voting, again referring only to those issues which they have agreed to in principle.[20] The point, again, being that since governments have agreed to the principles contained in the agreement, no one government should be able to block implementation.

Finally, governments should commit to have all the promises of the AIT fulfilled by the end of the fifth year of implementation, or 1 July 2000.

The federal government, constitutionally responsible for maintaining the economic union, should be willing to help certain jurisdictions to meet the costs of implementing the agreement and meet the necessary reporting requirements. In addition, since the agreement allows for the recovery of costs but not damages, the federal government should set up a one-off program of challenges designed to help firms, organizations and individuals, test the dispute settlement system, in the public interest, at a reasonable cost to them.[21]

Legislative Options

One key institutional weakness of the AIT is that its provisions have not been made generally applicable through implementing legislation in the various Canadian jurisdictions, unlike the way the European Single Market initiative and the NAFTA, for example, were implemented in their respective member countries. That is to say, AIT implementation remains almost entirely a matter of administrative fiat. Provinces have either passed minor changes to existing statutes or have passed implementing legislation covering mostly housekeeping provisions. Likewise, the federal legislation does not make the AIT directly applicable in federal law.[22] As Robert Howse explained, one way of making all or at least some of the AIT's obligations directly applicable would be to embody them in federal and provincial statutes. Of course, these could always be rescinded by the legislatures but, as Howse pointed out, this would attract more attention than flouting the provisions of a non-legally binding accord.[23] Some provinces could take the initiative by passing such laws which would take effect if a critical mass of others did the same thing.

While it is understandable that governments may not want to make all the provisions of this relatively new and untried agreement into law yet, a start could nevertheless be made in certain key areas, perhaps with legislation requiring that governments comply with the key reporting requirements provided for under the AIT.

A bolder avenue would be for the federal government to use its constitutional authority under sections 121 and 91(2) of the constitution, in order to seek the implementation of specific provisions of the AIT, where provinces cannot agree to do so.[24] Howse in particular has argued that the legitimacy of the federal government taking such action is actually reinforced by the existence of an AIT: that is, all the federal government would do in this instance is take action for ensuring that what has already been agreed to between it and the provinces is actually implemented. Clearly this is an important option, and one that the federal government should not be too shy of using if other avenues for improvement of the performance under the agreement cannot be taken. A private member's bill recently introduced in the House of Commons proposes that the federal government be able to do just that, provided that the proposal receives the approval of at least two-thirds of the province accounting for at least 50 percent of the Canadian population.[25]

Constitutional Options

Others, clearly frustrated, have suggested introducing a new binding authority, such as the Trade Council of the European Union and the Interstate Commerce Commission in the United States, capable of enforcing free internal trade. Thus, OWEC has proposed a Canadian Internal Trade Commission (CITC), which would be "an economic tribunal with judicial powers derived from the Constitution and independent of governments" to regulate all trade and commerce within the country.

Here the doubts expressed by the Macdonald Commission as to the possibility of enforcing full free trade through constitutional provisions alone come to mind.[26] But the commission itself also suggested that following a few years' experiment with an administrative agreement (such as the AIT), some of its provisions, if they were seen as functioning well, could be entrenched in the constitution.

CONCLUSION

In short, the story of the AIT so far, at least with respect to its provisions regarding non-discrimination between provinces, transparency, and dispute settlement, has been one of timid implementation and lack of reporting and dissemination of information concerning the steps taken by governments or private parties in order to ensure its implementation. If one considers that the agreement, as written, and especially in its general principles, strikes an appropriate balance between the need and responsibility of governments to strengthen the economic union on the one hand, and the legitimate differences that may occur from time to time in a wide range of policy areas under provincial jurisdiction on the other, one must view any significant deviation from the agreement as being detrimental to the well-functioning of Canada's economic union.

In order to speed up the pace of eliminating discriminatory barriers, and avoid the emergence of others in the future, Canadian governments should first ensure that all the information which they promised to make public when they signed the AIT be made available. In general, the agreement should be given a greater public profile, for example, by reporting on the progress of trade disputes. This should be accompanied by a strengthening of the AIT's institutional structure, in particular a greater monitoring and reporting role forthe secretariat and streamlined voting procedures, with a view to accelerate the pace of outstanding negotiations. As further steps, all the signatory governments should consider stronger legislation than is currently in place to implement key aspects of the agreement. If these steps do not result in a full implementation of the AIT within a reasonable period of time, the federal government should consider using its constitutional powers to ensure that this unanimous agreement among Canadian governments get fully implemented in practice.

NOTES

1. From this point on in the chapter, the word "province" will refer to both provinces and territories, unless otherwise indicated.

2. In this chapter, the words "parties" (to the agreement), "signatories" (to the agreement) and "governments" are used interchangeably, unless otherwise made clear.

3. See Thomas J. Courchene, "Analytical Perspectives on the Canadian Economic Union," in *Federalism and the Canadian Economic Union*, ed. Michael J. Trebilcock et al. (Toronto: Ontario Economic Council, 1983), in particular pp. 95-96; and Canada West Foundation, *The Canadian Common Market: Interprovincial Trade and International Competitiveness* (Calgary: Canada West Foundation, 1985).

4. Thus, the Canadian economic union allows enterprises to extend their operations from their local base without having to worry about the intricacies of a foreign legal system, possible protectionist actions under "trade remedy laws," the need to document the origin of their products, or the difficulties of enforcing judgements against foreign debtors. That such a trading facility particularly benefits small- and medium-sized businesses is shown by data collected by the Bureau de la Statistique du Québec, according to which 2,513 establishments in that province exported goods to other destinations in Canada in 1990, while 1,610 produced a roughly comparable dollar amount of exports to foreign countries. See, the Canadian Chamber of Commerce, *The Agreement on Internal Trade and Interprovincial Trade Flows: Building a Strong United Canada,* September 1996.

5. On this point, Michael A. Goldberg and Maurice D. Levi argue that "the accidental [i.e., provided by the political system] weights in the Canadian portfolio of provinces/territories provide an economic outcome that is close to the efficient frontier which designates economically efficient combinations of returns and risks, where 'return' relates to economic growth, and 'risk' to the volatility of economic growth," in "Growing Together or Apart: The Risks and Returns of Alternative Constitutions of Canada," in *Canadian Public Policy/Analyse de Politiques* 20, 4 (1994):341.

6. Notably the Western Agreement on Procurement in 1989, the Maritime Procurement Agreement in 1990, and the Intergovernmental Agreement on Beer Marketing Practices and Intergovernmental Agreement on Government Procurement in 1991.

7. See Robert Howse, *Securing the Canadian Economic Union: Legal and Constitutional Options for the Federal Government*, Commentary no. 81 (Toronto: C.D. Howe Institute, June 1996), pp. 4-6.

8. Such as, for example, a requirement that firms bidding on a federal government construction contract in a province be located in that province.

9. "Workers" is defined under the agreement so as to include virtually all persons in an employed situation: "an individual, whether employed, self-employed or unemployed, who performs or seeks to perform work for pay or profit" (Article 713).

10. *Agreement on Internal Trade, Chapter 7 — Labour Mobility: Annual Report 1995-96*, retrieved from Human Resources and Development Canada internet site, 4 July 1996, and "Government of Canada Announces Support to Facilitate Interprovincial Labour Mobility," Human Resources Development Canada press release, 12 February 1997.

11. The definition of agricultural and food goods for the purpose of this chapter excludes fish products and alcoholic beverages.

12. The last sentence of Annex 902.5 illustrates this perfectly: "The dates for the adoption of recommendations concerning imitation dairy products and butter blends are to be determined by the Ministers."

13. See Konrad Yakabuski, "Quebec Courts Margarine War," *The Globe and Mail*, 14 October 1997, p. B1.

14. See Robert Howse, "Between Anarchy and the Rule of Law: Dispute Settlement and Related Implementation Issues in the Agreement on Internal Trade," in *Getting There: An Assessment of the Agreement on Internal Trade*, ed. M. Trebilcock and D. Schwanen (Toronto: C.D. Howe Institute, 1995), pp. 178-90.

15. Ibid., pp. 183-86.

16. See Graham F. Parsons and Peter L. Arcus, *Interprovincial Trade and Canadian Unity* (Regina and Calgary: Organization of Western Economic Cooperation, 1996), p. 5; and in a news release accompanying the study.

17. See Alan Toulin, "Provincial Trade Pact Starting to Crumble," *The Financial Post*, 14 September 1996, p. 1.

18. See Andrew Coyne, "What Could the Premiers Deny Quebec That They Haven't Already Destroyed?" *The Globe and Mail*, 28 August 1995; and Armand de Mestral, "The Canadian Agreement on Internal Trade: A Comment," in *Getting There*, ed. Trebilcock and Schwanen, pp. 95-97.

19. Parsons and Arcus, *Interprovincial Trade and Canadian Unity*; and the Canadian Chamber of Commerce, *The Agreement on Internal Trade*.

20. In an earlier paper, I suggested that such a "qualified majority" could comprise 19 (two-thirds) of 28 provincial votes distributed as follows: Quebec and Ontario, four each; Alberta and British Columbia, three each; Prince Edward Island and the (soon three) territories, one each, and all other provinces, two votes. See "Open Exchange," in David M. Brown, Fred Lazar and Daniel Schwanen, *Free to Move: Strengthening the Canadian Economic Union*, Canada Round series no. 14 (Toronto: C.D. Howe Institute, 1992).

21. As proposed by Howse in "Between Anarchy and the Rule of Law," p. 186.

22. See Robert Howse, *Securing the Canadian Economic Union: Legal and Constitutional Options for the Federal Government*, Commentary no. 81 (Toronto: C.D. Howe Institute, 1996).

23. Ibid., p. 5.

24. Parsons and Arcus, *Interprovincial Trade and Canadian Unity*, p. 10.

25. Canada Bill C-203, *An Act to Amend the Agreement on Internal Trade Implementation Act*, Mr. Benoit, First Reading, September 1997.

26. Canada, Royal Commission on the Economic Union and Development Prospects for Canada (MacDonald Commission) *Report* (Ottawa: Minister of Supply and Services, 1985), vol. 3, p. 137.

7

Green Harmonization:
The Success and Failure of Recent Environmental Intergovernmental Relations

Patrick Fafard

L'inter gouvernementalisme a été une des caractéristiques définissantes des politiques environnementales canadiennes dans les années '90. Pendant les dernières années, les deux niveaux de gouvernements ont dévoués du temps et des efforts considérables à préparer des ententes intergouvernementales pour réglementer et restructurer leurs rôles et responsabilités respectives à l'égard de politique environnementale. À ce jour, cet effort n'a produit que de modestes résultats. Ce modeste succès est attribuable à une combinaison de facteurs sociaux, institutionnels et d'empiétement. Cependant, il faut porter attention tant aux succès qu'aux échecs. Même si rejetée par les Ministres, l'Entente [Environmental Management Framework Agreement (EMFA)], est un document compréhensif qui identifie les possibilités de politiques nationales et de prise de décision nationale d'où national n'était pas synonyme de fédéral. Les forces et les faiblesses de la EMFA sont importantes pour d'autres efforts à réaliser des ententes intergouvernementales compréhensives. En fait, l'expérience récente du domaine de la politique environnementale suggère que seuls des changements marginaux peuvent être accomplis par des négociations intergouvernementales et que de telles négociations posent d'importantes questions au sujet de la responsabilité démocratique.

INTRODUCTION

In their ongoing search for a new constitutional and institutional architecture, Canadians have debated a variety of changes to both the constitutionally entrenched division of powers as well as to the management of the existing allocation of responsibilities between Ottawa and the provinces. However, in recent years interest in formal constitutional change has declined and the debate has shifted to better management of the federation. The working assumption is that because the constitution cannot be easily amended, then

changes to the federal bargain should be achieved by intergovernmental agreement. Thus, while formal constitutional change was the order of the day in the
1980s, in the 1990s the focus has shifted to intergovernmental relations and
an effort to reinvent the cooperative federalism of the 1960s.

This renewed interest in intergovernmentalism has been evident in recent
interactions between Ottawa and the provinces across a range of policy fields.[1]
For example, intergovernmentalism is an integral part of many of the current
debates with respect to social policy and the social union, for example, the
deliberations leading to reform of the Canada and Quebec Pension Plans, and
the more recent efforts to mount a new national social program to combat
child poverty. Similarly, intergovernmentalism has been the hallmark of labour
market policy and has led to a series of federal-provincial agreements shifting
responsibility for labour market training from Ottawa to the provinces.[2]

Although it has not received as much public attention, intergovernmentalism
has been, and continues to be, the hallmark of environmental policy in Canada.
The most recent burst of intergovernmental cooperation began with the Statement on Interjurisdictional Cooperation in 1990, through the negotiations
leading to the rejected Environmental Management Framework Agreement
(EMFA), and finally to the Canada-Wide Accord on Environmental Harmonization, which was agreed to in principle by environment ministers in the fall
of 1996. In fact, the pattern of intergovernmental negotiation with respect to
environment policy and the resulting draft agreements are potentially as significant as anything being done in other policy fields. The central argument of
this chapter is that the recent patterns of intergovernmental relations with respect to environmental policy deserve scrutiny by those who seek clues as to
the more general patterns of reform to the Canadian federal bargain. And what
is more, the significance of environmental intergovernmentalism lies both in
the successes *and* the failures of the recent past.

The next section offers a short overview of recent intergovernmental negotiations with respect to environment policy, with particular emphasis on the
EMFA and the more recent Canada-Wide Accord. The central message here is
that governments have not been particularly successful in coming to a meaningful reallocation of federal and provincial responsibilities. The next part of
the chapter then seeks to explain these trends and in particular, the weakness
of the Canada-Wide Accord. The chapter then turns to a more detailed discussion of the EMFA. Although ministers rejected this agreement in 1996, it
deserves careful scrutiny. This agreement was an innovative effort to distinguish between federal, provincial, and *national* policies and programs. The
first two are the exclusive responsibility of the two orders of government while
the latter, national policies, would have been the joint responsibility of Ottawa and the provinces acting in concert. The importance of the EMFA lies in
the fact that, although the agreement was rejected, it did reintroduce into our
collective lexicon the concept of national policies which are not under the

exclusive jurisdiction of the federal government. The conclusion of the chapter offers some observations about the implications of a failed EMFA and a weak Canada-Wide Accord for the prospects of intergovernmental cooperation in other policy fields.

RECENT TRENDS

The question of the roles and responsibilities of Ottawa and the provinces with respect to the environment has received a great deal of attention in recent years. One of the reasons for this is a fair degree of ambiguity concerning the constitutional basis for federal and provincial activity in the areas of pollution control, ecosystem management and resource conservation. Of course, the environment is not included in the lists of powers assigned to each order of government according the *Constitution Act, 1867*. Nevertheless, the basis of provincial environmental legislation is relatively uncontroversial. Provinces legislate in the area of the environment based on their constitutional responsibilities for such things as local works and undertakings, property and civil rights, and the management of natural resources, the latter confirmed by the 1982 resource amendment to the *Constitution Act, 1867*. For its part, federal environmental legislation is based on varying combinations of the federal trade and commerce power, federal responsibility for the fishery and the conduct of international relations, and the federal power to legislate on the criminal law.[3]

Although both orders of government have the constitutional jurisdiction to act, on balance provinces have been more aggressive in asserting their jurisdiction. Whereas provincial governments have been keen to assert their authority, particularly with respect to the management of natural resources, the federal government has been comparatively timid and has not chosen to assert or even test the full extent of its constitutional authority.[4] The major exceptions have been when public concern about the environment has provided a strong incentive for federal action. This occurred most recently in the late 1980s when Ottawa enacted a series of new amended environmental statutes. This does not mean, however, that the two orders of government have not come into conflict with one another on matters of environmental policy. On the contrary, there is significant overlap between Ottawa and the provinces in several areas, notably with respect to environmental assessment (EA). Indeed, rationalization of "who does what" with respect to EA has proven to be one of the major reasons governments have sought to develop a new allocation of responsibilities with respect to environmental policy writ large.

TOWARD THE ENVIRONMENTAL MANAGEMENT FRAMEWORK AGREEMENT

Given this relative constitutional ambiguity, since the environment became an area of government activity in the late 1960s the relationship between Ottawa and the provinces with respect to environmental policy has been marked by periods of cooperation, conflict, and unilateral action.[5] Since the early 1990s, however, cooperation would *seem* to be the order of the day. This period of cooperation is in marked contrast with the conflict that marked the late 1980s and early 1990s with respect to environmental assessment and the development of the *Canadian Environmental Protection Act*.[6]

What appears to be cooperation may, however, be a combination of a variety of relationships and very different patterns of intergovernmental relations.[7] The intensive efforts of the past several years to achieve a comprehensive environmental management agreement have not produced very much more than a rather general statement of intent and best efforts. The basis for the current state of affairs and what might explain the lack of progress are worthy of some detailed attention.

In November 1993 the Canadian Council of Ministers of the Environment (CCME) met as part of an annual cycle of twice-yearly meetings.[8] At this particular meeting ministers agreed to make harmonization a top priority and directed their officials to work on a new "Environmental Management Framework for Canada." Over the next several months a Harmonization Task Group was established, bringing together officials from all provinces except Quebec. The task group developed a paper setting out a series of general principles to guide harmonization, which was presented to the CCME at its next meeting in May 1994. Ministers agreed with the general thrust of the paper and it was released for public comment.

Several months later the task group was dissolved and replaced by a more elaborate Lead Representatives Committee (LRC). The LRC took the lead in drafting what was to become the Environmental Management Framework Agreement (EMFA) and the 11 schedules that accompanied the agreement. The operating procedures of the LRC are notable because they reflect recent trends in intergovernmental negotiations in Canada where the emphasis is on transparency, public participation, and, unfortunately, considerable complexity. For example:

- The LRC brought together all provinces, including Quebec, and had an independent chairperson, an official from the Government of Alberta.[9]

- The LRC created a rather elaborate structure to assist it in developing an agreement. The LRC met monthly in different parts of the country. Fourteen subcommittees were created to work on different aspects of the main text and the schedules, and as many as 125 officials worked directly on the development of the agreement. This may explain why the text that was eventually produced was very complex and the agreement and the 11 schedules combined for a document of over one hundred pages.

- Early on, the Harmonization Task Group created a National Advisory Group (NAG) of 16 people from environmental non-governmental organizations (ENGOs), business, industry, municipalities, and universities. The NAG provided advice and feedback to the task group and later the LRC with respect to public consultation and the substance of the draft agreements.

- The work of the LRC was supplemented by public consultations. Individual members of the LRC and other officials met with stakeholders on request to discuss the work of the LRC and the development of the EMFA. Several public workshops were held to solicit input from stakeholders and interested parties. Also, the CCME Secretariat made extensive use of the Internet to disseminate draft copies of the EMFA and invite comments from stakeholders and the general public.

In other words, by the usual standards of intergovernmental negotiating, the development of the EMFA was a remarkably open and consultative process. However, these were intergovernmental negotiations about *environmental* policy. As a result, the process was also judged by the standards of recent environmental policymaking. In this regard, the EMFA process was found wanting.[10]

By December of 1994 a draft of the EMFA and four schedules were ready and ministers agreed to release the documents for discussion. Two months later, in February 1995, an invitational multistakeholder workshop was convened in Toronto. Approximately 55 people representing business, industry, environmental non-governmental organizations (ENGOs) and other groups came together to discuss and critique the draft agreement. Although industry representatives were either silent or generally supportive of the draft agreement, other participants, notably representatives of the environmental movement expressed a variety of concerns. For example, ENGOs were concerned that governments had not demonstrated that duplication and overlap existed in federal and provincial environmental regulations even though it was the problem that the EMFA was designed to address. Similarly, ENGOs were concerned that the EMFA would mean that the federal government would abandon its traditional roles with respect to environmental protection and that the agreement represented a *de facto* constitutional amendment.[11]

The consultation process was designed to feed into a revision of the draft EMFA for presentation to ministers at the next meeting of the CCME in May 1995. However, by this time the reform process was in jeopardy. The federal minister of the environment, Sheila Copps, was troubled by the concerns expressed by environmentalists and, in some cases, by industry. This was particularly the case with respect to issues relating to environmental assessment, an area that had been the subject of considerable intergovernmental

wrangling in the past. As a result, a revised draft of the EMFA was not released after the May ministerial meeting pending further revisions and
clarifications. At the October 1995 meeting of the CCME a revised draft and
ten of the eleven schedules were released for public comment. The schedule
dealing with EA was, perhaps not surprisingly, held back for further revisions.

In early 1996 environment officials held two more workshops in Edmonton
and Toronto to solicit comment and feedback on the revised draft of the EMFA
and the ten schedules. Strong criticism of the agreement was again voiced by
ENGOs and others, including representatives of Aboriginal Peoples who were
concerned that they had not been consulted in the drafting of the agreement
and they were not going to be parties to a new national framework for environmental policy in Canada. By this time the draft EMFA was all but dead.
When the CCME met in May 1996 to consider a final revised draft of the
agreement, ministers rejected the document and, with it, an ambitious recast-
ing of federal and provincial roles with respect to environmental management.
Instead, ministers instructed their officials to draft a new and simpler agreement. Interestingly enough, all jurisdictions, including Quebec, agreed to
participate in the new process.

A CANADA-WIDE ACCORD ON ENVIRONMENTAL HARMONIZATION

Notwithstanding the failure of the EMFA, during the spring and summer of
1996 there was continuing pressure for some sort of agreement with respect
to federal and provincial roles regarding the environment. Some of this pressure was coming from within the federal government itself which had embarked
on a major effort to recast the division of powers and shift responsibility to
the provinces in key areas, including the environment. For example, after being named minister of the environment in February 1996, Sergio Marchi was
later told by the Prime Minister's Office to secure an agreement with the provinces with respect to environmental management.[12]

Building on this pressure from the top and the months of work on the EMFA,
officials moved quickly and drafted a new Canada-Wide Accord on Environmental Harmonization. Drafts of the accord were once again released for public
consultation in August and September 1996. The text of the accord is quite
vague and represents a best-efforts approach on the part of Ottawa and the
provinces. At the same time, ENGOs again expressed concerns with the general thrust of the accord, once again raising concerns that the accord is designed
to address a problem, overlap and duplication, that either does not exist or,
may in fact be desirable.[13] Notwithstanding such concerns, Ottawa and the
provinces forged ahead and, in November 1996, environment ministers gave
agreement in principle to the accord. Ministers also released drafts of two
sub-agreements dealing with Inspections and Standards. Once again, environmental assessment proved to be a sticking point. Ottawa and the provinces

could still not agree on a rationalization of activity with respect to EA. In the absence of anything resembling consensus, ministers could only agree to release a discussion paper to once again elicit public comments.

The accord, in marked contrast to the EMFA, is only four and a half pages long and, similar to other intergovernmental agreements, does not bound the parties in any meaningful way and is hortatory rather than regulatory.[14] For example, pursuant to the accord, the federal and provincial governments agree that their environmental management activities will reflect a set of 13 principles. These principles are very general and include the proposition that pollution prevention is the preferred approach to environmental protection and that "working cooperatively with Aboriginal people and their structures of governance is necessary for an effective environmental management regime."[15] As was true for the EMFA, the substance of the Canada-Wide Accord, such as it is, lies in the sub-agreements. In the accord, governments state their intention to conclude such sub-agreements "on all areas of environmental management that would benefit from Canada-wide coordinated action."

Over the next several months officials forged ahead but, in contrast to the development of the EMFA, the process was somewhat less public and moved much more quickly. Attention focused on the draft sub-agreement on standards and the sub-agreement on environmental assessment. For example, in February 1997 a first draft of the EA sub-agreement was released for public comment and a revised draft was released in late March 1997. Similarly, in December 1996 the CCME Secretariat released a document with more specific details regarding the standards sub-agreement. The new document outlined a process for determining how standards might be set for a variety of substances including ground level ozone, dioxins and furans, benzene in air, and the remediation of sites contaminated with petroleum products. The CCME Secretariat convened a workshop in April 1997 to discuss Canada-wide standards in anticipation of final ratification of the sub-agreement by ministers at their meeting in May 1997.

Alas, the long-awaited May 1997 meeting of the CCME was cancelled because of the federal election. As a result, the decisions that were to have been made at that meeting were put off to the next scheduled meeting of the Council in the fall of 1997. However, the federal election also meant the arrival of a new federal minister of the environment, Christine Stewart, whose general orientation to decentralization is not clear. Similarly, the election meant the death of legislation before Parliament that would have significantly amended the *Canadian Environmental Protection Act*. These events have combined to put the whole process of environmental policy harmonization in abeyance as a new bill amending CEPA is drafted and the new minister decides where she wants to go with respect to harmonization. Thus, it is far from certain that there is still sufficient political will and momentum to allow ministers to ratify the Canada-Wide Accord.

In summary, the story of environmental federalism over the past several years has been one of thwarted ambition, varying degrees of consultation and openness, and a seemingly irresistible pressure to get some sort of agreement, however vague and unrealistic. In contrast to the intergovernmental conflict of the late 1980s and early 1990s with respect to environmental policy, the last several years have been marked by a considerable degree of cooperation, even if this cooperative spirit has not always resulted in a real change to the roles and responsibilities of Ottawa and the provinces. What might explain this shift in the overall tenor of federal-provincial relations with respect to the environment? The next section offers some possible explanations.

EXPLAINING RECENT EVENTS[16]

In seeking to understand the recent pattern of intergovernmental environmental relations, a range of societal, institutional and spillover factors help explain the relative lack of success in forging a new division of federal and provincial roles and responsibilities for environmental protection. The working assumption is that the patterns can be largely explained with reference to factors that are not unique to environmental issues. To go beyond this assumption is beyond the scope of this chapter.[17]

SOCIETAL FACTORS: PUBLIC OPINION

First, and perhaps most importantly, what happens with respect to environmental policy and intergovernmental relations (and indeed all intergovernmental relations) is the product of much more than the interactions among governments. The extent to which Ottawa and the provinces are able to harmonize environmental policy and programs is much influenced by a range of non-governmental or societal factors.

Contrary to the pattern of the late 1980s and early 1990s, the most important of these societal factors is no longer public opinion. As has been amply documented elsewhere, interest in, and concern about, the environment and environmental protection has fallen off in recent years following the green wave of the later 1980s and early 1990s. The recession of the early 1990s and the continuing levels of high unemployment have led to a situation where environmental issues are deemed less important than economic ones. This is particularly evident in British Columbia where a trade-off has been constructed pitting jobs against the environment and where concerns about jobs outweigh any concerns about the sustainability of forestry practices. More generally, in the January 1997 National Angus Reid/Southam News Poll, in response to an open-ended question about the most important issues for Canada today, only 4 percent of respondents identified the environment as an important issue.[18]

Given the relative lack of public concern about the environment, there is less public pressure for governments to do something substantive about the environment and environmental protection. This, in turn, allows governments and industry to redefine issues to emphasize competitiveness and jobs. Moreover, the relative lack of public concern makes it harder for ENGOs and others who oppose devolution of responsibility from Ottawa to the provinces.

However, it is easy to overstate the decline in public concern about environmental issues. Notwithstanding the polling results cited above, it would appear that there is latent public concern about the environment and environmental protection. Although respondents to polls are less likely to identify the environment as a priority issue, when prompted they will express high levels of environmental concern.[19] Thus, while public opinion, notably public concern about the environment, no longer drives the agenda of environmental policy, governments cannot simply ignore the issue.

Moreover, latent public concern about the environment and environmental protection does have an intergovernmental dimension, particularly when the issues are recast or linked to control over natural resources. Generally speaking, there is strong public support for continued *federal* regulation of environmental hazards. However, if the issues are redefined, not as matters of environmental policy but rather of natural resource development, the pattern shifts. In western Canada, in particular, the general public favours a predominant *provincial* role in the management of natural resources. Thus, provincial governments, if they are to appeal to public opinion, need to recast environmental issues as issues of economic development or control over natural resources. On these latter issues provinces are more likely to enjoy strong public support.

All of this should not be interpreted to mean that the public cares particularly about jurisdiction over environmental policy. On the contrary; despite a degree of latent concern and a public preference for provincial regulation of natural resources, for the time being anyway environmental policy does not register as a key issue for the general public. As a result, governments have relatively free reign to do what they want with respect to reallocating responsibility for the environment. In effect, jurisdiction over environmental regulation is not an issue that is likely to garner much public attention, at least not until the next wave of widespread public concern about environmental protection.

SOCIETAL FACTORS: ORGANIZED INTERESTS[20]

The strengths and weaknesses of the environmental movement are another important factor in explaining the recent pattern of environmental intergovernmental relations. It is clear that ENGOs do not have quite the same influence they did in the later 1980s and early 1990s. Once again, the backlash against Greenpeace's efforts to change forestry practices in British Columbia is a good example of this. More importantly, in recent years ENGOs have had fewer resources with which to lobby effectively. This is an even bigger problem when the issues at hand get caught up in the web of intergovernmental relations and effective lobbying requires intervening with several governments.

Yet the major ENGOs have done a very good job of marshalling their resources to fight the harmonization efforts of the two orders of government. The Canadian Environmental Network (CEN), with the strong support of the Canadian Institute for Environment Law and Policy (CIELAP) and additional analysis provided by the Canadian Environmental Law Association and the Canadian Environmental Defence Fund, led the way with several highly critical and detailed critiques of the harmonization process and both the EMFA and the more recent Canada-Wide Accord.[21] For example, submissions prepared by CIELAP argued repeatedly that the two orders of government had not demonstrated that harmonization is necessary or desirable and that the changes proposed under the rubric of harmonization would weaken rather than strengthen the environmental management regime in Canada. Canadian ENGOs have also been adept at ensuring that sympathetic media have tracked the development of the harmonization process. Thus, *The Toronto Star*, and in particular, columnist Rosemary Speirs, have run several items critical of the harmonization process.[22]

While Canadian ENGOs have not been successful in derailing the harmonization process altogether, they have been able to mount a serious enough critique to slow the process down. The ENGO critique has also contributed to a debate within the federal government on the merits of devolving more responsibility for the environment to provincial governments (this debate is further described below).

Conversely, organizations representing business and industry have not elaborated a strong position with respect to harmonization.[23] Although the elimination of overlap and duplication of environmental regulations is a long-standing priority for Canadian business groups, particularly resource industries, associations representing the sector have not used the harmonization process as a vehicle for pressing their claims. There are several possible explanations for this.[24]

First, it is likely that key resource industry associations are themselves divided on which order of government should do what. Firms that operate in only one province will have developed cooperative relationships with their provincial government and will likely support greater provincial responsibility for environmental regulation. Similarly, many firms, irrespective of size, perceive provincial governments to be more amenable to a resource exploitation agenda as compared to the federal government where Environment Canada retains some influence and resource development is more likely to be balanced against environmental concerns. Conversely, most of the major resource development companies in Canada have operations in several provinces. For these firms, different provincial regulatory structures are difficult to manage and they sometimes prefer to deal with a single federal regulatory authority. Thus, when many companies of different size and outlook come together in a single industry association, it makes it harder for the association to agree on the merits of federal versus provincial environmental regulation.

Second, although Ottawa and the provinces have been preoccupied with efforts to harmonize environmental responsibilities, harmonization is not a high priority for regulated companies. The latter are much more likely to be interested in pursuing various forms of deregulation, voluntary and negotiated compliance, and experiments with alternatives to command and control regulatory practices. Thus, the harmonization exercise is, for many firms, an interesting but relatively unimportant part of their overall relationship with governments.

Finally, harmonization has not been a big issue for business and industry interests because, irrespective of which order of government is responsible for environmental regulation, industry associations generally enjoy good working relationships with both orders of government. In the middle and late 1990s, in marked contrast to the late 1980s, economic development and jobs are a very high priority for governments at all levels. As a result, both Ottawa and the provinces are generally quite receptive to claims made by industry with respect to the competing goods of economic development and environmental protection. Either governments accept the proposition that one can have both public goods simultaneously, or they opt for jobs over the environment. As a result, for many firms, which order of government is primarily responsible for environmental policy is of little consequence. Many companies understand that economic development is very important and that resource exploitation will remain an integral part of any and all economic development strategy by either order of government.

INSTITUTIONAL FACTORS: DECISION RULE

A range of institutional factors are also important determinants of the overall pattern of federal-provincial environmental policy cooperation, even if little real reform has been achieved. For example, the Council of Ministers of the Environment has played a key role in the evolution of federal-provincial relations with respect to the environment. In marked contrast to several other policy fields, environment ministers meet twice a year, have a record of achievement (and failure[25]), are served by a national secretariat, and have developed considerable trust ties, particularly at the level of officials.[26] In those areas with a relatively low political profile, the CCME has made considerable progress.[27]

This pattern of intense interaction and the support of the national secretariat were key in the development of the Environmental Management Framework Agreement. However, recent cuts to the budget and staff of the secretariat may make similar intensive negotiations more difficult in the future.

Notwithstanding the incremental successes of the Council, the CCME has been unable to craft a significant amendment to the roles and responsibilities of the two orders of government. This is partly explained by the decision rule used by the Council. As with so many other intergovernmental bodies in Canada, the decisions of the CCME require the approval of all the members of the Council. As has been demonstrated elsewhere, a unanimity rule usually has the effect of strengthening the status quo and, by extension, those who will benefit from little or no change to the status quo.[28] In the case of decentralization and devolution, a unanimity rule favours the federal government or at least those ministers and officials who are keen to minimize a transfer of power and authority to the provinces.

INSTITUTIONAL FACTORS: FEDERAL LEADERSHIP

A unanimity rule also gives the federal government added influence since the federal government can block an initiative and argue that it is acting in the best interests of the country as a whole in marked contrast to any single province. This is particularly true in the case of environment policy where ENGOs and the general public look to Ottawa to exercise leadership and direction. As outlined above, the federal minister of the environment did try and slow down the deliberations of the environmental assessment schedule of the EMFA. More telling, the collapse of the EMFA is likely the result of, among other things, a desire by the federal government to not be seen to be "giving away the store" with respect to environmental policy. Because the federal Cabinet during this period was divided on where and how much power to devolve to the provinces,[29] this created an opportunity for the federal minister of the day, Sheila Copps, to pull back and limit the extent to which the federal government would retreat from regulating environmental matters.

SPILLOVER: NEW PUBLIC MANAGEMENT

A third set of factors help explain the preoccupation of the CCME to "harmonize" environmental policy while at the same time being unable to make significant progress on harmonization. As alluded to earlier, the making of environmental policy does not take place in a vacuum and is subject to other non-environmental agendas. Here I want to very briefly discuss two — the introduction of a new style of public management and efforts aimed at a non-constitutional renewal of the federation.

As has been well documented elsewhere, what governments do and how they do it has been much debated over the past decade under the general heading of "reinventing" government, or less dramatically, what others have called "the new public management."[30] The reform effort includes a preoccupation with streamlining operations, integrated service delivery, greater efficiency, and a stronger focus on "clients" or "customers." The reforms also involve identifying those activities and policy areas that are part of the core activities of a given order of government and those activities that can or should be devolved to another government or to the private sector. In the case of the federal government, one of the results of the reforms has been a move away from service delivery and/or experiments in "alternative service delivery" which often involve partnerships with other actors including, in some cases, provincial governments.[31]

These trends have several implications for the conduct of intergovernmental relations, and in particular, for the pattern of intergovernmental relations with respect to environmental policy. There is, for example, considerable pressure to pursue various forms of self-regulation,[32] or giving provincial inspectors the responsibility for enforcing federal regulations. Similarly, under a new public management ethos, regulation should be simpler and/or there should be a "single window" for regulated industries that deal with government. Thus, regulatory simplification and the search for just such a single window have been a central part of the harmonization exercise of the past several years.[33]

Unfortunately, establishing such single windows has proven quite difficult and they are not likely to be forthcoming as a result of formal, multilateral intergovernmental agreements. Although simpler more functional bilateral agreements are possible,[34] full-blown harmonization under the rubric of administrative and managerial reform is much harder to achieve. Much of the difficulty stems from the fact that the efforts to reshape public administration must contend with some basic realities of Canadian government, including federalism, and a strong tendency on the part of both governments and affected interests to resist major change. Reform of the administrative state is not simple or straightforward. In many cases, reform initiatives are undesirable or controversial. For example, "the new public management" all too often becomes nothing more than the application of private sector management techniques to the public sector. Such reforms conflict with the basic realities of responsible government, divided jurisdiction, and the need to manage public goods.[35] Thus, it is perhaps not surprising that, although the CCME has sought to harmonize environmental regulation in Canada, the road to harmonization has been long and bumpy. Harmonizing or rationalizing environmental policy and programs involves more than simply turning activities and responsibilities over to provincial governments or to the private sector in the name of administrative and regulatory reform.

SPILLOVER: RENEWAL OF THE FEDERATION

Notwithstanding the agenda for change in Canadian public administration, there is a similar if not more powerful agenda for change in the constitutional division of powers and the allocation of responsibility to the two orders of government. The process of "renewal of the federation" also has spillover effects on environmental harmonization.

Reform of the federation had been a long-standing priority of the Chrétien government, initially under the leadership of Marcel Massé. Moreover, some success had been achieved, for example in the area of pension reform where an elaborate and joint federal-provincial consultation exercise eventually culminated in changes to the Canada/Quebec pension plan. In the Speech from the Throne of February 1996, the reform effort was given renewed emphasis and the federal government promised to pursue a number of initiatives in response to the unsettling results of the November 1995 Quebec referendum. A new arrangement on environmental policy was part of the promised reform package.[36] Similarly, the issue of environmental harmonization was raised at the September 1995 Annual Premiers' Conference subsequent to the stalling of the process in May of that year. Following the meeting, the premiers wrote a letter to the prime minister requesting that the harmonization project be revived.[37] This focus on intergovernmental relations and on environmental policy continued through 1996. When the prime minister and the premiers met in June at a long-awaited First Ministers' Conference, they directed their environment ministers to make progress in harmonization by the November 1996 meeting of the CCME.

Thus, there has been considerable pressure from both the prime minister and the premiers encouraging their respective environment ministers to make a deal with respect to harmonization. A deal on environmental policy harmonization would serve as a good example of how the federation and the division of powers can be reformed and amended. However, although there has been pressure from the top, this has not translated into strong leadership by the federal government. In order to explain this failure it is useful to contrast the case of environmental policy with that of policies relating to labour market training and development.

In the case of training, Ottawa and the provinces have been able to negotiate a process whereby the federal government will transfer responsibility for the design and delivery of labour market training to those provinces that want to exercise these powers. Agreements have been signed with eight provinces, including Quebec.[38] As with environment, the reform agenda has been driven heavily by pressure from the top.[39] However, unlike environment, the progress on training was the result of: a very direct link to a broader national unity agenda, strong leadership from the federal minister, most recently Pierre

Pettigrew, and a lack of sustained opposition from interest groups outside the federal government.

Few, if any of these conditions apply to a putative agreement on environmental policy harmonization. First, the federal government was (and continues to be) unable to take the lead on environmental policy harmonization as a result of a sharp split between those who would decentralize power to the provinces and those who argued that the federal government should retain a leadership role in key policy areas.[40] This has created resistance in a number of policy fields including environment, an area where the federal government can legitimately claim a leadership role. The split is less significant when it comes to labour market matters because control over manpower is a long-standing demand from Quebec. Any losses in the ability of the federal government to exercise policy leadership with respect to labour market policy were believed to be strongly offset by the perceived advantages in terms of national unity. Such is not the case with environmental policy. Although control over the environment has been a traditional demand of Quebec, successive governments have not pressed the issue particularly hard. Unlike labour market training and development, jurisdiction over the environment was not part of the Meech Lake Accord, and did not figure prominently in the negotiations leading to the Charlottetown Accord.

Second, the federal government has not exercised the same leadership with respect to environmental policy harmonization as it did with respect to labour market matters. Sheila Copps, who as minister of the environment for much of the period leading up to the eventual rejection of the EMFA in the spring of 1996, was among those ministers who felt that the federal government should retain a leadership role in key areas. Thus, if the EMFA was eventually rejected, part of the reason lies in the fact that the federal side "got cold feet" and could not bring itself to sign a comprehensive agreement that would have significantly reduced the environmental policy role of the federal government either by transferring responsibility to the provinces or by creating mechanisms to develop and implement national policy.

Finally, in marked contrast to labour market training, in the development of environmental policy, strong, vocal interest groups are opposed to a change to the status quo.[41] Environmental groups are adamant that the federal government should retain a leadership role with respect to environmental policy. For their part, organizations representing business and industry, while generally supportive of anything that will reduce overlap and duplication, have not pressed hard for harmonization. In some cases this is because the industry association is split with some members close to a particular provincial government. In other cases, the lack of pressure from industry is the result of a focus, not on harmonization, but on deregulation or voluntary compliance with existing regulations.

OPPORTUNITY LOST: THE ENVIRONMENTAL MANAGEMENT FRAMEWORK AGREEMENT

The Environmental Management Framework Agreement is an impressive but flawed document that would have recast the roles and responsibilities of the federal and provincial governments with respect to environmental policy. The harmonization initiative itself was extraordinary in its scope and complexity. Federal and provincial officials were told that, short of a formal constitutional amendment, everything was on the table.[42] More significant perhaps, the EMFA would have formally introduced a distinction between federal, provincial, and "national" policies, the latter being jointly developed by Ottawa and the provinces acting in concert. It is this latter innovation that deserves particular attention, even though ministers ultimately rejected the EMFA.

The EMFA runs for more than one hundred pages and includes a short Framework Agreement and 11 schedules dealing with everything from the mundane (e.g., environmental education and communications) to the very important (e.g., the development of new guidelines and standards and the enforcement of existing regulations). In the Framework Agreement Ottawa and the provinces commit themselves to promoting predictability, clarity, and efficiency in environmental management (Preamble) and explicitly recognize that they share responsibility for ensuring that environmental matters are effectively managed (article 4.1). Although much of the agreement is concerned with defining the interests and responsibilities of the federal government (article 4.2) and the provincial governments (article 4.3), the EMFA does set out a process to develop "national" policies (article 5.2 and schedule VI).

In the Framework Agreement, a very strict distinction is made between federal, provincial, and "national" responsibilities. The latter term is explicitly defined and is said to mean that:

> the common interest is shared by federal, provincial and territorial governments, or that, even if one order of government had the lead role, shared decision-making is required or desired by that order of government. (article 1.1).

What is striking is that, in this agreement, the federal government was willing to distinguish between that which is "federal" and that which is "national." In a very explicit fashion Ottawa recognized that the policies and programs that it enacted, while applicable across the country, were not synonymous with national policies, the latter being the responsibility of both orders of government acting in concert. Moreover, in being party to the EMFA, the federal government would have acknowledged that for truly national policies to be initiated, some form of shared decisionmaking would be required.

WEAKNESSES OF THE EMFA

The EMFA, had it been signed, would have broken new ground in the conduct of intergovernmental relations in Canada. Nevertheless, the agreement as drafted had a number of weaknesses, which led, in part, to its rejection. First, the EMFA did not include a clear decision rule. Second, the agreement would, potentially, have been a *de facto* amendment to the constitution. Third, the EMFA would have created a series of powerful policymaking bodies only indirectly accountable to Canadian voters. I would like to briefly consider each of these weaknesses in turn.

NO DECISION RULE LEADING TO GRIDLOCK

Section 5.2 of the Framework Agreement very briefly sets out a process for developing national policies and allows for a national policy development process as set out in a separate schedule. Schedule VI, Policy and Legislation, describes a process for national environmental policy development where a primary clear goal is to minimize if not eliminate overlap and duplication in federal and provincial legislation (article 1). Unfortunately the Framework Agreement and Schedule VI are largely silent on the decision rule that will be employed in the development of national policies. The EMFA would have created a series of committees responsible for policy development, policy coordination, and implementation; but no where is there an explicit statement of the decision rule that would be employed. In the absence of a formal decision rule, it is almost certain that a unanimity rule would be used. This would have given Ottawa and each of the provinces a veto over the development and implementation of national policies. The net result would have likely been a very slow decisionmaking process. As CIELAP has argued, the EMFA would likely have increased the capacity for bureaucratic wrangling over environmental measures and starkly limited the chances that anything will be done to protect the Canadian environment.[43]

A *DE FACTO* CONSTITUTIONAL AMENDMENT?

As noted earlier, the EMFA would have allowed for national policies jointly decided by the two orders of government. Although this is arguably a useful innovation in the conduct of intergovernmental relations, for some critics of the EMFA this reference to national policies represents a *de facto* constitutional amendment.[44] Elsewhere critics argue that, by creating national decisionmaking processes, the EMFA would have created a new level of government, one that would be illegitimate, unaccountable, and unworkable.[45]

The fact that the EMFA would have had such a profound impact on the division of powers is very important given the current preoccupation with so-called non-constitutional changes to the federation. The working assumption is that a formal amendment to the constitution is all but impossible so that any significant changes to the roles and responsibilities of Ottawa and the provinces must be done by a series of administrative agreements and simple statutory changes. However, a formal amendment to the constitution is difficult if not impossible for at least two sets of reasons, only one of which is addressed by administrative agreements and statutory changes. First, it is simply very difficult to amend the constitution. Not only is the formal amending procedure quite rigid, the decision to hold a national referendum on the Charlottetown Accord means that a similar vote will be required for any significant amendments to the constitution. Moreover, in several provinces, ratification of a major constitutional change can only come after a province-wide referendum. Intergovernmental agreements such as the EMFA do get around this problem to some extent. Yet it is important to keep in mind that constitutional amendment is also difficult because of a lack of societal consensus on the desirability of such amendments. This applies particularly to formal changes to the division of powers, which would shift power from the federal government to the provinces. While such a shift is deemed desirable by many there is by no means consensus on this issue. Others are strongly opposed to anything that would further weaken the federal government. And in the particular case of environmental policy, there is even less consensus. While some deem a stronger provincial role to be desirable, others, notably the national ENGOs, are strongly opposed to anything that would further weaken the position of the federal government.

In sum, even though the EMFA would have meant a shift in the environmental policy regime and the creation of a process leading to national environmental policies, the fact that the agreement would have meant a *de facto* change to the division of powers is deemed by many to be a fundamental weakness.

ADDING TO THE DEMOCRATIC DEFICITS OF INTERGOVERNMENTAL RELATIONS

A third major criticism of the EMFA, one that would apply equally to the Canada-Wide Accord, is that these agreements add to the democratic deficits of Canadian governments. As CIELAP has argued, the EMFA would have created a shadow-level of government, unknown to most of the Canadian public, and unaccountable to any constituent save the other parties to the agreement.[46] Although the terms used by CIELAP may be a bit exaggerated, increased use of intergovernmental agreements does pose real challenges for democratic accountability. Simply put, intergovernmental policymaking, because it is one or more steps removed from the "regular" political process within a single jurisdiction, is less open, less transparent, and inherently less democratic. In other words, intergovernmental policymaking exacerbates the democratic deficit of contemporary governance.[47] Thus both the EMFA and the Canada-Wide Accord add to this democratic deficit because they are inherently intergovernmental in character and propose to give the CCME additional policymaking responsibilities.

' CONCLUSIONS

Since the early 1990s, intergovernmentalism has become one of the defining characteristics of Canadian environmental policy. The highlights of this emphasis on intergovernmental cooperation are arguably both the rejected Environmental Management Framework Agreement and the pending Canada-Wide Accord on Environmental Harmonization. Ironically enough, the cooperative spirit has not resulted in concrete progress. The federal and provincial ministers of the environment eventually rejected the elaborate and flawed EMFA and the accord is really only another best-efforts document.

This chapter has sought to explain the meagre returns of this renewed interest in cooperative federalism. The argument is that the federal and provincial governments have not been able to craft a new allocation of responsibilities as a result of a range of societal, institutional, and spillover factors. In summary, environment ministers have not been able to make a significant change to the status quo because of reduced public interest in environmental policy, strong opposition from ENGOs and only lukewarm support from business and industry groups. Moreover, progress has been difficult because decisions of the CCME must be unanimous, decisive leadership by the federal government has not been forthcoming, and because of the inherent complexity of any effort to move a single window approach to environmental management. Although the environmental policy harmonization efforts have benefited from the broader interest in non-constitutional changes to the division of powers, this has only meant pressure from the top to get a deal with little reference to the actual content of a harmonization of environmental policy in Canada.

Notwithstanding the meagre results, the intense intergovernmentalism of the past several years did produce the Environmental Management Framework Agreement, an innovative but flawed document that would have, had it been agreed to, created a new and distinct pattern of intergovernmental decisionmaking and governance. The importance of the EMFA lies in the fact that the agreement identified the possibility of national policies and national decisionmaking where national was not synonymous with federal.

The ultimate rejection of the EMFA has several implications for the conduct of Canadian intergovernmental relations over the next few years. The weaknesses of the agreement are clear. However, in rejecting it in favour of the subsequent Canada-Wide Accord, Ottawa and the provinces sent a strong signal about the likely pattern of intergovernmental relations in other areas. For example, the failure of the EMFA is likely to be telling for initiatives in other areas, notably social policy. Given the reluctance of the federal government to cede real authority over environment policy, Ottawa is unlikely to concede a provincial role in other areas; for example, in interpreting the *Canada Health Act*. Similarly, the very complexity of the EMFA may be partly an explanation of its downfall. However, the complexity of the agreement was the result of the magnitude of the changes being proposed to the roles and responsibilities of the two orders of government. This suggests that radical, wholesale change in the roles and responsibilities of the two orders of government is less likely than a continuing process of incremental change. Finally, the ENGO critique of the EMFA, notably the concerns raised about the increased reliance on intergovernmental decisionmaking, are likely to be repeated and amplified if and when the two orders of government seek to expand their reliance on intergovernmentalism. As Roger Gibbins has pointed out, intergovernmental forums are largely beyond the reach of electoral accountability. Gibbins asks, how, for example, could federal MPs be held accountable for programs and policies that were policed through intergovernmental forums? And for the same reasons, how could provincial governments be held responsible or accountable?[48]

Ultimately, the lesson of the EMFA and of the recent past of environmental federal-provincial diplomacy may be that ways must be found to reconcile two competing goods. On the one hand, intergovernmental decisionmaking creates the possibility for decentralization of power from Ottawa in a way that still allows for a national policy instead of a series of potentially conflicting provincial (or aboriginal) policies. On the other hand, intergovernmentalism must produce more than hopelessly complex agreements that do not specify a clear decision rule and make governments less, rather than more accountable to the electorate.

NOTES

Numerous colleagues offered comments on previous drafts of this chapter. I particularly want to thank Kathryn Harrison, Harvey Lazar and Katherine Sharf Fafard and the two anonymous reviewers who provided a variety of useful criticisms, comments and even kudos. Of course, the usual caveats apply.

1. See the chapters by Keith Banting, John Richards and Harvey Lazar in this volume for analysis of varying aspects of this renewed emphasis on intergovernmentalism.

2. See the chapter by Harvey Lazar in this volume and Herman Bakvis, "Federalism, New Public Management, and Labour-Market Development," in *Canada: The State of the Federation 1996*, ed. Patrick C. Fafard and Douglas M. Brown

(Kingston: Institute of Intergovernmental Relations, Queen's University, 1996), pp. 135-65. None of this is meant to suggest that a non-constitutional approach is sufficient to resolve the challenges facing the country.

3. For an introduction to the constitutional basis of provincial and federal activity with respect to the environment see, David Vanderzwaag and Linda Duncan, "Canada and Environmental Protection: Confident Political Faces, Uncertain Legal Hands," in *Canadian Environmental Policy: Ecosystems, Politics and Process*, ed. R. Boardman (Toronto: Oxford University Press, 1992); and A.R. Lucas, "Natural Resource and Environmental Management: A Jurisdictional Primer," in *Environmental Protection and the Canadian Constitution*, ed. D. Tingley (Edmonton: Environmental Law Centre, 1987), pp. 31-43.

4. With only some exaggeration, Vanderzwaag and Duncan argue that the approach of the federal government has been one of deference, and the federal power to act has in practice been dealt away by federal-provincial agreement. Vanderzwaag and Duncan, "Canada and Environmental Protection," p. 23.

5. For a summary of the shifting patterns of intergovernmental relations with respect to the environment, see Kathryn Harrison, "Prospects for Intergovernmental Harmonization in Environmental Policy," in *Canada: The State of the Federation, 1994*, ed. Douglas M. Brown and Janet Hiebert (Kingston: Institute of Intergovernmental Relations, Queen's University, 1994), pp. 179-99; and Kathryn Harrison, *Passing the Buck, Federalism and Canadian Environmental Policy* (Vancouver: University of British Columbia Press, 1996).

6. See Harrison, "Prospects for Intergovernmental Harmonization in Environmental Policy."

7. For a discussion of the different possible patterns of intergovernmental relations with respect to environment policy, see Patrick Fafard and Kathryn Harrison, "Intergovernmental Relations and Environmental Policy: Concepts and Context," a paper presented to a conference, "The Environment and Intergovernmental Relations," Queen's University, 13-15 February 1997.

8. The following account of recent intergovernmental relations with respect to the environment draws primarily on Gerry Fitzsimmons, "Harmonization Initiative of the Canadian Council of Ministers of the Environment," a paper presented to the 1995 IPAC National Forum, mimeo, August 1995; Canadian Institute for Environmental Law and Policy, "Harmonizing to Protect the Environment? An Analysis of the CCME Environmental Harmonization Process," mimeo, November 1996; and Canadian Council of Ministers of the Environment, *Background on the Harmonization Initiative*. The latter can be found on the CCME web site at http://www.ccme.ca/ccme/background.html.

9. Alas, the participation of Quebec was not to last. In November 1994 the Quebec government announced it was withdrawing from the LRC, citing the federal government's proclamation of the *Canadian Environmental Assessment Act*.

10. For example, in a commentary on the EMFA, the Canadian Institute for Environmental Law and Policy argued that the EMFA was prepared in the absence of appropriate mechanisms for meaningful consultation with non-governmental organizations and other stakeholders. See CIELAP, "The Environmental

Management Framework Agreement — A Model For Dysfunctional Federalism? An Analysis And Commentary," CIELAP Brief Number 96/1, February 1996. This document can be found at the CIELAP Web site: http://www.web.apc.org/cielap.

11. "Environmental Harmony or Environmental Discord? An Analysis of the Draft Environmental Management Framework Agreement and a Statement of Principles for the Protection of Canadas Environment," mimeo, April 1995. This document was signed by 65 national, provincial, and local ENGOs.

12. Rosemary Spiers, "Environmental safety sacrificed for harmony," *The Toronto Star*, 2 July 1996.

13. Canadian Institute for Environmental Law and Policy, "Harmonizing to Protect the Environment? An Analysis of the CCME Environmental Harmonization Process," mimeo, November 1996.

14. On the hortatory nature of intergovernmental agreements and, in particular, the standards sub-agreement to the Canada-Wide Accord, see Alastair R. Lucas, "Underlying Constraints on Intergovernmental Cooperation in Setting and Enforcing Environmental Standards," paper presented to a conference, "The Environment and Intergovernmental Relations," Queen's University, 13-15 February 1997.

15. "Harmonization Accord Draft Text: A Canada-Wide Accord on Environmental Harmonization," mimeo, 1997. The draft text of the accord can be found on the CCME Web Site at: http://www.mbnet.mb.ca/ cme/accord_draft.html.

16. This section also builds on a similar analysis found in Harrison, "Prospects for Intergovernmental Harmonization in Environmental Policy." However, a somewhat wider range of explanatory factors are considered here.

17. As one of the reviewers of this chapter observed, maintaining ecosystem integrity over the long term is a highly complex matter that challenges the capacity of the existing institutions of intergovernmental relations and public administration generally. To put it differently, intergovernmental relations are based on a federal system of government, which privileges a territorial definition of the Canadian polity. A more expansive, ecological point of view places much less emphasis on territory and takes a broader frame of reference. Such a broader frame of reference *is* needed to explain the challenges of making environmental policy and actually improving the quality of the environment. However, it is not likely to be needed to explain the recent patterns of intergovernmental relations, which are the focus of this chapter.

18. Angus Reid Group Inc., *The Federal Political Scene, The Public Agenda, The National Angus Reid Southam News Poll,* Public Release Date: Thursday, 30 January 1997. This National Angus Reid/Southam News Poll was conducted by telephone between 21-27 January 1997 among a representative cross-section of 1,519 Canadian adults. With a national sample of 1,519, one can say with 95 percent certainty that the results are within +2.5 percentage points of what they would have been had the entire adult Canadian population been polled. In a similar poll in July 1989, 31 percent of respondents identified the environment as the most important issue. The poll results can be found at: http://www.angusreid.com/pressrel/fedpolscenejan97.html.

19. See Harrison's discussion of public opinion, "Prospects for Intergovernmental Harmonization in Environmental Policy," pp. 189-91.

20. Much of the following is taken from Patrick Fafard, "Groups, Governments and the Environment: Some Evidence from the Harmonization Initiative," paper presented to a conference, "The Environment and Intergovernmental Relations," Queen's University, 13-15 February 1997.

21. See, for example, "The Draft Environmental Management Framework Agreement and Schedules: A Commentary and Analysis." CIELAP Brief 95/1; and "The Environmental Management Framework Agreement — A Model for Dysfunctional Federalism?"

22. See, for example, Rosemary Spiers, "Environmental safety sacrificed for harmony." However, *The Toronto Star* is somewhat unique in this regard and the harmonization process has not captured the attention of the national media.

23. Personal communication with Mark Winfield, Director of Research, Canadian Institute for Environment Law and Policy, March 1996.

24. What follows is drawn in part on Fafard, "Groups, Governments and the Environment."

25. See Heather A. Smith, "The Provinces and International Environmental Policy Making: The Case of Climate Change," a paper presented to a conference, "The Environment and Intergovernmental Relations," Queen's University, 13-15 February 1997.

26. J. Stefan Dupré, "Reflections on the Workability of Executive Federalism," in *Intergovernmental Relations*, ed. Richard Simeon, Vol. 63, Research Studies, Royal Commission on the Economic Union and Development Prospects for Canada (Toronto: University of Toronto Press, 1985), pp. 1-32. A revised version of this paper also appears as "The Workability of Executive Federalism in Canada," in *Federalism and the Role of the State*, ed. Herman Bakvis and William M. Chandler (Toronto: University of Toronto Press, 1987), pp. 236-58.

27. For example, the CCME runs pollution prevention awards program, has drafted water quality guidelines, and has developed a National Packaging Protocol.

28. See Kathryn Harrison, "The Regulator's Dilemma: Regulation of Pulp Mill Effluents in the Canadian Federal State," *Canadian Journal of Political Science* 29 (1996): 469-96.

29. See David Cameron, "Does Ottawa Know it's Part of the Problem?" in *Québec-Canada: What is the Path Ahead?* ed. John E. Trent et al. (Ottawa: University of Ottawa Press, 1996), pp. 293-98.

30. For an introduction to the new public management see *inter alia*, Andrew Gray and Bill Jenkins, "From Public Administration to Public Management: Reassessing a Revolution?" *Public Administration* 73 (Spring 1995): 79-99; and Donald Savoie, "Public Administration: A Profession Looking for a Home," in *Policy Studies in Canada: The State of the Art,* ed. Laurent Dobuzinskis, Michael Howlett and David Laycock (Toronto and Buffalo: University of Toronto Press, 1996), pp. 125-46.

31. For an introduction to ASD, see Robin Ford and David Zussman (eds.), *Alternative Service Delivery: Sharing Governance in Canada* (Toronto: KPMG Centre for Government Foundation, 1997).

32. See Michael D. Mehta (ed.), *Regulatory Efficiency and the Role of Risk Assessment* (Kingston: School of Policy Studies, Queen's University, 1996).

33. For an overview of the evolution of environmental regulation in Canada see Kathryn Harrison, "Retreat from Regulation: Evolution of the Canadian Environmental Regulatory Regime," in *Canadian Regulatory Institutions: Globalization, Choices and Change,* ed. G. Bruce Doern et al. (Toronto: University of Toronto Press, forthcoming.).

34. In Winnipeg, the federal and provincial ministries of the environment and the Secretariat of the CCME have relocated to a single location and are working toward a single administrative structure and shared resources. Personal communication from Liseanne Forand, CCME Secretariat.

35. For a critical discussion of the weaknesses of the "new public management" see Donald Savoie, "Public Administration: A Profession Looking for a Home."

36. See Canada, Office of the Prime Minister, *Speech from the Throne, Ottawa, Ontario February 27, 1996.* A copy of the speech can be found at the web site of the prime minister: http://pm.gc.ca.

37. Canadian Institute for Environmental Law and Policy, "Harmonizing to Protect the Environment? An Analysis of the CCME Environmental Harmonization Process," p. 6.

38. Human Resources Development Canada, "Canada and Québec Sign Historic Labour Market Agreement," News Release 97-28, 21 April 1997. A copy of the release can be found at: http://www.hrdc-drhc.gc.ca/hrdc/ei/lma/qc/9728_e.html

39. See the chapter by Harvey Lazar in this volume. See also Bakvis, "Federalism, New Public Management, and Labour Market Development."

40. See Cameron, "Does Ottawa Know it's Part of the Problem?"

41. The following is taken from Fafard, "Groups, Government and the Environment."

42. I am indebted to Kathryn Harrison for bringing this to my attention.

43. "The Environmental Management Framework Agreement — A Model for Dysfunctional Federalism? An Analysis And Commentary," CIELAP Brief Number 96/1, February 1996, p. 9.

44. See "Environmental Harmony or Environmental Discord? An Analysis of the Draft Environmental Management Framework Agreement and a Statement of Principles for the Protection of Canadas Environment," mimeo, April 1995, p. 1.

45. "The Environmental Management Framework Agreement — A Model for Dysfunctional Federalism?" p. vii.

46. Ibid., p. 16.

47. The term democratic deficit or democracy deficit is usually used as part of a critique of decisionmaking in the European Union. For an introduction to the issues in an EU context see Michael Newman, "Democracy and the European

Union," in *The Future of Europe*, ed. Valerie Symes et al. (London: Macmillan, 1997), pp. 15-42. For a discussion of the inherent democratic deficit of Canadian intergovernmental relations, see Roger Gibbins with the assistance of Katherine Harmsworth, *Time Out: Assessing Incremental Strategies for Enhancing the Canadian Political Union.* Commentary 88 (Toronto: C.D. Howe Institute, 1997).

48.   Roger Gibbins, *Time Out: Assessing Incremental Strategies for Enhancing the Canadian Political Union,* p. 19.

8

Federalism and Aboriginal Relations

Audrey Doerr

Cet article examine le contexte des relations intergouvernementales en ce qui concerne les gouvernements autochtones. Il souligne quelques initiatives intergouvernementales clefs impliquant les gouvernements autochtone, fédéral et provincial dans les domaines des réclamations territoriales des autochtones, des développements économiques et de l'éducation. Les exemples de coopération tripartite n'ont pas l'intention d'être exhaustifs mais plutôt des exemples des quelques activités nonconstitutionnelles courantes en cours qui appuient le progrès de l'autonomie gouvernementale autochtone. Ils démontrent aussi l'usage et l'adaptation des mécanismes intergouvernementaux dans ces domaines de politiques gouvernementales.

INTRODUCTION

The inclusion of aboriginal self-government as an inherent right and as a third order of government in Canada in the 1992 Charlottetown Accord was a demonstration of the effectiveness of aboriginal leadership working within the machinery of executive federalism.[1] With the defeat of the referendum on the accord, combined with general constitutional fatigue on the part of the electorate, the discussion of these and other constitutional issues fell by the wayside. Perhaps because of this, the constitutional proposals of the federal Royal Commission on Aboriginal Peoples (RCAP), established in August 1991, have not provided the basis for an ongoing political debate of aboriginal constitutional issues. The response of the federal government to the report when it was released in November 1996 was cautious.[2] In the absence of any strong federal response, few provincial governments made comments.[3]

These reactions may also be explained in part by the numerous undertakings being pursued on a non-constitutional, intergovernmental basis. Upon its election in 1993, the federal Liberal government committed itself to a policy that recognized that the inherent right to self-government already existed within section 35 of the *Constitution Act, 1982*. A number of program initiatives — especially in the areas of land claims, economic development, and education — were also proposed. And, like its predecessor, the Liberal government distanced itself from the issues and alliances of the previous administration.[4]

During the federal Liberal government's first term, the then minister of Indian affairs and northern development, the Honourable Ron Irwin, undertook an ambitious campaign to pursue the "practical agenda" of the *Red Book* by making agreements with willing aboriginal groups, and, wherever possible, provincial governments, on a broad range of initiatives.[5] Diversity in approaches was encouraged and new alliances between Ottawa and regional aboriginal leaders were forged. It also became evident that Prime Minister Chrétien favoured an incremental rather than a wholistic approach to aboriginal issues and wished to avoid any national process that would add pressures on his government.[6] As a measure of ministerial political effectiveness, it could be argued that First Nation and aboriginal issues were effectively managed or that the federal Liberal government read accurately public opinion on these issues, or both, given that aboriginal issues hardly surfaced during the federal election campaign of 1997.

By pursuing non-constitutional processes on a regional basis, a diverse range of issues has emerged from an always crowded, aboriginal agenda. While the traditional provincial view has been that the federal government has legislative authority for Indians and lands reserved for Indians under section 91(24) of the *Constitution Act, 1867*, provincial governments have become increasingly involved in aboriginal issues. In particular, the entrenchment of aboriginal and treaty rights in sections 25 and 35 of the *Constitution Act, 1982* has broadened that responsibility to include provincial governments on an increasing number of legal and practical issues. For example, the constitutional recognition of aboriginal and treaty rights has led to a more active role for provinces, especially on matters of implementation of those rights as well as matters involving provincial interests in land claims and self-government negotiations. Furthermore, provinces have to deal with municipal concerns about federal or provincial negotiations with neighbouring aboriginal communities. And provincial governments continue to spend on programs targeted to Aboriginal Peoples including First Nations individuals on reserve.

The following discussion is intended to provide the reader with an introduction to current directions of intergovernmental activities and initiatives involving First Nations. The scope of the chapter, nevertheless, is limited to a few key subject areas with examples that typify constructive intergovernmental cooperation that enhances First Nation control over their affairs through non-constitutional means. It does not provide an exhaustive survey province by province or territory by territory, but rather selects a number of initiatives across the country to demonstrate the nature of intergovernmental collaboration with First Nations. The process of institution-building involving partnerships with the private sector is also noted to demonstrate how these activities, in turn, can strengthen the position of First Nations in their dealings with other governments.

As the First Nation population continues to increase at a rate that is estimated at twice Canada's national average, First Nation leaders are faced with growing pressures from community members for social and economic improvements to support the well-being of their communities.[7] The leaders must often work with non-aboriginal governments to bring about improvements in social and economic circumstances. For their part, non-aboriginal governments are often pressured by third-party interests to resolve outstanding issues respecting aboriginal rights or to find the means of supporting aboriginal efforts to advance their economic interests. But the fact that tripartite participation may be driven by pragmatic motivations on the part of each of the parties does not detract from these undertakings.

INTERGOVERNMENTAL RELATIONS

In the past, many First Nation communities existed largely in isolation from mainstream society. As a result, the interest, let alone the opportunity, for contact with provincial governments and municipalities was limited and the relationships with the federal government were characterized, at best, as paternalistic. In the years after the Second World War, the situation began to change and gradually the federal government took steps to encourage greater Indian participation in their own affairs. The right of status Indians to vote in federal elections, for example, was legislated in 1960. But the federal government's White Paper of 1969, which proposed wide-ranging recommendations to give First Nations "equal status" in society, was rejected by the leadership.[8] This led to the development of a more united and more aggressive approach by First Nation leaders in demanding recognition of their aboriginal rights and more control and responsibility for their affairs. As a result, there was also an increasing level of direct contact between aboriginal leaders and provincial governments and municipalities even though many First Nation communities, especially the Treaty First Nations in western Canada, emphasized the bilateral relationship with the federal Crown, i.e., the federal government.

Just as the Canadian federal system has been made to work through the accommodation of jurisdictional interests by employing a wide range of administrative mechanisms, the introduction of aboriginal governments into the intergovernmental milieu follows similar patterns. At the ministerial level, the participation of aboriginal representatives at First Ministers' Conferences on Aboriginal Constitutional Affairs and in subsequent constitutional fora in the 1980s and 1990s, gave aboriginal groups the opportunity to gain experience with the formal political processes of executive federalism. At the administrative level, there are federal-provincial-aboriginal agreements, joint boards and councils, and a range of cost-sharing agreements respecting government programs. In brief, every means of cooperative undertaking is available to non-aborignal and aboriginal governments to enhance the participation of First Nation leadership in intergovermental affairs. The use of these techniques reflect the practical necessity of collaborative effort in particular circumstances. The examples below, for the most part, reflect tripartite processes although in other areas First Nation communities may prefer to relate on a bilateral basis with federal and provincial governments respectively. Let us consider some of the undertakings:

LAND CLAIMS

Access to land and resources for Aboriginal Peoples is important to them to correct injustices from the past and to provide an economic base in the present and future.[9] Land-claims negotiations have attempted to resolve long-standing issues in many parts of the country. In the Northwest Territories, the long-held dream of an Inuit "home land" is finding reality in the establishment of Nunavut in the eastern Arctic, which will be a public government with the status of a territory. In northern Quebec, First Nation and Inuit leaders have been able to use the compensation and resources obtained through their land-claims settlements to advance the well-being of their communities. In many areas in southern Canada, however, terms and conditions in First Nation land agreements and treaties of the past restrict the claims that governments are prepared to accept and negotiate. There are two federal claims policies, comprehensive claims and specific claims, which are used and adapted to meet differing circumstances and legal obligations.[10] Most provincial governments have tended to develop and apply a single policy or policy framework for land-claims negotiations or have dealt with issues on a case-by-case basis. Some examples of current intergovernmental claims processes are the following.

In *British Columbia*, with the exception of a small part of Vancouver Island and an area in northeastern British Columbia, no land treaties were ever signed with First Nations. Following the Report of the British Columbia Claims Task Force in 1991, an agreement was reached in 1992 between the governments of Canada and British Columbia and the First Nations of British Columbia to establish the British Columbia Treaty Commission (BCTC). Subsequently, both federal and provincial governments passed legislation to establish the commission and the First Nations' Summit of British Columbia chiefs formally endorsed its establishment.

The commission acts as a coordinating body for the start-up of negotiations and as a monitoring body which also has authority to allocate funds to

First Nations for their participation in these processes. The process itself involves six stages which range from submitting a statement of intent to the negotiation of final agreements and implementation of the treaty. To make negotiations comprehensive, self-government has been included in the subject matters for negotiation. Regional Advisory Committees have been established in each treaty negotiation area and provide a means for third-party interests to become informed on the negotiations and to advise the negotiators for the federal and provincial governments and the First Nation involved. Public information sessions are also a common feature of individual negotiations. Currently, there are 46 First Nation groups representing over 70 percent of British Columbia First Nations involved in the BCTC process.[11]

One of the first groups to reach an agreement-in-principle(A-I-P) with Canada and British Columbia was the Nisga'a First Nation in 1996. This A-I-P provides the framework and basis for substantive negotiations on a range of specific subject matters. With negotiations for a final agreement underway, the British Columbia government established a Select Standing Committee on Aboriginal Affairs to conduct hearings into the treaty process and subjects arising from the Nisga'a agreement-in-principle in the fall of 1996. These public hearings which took place throughout the province were concluded in March 1997. As well, provincial ministries have conducted studies to assess the socio-economic effects of the agreements.[12] Generally, these agreements are perceived as being beneficial to all parties.[13]

The conduct of tripartite negotiation processes in British Columbia may be viewed as a real breakthrough in intergovernmental cooperation. After years of denying the existence of any aboriginal rights and any need for provincial involvement in earlier federal negotiations with First Nations, the province is a full partner at the negotiating table. It also participates, with the federal government, in a cost-sharing agreement to support the negotiations. While the BC treaty process holds promise for future resolution of aboriginal claims in that province, it will be a process that can be expected to take time even with continued public support. Some First Nation groups may be interested in moving quickly whereas others can be expected to be cautious or have differences which may be difficult to resolve. But the process has a statutory basis and it can be expected to provide an ongoing, formal mechanism for addressing these claims.

In the *Prairie provinces*, where First Nations are parties to treaties that involve land, many specific claims have been negotiated through a process called Treaty Land Entitlement. These types of claims arise when a First Nation has not received all of the land it is owed under treaty provisions to which it is a party and submits a claim to the federal government for negotiation.[14] Negotiations on these issues with First Nations in Alberta, Saskatchewan, and Manitoba go back many years but only recently have a significant number of agreements been reached among federal and provincial governments and claimant First Nations in those provinces. Provincial participation is needed, for the negotiations usually involve the transfer or purchase of provincial Crown land. Furthermore, the implementation process requires coordination and co-operation between federal and provincial and municipal governments.[15] In 1996, an agreement-in-principle among negotiators for Canada, Manitoba, and 19 First Nations on treaty land entitlement issues for those communities was announced. These negotiations are reported to be the last set of contested claims of this nature.[16]

The Saskatchewan government has also agreed recently to play a formal role in broader treaty-based discussions including self-government issues. An Office of Treaty Commissioner in Saskatchewan, first established in 1987 by the federal government, was given a new mandate in 1996 to faciliate self-government negotiations and to assist with exploratory discussions on treaty issues. The agreement was supported by both the governments of Canada and Saskatchewan.[17] The active involvement of the province in the renewal of the Office marks another advance for intergovernmental approaches to these issues. A third example of tripartite approaches to land-claims issues is the Indian Commission of Ontario. Established in 1978 by federal and provincial Orders-in-Council, this tripartite body, among other roles, facilitates tripartite negotiations of many of the specific land claims in the province. Many of the claims in southern Ontario involve pre-Confederation treaties and land settlements devised by colonial governments in Upper Canada, which subsequently became the province of Ontario. In addition, the negotiation of post-confederation treaties in northern Ontario and the accompanying legal cases, created special provincial interests in traditional or treaty area lands especially concerning the natural resources on those lands.[18] The interest and willingness of successive provincial governments in Ontario to address First Nation land issues has ebbed and flowed over recent years. The problem that Ontario governments often face in moving expeditiously is opposition from third-party interests such as the Ontario Anglers' and Fishermen's Association and other groups of this nature. While the Indian Commission of Ontario continues to provide a formal forum for tripartite discussion, First Nations in Ontario are frequently frustrated with what they perceive as a lack of political will, especially on the part of the province, to settle claims. It appears that the current provincial government, with its particular ideological outlook, has not given any strong indication of its interest in addressing major issues. Rather, its emphasis has been on specific, practical problems involving the parties.

Aboriginal land claims can be expected to remain an ongoing issue for all parties. For First Nations, land-claims settlements hold out the possibility of developing a stronger economic base. For non-aboriginal governments, settlements are intended to provide certainty over the status of the land and certainty against future claims and, in turn, address third-party interests. The fact that the main elements of major agreements receive constitutional protection under section 35 of the *Constitution Act, 1982* also enhances their importance in intergovernmental relations in Canada.

In the final analysis, claims-settlement processes must be viewed from a long-term perspective. It is important to remember that for the First Nations, treaty-making processes are the basis of an ongoing relationship, especially with the federal government. Agreements reached at particular points in time are milestones but not necessarily conclusions of the process. For non-aboriginal governments, finality is often the main objective and government representatives are frequently perplexed when issues are raised after agreements are reached. To the extent that land-claims agreements have been reached or that claims are under negotiation in those regions of Canada where treaties had not been reached previously, it could be argued that this is an indication of good progress on these issues. For many of the First Nation groups, the compensation and benefits afforded by the claims settlements have helped to narrow the economic gap and allow First Nation leaders to keep pace with socio-economic pressures from their communities associated with population growth. And the experience gained through the intergovernmental negotiation processes has also helped build and maintain ongoing working relationships, processes, and even structures of intergovernmental cooperation.

ECONOMIC DEVELOPMENT

Economic self-sufficiency is considered a basic prerequisite of self-government.[19] Yet, First Nations have often been limited in pursuing opportunities for economic development by the complex, legal restrictions of the *Indian Act*.[20] In addition, the lack of management experience and lack of equity funding have been particularly difficult issues for First Nation entrepreneurs. But increasingly, there are indications that some of these obstacles are being removed. As First Nations develop their own economic institutions, their ability to interact with other governments is enhanced. Furthermore, federal and provincial governments have facilitated First Nation initiatives to expand business opportunities with other players with their current emphasis on partnerships with the private sectors and other organizations.

An example of an emerging First Nations' economic institution in the resource sector is Indian Oil and Gas Canada (IOGC). Created in 1987 as an agency within the federal Department of Indian Affairs and Northern Development, steps are now being taken to transfer control to First Nations. In June 1996, the federal government signed an agreement with the Indian Resource Council, the First Nation organization representing First Nations with oil and gas interests, to establish a Board of Directors to co-manage the oil and gas resources located on Indian reserve lands.[21] During the co-management phases, the authority and decisions of the board require the approval of the executive director of IOGC and operations will continue in accordance with the existing *Indian Oil and Gas Regulations, 1995* and *Indian Oil and Gas Act.* For the Indian Resource Council to assume full control, regulatory and legislative changes to the existing laws will be undertaken.

The natural gas and oil sector is an important component of provincial economies, especially in Alberta. The operations of this First Nation company, with headquarters located in Calgary, position it to become a leading aboriginal resource agency in that region as well as across Canada. Currently, it manages assets valued at more than $1.1 billion.[22]

Historically, First Nation enterprises have had limited access to financial capital through non-aboriginal lending institutions. In recent years, many Canadian chartered banks have begun to recognize the potential of cultivating aboriginal clientele, as evidenced by more and more examples of chartered banks opening branches in First Nation communities. But until the past year, the only First Nation financial institution in Canada was the Peace Hills Trust company in Alberta.

The creation of a *First Nation Chartered Bank* grew out of a commitment in the 1993 Liberal *Red Book* to establish a national aboriginal financial institution. On 6 December 1996, the federal government announced that the Federation of Saskatchewan Indian Nations (FSIN) and its financial arm, the Saskatchewan Indian Equity Foundation, and the Toronto Dominion Bank would jointly invest in a chartered First Nation Bank of Canada (FNBC). To that end, the Indian Equity Foundation committed $2 million and the TD Bank committed $8 million investment in the First Nation Chartered Bank. The Department of Indian and Northern Affairs provided $511,000 in initial developmental costs.[23] The first branch of the FNBC opened in early 1997 in Saskatoon, Saskatchewan. It offers a full range of banking services, administration and financial support services. Its western Canadian location is a reflection of the proactive leadership role taken by the Federation of Saskatchewan Indian Nations to help advance economic development and to provide services to First Nation clientele.

Another example of an aboriginal financial agency is *the Indian Taxation Advisory Board* (ITAB). Created in 1989 by the Department of Indian Affairs and Northern Development to provide the minister with advice on the approval of property taxation by-laws, it has promoted real property taxation by First Nations and assists in the development of policies and procedures. With the assistance of ITAB, more than 50 First Nations have enacted by-laws taxing real property interests on reserve lands. First Nation revenues raised by these taxes are estimated to exceed $12 million.[24]

The work of ITAB has also led to an interesting example of intergovernmental cooperation. In June 1996, a Centre for Excellence in Municipal-

Aboriginal Relations was announced by representatives of the federal government, the Federation of Canadian Municipalities [FCM], and the Indian Taxation Advisory Board.[25] Funded by the federal government and the FCM-member municipalities, this centre is designed to offer opportunities for municipalities to share with aboriginal governments their best practices in financial management, service delivery, and political accountability. It acts as a national body which provides a forum for exchange of information and research on issues such as municipal-aboriginal intergovernmental relations, taxation governance, and service delivery. Given the concerns that have been expressed by municipal governments about the role of local aboriginal governments in economic development in recent years through the Federation of Canadian Municipalities, this kind of initiative provides excellent opportunities for improved relations, especially in relation to concerns about local taxation.

While economic and financial institution-building helps strengthen the economic base for First Nations and position them for more effective interaction with other governments and organizations, there are also examples of intergovernmental cooperation on economic development initiatives. In addition, economic development is one area where federal and provincial governments have worked closely in recent years to reduce overlap and duplication in programming and to improve service to the client through program coordination. An example of how First Nations can participate in intergovernmental collaboration, in private sector partnership and in streamlining government processes is the New Brunswick Federal-Provincial-Aboriginal Joint Economic Development initiative (JEDI). Since 1994, federal, provincial and aboriginal representatives have worked together to identify and pursue undertakings that will contribute to aboriginal economic development in New Brunswick and have put in place a number of joint program initiatives. For example, there is a three-year Strategic Aboriginal Employment Placement plan involving governments and the private sector in partnership. The Union of New Brunswick Indians was funded to conduct job opportunity analyses in the region. Joint public sector-private sector funding has supported training iniatives for employment for Aboriginal People in chartered banks, as teachers' aids in provincial schools and as business entrepreneurs. With support from the New Brunswick Regional Development Corporation, Atlantic Canada Opportunities Agency and the Royal Bank, a Native Youth Entrepreneurship Loan program for on-reserve aboriginal youths is being administered by the Ulnooweg Development Group Inc., an Aboriginal Capital Corporation. There are currently some 50 business projects, the development of which is being facilitated by the Atlantic Canada Opportunities Agency and the New Brunswick Department of Economic Development.[26]

Many other examples of success stories of First Nation entrepreneurship and enterprise can be found. Annual Aboriginal and First Nation business award events are held nationally and, in some cases provincially, to acknowledge the achievement of aboriginal business leaders. These efforts to enhance the economic status of First Nations helps, directly and indirectly, to strengthen the role their governments play in relations with non-aboriginal governments and with the private sector.

EDUCATION

Education provides an interesting example of evolving federal-provincial-First Nations relations. Contrary to some perceptions, the administration of Indian education has always involved federal and provincial governments. In the *Indian Act*, the federal government has legislated on schools and matters related to their operation and the attendance of students.[27] The provincial governments have responsibility for such matters as curriculum, standards, and certification of teachers. With respect to postsecondary education, the federal government has provided funding to eligible Indian and Inuit people through its Post-Secondary Student Support Program introduced in 1985 but formally accepts no jurisdictional responsibility in this area.[28]

If a First Nation government wants to assume jurisdiction and control over education for its members, it will need to negotiate with both federal and provincial governments. And with the introduction of the federal government's Inherent Right policy introduced in 1995, it is now possible for a First Nation to negotiate First Nation jurisdiction over education including curriculum with willing provincial governments as well as control over administration and operations of schools with the federal government.[29]

The Mi'kmaqs of Nova Scotia are an example of this. On 14 February 1997, Mi'kmaq Chiefs of Nova Scotia, the federal minister of Indian and northern affairs and the provincial premier of Nova Scotia signed an agreement that transferred jurisdiction for education to the First Nations. The agreement allows for the transfer of approximately $140 million to the First Nations for education over a five-year period.[30] Programs covered under this agreement include primary and secondary education on-reserve and postsecondary education funding to band members on and off-reserve. The funding will also provide for the operation and maintenance of facilities, band administration, and capital. Legislation will be passed to formalize the agreement.

The agreement goes beyond devolution of administrative responsibility to the First Nations. It provides for full transfer of responsibility and control over education by the community. In this way, it simplifies the provisions of educational services which in the past have involved the two levels of government by recognizing the jurisdiction of the First Nation government for education.

CONCLUSIONS

Any attempt to assess the success of these initiatives may be tempered by the perspective of the individual reader. Success or failure in land-claims negotiations or with economic development or educational initiatives may also be judged differently by different players in the processes themselves. On balance, however, it could be argued that the undertakings that are there, especially in the area of land claims and economic development and increasingly in the area of education, indicate significant progress in intergovernmental relationships between First Nations and other governments. In turn, these relationships have helped enhance the capacity of First Nations to address social and economic issues in their communities as well as strengthen their position in dealings with other governments.

In a recent article which provided a macro-assessment of federal government activities in past decades, Arthur Kroeger, a former deputy minister of Indian affairs and northern development noted the federal government's past inability to solve aboriginal socio-economic problems with expensive social programs.[31] The direct participation of First Nation governments as an equal party in intergovernmental processes may help to provide different approaches and, hopefully, solutions to long-standing socio-economic problems. The examples provided here also demonstrate that with the various governmental and business institutions which are emerging there will be a need for ongoing intergovernmental collaboration. In sum, the place of aboriginal governments in Canadian federalism is starting to have a clearer, practical definition as institutions are established and formal processes produce legally-binding agreements. And, non-aboriginal governments generally seem to be supportive of intergovernmental undertakings of a practical nature.

Although constitutional issues have not been high on the agendas of non-aboriginal governments, the recommendations of the Report of the Royal Commission on Aboriginal Peoples have brought back to the table the outstanding constitutional issues, including aboriginal sovereignty, the creation of a third order of aboriginal governments, and an aboriginal Parliament. Whether the federal and provincial governments will be interested or willing to pursue discussions on these subjects may, like many instances in the past, be influenced by the force and confluence of political events at a particular point in time. What can be expected is that both federal and provincial governments will use the results of the non-constitutional processes as evidence that progress can be made without constitutional reform.

In the meantime, provincial governments remain cautious about their participation even in non-constitutional undertakings and often comment with concern, perceived or real, that the federal government may be trying to off-load responsibility for First Nations to them. Notwithstanding the constitutional discussions of recent decades, provincial governments, for the most part, continue to view responsibility for First Nations as a federal responsibility, especially as it relates to funding programs and services. Often the federal government has had to bring pressure to bear to obtain provincial participation in discussions involving First Nations. But where there is a common practical interest and political will, progress can be made on negotiating and supporting agreements that have a mutual benefit to all parties.

In the immediate future, the role that First Nation leaders, especially those in Quebec, will play on national unity issues will be important to watch. While the issue of Quebec sovereignty was used by First Nation leaders to argue for the recognition of aboriginal rights in the 1970s, paradoxically, today, questions are being raised by some First Nation and Inuit leaders in Quebec about whether Quebec has a legal right to declare independence unilaterally. Prior to the 1995 Quebec referendum, both Inuit and First Nation communities in the province conducted their own referenda which resulted in an overwhelming response by aboriginal voters to remain a part of Canada.[32] If a constitutional process is renewed, First Nation leaders will want to be strategically positioned. Practical achievements that support stronger First Nation economic base and institutions of self-government will also enhance the influence that First Nation leaders may have in any intergovernmental discussions about the future of Canadian federalism.

We are in an era in which aboriginal governments, whatever their particular institutional structure and authority, are going to be increasingly active participants on the intergovernmental landscape along with all the other types and forms of governments and governing authorities in Canada. We are going to have to continue to find creative solutions to accommodate First Nation communities within our federal system. This may result in radical surgery to our constitutional framework to accommodate the diversity. But pragmatism has always been a vital element of good government in Canada and the means of finding solutions to our challenges of governance.

NOTES

1. See the *Draft Legal Text, 9 October 1992*. As the text states: "[This] text is based on the Charlottetown Accord of 28 August 1992. It is a best efforts text prepared by officials representing all the First Ministers and Aboriginal and Territorial Leaders." See pp. 1, 3, 37, and 38 in particular.

2. The report was released on 21 November 1996. See Canada, Royal Commission on Aborginal Peoples (RCAP), *Report* (Ottawa: Canada Communications Group,

1996). The five volumes included: Volume 1: *Looking Forward, Looking Back*; Volume 2: *Restructuring the Relationship*; Volume 3: *Gathering Strength*; Volume 4: *Perspectives and Reality*; and, Volume 5: *Renewal: A Twenty Year Commitment*. The federal response was threefold. First, the minister indicated that it was not possible to increase program expenditures as recommended; but, second, the report would be reviewed. See Scott Feschuk, "Cost of reforms $30-billion, report on aboriginals says," *The Globe and Mail*, 22 November 1996, p. A9. Third, the department issued a report outlining government achievements from 1993. See Department of Indian Affairs and Northern Development, "Aborginal Agenda: Three Years of Progress" (Ottawa: Public Works and Government, 15 November 1996), mimeo.

3. Alberta Social Services Minister Stockwell Day questioned the report's recommendations that the province should share the cost for any increases in program spending. See Larry Johnsrude, "Minister fears Ottawa's aims," *Calgary Herald*, 22 November 1996, p. A3.

4. The relationship between successive ministers of Indian affairs and northern development and the national chief of the Assembly of First Nations(AFN) is shaped by politics and personality. At the end of the Liberal regime in 1984, there was a close alliance between the two respective incumbents. With the change of government in September 1984, the Progressive Conservative minister, David Crombie, chose to travel out to the communities rather than focus on the national leadership. But the AFN leadership also changed and a new rapport was established. By 1993, however, the then AFN national chief, Ovide Mercredi, had been working closely with the Progressive Conservative government on a number of issues not the least of which had been the Charlottetown Accord. With the election of the Liberal government in 1993, the relationship between the national chief and Minister Irwin was problematic from the beginning. The national chief's interest in constitutional issues and Minister Irwin's general disinterest in these issues was only one of many differences between them which emerged over the following three years, and were never reconciled.

5. See "Aboriginal Agenda." Sixty-seven initiatives are listed in this report.

6. For example, see Edward Greenspon, "PM's past suggests caution," *The Globe and Mail*, 22 November 1996, pp. Al and A7.

7. See Royal Commission on Aboriginal Peoples, *Looking Forward, Looking Back*, p. 15.

8. See Audrey Doerr, "Indian Policy," in *Issues in Canadian Public Policy*, ed. G.B. Doern and V. S. Wilson, (Toronto: Macmillan, 1974), pp. 36-54.

9. See RCAP, *Restructuring the Relationship*, Part 2.

10. The federal comprehensive claims policy addresses the negotiation of claims with aboriginal groups where rights of traditional use and occupancy of the land had been neither extinguished by treaty nor superseded by law. Specific claims policy deals with claims relating to outstanding lawful obligations of the federal government whether under the terms of treaties, obligations of the *Indian Act*, or the proper discharge of responsibility for reserve lands.

11. See Department of Indian Affairs and Northern Development, "Yale First Na-
     tion, Canada, and British Columbia Sign Framework Agreement," 12 February
     1997, news release, mimeo.

12. See Federal Treaty Negotiation Office, *Treaty News*, March 1997 on Indian and
     Northern Affairs WorldWideWeb Site.

13. For an academic assessment of the process see Christoper McKee, *Treaty Talks
     in British Columbia: Negotiating a Mutually Beneficial Future* (Vancouver: Uni-
     versity of British Columbia Press, 1996).

14. See Department of Indian Affairs and Northern Development, "Treaty Land
     Entitlement in Manitoba," Ottawa, *Backgrounder,* 21 June 1996, mimeo. Land
     allotments under most of the numbered treaties signed by the First Nations of
     the Prairies and the Canadian government were based on population. However,
     population counts used by early surveyors as a means of determining land quan-
     tum for reserves were often only rough estimates of the land entitlement and
     these calculations did not always provide for the full entitlement of land under
     the treaty.

15. For a discussion of the types of issues, see an article by Theresa M. Dust, Q.C.,
     entitled "The impact of aboriginal land claims and self-government on Cana-
     dian municipalities," *Canadian Public Administration*, forthcoming 1997. The
     paper is based on a study done for the Intergovernmental Committee on Urban
     and Regional Research, Toronto, Ontario in 1995.

16. It should be noted that these particular negotiations in Manitoba had been stalled
     since 1984 largely as a result of differences between federal and provincial gov-
     ernments. See Department of Indian Affairs and Northern Development, "Treaty
     Land Entitlement in Manitoba."

17. Department of Indian Affairs and Northern Development, "Historic Agreements
     Signed by Canada, Saskatchewan and Federation of Saskatchewan Indian Na-
     tions," news release, 31 October 1996, mimeo.

18. See Bradford W. Morse (ed.), *Aboriginal Peoples and the Law: Indian, Métis
     and Inuit Rights in Canada* (Ottawa: Carleton University Press, 1985), for dis-
     cussion of *St. Catherine's Milling Co. v. the Queen*, 1888, pp. 96-99; and for
     discussion of federal-provincial agreements respecting Indian Reserve Lands,
     pp. 487-500.

19. See Special Committee on Indian Self-Government, *Report* (Ottawa: Minister
     of Supply and Services, 1983); and RCAP, *Restructuring the Relationship*, ch. 5.

20. See Shin Imai and Donna Hawley, *The 1995 Annotated Indian Act* (Toronto:
     Carswell, 1994). For example, legal title to First Nation land is "vested in Her
     Majesty." The use or disposition of that land is therefore subject to a variety of
     restrictions and regulations. The legal status of a Band Council is also limited
     under the Act. There are, for example, numerous cases in law dealing with the
     extent of the legal status of a band, whether it can be sued or sue, whether it can
     acquire or hold real property and the extent of its liability. See ibid., pp. 6-9.

21. Department of Indian Affairs and Northern Development, "Government/First
     Nations Management Board," Ottawa, *Backgrounder*, June 1996, mimeo.

22. Information obtained from the Office of the Executive Director, Indian Oil and Gas Canada, 6 August 1997.

23. Ibid., "Federal Government Congratulates Federation of Saskatchewan Indian Nations and the TD Bank on Launch of First Nations Bank of Canada," news release, Ottawa, 9 December 1996, mimeo.

24. The Indian Taxation Advisory Board reports that some 57 First Nations in British Columbia and Alberta have enacted taxing by-laws. Source: Indian Taxation Advisory Board Web Site on INAC WorldWideWeb site.

25. Department of Indian Affairs and Northern Development, "Centre for Excellence in Municipal-Aboriginal Relations Announced," news release, Calgary, 3 June 1996, mimeo.

26. "New Brunswick Federal-Provincial-Aboriginal Joint Economic Development Initiative (JEDI)," *Backgrounder*, Ottawa, March 1997, mimeo.

27. *Indian Act*, pp. 115-19.

28. Federal funding is approximately $247 million nationally and provided support to more than 27,000 aboriginal students in 1996-97. In recent years there has been some 3,500 graduates a year. See Department of Indian Affairs and Northern Development, "Increase in Post-Secondary Education Enrollment," Ottawa, 1997, mimeo.

29. See Canada, Department of Indian Affairs and Northern Development, *Federal Policy Guide: Aboriginal Self-Government: Government of Canada's Approach to Implementation of the Inherent Right and the Negotiation of Aboriginal Self-Government* (Ottawa: Minister of Supply and Services, 1995).

30. Department of Indian Affairs and Northern Development, "Education Jurisdiction Transferred to Mi'kmaq of Nova Scotia," news release, Ottawa, 14 February 1997, mimeo.

31. See Arthur Kroeger, "Governing in the Millennium: How *Much* less Government" (Ottawa: Research Group of Canadian Centre for Management Development, 1996), as reported in Canadian Centre for Management Development, *Executive Leadership* 9, 3, p. 7.

32. There is also a growing policy interest in these issues. Among other publications, the Institute for Research on Public Policy has a Quebec-Canada series on *Aboriginal Peoples and the Future of Quebec*. One of the RCAP studies was also focused on some of these issues. See Renée Depuis and Ken McNeil, *Canada's Fiduciary Obligation to Aboriginal Peoples in the Context of Accession to Sovereignty by Quebec*, Vol. 2. *Domestic Issues* (Ottawa: Minister of Supply and Services, 1995).

III

Intergovernmental Diplomacy

9

Alberta's Intergovernmental Relations Experience

Roger Gibbins

Cet article trace l'histoire du département des affaires fédérales et intergouverne-mentales de l'Alberta (FIGA) de 1972 à aujourd'hui, et le fait dans le but d'explorer l'évolution plus générale des relations intergouvernementales dans la province. Cette évolution peut être expliquée comme une réponse stratégique à la position politique et démographique de l'Alberta à l'intérieur de l'état fédéral canadien. Plus spécifique-ment, le gouvernement provincial a utilisé les relations intergouvernementales comme l'endroit préféré dans lequel faire avancer une vision constitutionnelle clairement définie. On fait aussi l'argument que le comportement intergouvernemental de l'Alberta parallèle étroitement celui du gouvernement canadien en essayant de gérer ses liens avec les États-Unis. À cet égard, les relations intergouvernementales dans l'Alberta peuvent être perçues comme une politique étrangère canadienne en plus petit. Cet article conclut en suggérant que plusieurs des défis intergouvernementaux dont l'Alberta fait face, seront dans un avenir rapproché affrontés par les gouvernements provinciaux à travers le pays, et que, par conséquent, l'expérience de l'Alberta a une applicabilité canadienne élargie.

INTRODUCTION

Other chapters in this volume have addressed the ongoing and potential re-form of the Canadian federation through non-constitutional means. In practice, this means reform *of* and *through* intergovernmental relations. Within this context, the Alberta experience looms large. Historically, the province has carried disproportionate weight within intergovernmental councils, and has played an active role in shaping the norms and practices of intergovern-mentalism. In the contemporary era, Alberta has taken a leadership role in reforming the intergovernmental aspects of social policy, and has been at the forefront of provincial involvement in trade policy and promotion. Alberta was quite likely the central player in the intergovernmental negotiations lead-ing up to the Agreement on Internal Trade. In short, if we are to understand the intergovernmental aspects of non-constitutional reform, Alberta's experience is a good place to start.

As is so often the case, to understand the present we must begin with the past. Two coincidental events in 1972 have come to play an important role in shaping our conceptual understanding of Canadian intergovernmental relations and the institutional realities of those relations. The "conceptual" event was the publication of Richard Simeon's *Federal-Provincial Diplomacy: The Making of Recent Policy in Canada*, which grafted the analytical framework and political imagery of international relations onto the study of Canadian federalism. The "institutional" event was the establishment of Alberta's Department of Federal and Intergovernmental Affairs (FIGA), a new central agency designed to coordinate the province's growing engagement in intergovernmental relations and to yoke that engagement to Alberta's larger strategic objectives. This chapter brings these two events together by showing that Alberta's experience with *intergovernmental* relations bears a striking resemblance to Canada's experience with *international* relations.

The primary tasks of this chapter are to provide (a) an explanation of the contemporary intergovernmental relations scene in Alberta, (b) a brief discussion of intergovernmental challenges on the horizon, and (c) some concluding commentary on the extent to which one can generalize from Alberta to the larger intergovernmental experience. These can best be accomplished by starting with an historical overview of two sides of the same coin: intergovernmental relations in the province, and FIGA as their institutional expression. This overview is particularly relevant to our understanding of contemporary intergovernmentalism because there is a consistent story line to the province's experience, one embedded in the evolution of FIGA. For all governments in Canada, intergovernmental relations constitute an ongoing, complex and increasingly important activity. But for Alberta, the practice of intergovernmental relations is much more. It is a philosophy of government and a strategic response to the province's perceived (and demonstrated) weakness within parliamentary institutions. As a consequence, there is a coherence to the Alberta experience which may not be typical.

It should be noted, of course, that FIGA does not manage the totality of Alberta's intergovernmental relations. A good deal of the intergovernmental load, indeed the bulk of that load, is carried by the line departments which have developed their own intergovernmental experience, capacity and expertise. Many of the larger intergovernmental conflicts over such issues as gun control, health-care extra-billing, potential carbon taxes, and the Canadian Wheat Board have taken place through line departments with limited involvement from FIGA. Nonetheless, it is FIGA that pulls this larger picture into focus, and it is through an examination of FIGA that the broad story of Alberta's intergovernmental experience can be most easily detected.

THE INTERNATIONAL MODEL

If there has been a clear theme to Canadian foreign policy since the end of the Second World War, it can be found in the attempt to embed bilateral relations with the United States into an institutionalized, multilateral environment.[1] Canadian governments have realized that formal bilateral relationships with the United States are best avoided because of the ten-to-one disparity in population and economic power. Canada will always be out-gunned (figuratively) in a bilateral relationship. There is also no room for creative alliance-building in a bilateral relationship, except in circumstances where domestic American allies can be found. (Canadian governments, for example, were able to harness American environmentalists to their acid rain agenda, whereas domestic allies have been difficult to find in the Pacific salmon dispute.) As a consequence, Canada has been an enthusiastic supporter of multilateralism — the United Nations, NATO, the Organization of American States, and NAFTA instead of the FTA. Lying behind this enthusiasm has been a consistent effort to ensure that bilateral Canadian-American relations are conducted *by the rules* and *through the institutions* of multilateralism. The Canadian mouse has neither the domestic clout within the US nor the population and economic resources that would be necessary to have faith in bilateral relations with the American elephant.[2]

Now, just as Canada's population is only one-tenth that of the United States, Alberta contains just under one-tenth (9.3 percent) of Canada's population. And just as Canada lacks effective political clout within American congressional institutions, so too has Alberta traditionally lacked effective clout within Canadian parliamentary institutions. Now care must be taken not to exaggerate the parallel, for even in the worst of times Alberta's influence within parliamentary institutions has surpassed Canada's influence within congressional institutions. Nevertheless, the *perceived* exclusion from national decisionmaking captures a foundational element in Alberta's political culture and the regional culture of the west. It is the genesis and rallying cry of western alienation: "The West Wants In!" Furthermore, just as Canada has tried to avoid formalized bilateral relations with the United States and has pursued instead a policy of multilateralism, so too has Alberta pursued an analogous strategy of intergovernmentalism. In short, Alberta has approached its place within the Canadian federal state as Canada has approached its place within North America. Intergovernmentalism in Alberta's case is Canadian foreign policy writ small.

Admittedly, this model of the Alberta experience cannot simply be asserted, and the first part of the chapter is designed to provide substantiation. However, in assessing the evidence the reader should keep in mind the role social science models play. They are not meant to incorporate the full complexity of political reality, but rather are designed to throw into relief general patterns of experience, highlighting central features while leaving many of the nuances in shadow. The present model provides only a broad conceptual understanding of the Alberta intergovernmental experience, and suggests how that experience sheds light on the larger Canadian case. It abstracts from the Alberta experience, and thereby imposes a measure of coherence that may not have been apparent to or even planned by the governments of the day.

HISTORICAL EVOLUTION OF INTERGOVERNMENTALISM IN ALBERTA

The recent history of intergovernmentalism in Alberta spans the three Progressive Conservative administrations of Peter Lougheed (1971-1985), Don Getty (1985-1992), and Ralph Klein (1993 onward). We will look at these in turn, paying particular attention to the patterns of continuity that sweep across the three administrations.

THE LOUGHEED YEARS

Our story begins in 1971 with the election of Peter Lougheed's Progressive Conservatives, ending 36 consecutive years of Social Credit government. A partisan change in government is unusual in Alberta; indeed, it had happened only twice before 1971 — in 1921 and 1935 — and has not happened since. As a consequence, changes in government are inevitably seen as milestone events, and the 1971 election was no exception. It signaled the beginning of a determined effort by the government and people of Alberta to leave their mark on the national scene, to put aside the province's economic and political marginalization. And, within Lougheed's first term, external events in the international oil market were to provide Alberta with the financial wherewithal to be taken seriously within the national community. In short, Lougheed's election marked the dawn of the "new West" as the province shook off the lingering dust of the Great Depression and the ideological inertia of Social Credit.

But there was a problem. Shortly after the Progressive Conservatives came to power provincially, the 1972 federal election left Alberta without representation on the government side of the House of Commons. If Alberta was to establish an effective political presence on the national scene, it would have to be done through the premier and intergovernmental relations rather than through elected representatives in the House. Thus the establishment of FIGA had been opportune.[3] It should be stressed, moreover, that the 1972 election was seen not as an aberration but as a dramatic confirmation of a regional critique of parliamentary institutions that reached back at least to the Progressives and the United Farmers of Alberta in the early 1920s.

Parliamentary institutions, it was believed, would inevitably reflect the demographic weight and hence economic interests of the central Canadian provinces. Here readers will recognize the now-classic distinction between intrastate and interstate federalism. Albertans believed that intrastate federalism — the expression of regional interests within the parliamentary institutions of the national government — was so badly flawed that only an interstate strategy — relying on government-to-government relations — offered any realistic prospect of success.

A practical reason for strengthening the province's intergovernmental capacity should also be noted. The 1973 Western Economic Opportunities Conference, held in Calgary and attended by representatives from the federal, western provincial and territorial governments, demonstrated that the western provinces could be brought together in a united front if there was the political will, leadership and institutional capacity to do so.[4] At the same time, it also demonstrated that Ottawa would overwhelm provincial delegations in federal-provincial forums unless those delegations were well-prepared, thoroughly briefed, and aggressively led. Playing effectively on the intergovernmental stage, therefore, required bureaucratic resources of the sort rapidly put into place through FIGA. At the time of FIGA's founding, however, it was not assumed that such resources would be necessary over the long haul. FIGA's first annual report struck a touching note of optimism: "It must be remembered ... that many issues of intergovernmental affairs are of a perennial nature and will not disappear by waving a wand, but will instead require *several months or even years* of study and negotiation" (emphasis added).[5]

Although FIGA was by no means unique, it provided an example of a top-flight intergovernmental "shop." FIGA, like most central agencies, was never a big player in terms of budget or staff; its influence within the provincial government depended on the political authority it was able to command. Thus it is important to note that FIGA's first minister was Don Getty, widely seen at the time of his appointment as a central and influential figure in the Lougheed Cabinet, as was Lou Hyndman, FIGA's second minister. Their appointments signaled the importance the premier was perceived to place in FIGA. It should also be stressed that Lougheed's extensive involvement in intergovernmental relations meant that FIGA served the premier along with its minister.[6]

Alberta's dilemma with intrastate federalism, and its exclusion from the federal Cabinet, only deepened in the years following FIGA's creation. In the federal election of 1974, Albertans again did not elect an MP on the government side of the House, and the provincial government's concern about Ottawa's propensity for unilateral action increased. As FIGA's minister, Lou Hyndman, stated in the Alberta Legislature:

> I think it's clear that as a government we must be wary of new federal initiatives in a host of areas in which they are moving ... Certainly, as a province we're

prepared to co-operate in any way we can on a reasonable basis. We're prepared
to negotiate. We're prepared to go to meetings and have discussions. But as a
province we're not prepared to accept unilateral decisions from Ottawa.... That's
not the kind of confederation we see. That's not the kind of Canada we, and I
think other provinces, envision.[7]

Then, after the 1979 election of Joe Clark's minority Progressive Conservative government, Alberta was not only on-side but the prime minister himself
was from the province, although not necessarily in line with the provincial
government's thinking of energy pricing. If the Clark government had lasted,
Alberta's intergovernmental strategy would have been tested; it is more difficult to argue that intrastate federalism does not work when the prime minister
is from your province, although Quebec governments have shown that it is
not impossible to do so. But Clark did not last, and the strategy was not put to
the test. Instead, the election of the Trudeau Liberals in 1980, again without a
Liberal MP from Alberta (or for that matter from anywhere west of Winnipeg), soon led to the most graphic failure yet of Canadian federalism, at least
from the perspective of Albertans. The 1980 National Energy Program was
seen as an unprecedented attack by the federal government on Alberta's wealth
and, more fundamentally, on the constitutional division of powers. The federal government, it appeared, was ignoring the constitutional rules of the game.
When Ottawa also announced in the fall of 1980 its plan to unilaterally repat-
riate and amend the constitution, Albertans' views on federalism bordered on
paranoia.

The problem was how to rein in a federal government that was bent, hell-
bent it seemed, on unilateralism. The answer was to be found in
alliance-building with other provincial governments, a strategy that was possible within the context of intergovernmentalism. FIGA facilitated an
aggressive alliance-building strategy whose objective was to use
intergovernmentalism just as Canada used multilateralism on the international
stage, to create interprovincial alliances that would offset or at least temper
the political power of the federal government. In this respect, Alberta worked
not only with the other three western provinces but also with Quebec. Although in the popular political culture Quebec and Alberta were generally
seen to be at odds, there was a good measure of commonality at the governmental level. Both governments resisted unilateral action by the federal
government, and both sought to rollback federal intrusions into provincial
fields of responsibility. It was only when Alberta's insistence on the constitutional equality of the provinces ran up against Quebec's quest for recognition
as a distinct society, and when institutional reforms such as Senate reform
were on the table, that the two diverged.

It was in the intergovernmental negotiations of 1981-82 that Alberta scored
perhaps its biggest constitutional success by orchestrating a new amending
formula in which all provinces were treated equally. The formulas built into

the 1982 *Constitution Act* had the great virtue, from Alberta's perspective, of not singling out any province for special treatment. The 7/50 requirement denied any one province a veto, and where a veto was provided in other sections, it was provided to all. Thus the Act recognized the constitutional equality of the provinces, and built in additional protection for provincial jurisdiction with respect to natural resources. It staved off the unilateral inclinations of the federal government of the day, and prevented unilateral constitutional amendment in the future.[8] Therefore the Act, including the intergovernmental process leading up to it, reflected Alberta's strategy of locking the federal government into an intergovernmental web; Ottawa could neither act unilaterally nor appeal directly to the people over the heads of the provincial governments.

The Lougheed years saw FIGA's international expansion as Alberta began establishing offices in London, New York, Los Angeles, Houston, Tokyo, Hong Kong, and Seoul.[9] (Alberta, nevertheless, was a relatively small provincial player on the international stage; Quebec had 29 offices abroad, Ontario 19 and British Columbia 9 at their respective peaks.[10]) In some respects, an international presence made sense for a province so heavily dependent on international trade. FIGA's offices abroad were mandated to promote the sale of Alberta products, encourage investment in and business immigration to Alberta, provide strategic trade advice to the Alberta government, market Alberta as a tourist destination, promote technology transfer, and arrange for scientific, cultural, and academic exchanges.[11] Although all this was appropriate for a province with an export-based economy, it can also be argued it would not have been necessary in a well-functioning federal system in which the national government and its external representatives were alert to regional interests and priorities. However, this presupposes an effective intrastate regime in which regional representatives can monitor the national government's external performance. Instead, Alberta pursued an intergovernmental strategy and mandated its international offices to "keep Canadian diplomats informed of Alberta's interests, priorities, and expertise, so that they, too, can work on Alberta's behalf."[12]

In his last intergovernmental appearance at the 1985 First Ministers' Conference on the economy, Peter Lougheed threw his considerable weight behind the initiation of free trade negotiations with the United States. This initiative was quickly picked up by the Mulroney government, and when the negotiations began Alberta entered an important new stage in the evolution of intergovernmental relations, and did so with a new premier at the tiller.

Given that there has been no change in Alberta's governing party since the 1971 election, it is important to ask whether there was significant policy or strategic change associated with the leadership transition from Peter Lougheed to Don Getty. The basic answer is that change had an effect, but not to the extent of seriously disrupting the intergovernmental strategy put in place by Lougheed. Although Lougheed was the primary architect of this strategy for securing provincial influence on the national scene, Don Getty was to solidify it throughout the negotiations leading to the Free Trade Agreement (FTA) and the North American Free Trade Agreement (NAFTA). His primary strategic departure was to champion Senate reform (discussed below) or, in more conceptual terms, the reform and reinvigoration of intrastate federalism. Alberta's first and to this point only Senatorial "selection" was held during Getty's term of office. However, he did not abandon intergovernmental relations in his pursuit of Senate reform; instead, he opened up a second and eventually unsuccessful front in Alberta's ongoing pursuit of effective political influence and thereby economic protection on the national stage.

Canada entered free trade negotiations with the United States in large part because of the growing fear of unilateral action by the American Congress; a free trade agreement was seen as the best device to tie the hands of Congress. Alberta, for its part, expressed a similar concern about unilateral action by the federal government. The fear was that Ottawa would use trade agreements to strengthen its control over the internal economy. Alberta was determined that freer trade not provide a mechanism for greater federal encroachments on provincial fields of jurisdiction. The province was prepared to surrender control to the marketplace, but not to Ottawa.

During the negotiations surrounding the proposed FTA, and then surrounding NAFTA, the Alberta government realized that it had an important stake in the *process* as well as the outcome. On the outcome side, the position of the Alberta government was straight-forward; it wanted as broad and deep a free trade agreement as possible. On the process side, it wanted to ensure that any agreement would not provide a mechanism through which future federal governments might intrude on provincial areas of jurisdiction. Thus Alberta was more concerned about protecting itself from Ottawa than it was about protecting the province's economic interests from the United States; the latter was seen as a non-issue.

This set of process concerns spilled over into the negotiations on internal free trade that were spawned by the continental free trade agreements and growing economic impact of globalization. Here again, Alberta was concerned that if the provincial governments could not act in concert to promote internal free trade, their failure to do so might provide an excuse for unilateral action by the federal government. Once more, multilateral action by provincial governments was promoted as an alternative to unilateralism by the federal government, potentially reinforced by constitutional amendments to strengthen Ottawa's powers of economic management. The provinces, it was hoped, could play a creative role rather than simply reacting to the federal government.[13] While Alberta was concerned about the substance of the eventual Agreement on Internal Trade, its primary concerns were with the process, with the institutional mechanisms that might evolve to handle conflict resolution, and with denying the federal government the opportunity or rationale for further economic intervention.

The Getty years are difficult to summarize with respect to intergovernmental relations. In terms of the FTA and NAFTA, Alberta was successful in achieving both its primary economic goal (broader free trade) and its intergovernmental objectives; Ottawa brought the provinces into the free trade negotiations, and the agreements did not strengthen Ottawa's economic powers vis-à-vis the provincial governments. With respect to internal free trade, Alberta and the other provinces denied Ottawa the opportunity to step in as the only political actor capable of cutting through a slew of provincial trade barriers. While the Agreement on Internal Trade was neither as deep nor as broad as Alberta would have preferred, it was nonetheless an intergovernmental success in that Ottawa was unable to assume leadership for the reduction of internal trade barriers. The failures of the Getty years came on the national unity front; the alliance with Quebec that helped create the Meech Lake Accord was unable to ensure its passage, and hopes for Senate reform were dashed when the Canadian and Alberta electorates defeated the 1992 referendum on the Charlottetown Accord. However, these failures were not Getty's alone; he was far more instrumental in the construction of constitutional packages than he was in their ultimate rejection.

THE KLEIN YEARS

What happened when Ralph Klein replaced Don Getty as premier of the province? Klein immediately abandoned Getty's pursuit of constitutional reform, and thus of Senate reform. He returned to a purely intergovernmental strategy, and in this he had lots of company. Klein, after all, was elected leader of the Alberta Progressive Conservatives less than two months after the referendum defeat of the Charlottetown Accord. In the wake of that defeat the country as a whole turned its back on constitutional reform, and the populist Alberta premier was no exception. His focus was on *rebalancing* achieved through non-constitutional change. In effect, Klein argues that the constitutional status quo should be respected, not changed. In this regard he is in line with the arguments made by Peter Lougheed that the province's ownership of natural resources and its programmatic jurisdiction were not being respected by a federal government that ignored the rules of the game in its pursuit of

unilateralism. Although the NEP dragon was slain by the Mulroney government, other dragons were to be found in Ottawa's unshackled spending power
and unilateral cuts to transfer programs. Here the 1995 federal budget and its
unilateral changes to interprovincial transfers — the CHST initiative — was a
watershed event in the eyes of the Alberta government.

If one looks back prior to the 1971 election, there is little evidence that
Alberta sought a fundamental redistribution of powers between the federal
and provincial governments. Conflicts, when they arose, related to a perception that Alberta was not being treated equally with other provinces (e.g., the
Natural Resources Transfer Act) or that the province's constitutional authority was not being respected (e.g., Premier Ernest Manning's opposition to
national medicare). When Peter Lougheed came to power, there was little significant change in these respects; the new premier's primary concern was with
the *protection* rather than *expansion* of provincial powers. Alberta premiers
reflected a conclusion drawn across the west that the primary need was for
greater regional influence on the exercise of federal government powers rather
than for the transfer of powers to the provincial governments. It is worth noting in this context that the constitutional position paper released by the Alberta
Legislature in March 1992 did not call for any change to the division of powers, but only for a clarification of federal and provincial roles and
responsibilities.[14]

The west's position in this regard is quite different from Quebec's. At least
until recently, the west has sought power at the centre rather than devolution,
whereas Quebec has used its formidable power at the centre to pursue devolution. Quebec has married its intergovernmental relations strategy to its political
strength within parliamentary institutions and the federal Cabinet, whereas
Alberta's intergovernmental relations strategy has been used to compensate
for its chronic weakness at the centre. Quebec's is an insider strategy, Alberta's an outsider strategy. And, Quebec's strategy has been used as a bridge to
independence, whereas Alberta's strategy has been used to ward off a federal
government within which Quebec leaders have been the principal players.

But what about Klein's emphasis on rebalancing? Should this be seen as a
major departure, as a quest for more provincial power? Here the point to stress
is that rebalancing as envisioned by Klein need not entail constitutional change.
Indeed, rebalancing is appealing because it can be achieved without constitutional change; it is about making existing governments work, and work better.
All that is required is for the federal government to respect the existing division of powers and butt out of provincial responsibilities, such as the
management of the health-care system. The case for rebalancing is basically a
case for the constitutional status quo. The argument is not that the provinces
should do more, but that Ottawa should do less. And what it does do, it should
do in *intergovernmental concert* with the provinces. This was the position
adopted by nine of the ten premiers at the 1996 Premiers' Conference in Jasper.

Premier Klein has been instrumental in getting rebalancing on the country's intergovernmental agenda, establishing the terminology (Ottawa preferred "improving the efficiency of the federation" to "rebalancing") and articulating a rationale built on public accountability (badly blurred in the past by the spending power) and the elimination of waste springing from duplication. He has been effective in harnessing the federal government's retreat from constitutional reform and its near-desperate search for non-constitutional national unity solutions to his own intergovernmental agenda. Alberta's concern with overlap and duplication with respect to labour market training has been long-standing, and when the attempt to address this issue through the Charlottetown Accord collapsed, Alberta came back to it through the rebalancing initiative. More generally, the communiqué of the 1994 Annual Premiers' Conference set out to establish provincial leadership in the non-constitutional reform of social programs falling within provincial jurisdiction, and Alberta set out to be a leader among the provinces. The premiers collectively were concerned with much more than financial transfers and penalties. The Canadian identity, it has frequently been argued, is bound up in the nature of social programs, and thus the premiers were determined to show that the Canadian identity could be as well protected through intergovernmental agreements as it could through federal government encroachments in provincial areas of jurisdiction. Simply put, they were unwilling to concede the high ground of national unity to the federal government. Note, for example, a September 1996 speech by Premier Klein.

> I mentioned a moment ago that Canada is internationally acclaimed for its social programs, and on this point [the premiers] agree with the federal government — that our social programs truly do define us as Canadians. In an "Issues Paper on Social Policy".....the Premiers have proposed a specific eight-point plan for the reform and renewal of social policy in Canada. Some in the federal government simply respond with the tired old line about "Provinces wanting to dismantle health care, social services, etc., etc." That response is unbecoming of the national government.[15]

In these respects, Klein is expressing well-established Alberta themes. For example, the 1992 Select Special Committee on Constitutional Reform stated that "Canada's network of social security and social service programs are an integral component of the Canadian identity, and maintenance of these programs is essential to the well-being of Canadians."[16] However, while the committee called for common, nationwide standards for education, health care, and social services, it recommended that "in areas of exclusive provincial jurisdiction, standards should be formally established through interprovincial agreement."[17]

Throughout the rebalancing discussions, Premier Klein has played a major public role and FIGA has played a major bureaucratic role in maintaining momentum for the initiative among provincial governments across the country.

Throughout, Alberta has advanced a consistent set of themes: although both orders of government may remain active in some fields, there should be less duplication; the constitutional division of powers should be respected; the governments with the jurisdictional authority should have the financial resources to do the job; and unilateral action, particularly by the federal government, must be avoided at all costs. The search is for harmonization arrived at through intergovernmental negotiation.

The rebalancing initiative fits within the international model developed at the outset of this chapter. In Premier Klein's vision, rebalancing means only that Ottawa respect the constitutional authority of the provinces in such fields as health care and social policy; his concern is with unilateral action by a federal government that does not respect the rules of the game. This, I would suggest, is a constant fear of small states such as Canada when dealing with superpowers such as the United States. Hence the desire to tie superpowers down through international agreements and the rules that follow in their wake; to constrain, for example, the US Congress through the obligations of GATT, the WTO, and NAFTA. The Alberta government seeks a federal system of rules and institutionalized consultation; it fears unilateral actions by a federal government within which it exercises little influence. Alberta looks upon Ottawa as Ottawa looks upon Congress, and responds in a similar way. In both cases, the best line of defence against unilateralism is effective intergovernmental relations.

The Klein government's push, in concert with Ontario, for greater provincial input into the determination of national standards for social programs fits neatly into the international model. National standards set by Ottawa and enforced by the spending power allow for unilateral federal action, including retaliatory action against provinces not abiding by Ottawa's interpretation of the standards. Hence the interest in having truly *national* standards — not *federal government* standards — set and policed through intergovernmental mechanisms. The federal government might still participate, but it would have to play by multilateral rules. It would be constrained in a way analogous to how NAFTA constrains the US Congress. What Klein resents more than anything else is the presumption that Parliament can and should police provincial governments operating within their own constitutional domain. As the premier stated just prior to the 1996 Annual Premiers' Conference, the provinces "are not criminals."[18] While in theory Klein rejects the need for *any* external review of provincial government performance, he is willing to accept intergovernmental mechanisms if these can screen the provinces from unilateral intervention by the federal government.

Premier Klein, therefore, has not abandoned Premier Getty's intergovernmentalism strategy; he has simply changed its focus from international and internal free trade negotiations to social policy.[19] In effect, he is broadening and deepening the existing strategy.[20] Throughout, however, the premier confronts a leadership dilemma that also bedeviled his predecessors. The problem is how to assert leadership without having initiatives dismissed as reflecting the idiosyncratic interests of one of Canada's wealthiest provinces. To avoid this stigmatization, Alberta premiers must "hide their light under a bushel," as Lougheed did in orchestrating the 1982 amending formulas. This in turn means that FIGA's role becomes even more important. Effective work behind the scenes, in the bureaucratic trench warfare of intergovernmental relations, is essential.

One of Klein's more interesting intergovernmental innovations is in the field of aboriginal affairs.[21] If there is a clear "growth area" in intergovernmental relations, it is in aboriginal affairs. The movement toward self-government implies a greater provincial institutional capacity for government-to-government relationships with Aboriginal Peoples. As aboriginal governments take on greater political legitimacy, jurisdictional control and bureaucratic muscle, the need for effective government-to-government relationships will become pressing. In this respect, FIGA's recent merger with Aboriginal Affairs[22] marks a significant development in the Canadian practice of intergovernmentalism. Of course, the merger is still in embryonic form, and there are conceptual problems yet to be worked through, along with their institutional consequences. Will aboriginal governments be treated in the same way as provincial governments? Will the same protocols be followed? The same files kept? Will intergovernmental relations with First Nations have the same routing within FIGA? How will FIGA orchestrate its relations with aboriginal organizations inside and outside the province?

Ralph Klein's approach to alliance-building has also been somewhat different from his predecessors, in part because the Quebec governments led by Jacques Parizeau and Lucien Bouchard (notwithstanding some difference between them as discussed by Réjean Pelletier in this volume) have withdrawn from intergovernmental relations to an unprecedented degree. The problem, therefore, has been to find an ally in the intergovernmental arena to replace Quebec. Ontario has been courted for this role, even though during the Lougheed and Getty administrations the Ontario governments appeared to be wedded to a relatively centralized model of federalism that Albertans found difficult to accept. Now, with evidence of ideological convergence between Alberta's Ralph Klein and Ontario's Mike Harris, and with Ontario's apparent embrace of a more decentralized federal state, the opportunities for alliance-building are reasonably good. The other potential ally is British Columbia. However, BC's potential is problematic given its quirky performance on the national stage. For reasons too complex to be explored here, BC has not carried the weight in national political life one would expect from Canada's third largest province. Its premiers, lacking the type of continuity and ballast that FIGA provides for Alberta premiers, have vacillated between disengagement from national political life, on the one hand, and erratic participation, on the other. (The recent Pacific salmon dispute is an illustration of the latter.) In recent times, the BC government has been preoccupied with a domestic political agenda that has little in common with Alberta's and therefore provides little foundation for alliance-building. The upside of this for Alberta is that BC's performance has created space for Alberta to exercise regional leadership; it has been easier for Alberta premiers to "speak for the west" when BC premiers have been disinclined or unable to do so. Peter Lougheed was particularly fortunate in not having to compete with a strong voice from BC when speaking for the west on the national stage. The downside is that BC is at best an unreliable intergovernmental ally. As a consequence, a strong western Canadian coalition has been difficult to forge, and thus Alberta's still tenuous alliance with the Harris Progressive Conservatives is all that more important.

There is one final detail to note about Klein's intergovernmental record, and that is the winding down of FIGA's international trade promotion activities. The European and American offices have been closed, and only the Asian offices kept open. These cuts coincide with the general budgetary restraint the provincial government has imposed, but balancing the budget was not the prime driver. Of greater significance has been the change in Ottawa's approach to international trade. The current Liberal government has made a concerted attempt to bring the provincial governments into play, an attempt symbolized by the Team Canada trade missions so heartily endorsed by Ralph Klein.[23] Thus there is less need for an independent provincial voice on the trade promotion front. As a senior FIGA official put it, "there is no need to stand up and be heard because we *are* being heard." However, while this may be the situation in trade promotion, Alberta still believes that more could be done regarding provincial involvement in trade policy and trade negotiations. Movement on these fronts remains a priority with Alberta.

It should also be mentioned, with respect to trade promotion, that the business environment has changed. It is no longer the case that Alberta businesses need government help in dealing with European and American markets; the value-added of FIGA's expertise has been reduced to the point where the international offices no longer have a useful role to play. Rather than having the premier speak for the interests of the Alberta business community abroad, as Lougheed did in lobbying Congress, organizations such as the Canadian Association of Petroleum Producers now conduct Alberta's "foreign policy." Only in Asia, where government-to-government relations still play an important role in the economy, is there a continuing rationale for such offices, although even here there has been increased integration with Canada's external representation.

The Klein government's approach to intergovernmental relations can be briefly summarized by noting its general correspondence with Alberta's policy in the past. There has been a consistent attempt to draw the federal government into multilateral arrangements, and to resist unilateral action by Ottawa. The premier's primary focus, like that of Mr. Lougheed, has been on intergovernmental relations rather than on institutional reform. As a consequence, FIGA continues to play an important role, and it has spearheaded Alberta's involvement in social policy reform. Although its international activities have been reduced, it has taken on the potentially vast responsibilities for intergovernmental relations with aboriginal governments. Finally, FIGA has maintained its constitutional poise, experience, and readiness should Alberta once again be thrust into national unity negotiations in the wake of the Calgary Declaration.

STAYING THE COURSE

The history of Alberta intergovernmental relations sketched in above has been marked by a great deal of continuity. To explain this continuity over the past 26 years, a number of factors need to be brought into play:

- there has been, not surprisingly, a basic continuity in the province's demography and economy. Despite widespread perceptions by Albertans of their province's steady growth, Alberta's share of the national population has not changed appreciably over the past 30 years.[24] And, although the Alberta economy was badly rocked in the early 1980s, economic performance generally remains above the national average.

- there has been no partisan change of government over this period, and only two changes in premier.

- there has been considerable continuity in Alberta's weaknesses within the country's governing party, and thus within the federal Cabinet. Reform's success in the 1997 federal election confirms the general pattern of chronic weakness on the government side of the House. However, the notable exception of the Mulroney years, when Alberta ministers Harvey Andre, Joe Clark and, most importantly, Don Mazankowski were leading figures in the federal Cabinet, shows that there is more to the Alberta story than simply weakness within the national government. When that weakness was replaced by disproportionate strength between 1984 and 1993, the by-then well-established patterns of intergovernmentalism were not significantly disrupted. Thus the strategy described in this chapter may now be more than a necessity: it may be seen as preferred and optimal.

- there has been a great deal of continuity in FIGA's personnel. Many of the key players have had decades of experience with FIGA, and thus with the broader intergovernmental system. Oryssia Lennie, for example, was in place by 1971, before the department even existed, and did not leave until the spring of 1997 when she resigned as FIGA's deputy minister to take up a position with the Office of Western Economic Diversification. FIGA's principal international trade expert, Helmut Mach, has been with the department since 1973; Garry Pocock, who heads the Canadian federalism team, has been with FIGA for close to 20 years, and Francie Harle, a central player in the reform of social policy, has extensive experience. Note should also be made of long-serving ministers, particularly Jim Horsman.

- the consistent intergovernmental relations strategy is based on a well-articulated understanding of Canadian federal institutions. In part, this intellectual coherence was the product of Dr. Peter Meekison's long tenure as deputy minister, although it is clearly manifest throughout the department.

It is important, however, not to overstate the consistency, for there have been some important tensions. If we look back at the evolution of Alberta's intergovernmental strategy, two apparent incongruities must be addressed. The first arises from the province's renowned enthusiasm for Senate reform,[25] and the second from its populist tradition. At first glance, both would appear to be inconsistent with a heavy emphasis on intergovernmentalism.

It has long been recognized in the province that intergovernmentalism, as expressed through First Ministers' Conferences and the like, fails to address a critical issue of institutional design, and that is the provision of adequate regional representation *within* the councils of the federal government. No matter how elaborate the mechanisms of intergovernmental consultation and negotiation, or how extensive the devolution of powers, there is still a need for effective regional representation within the national government. If this need is not met, then the federal government will be captured by those regional interests — read central Canadian interests — that are represented within its ranks. The Alberta government's first and still preferred solution to this problem was an intergovernmental solution. In 1982 Alberta first advanced a proposal to replace the Senate with a House of the Provinces in which the provincial governments, through their appointed senators, would be brought into the federal Parliament.[26] Thus the House of Commons and the federal Cabinet would be constrained by provincial government representatives *in Parliament*. The House of the Provinces, therefore, would complement other forms of intergovernmentalism. It would expand, rather than challenge, intergovernmentalism as a model of governance for the Canadian federal state.

Initially, then, there was no conflict between the province's intergovernmental strategy and the pursuit of Senate reform; they were two sides of the same coin. However, the House of the Provinces model failed to attract public support, and in 1983 a legislative committee chaired by MLA David Anderson held public hearings across the province to determine what type of Senate reform Albertans would support. The committee returned with clear and unequivocal public support for an *elected* Senate. The premier at the time, Peter Lougheed, was aware that an elected Senate could be a powerful competitor to provincial governments, and that elected senators would diminish the political authority and influence of provincial premiers as regional spokespersons. More broadly, and as the American experience suggests, an elected Senate would weaken intergovernmentalism by strengthening the capacity of the federal parliament to reflect regional interests and diversity. However, these concerns were difficult to inject into the public debate, and Lougheed was left with no option but to sign on as a reluctant supporter of a Triple E Senate — elected, equal, and effective. The premier had been blind-sided by his electorate, and by a public debate beyond his control mobilized by non-governmental actors such as the Canada West Foundation and the Committee for a Triple E Senate, and then later and with much greater force by the Reform Party of Canada.

The real anomaly with respect to Senate reform was not Lougheed's House of the Provinces, which would have strengthened intergovernmentalism as a mode of government, but rather Don Getty's enthusiasm for a Triple E Senate. Whether he was oblivious to the likely impact of a Triple E Senate on Alberta's intergovernmental strategy, or whether he simply did not care, whether he believed in a larger constitutional and national unity good that might be promoted through Senate reform, is still unclear. It should also be noted, however, that by the time he became premier, public opinion within the province was solidly behind the Triple E model, and it is unlikely that Getty had any alternative but to join the parade he then led through intergovernmental negotiations. Even the formidable Peter Lougheed had been unable to control or direct the Senate reform debate. The more general point is that the Alberta government is no longer a hegemonic player with respect to constitutional politics in the province. Albertans rejected its proposal for a House of the Provinces, would have rejected the Meech Lake Accord had they been able to get their hands on it, and then voted against the Charlottetown Accord despite Getty's (admittedly lukewarm) support. When the Alberta government takes its intergovernmental strategy out in public, it routinely encounters a very rough reception indeed.

The second incongruity arises from Alberta's populist tradition. Intergovernmentalism as a model of governance stands at the polar extreme from populism. By its very nature, intergovernmentalism takes place away from the public eye. It is everything the public came to despise about the process that gave birth to the Meech Lake Accord: secretive, carried out by men (and an increasing number of women) in suits, and averse to public ratification. How, then, do we explain the Alberta government's commitment to a style of governance so at odds with populist traditions? Part of the answer comes from realizing that the populism generally practised in the province has been a form of *executive populism* that is not mediated through legislative assemblies[27] or, for that matter, through political parties. Premiers have eschewed the populism of direct democracy for a personal relationship with the electorate that does not require verification through legislative debate or referendums. This style of populism, where premiers speak for the province in intergovernmental forums, is quite compatible with intergovernmentalism as a style of governance and as the primary means by which Alberta's presence is asserted on the national stage. It was perfected by Lougheed, although adopted with less comfort by Getty and much less comfort by Klein.

Yet this is only part of the answer, and the tension between populism and intergovernmentalism remains. To this point, however, it is the Reform Party that has effectively mobilized more conventional populist sentiment, leaving the provincial government and its premier free to follow executive populism that by-passes the legislature and relies on public consultation through government-appointed boards and tasks forces. (In the fall of 1997, for example, the provincial government hosted a hand-picked economic summit as an alternative to a fall session of the legislature.) Where executive populism and Reform's more conventional populism are likely to collide is in any public debate within the province on constitutional reform. Premier Klein's intergovernmental hands may be tied with respect to constitutional politics by his determination not to discuss the constitution behind closed doors, and by his insistence on public ratification of any constitutional deal that might be struck. As he stated at the Edmonton Premier's Dinner on 8 May 1997, there will be no backroom deals, no closed-door negotiations and, most importantly, "no constitutional changes will occur unless approved by Albertans in a referendum." Thus on the constitutional front Klein is prepared to accommodate the populist impulse of the province, although his active participation in the process leading up to the Calgary Declaration shows he is not stridently opposed to the more conventional aspects of intergovernmentalism.

FUTURE CHALLENGES

The short-term future of FIGA and the province's intergovernmental strategy have been laid out in FIGA's most recent business plan, tabled during the spring 1997 session of the legislature.[28] The *Business Plan* identifies a number of goals that flow naturally from Alberta's experience over the past 26 years:

- a restructured federal system that "more clearly defines the roles of federal and provincial governments, reduces intergovernmental overlap and duplication, and provides greater clarification of responsibility and accountability;"

- effective strategies for strengthening national unity, and asserting "Alberta's long-term interests as an equal partner in Confederation;"

- an open domestic and world trading system;

- an active, targeted international role for Alberta;

- enhanced aboriginal participation in government processes and the economy; and

- helping Métis settlements become self-reliant communities.

Former premiers Peter Lougheed and Don Getty would have been perfectly happy with these goals.[29] Beyond this agenda, however, there are also a number of other issues on the intergovernmental horizon:

- the integration of aboriginal governments into the routine structures and operations of intergovernmental relations;

- the development of outcome indicators that can effectively assess intergovernmental performance. This is not an easy thing to do. How does one assess to what extent Alberta, as one of 13 Canadian governments, shaped the Tokyo round of GATT negotiations? Was the defeat of the Charlottetown referendum in Alberta a black mark against FIGA, or was it ultimately a good thing? Is FIGA accountable for the state of national unity? How does one measure the informal leadership FIGA personnel might provide in intergovernmental councils?[30] How do you measure performance when the objective is to stop something from happening?

- keeping the rebalancing initiative alive now that the federal government is no longer under such intense financial pressure and has money in its pocket;

- avoiding intergovernmental polarization between the have and have-not provinces, and thus avoiding Alberta's potential isolation in the intergovernmental community; and

- bringing Quebec back into the intergovernmental fold and, if not, preventing the evolution of intergovernmental mechanisms exclusive of Quebec from providing the *de facto* foundation for a Quebec-less Canada and an independent Quebec.

Most of these challenges illustrate Alberta's continuing exposure to developments on the national scene. As we would expect, Alberta is shaped by more than it shapes the national scene. However, this is not to suggest that the rest of the country has little to learn from the Alberta experience.

GENERALIZING FROM THE ALBERTA CASE

Any discussion of the future of intergovernmental relations in Alberta takes on additional weight if the argument can be made that Alberta foreshadows the future of intergovernmental relations in the country at large. Traditionally, however, it has been difficult to make the argument that the Alberta experience is useful in interpreting the broader Canadian experience. Alberta, it is asserted, is too idiosyncratic; the province is too rich, too conservative (and Conservative), too right-wing, too Reform, or just too weird. It is suggested, therefore, that if one wants to understand the national experience, it is better to start with a more typical province.[31]

In this case, however, the Alberta experience does capture some of the flavour of the more general Canadian experience with intergovernmental relations. In addition, there is little that is idiosyncratic about the challenges looming on Alberta's intergovernmental horizon. Most provinces, for example, will have to find some way to fold aboriginal governments into the patterns and conventions of intergovernmental relations. Performance indicators will not be unique to the Alberta case, nor will Quebec's ongoing challenge to intergovernmental structures and agreements. The challenges Alberta and FIGA are wrestling with are national in scope and implication.

Where the Alberta case is idiosyncratic is in its political environment, although even here Alberta shares some similarities with other provinces. In bringing this discussion to a close, therefore, it is important to mention two major environmental changes that have occurred. In the past, and particularly during the tenure of Peter Lougheed, the Alberta government's ability to speak for the west in national politics was facilitated by British Columbia's erratic and/or subdued intergovernmental performance. Alberta's star shone so bright in part because British Columbia's star shone so dim; BC premiers never achieved the national stature enjoyed, for instance, by Lougheed. However, it appears that the current government of British Columbia is determined to be a more assertive player, if not necessarily a more constructive player, on the national political stage. Certainly it is difficult to look at the recent salmon dispute and come to any other conclusion. The challenge for Alberta will be to yoke a more engaged and assertive British Columbia to its own federal vision and provincial interests.

Second, Alberta's intergovernmental strategy was developed during a time when there was no strong federal partisan voice for the west. In terms of federal parties, the west spoke with a fractured and/or ineffective voice. The federal Liberals were relatively weak across the region, although more so in Alberta than elsewhere; the New Democrats had a relatively weak Ottawa presence; and the Progressive Conservatives were on the opposition side of the House for a good deal of the time. Thus premiers in the west, and Alberta premiers in particular, did not have to compete with strong federal partisan voices from the region. This has changed with the arrival of Reform, and with the almost hegemonic presence of Reform MPs in Alberta and British Columbia following the 1997 general election. Thus premiers will have to compete with Preston Manning in speaking for the west, and Manning has demonstrated great ability in mobilizing regional opinion. Admittedly, Peter Lougheed had to compete with Joe Clark from 1976 to 1983. However, Clark led a more broadly based national party than does Manning, and was therefore more constrained as a regional voice. If Reform is able to establish a bridgehead in Ontario, Manning may also be constrained. Indeed, even the attempt to establish a bridgehead may soften Reform's regional voice, and thereby give more room for Ralph Klein. Nonetheless, a strategy that relies so exclusively on intergovernmental relations may make less sense at a time when Reform has such a powerful regional presence in the House of Commons.

Finally, it should be stressed that the dilemma Klein faces in reconciling a populist political culture with intergovernmentalism is not his dilemma alone. Since the engagement of the Canadian electorate in the 1992 referendum on the Charlottetown Accord, it has become increasingly difficult to exclude the general public from intergovernmental affairs. At the very least, this is the case in the constitutional arena, and the effects of public participation in constitutional decisionmaking could well ripple throughout the political system more broadly defined. In the extreme, one could argue that there is a growing gulf between the intergovernmentalism preferred by political elites and the populist impulse of the mass public. What makes this gulf even more problematic is that powerful partisan actors, most notably Reform but also the Parti Québécois and the Bloc, will act as watchful policemen to ensure that the public is in fact involved. Therefore Premier Klein's balancing act in the years to come between intergovernmentalism and populism may have important lessons for the country at large.

NOTES

I would like to thank Wayne Clifford, Francie Harle, Oryssia Lennie, Helmut Mach, Jim Ogilvy, Garry Pocock and Paul Whittaker for sharing their insights into the evolution of intergovernmental relations in Alberta. Of course, they should not be held responsible, either singly or collectively, for the conclusions of this paper, the assessment of FIGA, or any errors or omissions. I would also like to thank Nancy MacDonald Lizotte for her assistance and guidance.

1.   This modeling exercise comes from an observer of domestic politics and should be taken with a large grain of salt by students of Canadian-American relations. The objective of the present exercise is to shed light on Canadian intergovernmental relations, and not on the Canadian-American relationship.

2.   In practice the mouse may try to cozy up to the elephant in all sorts of ways, including by playing golf. Canada's avoidance of bilateralism has often been

3.   coupled, although not comfortably, with the claim to a special relationship with the United States.

3.   FIGA was not the only department of intergovernmental relations to be established during this time, and indeed was patterned after an earlier Quebec initiative. However, in no other case was such a department so central to its province's political strategy on the national scene.

4.   The three prairie provinces had met before as the Prairie Economic Conference. WEOC marked BC's first participation, and paved the way to the annual Western Premiers' Conference.

5.   Department of Federal and Intergovernmental Affairs, *First Report*, 13 January 1975, p. 19.

6.   When Ralph Klein became premier, he also acted as FIGA's minister, thereby reinforcing FIGA's established institutional position at the heart of the provincial government.

7.   13 May 1976. Cited in FIGA's Fourth Annual Report, 31 March 1977, pp. 1-2.

8.   As it turned out, this is not quite true; federal legislation in 1995 which "lent" Parliament's veto to each of the five regions in effect altered the amending formula.

9.   Small operations predated the Lougheed years, but took on a much greater role during those years. Alberta first appointed an Agent General in London in 1925, although the position was then left vacant from 1931 to 1948. A Tokyo office was opened in 1970.

10.   Alberta Federal and Intergovernmental Affairs, *Alberta's International Offices: Report to the Alberta Legislature*, Edmonton, April 1991, Appendix V.

11.   Ibid., p. 2.

12.   Ibid., p. 13.

13.   This hope is picked up as a consistent theme in FIGA's annual reports. Note, for example, the third report: "The recent pattern of federal-provincial relations suggests that the provinces have had a more significant role in shaping national policy decisions than in previous eras. As the provinces have gained experience and confidence in negotiating they have been more successful in contributing to final decisions rather than simply reacting to federal initiatives." September 1977; p. 27.

14.   Alberta Select Special Committee on Constitutional Reform, *Alberta in a New Canada: Visions of Unity* (Edmonton, March 1992), p. 13.

15.   An address by the Honourable Ralph Klein to the National Chapter of Dialogue Canada, Ottawa, 26 September 1996.

16.   *Alberta in a New Canada*, p. 20.

17.   Ibid.

18.   Robert Mason Lee, "The Plan to Replace Momma Ottawa with Executive Provincialism," *The Globe and Mail,* 24 August 1996, p. D2.

19. Klein, however, has abandoned Getty's enthusiastic interest in Senate reform. The 14 September Calgary Declaration so strongly endorsed by the Alberta premier is silent with respect to institutional reform.

20. The National Child Benefit initiative, described by Lazar in this volume, neatly captures Alberta's approach to social policy reform. Ottawa is to provide more money for income support, but social services support programs will be under provincial control, with national standards set by intergovernmental agreement.

21. Although Premier Klein's personal interest and involvement in aboriginal affairs is a departure, it should be noted that Don Getty chose to become directly involved in the Lubicon dispute.

22. This merger has been described as the guppy swallowing the whale, given the much larger budget of Aboriginal Affairs. However, FIGA's staff resources were larger. Shortly after Alberta's lead, Saskatchewan and New Brunswick announced that they, too, would be moving in the same direction.

23. The communiqué issued at the conclusion of the 1995 Western Premiers' Conference in Yorktown, Saskatchewan, notes that the Team Canada concept "originated with British Columbia and was brought to the First Ministers' table by the Western Premiers," 2 November 1995, p. 3.

24. Alberta's share of the national population has increased from 7.5 percent in 1971 to 9.3 percent in 1996.

25. For the best statement on Alberta's Senate reform position, see *Alberta in a New Canada: Visions of Unity*.

26. Government of Alberta, *Harmony in Diversity: A Reformed Senate of Canada* (Edmonton: Government of Alberta, 1982).

27. The provincial treasurer has just announced that the Alberta legislature will meet only once a year.

28. Federal and Intergovernmental Affairs, *Business Plan 1997-1998 to 1999-2000*, tabled in the Legislative Assembly, 21 April 1997.

29. A similar set of goals is identified in FIGA's Twenty-Third Annual Report, tabled 31 March 1996.

30. To this point, FIGA has relied on a five-point client satisfaction rating as its primary performance indicator.

31. This could not be an Atlantic province (which would be too small and too poor), Quebec (which, after all, is distinct, or at least unique), Manitoba or Saskatchewan (which are too rural) or British Columbia (which is too weird). The appropriate national template must therefore be found in one of the other provinces.

10

Ontario and the Federation at the End of the Twentieth Century

Sid Noel

Cet article analyse le rôle changeant de l'Ontario dans la Confédération. Il porte une attention particulière aux effets de la volatilité électorale de la province depuis 1985 et aux pressions externes auxquelles la province a de plus en plus été sujettes, notamment les tendances vers la globalisation de la production et des marchés et le choc du référendum québécois de 1995. Il trace les changements et les continuités du rôle de l'Ontario dans la fédération sous le gouvernement de Harris, avec une attention particulière aux questions fiscales et constitutionnelles. L'article argumente que l'Ontario va probablement continuer à cultiver des liens économiques et politiques plus étroits avec les états américains voisins dans la région des Grands Lacs, mais que la nature et la proximité de ces liens, et que la place future de l'Ontario dans la Confédération, dépendront probablement de façon significative sur si le Québec demeure partie du Canada.

> For five generations Ontario has always been seen as the big guy at the end of the bar who would pick up the tab at the end of the night. Those days are gone.
>
> *Bob Rae, 1994[1]*

INTRODUCTION

Ontario's role in Confederation is commonly held to be a function of its disproportionately large population and economic strength. With approximately 11 million people, it is home to more than 37 percent of the Canadian population, which makes it more than 50 percent larger than Quebec, the province with the second-largest population; it produces more than 40 percent of Canada's gross domestic product; and it is the country's dominant financial, communications, and manufacturing centre. Politically, it occupies a large and sometimes seemingly commanding position in the national government — as at present, when, as a result of the 1997 federal election, 101 of the 155 seats held by the governing Liberal party are in Ontario.

Facts of this kind, however, while useful as background, by themselves explain very little. Ontario's relations with the federal government, for example, have never varied significantly according to the number of Ontario representatives in the federal governing party. Nor have its relations with the other provinces ever been simply a matter of demographic or economic *force majeure*.[2] Rather, both sets of relations have typically been complex and multi-faceted, shaped by institutions and experience, by transformative events such as the energy crises of the 1970s, the constitutional changes of 1982 and the Quebec referendum of 1995, by trade-offs and exigencies that often run counter to the seemingly intractable facts of demography and economics — and even, at times, by the party in power.

INTERNAL TENSIONS AND EXTERNAL PRESSURES

What I wish to show in this chapter is that Ontario's federal-provincial and interprovincial relations at the end of the twentieth century are being radically refashioned, primarily through a conjunction of internal political and cultural tensions and external threats and pressures. The internal tensions arise from the growing dissonance between two of Ontario's most deep-seated values, both of which have roots that go back far in the province's history and remain firmly imbedded in its political culture. The first of these values is the strong, patriotic attachment of the Ontario people to the Canadian nation. The second is their widely shared consensus on the primacy of economic goals, for themselves as individuals and for their communities — in other words, their "imperative pursuit of economic success."[3] The external pressures arise from the threat of national disintegration, which the Quebec referendum shock of 1995 raised to an unprecedented level; from the southward pull of the United States, which has grown steadily more powerful and pervasive — economically, culturally, and politically — since the Canada-US Free Trade Agreement of 1988; and more generally from trends toward the globalization of production and markets.

During most of the past century, Ontario's attachment to Canada and its economic aspirations have generally been compatible, or at least not obviously in conflict. The only extended period of constitutional and political conflict between Ontario and the federal government occurred in the 1870s and 1880s, over the province's disputed claims to civil jurisdiction and territory.[4] By 1890, however, those disputes had been resolved in Ontario's favour, thus giving successive Ontario governments of whatever party little reason to be dissatisfied with the basic structure or operation of the federal system. As a result, there evolved a distinctive Ontario approach to Confederation that may be characterized as supportive and conciliatory — but also more than a little proprietorial and backed by a strong presumption of leadership (typically exemplified by the Ontario premier) in the promotion of national unity.

There were, of course, exceptions to this general pattern. Disputes between the Ontario and federal governments over fiscal and social policy issues were not uncommon. For example, in the late 1930s there was a fierce confrontation between the Hepburn government and Ottawa over the funding of "relief" (welfare) expenditures, the division of tax powers, and virtually every other aspect of what were then called "Dominion-Provincial" relations.[5] Three decades later the Robarts government engaged Ottawa in a war of words over the financing of medicare.[6]

In more recent times, there were two major rifts that had wide political ramifications for the federation. The first rift came in the 1970s and early 1980s and was more interprovincial than federal-provincial: when the Davis government supported the federal government against the Alberta government on the federal National Energy Policy.[7] The second, and more politically divisive within Ontario, was the brief but acrimonious skirmish between Ontario and the federal government (and to a certain extent between Ontario and most of the other provinces) over Canada-US free trade in 1988, which the Peterson government vociferously opposed.[8]

In the following years, however, a looming constitutional crisis increasingly overshadowed all other issues. Though lingering disputes over economic, fiscal, and social policies remained, they had little or no effect on Ontario's constitutional stance, which remained constant even through changes of government and under premiers of different political stripe: Liberal David Peterson played a constructive and highly conciliatory role in efforts to rescue the doomed Meech Lake Accord in 1990 and his successor, New Democrat Bob Rae, played a similar role in support of the equally doomed Charlottetown Accord in 1992.

In retrospect, the failure of those two major constitutional initiatives may be seen as marking a turning point in Ontario's relations with the federation. Successive Ontario premiers had played leading national roles in support of measures that they believed were not only or even primarily in Ontario's interest, but in the general interest of Canada. While their aim, above all, was to accommodate Quebec and secure its formal assent to the 1982 *Constitution Act*, in the negotiations leading to the Charlottetown Accord, Premier Rae had also played a key role in securing the adoption of additional clauses designed to recognize the claims of native peoples and strengthen the economic and social bonds of Canadian union. Both Peterson and Rae had shown a degree of personal commitment to the respective accords that was matched by few other premiers or even members of the federal Cabinet; both had campaigned passionately across the country and in the full glare of the national media, even as opposition mounted; and both had spent freely of their own and Ontario's political capital in the process.[9] But in the end their efforts had proved futile and perhaps even counter-productive, since the intervention of Ontario premiers is not unknown to cause resentment in other provinces. In a final irony, both Meech Lake and Charlottetown, which were supposed to promote national unity, proved hugely divisive even within Ontario. Their eventual defeat, moreover, had dire consequences. In effect, after the failure of the Meech Lake Accord to secure ratification, and the rejection of the Charlottetown Accord in a national referendum (in spite of being approved in Ontario by the narrowest of margins), Ontario's approach to Confederation lay in ruins.

The Rae government had no alternative to offer. Exhausted and financially beleaguered, its only recourse on the intergovernmental front was to engage the federal government in a series of acrimonious fiscal disputes, centring mainly on the costs to the Ontario treasury of federal cuts to transfer payments to the province in the areas of health, education, and social welfare.[10] In 1995 — like the Peterson government in 1990 — it suffered a crushing electoral defeat.[11]

ENTER THE COMMON SENSE REVOLUTIONARIES

The new government of Mike Harris that swept into power at Queen's Park in June 1995, winning 82 of 130 seats, represented a new force in Ontario politics. While nominally Progressive Conservative, it bore little resemblance to the moderate, centrist, pragmatic PC dynasty that had governed Ontario from 1943 to 1985.[12] After 1990, under Harris's leadership, the PCs had been recast as a party of the conservative right — a party whose ethos and policy prescriptions more closely resembled those of state Republican parties in Michigan and New Jersey, the Klein government in Alberta, and the federal Reform Party of Preston Manning, whose mixture of anti-government rhetoric and populist sentiments it faithfully echoed. In the 1995 election campaign, it all but dropped the word "Progressive" from its label (in favour of "Conservative" or "the Harris party"). It also assigned great prominence to its manifesto, a document titled *The Common Sense Revolution*, which outlined in bold relief an agenda of radical right-wing reform for Ontario.

During its first two years in office, the Harris government pushed ahead with its agenda with revolutionary zeal — repealing the previous NDP government's labour and social legislation, cutting taxes, drastically reducing the size of the public service, and fundamentally restructuring the whole system of public administration and finance of the province, from welfare to heath to education to local government.

These initiatives were all domestic. *The Common Sense Revolution* had included no mention of federal-provincial relations or the constitution, and from the start the Harris government seemed determined to give such matters the lowest possible priority. Unlike Bob Rae, who had combined the post of minister of intergovernmental affairs with the premiership, Mike Harris, in forming his Cabinet, combined it with the women's issues portfolio (another area not held in notably high regard by Conservatives) and awarded it to Dianne Cunningham, a London MPP and former PC education critic. She was also one of the few unrepentant progressive conservatives left in the party after 1990, when she had run against Harris for the party leadership.[13] The outlook for her ministry did not seem auspicious. But on the few occasions when intergovernmental issues did arise, Cunningham proved to be a steady back-up performer to Harris (playing *pianissimo*, as it were, to the premier's *basso profundo*), and events were unfolding that would soon improve her ministry's prospects.

The politics of the federation have a way of intruding upon domestic agendas — as the Harris government discovered in October 1995, barely four months after taking office. This time the intrusion came with a jolt, rudely delivered by the Quebec sovereignists. The Quebec referendum had for the most part been viewed complacently in Ontario, at least until the very end, when it appeared that the unthinkable might happen and the sovereignist side might actually win. As it turned out, the federalist side won by a mere 54,288 votes out of more than 4,757,509 cast and with the support of only 40 percent of francophones — a shocking reminder of the country's parlous state of near-disintegration. The national unity issue was again unavoidably a matter of urgent concern, and however unwelcome the prospect, over the next two years the Harris government was forced to grapple with it. What gradually emerged from the Premier's Office and the Ministry of Intergovernmental Affairs — after some initial floundering — was a reappraisal of Ontario's core interests and the outline of a radical new approach to Confederation.

THE PREMIER SPEAKS

Every Ontario premier is expected to play a prominent role in constitutional and intergovernmental affairs, as perhaps befits the sense Ontarians have of their province's preeminence in the federation and the large economic and emotional stake that they have traditionally invested in its continuing viability. But the cruel reality is that these areas have become a source of intractable contestation within Ontario, and for successive premiers they have led only to political failure and frustration. Unlike Oliver Mowat — who in 1884 had basked in public adulation following his constitutional victories over the federal government, being feted from town to town and paraded like a conquering hero through the streets of Toronto[14] — no modern premier, except perhaps John Robarts, has made any political gain from involvement in intergovernmental affairs, and most have suffered losses. For David Peterson and Bob Rae, the losses were politically devastating.

Mike Harris thus had good reason to avoid becoming too deeply involved in intergovernmental affairs, especially those involving constitutional issues; but, as Ontario's premier, he could not avoid them completely or for very long. His first intervention, on 10 June 1995, just two days after the election, was brief but revealing: the way to make Confederation work, he said, was to demonstrate that "we can make changes in federal-provincial powers and jurisdictions ... I think this will go a long way to convincing Quebecers that Canada can work as a country." On fiscal matters, he expressed no objection to the federal cuts in transfer payments that had so antagonized Bob Rae. He himself had run on a platform of deficit reduction, and he professed only sympathy with the federal government's deficit reduction efforts. But, he pointedly added, in the fields of health care and social programs "I think it will be incumbent upon the premiers to take a leadership role in setting national standards ... They [the federal government] don't have the dollars any more, so they're saying to us, 'Look, we want out of a number of these areas'."[15]

These statements accurately signalled the key elements in the Harris government's future approach to intergovernmental relations: its preference for reforming Confederation through non-constitutional means, its insistence on the need for a rejigging of program responsibilities and for greater flexibility in federal-provincial financial arrangements, and its expectation of a *quid pro quo* from the federal government in return for Ontario's assuming an increased share of the costs of social programs. This approach was more fully elaborated during the following months.

In August, shortly before attending his first premiers' conference, Harris stated "I think that it is very clear that the status quo is not acceptable to Ontarians ... we're prepared to look at changes in the way the federal government and the provinces operate." At the conference, he was more specific: in his view Ottawa had "disqualified itself" from having a major role in overseeing social programs. "We believe, he stated, "that if the federal government withdraws more and more dollars from social programs and from health care ... we require increased flexibility as to how those dollars are spent and how we meet objectives."[16] The conference ended with the premiers divided over the future federal role along predictable "have" and "have not" lines.

In October, shortly before the Quebec referendum, Harris made his first direct foray into the national unity debate, in a speech delivered before the Canadian Club of Toronto. He avoided long-standing and contentious constitutional issues, such as the recognition of Quebec as a "distinct society." Instead, he delivered what was obviously intended as a "common sense" warning to Quebecers. If they voted yes, he said, they would be voting to deprive themselves of "the Canadian advantage," for, "if Quebec separates, there would be international borders between Ontario and Quebec. And borders do matter." From Ontario's point of view, he added, the sovereignist "partnership" proposal (referred to as an "agreement" in the referendum question) was simply a "non-starter." Then, warming to his favourite theme, he proposed as an alternative to separation "a more functional federation, that streamlines governments, that eliminates waste and duplication of services. This kind of change will be supported by Ontario. Change that gives better value to the taxpayer."[17]

"I have to get a grip on my natural tendency to laugh at that," Jacques Parizeau derisively responded.[18] But on referendum night, after the votes were counted, it was a very different "natural tendency" that the Quebec premier displayed. "Money and the ethnic vote," he famously alleged, were responsible for the yes side's narrow loss. Soon thereafter he resigned and was replaced by his ally and nemesis, Lucien Bouchard.

THE REFERENDUM SHOCK AND ONTARIO'S RESPONSE

Prior to the referendum, the Harris government's relations with the federal government had been generally low-key and amicable, if not entirely harmonious. The open hostilities that had existed during the latter part of the Rae government's tenure, for example, were conspicuously absent. As Ottawa wished that all premiers would do, Harris had largely stayed out of the national unity debate, apart from his Canadian Club address, but in it he had said nothing that could not equally have been said by Jean Chrétien. And on a range of practical issues, Intergovernmental Affairs Minister Dianne Cunningham and Finance Minister Ernie Eves had been quietly building better relations with their federal counterparts. Eves, for example, had been receptive to the idea of a blended consumption tax to replace the GST (which, among other benefits, would relieve the federal Liberals of one of their more awkward election promises).

In the aftermath of the referendum, however, Ontario-Ottawa relations quickly soured. Late in the referendum campaign, with a yes vote seeming more likely with each poll, Prime Minister Chrétien had suddenly promised to support the constitutional recognition of Quebec as a "distinct society" if Quebecers voted no — a promise that was empty without Ontario's cooperation, since, under the amending formula, the approval of seven provinces containing 50 percent of the population was required.[19] Harris, however, resolutely resisted being drawn into the "distinct society" camp, no doubt in part because of the unfortunate examples of Peterson and Rae, but more immediately, and probably more importantly, because of the informal alliance that existed between his provincial PC party and Preston Manning's Reform party. "Unless you have that coalition, you don't get elected," Harris once candidly explained.[20] Reform had surged in popular support in the west, and to a lesser but still substantial degree in Ontario, in part by channelling popular opposition to the constitutional recognition of Quebec's distinctiveness, and there had been considerable clamour by Ontario Reformers to contest the 1995 Ontario election. But Manning had vetoed the project, and without their own party's candidates in the field, which would have split the right-wing vote, Ontario Reformers had swung massively behind Harris and were an important factor in his victory.

Following the referendum, therefore, Harris found himself classically cross-pressured between the Reform component in his Conservative coalition and the Liberal federal government. Not surprisingly, he refused to support the latter's proposed distinct society amendment. Had he done so, he would have split his party and, in any case, it was probably not his inclination. Prime Minister Chrétien and his government were thus placed in an embarrassing position, albeit one that was primarily of their own making, and ended up lamely substituting a parliamentary resolution for the promised amendment.[21]

Inevitably, the Quebec referendum raised serious doubts about the way Chrétien and his advisers had handled the national unity issue. Their overconfidence and miscalculations, Preston Manning rather too gleefully reminded them, had led to a "near death experience." The Harris government appeared to agree. After the referendum, it became noticeably less accommodating in its dealings with Ottawa,[22] more open to overtures from Quebec, and more concerned to redefine and ensure the security of Ontario's core interests.

ONTARIO AFTER NAFTA

Paradoxically, any reappraisal of Ontario's position in Canada has to begin with its relationship with the United States. Ontario has always possessed a locational advantage that allowed it to develop important and lucrative economic ties with the US, as exemplified in the twentieth century by integrated auto production under the Canada-US Auto Pact. At the same time, Canadian tariff protection helped to establish Ontario's place as the dominant supplier of manufactured goods to the Canadian market. Hence, it was commonly held, Ontario enjoyed the best of both worlds, which accounted in large measure for its enduring prosperity, political stability, and untroubled identification with the Canadian nation. By extension, it could afford to be the largest net contributor to the federal treasury, since the bulk of federal equalization payments and other transfers to the poorer provinces eventually recirculated back to Ontario through the purchase of Ontario-made goods. In other words,

Ontario's political and economic interests were assumed to be practically synonymous.

By the mid-1980s, however, this assumption had become more than a little suspect. The Ontario economy had drifted far toward economic integration with the US, trade was becoming globalized, and the bonds of Canadian unity had become frayed and tenuous. Ontario's opposition to the Canada-US Free Trade Agreement of 1988 is not easily explained in purely economic terms.[23] The business community was strongly in favour of the FTA, and while free trade was expected to cause serious problems in some industries, the Ontario economy as a whole was well-positioned to reap major benefits, as eventually it did. Ontario's opposition, then, may be seen as primarily a matter of culture and identity — an unwillingness to see Canada become more like the US in social and political values, or to dissolve the east-west economic bonds that still symbolized for Ontarians the ideal of a transcontinental Canadian state.

Nevertheless, by 1995, after a turbulent decade of political and economic upheaval, the direction of Ontario's future trading pattern had been settled. Under NAFTA it had become overwhelmingly north-south.[24] And without a Canadian tariff wall, there was no longer any assurance that federal transfers to the poorer provinces would eventually flow back to Ontario. Though a substantial portion continued to do so, they might now as easily flow to the United States, or for that matter, as global trade increased, to Europe or Asia. The result was a decoupling of Ontario's economic and political interests — a decoupling accentuated by growing regional tensions, fiscal pressures, the resurgence of Quebec separatism after the defeat of Meech Lake, and finally, the cliffhanger Quebec referendum.

The electoral realignment that brought the Harris government to power in 1995 is in certain key respects, a political reflection and counterpart of the economic realignment that had taken place in Ontario during the previous decade. The Harris government, in striking contrast to its predecessors, not only accepts free trade but positively welcomes its effects. Those effects it sees mainly as opportunities — but only if Ontario radically changes its social and political institutions in order to become more competitive. Hence, the consistent thrust of the Harris government's domestic "restructuring" agenda is to bring Ontario into line with "post-NAFTA realities," and in particular with the taxation and social welfare regimes of its American neighbours (and competitors) in states such as Michigan and Pennsylvania. This approach is clearly signalled in the PC election platform, *The Common Sense Revolution*: "We do know that many employers looked at Ontario as a prospective location for expansion or new investment, compared us to other provinces and U.S. states, and then gave us a pass. It doesn't have to be like this."[25]

The Harris government, moreover, is generally inclined toward an American neoconservative outlook that draws its intellectual inspiration, and its vocabulary, mainly from American models. Implicit in this view is the notion that Ontario would be a better and more productive place if Ontarians would only become more individualistic and less reliant upon government — in other words, if their post-NAFTA culture matched their post-NAFTA economic environment. It therefore tends automatically to clamp a neoconservative, anti-government, market-based framework upon questions of public policy and to reject, or be uncomprehending of, other approaches. This considerably simplifies governing, since it means that in practice government should always do less and taxes should always be lower. But it also means that its approach to questions of the constitution and national unity, which unavoidably involve complex issues of culture and identity, tends to be narrowly conceived.

ONTARIO AND QUEBEC

In the year after the Quebec referendum, the Harris government's domestic agenda found an unexpected echo in Quebec. During the referendum campaign, Harris's cuts to the public sector had been repeatedly the target of separatist attacks — held up by Lucien Bouchard, for example, as a warning to Quebecers of what they might expect if they remained in Canada.[26] As premier, however, Bouchard (who has been known to change his mind on occasion) emerged as a champion of public sector downsizing for Quebec and of the need for more competitiveness — thus apparently placing himself on side with his formerly reviled Ontario counterpart. That, at any rate, was the way the story was spun in the Toronto media, which tended to ignore some salient differences, such as the fact that Bouchard's plan included no large tax cuts and that he had little choice, given what other province's had already done to reduce their deficits.

Harris, meanwhile, had been endeavouring to limit damage to Ontario economy from the referendum result by downplaying, or even denying, its seriousness in speeches to American and Asian investors. "The chances of a separation of Quebec from the rest of Canada are absolutely zero," he proclaimed on one occasion, before an audience of no doubt bemused New York financiers.[27] Bouchard's alleged conversion to the tenets of the Common Sense Revolution (or at least to a passable facsimile) was therefore a most fortuitous development. It not only reassured nervous Quebec bondholders that it would likely be "business as usual" whether Quebec separated or not, it also lent valuable credibility to Harris's main point: namely, that Ontario remained an attractive place for international investment.

During 1996 and early 1997 a personal rapprochement of growing warmth developed between the two premiers, including exchanges of family visits and the careful projection in the media of an image of "normal" intergovernmental relations.[28] Initially, the national unity question was strictly "off the agenda." At their Quebec City meeting, in May 1996, Harris and Bouchard focused on very specific concerns, such as their common objection to federal compensation payments to the Atlantic provinces in return for the blending of their sales taxes with the GST. "It's not a secret that on sovereignty or federalism we may have different views," Harris summed up, "but we're here today to talk about things that we agree on, those things that we think are of significant mutual benefit to Canada's two largest and most important provinces."[29] Subsequently, however, their rapprochement was underlined by Harris's increasingly vehement rejection of the usefulness of entrenching a distinct society clause in the constitution. Coincidentally, perhaps, but also symbolically, Bouchard was paying a return visit to Harris in Toronto, in March 1997, on the very weekend that the Quebec Liberal party was meeting to adopt a new platform calling for the constitutional recognition of Quebec as a distinct society.[30]

While Harris is open to attack for "naively playing the separatist game"[31] — that is, for appearing to reinforce Bouchard's assurances to Quebecers that a sovereign Quebec will continue to enjoy normal, friendly relations with Ontario — there can be no doubt that he has effectively repositioned Ontario on the national unity front. That repositioning shows a marked independence from Ottawa, an implicit willingness to contemplate the possibility of Quebec separation (*pace* the premier's "zero chance" prognostications), and a determination to protect Ontario's specific interests in investment and trade.

ONTARIO AND OTTAWA

Relations between Queen's Park and Ottawa are conducted at so many levels, and through so many channels, that any brief account of them is bound to be incomplete. The following, therefore, is not meant to be a representative, or still less a comprehensive, survey; rather, it is a selective look at three areas of key importance.

FISCAL ISSUES

"We accept a reduction of transfers from the federal government, providing those dollars are going towards the deficit. I'm satisfied to date that they are," Harris stated in June 1995.[32] This represented nothing less than a revolution in Ontario's attitude — a 180-degree turn from the position taken by the NDP government of Bob Rae. What made the premier's statement all the more remarkable was that it came just a few months after the federal government's 1995 budget in which a new transfer regime — the Canada Health and Social Transfer (CHST) — had been introduced. The CHST had built into it all of the features that had worked to Ontario's disadvantage under the old regime and that had been so strenuously protested by the Rae government. And, adding injury to insult, it also slashed payments to the provinces by a massive amount, with Ontario taking by far the biggest cut — no less than 54 per cent of the total for the entire country.[33]

It is illuminating to review the immediate background to this issue, and in particular to recall the basis of the Rae government's protests: it was not just that the federal government was downloading the costs of deficit reduction onto the provinces, it was that in the process Ontario was being made to bear more than its fair share. In effect, as Queen's Park demonstrated again and again, Ontario was being systematically short-changed under virtually every transfer program; and virtually every program, whatever its original purpose, tended to turn into an "equalization" program, with Ontario paying a disproportionately large share of costs and receiving a disproportionately small share of benefits. The federal cap on Canada Assistance Plan (CAP) payments, for example, meant that while all other provinces except British Columbia received 50 percent of the costs of social assistance, Ontario received only 29 percent. The total cost to the Ontario treasury was billions of dollars — $1.7 billion in 1994-95 alone, and $7.7 billion over five years. Ontario received 53 percent of new immigrants, yet received only 38 percent of federal funding for their resettlement and training (while Quebec, by contrast, received 12 percent of immigrants and 37 percent of funding). Hence, the Ontario government charged, "in the six years between 1990-91 and 1995-96, federal government discrimination against Ontario in job training, immigration and social assistance alone has cost Ontario taxpayers $12.4 billion, including interest costs."[34] A substantial portion of Ontario's budget deficit could thus be directly attributed to shortfalls in federal transfers. "The systematic discrimination against this province has to stop," Rae had declared.[35] After the election of the Chrétien government in 1993, "a fair share for Ontarians" was Rae's constant refrain in his attempts to obtain financial redress from Ottawa.[36] But it was a refrain that fell on deaf ears: each Liberal budget made matters worse.

This was the situation the Harris government faced with apparent equanimity in June 1995. A new era of fiscal harmony indeed seemed at hand. By the following June, however, after a year of largely fruitless fiscal negotiations over tax policies and fiscal transfer issues, it was clear that the Harris government had effected another 180-degree turn and was now taking a much tougher, more confrontational line in its dealings with Ottawa — an approach that in no essential respect differed from Bob Rae's.

The breach that occurred between Queen's Park and Ottawa over GST/sales tax harmonization is symptomatic of the turnabout. Initially a spirit of optimism and good will had prevailed, as both Harris and Finance Minister Ernie Eves favoured harmonization; but negotiations had stalled in the soured atmosphere of post-referendum politics and, perhaps inevitably, the tax harmonization issue became entangled with the much larger issue of fiscal fairness. The federal proposal, Eves concluded in December 1995 (echoing former NDP finance minister, Floyd Laughren), amounted to a tax-shift from business to consumers that would cost Ontarians $3 billion per year "and that is unacceptable."[37] Harris and Chrétien met in March 1996, in a final effort to break the impasse but no new proposal emerged. The gulf between the two sides proved unbridgeable, not least because Ottawa showed no inclination to understand the perspective of Ontario's Common Sense Revolution. As an exasperated Eves later commented, "We're not into increasing taxation. We're into reducing taxation.[38]

Eventually, facing an election with a key promise unkept, the Chrétien government gave up on Ontario and struck a deal with three of the Atlantic provinces (all except Prince Edward Island). That deal, however, was cemented by the promise of federal subsidies, a large portion of which Ontario taxpayers would end up paying, thus further aggravating relations between Queen's Park and Ottawa.

In a speech on 14 June 1996, somewhat ironically delivered before the Council for Canadian Unity, Dianne Cunningham laid out the revised (but also familiar) Ontario line. Her theme was the need for greater fairness in transfer payments and an end to the discriminatory treatment of Ontario. She then proceeded to list, as Rae had done so many times, specific areas where Ontario suffered serious shortfalls, such as Unemployment Insurance and the CHST. Ontarians, she said, had always supported straightforward equalization payments to the poorer provinces, but cannot support the "continued discrimination against our province in other program areas." Revenue shortfalls and discrimination, she argued, were the result of a pattern of flawed, unilateral decisionmaking by the federal government: "This unilateralism has undermined fairness, coherence and stability. It has resulted in an atmosphere of federal-provincial acrimony."[39] So much for the new era of fiscal harmony.

REBALANCING

The core of the Harris government's domestic agenda reflects the belief that Ontarians are overgoverned and overtaxed, and that the problem stems from too much bureaucracy and too much duplication and overlap between different levels of government. Its domestic solution, therefore, is a drastic administrative "restructuring." This includes cutting everything from the number of members of the legislature to the number of school boards, "disentangling" the functions and tax powers of the province and its municipalities, and amalgamating many of the latter into larger and supposedly more efficient units.[40] It would be surprising if so radical an agenda, toward which the government has shown total commitment, did not find a parallel in its intergovernmental relations. In fact, the parallel is extremely close. In intergovernmental affairs, the Harris government's equivalent watchword to "restructuring" is the "rebalancing" of federal and provincial responsibilities. It is precisely in this area that the Harris government's demands for change differ most strikingly from those of its NDP predecessor. Bob Rae's concept of "fair shares federalism," for example, was not linked to a demand for less government or greater decentralization or more interprovincialism.

The inspiration for rebalancing obviously derives from the Common Sense Revolution, but almost from the start it was also presented as an alternative to constitutional change. "We've got massive duplication. We are over-governed and over-regulated," Harris reportedly told Chrétien in January 1996 (in the unlikely setting of a flight to Bombay as part of a "Team Canada" trade mission), adding, in reference to the Quebec problem, "We've learned that we can't grab the whole enchilada in one package ... So I think we should go at it in bite-size pieces." He left no doubt as to where the first bite should be taken. "Getting rid of government duplication ... will lead to some successes that are more easily achievable (than a constitutional amendment), and the rest will follow," he confidently predicted.[41] Chrétien's response, if any, was not reported.

The force and radicalism of Ontario's rebalancing ideas became more evident in August, at the Annual Premiers' Conference held in Jasper, Alberta. Harris's opening salvo is worthy of note. "I think we can do a lot better than the federal government. The federal government is bankrupt," Harris told the Calgary Chamber of Commerce on the eve of the conference. "It has no dollars. Its ability to intervene financially ... is diminished. Times are changing. It's time for provinces to step forward." Stepping forward, he made clear, meant taking over the setting of national standards in social programs: "While some top-down federalists claim the provinces can't or won't take a national approach, I say we can ... national standards do not have to be federal government standards."[42]

Harris's speech, while blunt and aggressive, was not mere bluster. In preparation for the meeting, the Ontario government had commissioned a policy paper by Queen's University economist Thomas Courchene, and it was Courchene's paper that underpinned the premier's remarks. The Ontario initiative also built on a proposed set of principles for social programs that had been presented to the first ministers in June in a bland document titled *Report to Premiers*.[43] Though little remarked upon at the time, the report was potentially significant because its proposed "mutual consent principles" were defined in such a way as to leave the door ajar to a much greater degree of decentralization.

Courchene's paper, titled "ACCESS" (A Convention on the Canadian Economic and Social Systems), seeks to push the door to decentralization wide open by means of a far-ranging and original analysis that puts specific policy flesh on the bare bones of the *Report to Premiers*. Courchene approaches the issue from the perspective of "global determinism" — a staple of late twentieth-century conservative ideology. "The assumption," he writes, "is that social policy is undergoing substantial, indeed unprecedented decentralization and the question is: How, in light of this decentralization, do we Canadians reconstitute our internal common markets in the socio-economic arenas?"[44] The answer, he argues, it to bow to the inevitable and rebalance the federal system to give the provinces a greatly enlarged role in "preserving and promoting the Canadian economic and social union."[45] Responsibilities in some (mainly financial) "arenas," such as securities regulation, he suggests, might usefully be shifted upwards to the federal government; but the dominant thrust of his recommendations is toward the decentralization of social programs, accompanied by greater interprovincialism in the setting of standards. This, he states, is dictated by "north-south" economic realities, and the implication is unavoidable: it means "that any notion of identical standards across all provinces is a non-starter — much of the negotiation will have to be in terms of principles and 'equivalencies'."[46] What is needed to ensure the future of "social Canada" is thus the negotiation of a formal (but non-constitutional) "convention" that would form the basis for a fundamentally restructured federation.

Interestingly, Courchene's proposal is very much in keeping with the thought on this subject of an earlier economist, Professor Kenneth Taylor of McMaster University, who was an adviser to Premier Mitch Hepburn and whose views were reflected in Hepburn's speech to the Royal Commission on Dominion-Provincial Relations (Rowell-Sirois) in May 1938. According to Taylor's calculations, Ontario was contributing over 45 percent of federal revenues while receiving only 28 percent of federal expenditures, and was being short-changed across the board. "We are not Midas," Attorney General Gordon Conant told the commission. From the Hepburn government's point of view, the unfair treatment of Ontario resulted from the excessive centralization of powers and both were unacceptable. Hepburn's contribution was to deliver a rambling diatribe in which he argued, *en passant*, that if national programs were essential, then perhaps they would be "better arranged by compact."[47]

ACCESS discusses in complex detail the administrative and legal provisions that such a compact or convention might embody — including possible "framework axioms" and "compliance and enforcement" mechanisms — but its political thrust is uncomplicated. It complements the Harris government's domestic agenda and represents a powerful rationale for the extension of that agenda into the intergovernmental sphere.

Harris's Calgary speech and Courchene's ACCESS paper provoked a predictable furore among the premiers of the have-not provinces,[48] as the Ontario delegation must have known they would. Harris later diplomatically downplayed his commitment to the ideas expressed, but discussion of them had dominated the conference. Ontario had delivered its new message, loud and clear.

NATIONAL UNITY

Rebalancing the federation by non-constitutional means and altering it by constitutional amendment are not mutually exclusive alternatives, but, as the Ontario position crystallized, they were treated more and more as though they were. As early as her June 1996 speech to the Council for Canadian Unity, which mainly dealt with fiscal issues, Dianne Cunningham had expressed Ontario's preference for "practical reforms that do not carry the symbolic freight associated with constitutional reform." Premier Harris's view "is that this is not the time for grand pronouncements matched by inaction,"[49] she had pointedly warned the federal government.

By October, in the wake of Ontario's Jasper initiative, her position had hardened and her tone had become more acerbic. "At the end of the day, I have to tell you, there are questions about how serious the federal government is about finding ways of managing our country based on principles that all the partners in the federation know and accept," she said in a speech to the Metropolitan Toronto Board of Trade. Ontario, she estimated, made a net contribution to the have-not provinces of almost $15 billion, or 5.2 percent of its GDP. "That is an amount which is roughly equal to our provincial spending on schools, colleges, universities and hospitals combined. Some of this represents a legitimate sharing of the wealth. Some of it does not." She then proceeded to a point by point reiteration of the Jasper initiative. Progress toward rebalancing, she strongly implied, was regarded by Ontario as a test of good faith and a *sine qua non* for Ontario's future cooperation in constitutional matters. Rather than constitutional reform, efforts to "reform the way governments do business with each other" are the way to strengthen the unity of the country. "The time for the grand gestures of the past is long gone. Our Government wants to see some non-constitutional successes before embarking on any constitutional changes."[50]

The rancorous federal election campaign during the spring of 1997 only underlined the deterioration of Ottawa-Queen's Park relations. A shared-cost infrastructure program, for example, prompted a furious response from Finance Minister Eves when it emerged that Ottawa was planning to by-pass Queen's Park and deal directly with Ontario municipalities. Liberal MPs, Eves charged, wanted to use the program as a "slush fund" and go around handing out "little election goodies, door-to-door, municipality to municipality."[51] The election also reopened the split between PCs and Reformers in the ranks of Ontario's Conservative coalition — a split that even members of Harris's caucus flagrantly displayed by taking opposite sides. And, exacerbating matters still further, Preston Manning and the Reform party managed once again to escalate "Quebec" and "distinct society" into visceral "hot button" issues. With little choice if he wished to avoid a split with Manning, Harris refused to endorse federal PC leader Jean Charest,[52] whose party was pledged to the constitutional entrenchment of a distinct society clause.

His refusal came as no surprise. Early in April, in Vancouver, he had told a receptive Fraser Institute audience that distinct society "is an old fashioned term for an old-fashioned policy that was a disaster ... Liberals, Conservatives, *The Toronto Star*, all the elites, labour leaders, academics, all said the right policy was appeasement for Quebec and they were all wrong. They were proven wrong."[53] Speaking in North Bay on 27 April, on the very eve of the campaign, he again blasted supporters of the notion. "I will say this, and some may consider it controversial," he is reported to have said, "but quite frankly I think those who advocate (distinct society) the most are those who feel guilty about Meech Lake." Ostensibly, the target of his attack was Prime Minister Chrétien: "He wasn't there when we needed him. He was not there! And now he's trying to relive the past. We need somebody to talk about the future." That somebody, implicitly, was not Jean Charest: "I believe any politician who uses those words (distinct society) is not contributing to national unity." Harris's visits to Lucien Bouchard, he evidently believed, had given him a grassroots feel for the issue. "Generally what I hear from Quebecers," he said, "is that when separatists ... hear a politician talk about distinct society, they say 'Boy, are they out of touch'."[54]

ONTARIO'S FUTURE IN (OR OUT OF) CONFEDERATION

In July 1997 Harris and Bouchard were meeting again. This time, they were representing their provinces at the annual Council of Great Lakes Governors in Erie, Pennsylvania.[55] Their presence at the meeting serves as a useful reminder that Ontario and Quebec both have vital economic, environmental, and other interests at stake in the Great Lakes region, and hence with one another — interests that their governments will have to attend to whatever may be the eventual fate of the Canadian federation.

There is no evidence that the Harris government has taken any concrete steps to prepare a "Plan O" — that is to say, a deliberate strategy to protect Ontario's interests in the event that Quebec votes yes in the next referendum — though it has commissioned studies of possible financial and other impacts of Quebec separation that could form the basis of such a plan.[56] Meanwhile, the threat of a yes vote hangs uncertainly over Ontario's relations with both Quebec and the federation.

There can be no doubt that the vast majority of Ontarians devoutly hope that Confederation can somehow survive — but beyond that, they share no consensus on what they, or their government, might usefully do to bring about the desired result. Thus, while their traditional sense of attachment to the

Canadian nation remains strong, it is now being tested by their unresolved internal political divisions, and perhaps even more, by the disturbing spectacle of a weakened and regionalized federation whose future is problematical at best.

Since 1985, moreover, Ontario has elected a series of activist governments, each one with an agenda of change seemingly more challenging and conflict-generating than the one before. This has naturally made Queen's Park a prime focus of media attention, in a city that is home to a vast and influential media industry. Over the past decade, therefore, Ontarians have been bombarded by reminders of the importance of Queen's Park in their lives — unlike the preceding four decades of generally bland politics — and the effect has been galvanizing. It has re-connected Ontarians to their provincial government, either as supporters or opponents, and in a curious unintended way, has restored Toronto's status as a major political centre — a genuine capital city. Whether Quebec secedes or not, these developments of the past decade will have an important bearing on Ontario's future intergovernmental relations.

If Quebec does secede, Ontario's immediate reaction will almost certainly be an avowal of renewed support for Canada. At the popular level, the impulse toward a flag-waving show of national unity will be strong, as Ontarians, like other Canadians, will wish desperately to salvage something positive from the ruins of Confederation. At the governmental level, the party in power at Queen's Park will have no choice but to maintain a facade of stability in hope of calming anxious citizens and international financial markets. But once the immediate crisis is over, and the repercussions have been more or less absorbed, deep and perhaps irreconcilable divisions are likely to emerge among the remaining provinces over the federation's future constitutional and financial arrangements.

Ontario's role in a truncated Canadian federation is itself likely to be a divisive issue. Within the province, there would be many who would object to taking on unlimited liability for a union that will be seen as costly to maintain, politically confining, and of dubious economic benefit. In the other provinces, any political arrangement that reflected Ontario's hugely disproportionate population and economic weight would be likely to cause resentment and deepening of current regional antagonisms. If other provinces begin to agitate for the carving up of Ontario in order to "rebalance" the federation (as they may well do, no doubt with the aid of much expert map-making advice), they are likely only to trigger Ontario's determination to preserve its unity — either by insisting on a degree of control over its own affairs that would make the Jasper initiative seem modest, or by its departure. In either case, Ontario would find an attractive and viable alternative at hand. In particular, it might well find that its core interest lies not in preserving at any cost its traditional ties with the west and Atlantic Canada, but rather in using its new-found autonomy to cultivate its emerging role as a "North American region state,"[57] with a range of associational intergovernmental relations with other similar states, including Quebec. The economic and political advantages of such a re-orientation would be considerable, quite apart from containing the damage that would result from Quebec's secession. It would allow Ontario to get a better grip on its public finances for example, by converting its present open-minded commitment to the financing of redistributive federal programs into straightforward "grants-in-aid" and perhaps redirecting a larger portion of program spending to its own "have-not areas" or to specific priorities, such as the resettlement of new immigrants. Post-NAFTA Ontario already has in place many of the requisites for economic success in such a role, and, with more than 11 million people, the potential to be a political actor of consequence. Historically, Ontario has never permitted its economic and political interests to be out of sync for very long, and the secession of Quebec would very likely accelerate a new convergence.

Alternatively, if Quebec is somehow accommodated, whatever the specific nature of the accommodation might be, it is likely to involve greater provincial autonomy, at least for provinces that have the wherewithal to exercise it — as Ontario, of all provinces, uniquely does. Again, Ontario would have a strong interest in strengthening its association with Quebec and neighbouring US states in the Great Lakes region. The Canadian political context, however, despite its tensions — of which there would no doubt be many, for it would take nothing less than a political miracle to accommodate Quebec without at the same time opening up other deep divisions — would be more hopeful than that which would prevail in the aftermath of a Quebec secession. For Ontario, the federation would again be by far the most important, though no longer the only, focus of its intergovernmental concerns. Confederation and its fractious partners would have survived to fight another day, and that would make all the difference.

NOTES

I am grateful to officials in the Ontario Ministry of Intergovernmental Affairs for their help while I was working on this chapter. My thanks in particular to Cameron Fowler, Craig McFadyen and Bill Forward for meeting with me at short notice and members of the ministry staff for promptly supplying me with the texts of speeches and other documents. They, of course, bear no responsibility for the contents of this essay. I wish also to thank Leslie Coventry for her research assistance; Bob Young and Peter Neary for their helpful comments on an earlier draft; and Tom Courchene for allowing me to read the manuscript of his stimulating new book (with Colin Telmer), *From Heartland to North American Region State: An Interpretative Essay on the Social, Fiscal and Federal Evolution of Ontario* (forthcoming).

1.   *The Globe and Mail*, 7 October 1994, p. A4.

2.   For a brief overview of Ontario's modern intergovernmental relations, see David Cameron and Richard Simeon, "Ontario in Confederation: The Not-So-Friendly Giant," in *The Government and Politics of Ontario*, 5th ed., ed. G. White (Toronto: University of Toronto Press, 1997), pp. 158-85. For the earlier history see Christopher Armstrong, *The Politics of Federalism: Ontario and the Federal Government, 1867-1942* (Toronto: University of Toronto Press, 1981).

3.   This, I have argued elsewhere, is one of the key "operative norms" of the Ontario political culture. For further discussion, see my essay "The Ontario Political Culture — An Interpretation," in *The Government and Politics of Ontario*, ed. White, pp. 49-68.

4.   Sid J.R. Noel, *Patrons, Clients, Brokers: Ontario Society and Politics, 1791-1896* (Toronto: University of Toronto Press, 1990), pp. 249-60.

5.   See John T. Saywell, *'Just call me Mitch': The Life of Mitchell F. Hepburn* (Toronto: University of Toronto Press, 1991), pp. 376-84.

6.   See Allan K. McDougall, *John P. Robarts: His Life and Government* (Toronto: University of Toronto Press, 1986), p. 217.

7.   See Claire Hoy, *Bill Davis* (Toronto: Methuen, 1985), pp. 332-48.

8.   Peterson "took part in the popular provincial pastime of Fed-bashing, with free trade the issue." Georgette Gagnon and Dan Rath, *Not Without Cause: David Peterson's Fall From Grace* (Toronto: HarperCollins, 1991), p. 94. See also G. Bruce Doern and Brian Tomlin, *Faith and Fear: The Free Trade Story* (Toronto: Stoddart,1991), pp. 143-49.

9.   Bob Rae later wrote in his memoirs: "I had used up my negotiating resources in the year of Charlottetown ... and just didn't have enough left for what was to follow," *From Protest to Power* (Toronto: Viking, 1996), p. 201.

10. The Rae government's position in these disputes became known as "Fair Shares Federalism." It was backed by extensive statistical research commissioned from Informetrica, an Ottawa consulting firm, and ably presented by Rae himself. See, e.g., his statement entitled "Federal-Provincial Jurisdiction," Ontario Legislative Assembly, *Debates*, 20 April 1994, pp. 5737-38.

11. This is not meant to suggest that the defeat of either the Peterson or the Rae government was *directly* caused by their failures in the intergovernmental sphere, though in both cases those failures were an important *indirect* cause. See Gagnon and Rath, *Not Without Cause*, p. 86; and Rae, *From Protest to Power*, pp. 193-201.

12. Peter Woolstencroft, "More than a Guard Change: Politics in the New Ontario," in Sid Noel (ed.), *Revolution at Queen's Park: Essays on Governing Ontario* (Toronto: Lorimer, 1997), pp. 38-54.

13. Cunningham, a former London school trustee and the only candidate to run against Harris, was backed by the "Red Tory" wing of the PC party. She ran a strong campaign, losing by 1,472 votes (8,881 to 7,189).

14. Noel, *Patrons*, pp. 261-62.

15. *The Toronto Star*, 10 June 1995, p. A12.

16. *The Globe and Mail*, 15 August 1995, p. A3.

17. Ontario, Premier's Office, Notes for an Address by the Hon. Mike Harris, The Canadian Club, Toronto, 12 October 1995.

18. *The Globe and Mail*, 13 October 1995, p. A4.

19. *Montreal Gazette*, 23 October 1995, p. A10. Technically, a constitutional amendment could have passed without Ontario's support if it had the support of Quebec and six other provinces, but since there was no possibility that Bouchard would support such an amendment, Harris's support was crucial.

20. *The Globe and Mail*, 5 April, 1997, p. A4.

21. Canada, House of Commons, *Journals*, 11 December 1995, p. 2232. Kenneth McRoberts writes that "Chrétien felt compelled to keep the promise he had made in the panic of the referendum campaign's last week. After failing to persuade enough provincial premiers to support constitutional recognition of Quebec as a "distinct society," Chrétien resolved to deal with the matter through non-constitutional action." Kenneth McRoberts, *Misconceiving Canada: The Struggle for National Unity* (Toronto: Oxford, 1997), p. 236.

22. By early 1996, Ottawa and Queen's Park were openly feuding. In response to Ottawa's leaked complaints about "lack of co-operation" from Queen's Park, Harris responded that Ottawa was not dealing "straight up" with Ontario. "There are some around the Prime Minister who play the old political game ... The truth is, we've accommodated the federal government far more than they've accommodated us." *The Toronto Star*, 7 April 1996, p. D1.

23. See Donald. E. Abelson and Michael Lusztig, "The Consistency of Inconsistency: Tracing Ontario's Opposition to the North American Free Trade Agreement," *Canadian Journal of Political Science* 29, 4 (1996): 681-98.

24. In 1981, Ontario's exports were roughly in balance between the other provinces of Canada and the rest of the world. By 1994, while the value of exports to both had grown, only 32 percent of Ontario's exports went to the other provinces and 68 percent to the rest of the world (mainly to the US). Statistics Canada, Provincial Economic Accounts, *Annual Estimates*, 1981-94, Table 3.

25. Ontario Progressive Conservative Party, *The Common Sense Revolution* (Toronto: Ontario Progressive Conservative Party, 1994), p. 14.

26. *Montreal Gazette*, 24 October 1995, p. A10.

27. *The Globe and Mail*, 7 June 1995, p. A8.

28. Harris's amicable dealings with Bouchard contrast sharply with Bob Rae's attitude. Rae saw Bouchard as an unmitigated menace: "if his vision is realized, he's going to hurt us. He's going to hurt all of Canada terribly ... I think he's deluding himself if he thinks that the rest of the country is going to sort of sit back with some quiet resignation and accept the breakup of the country. I don't intend to." *The Globe and Mail*, 8 November 1993, p. A1. See also Rae, *From Protest to Power*, p. 268.

29. *The Globe and Mail*, 31 May 1996, p. A4.

30. *The Globe and Mail*, 8 March 1997, pp. A5-6.

31. "Mr. Bouchard has quite adroitly played the gullible Mr. Harris for a sucker," columnist Jeffrey Simpson wrote. *The Globe and Mail*, 16 April 1997, p. A18.

32. *The Globe and Mail*, 29 June 1995, p. A1.

33. Canada, Department of Finance, *Budget 1995* (Ottawa: Department of Finance, 1995), Table 1.

34. Government of Ontario, "Ontarians Expect Fairness from the Federal Government," April 1995 (pamphlet).

35. Ontario, Legislative Assembly, *Debates*, 20 April 1994, p. 5738.

36. Rae, for some reason, believed that the Chrétien government would be more sympathetic to Ontario's case than the Mulroney and Campbell governments. But he kept insisting that Ottawa review the numbers, while the federal government would discuss only the generalities of program reform. "Talking about social reform without talking about the numbers is a little bit like talking about *Moby Dick* without talking about the whale," Rae complained. *The Globe and Mail*, 7 October 1994, p. A1.

37. *The Toronto Star*, 14 December 1995, p. B1.

38. *The Globe and Mail*, 28 March 1996, p. A2.

39. Ontario, Ministry of Intergovernmental Affairs, Speech by Hon. Dianne Cunningham, Council for Canadian Unity, Toronto, 14 June 1996.

40. For an account of the domestic politics of restructuring, see my essay "Ontario's Tory Revolution," in *Revolution at Queen's Park*, pp. 2-17.

41. *The Toronto Star*, 11 January 1996, p. A12.

42. *The Toronto Star*, 21 August 1996, p. A1; Ontario, Premier's Office, Speech by the Hon. Mike Harris, Calgary Chamber of Commerce, 20 August 1996.

43. Ministerial Council on Social Policy Reform and Renewal, *Report to Premiers*, Ottawa, 1996.

44. Thomas J. Courchene, "ACCESS: A Convention on the Canadian Economic and Social Systems," (Toronto: Ontario Ministry of Intergovernmental Affairs, 1996), p. 2.

45. Ibid.

46. Ibid., p. 5.

47. Saywell, *"Just call me Mitch,"* pp. 380-84. After listening to Hepburn's astonishing 90-minute rant, Commissioner N.W.Rowell suffered a heart attack followed by a stroke from which he never recovered. (Margaret Prang, *N.W.Rowell: Ontario Nationalist* (Toronto: University of Toronto Press, 1975), pp. 496-97. As far as is known, none of those in attendance at the Jasper conference suffered any ill effects.

48. "The premiers of New Brunswick, Newfoundland and Saskatchewan led the charge against the proposals..." *The Globe and Mail*, 22 August 1996, p. A1.

49. Cunningham, Speech, Council for Canadian Unity, 14 June 1996.

50. Ontario, Ministry of Intergovernmental Affairs, Hon. Dianne Cunningham, Speech to the Metropolitan Toronto Board of Trade, 30 October 1996.

51. *The Globe and Mail*, 18 April, p. A7.

52. One of Manning's tactics was to endorse Harris, thus implying that the endorsement worked both ways. In a rally in Harris's home town of North Bay, Manning had declared that he (not Jean Charest) would "bring the Common Sense Revolution to Ottawa." *The Globe and Mail*, 16 April 1996, p. A4. When Harris made an appearance at an Ontario PC party fundraiser in Ottawa, "Manning was there, shaking hands and making himself conspicuous... Reform recruiters stood guard at the escalator...steering Harris supporters to a reception room marked with signs that read: OK Preston, Sign Me Up." *Globe and Mail*, 19 April 1997, p. A4.

53. *The Globe and Mail*, 5 April 1997, p. A4.

54. *The Toronto Star*, 27 April 1997, p. A1.

55. *London Free Press*, 12 July 1997, p. A6.

56. Partial release of these documents was ordered by the Ontario Information and privacy Commissioner, following a request by *The Globe and Mail*. The commissioner ruled that only two of the ten documents requested should be released in their entirety, along with portions of seven others, but that the whole of a document "about relations between Ontario and its investors" could be withheld. *The Globe and Mail*, 28 May 1997, p. A4. At the time of writing, the documents ordered released had not yet been made available.

57. This phrase is Tom Courchene's, from the title of his forthcoming book.

11

From Jacques Parizeau to Lucien Bouchard: A New Vision? Yes, But ...

Réjean Pelletier

Devant l'impasse constitutionnelle qui perdure depuis l'échec de l'Accord de Charlottetown en 1992, on a exploré une autre voie de renouvellement de la fédéra-tion canadienne, soit celle d'ententes administratives conclues entre le fédéral et les provinces. Avec l'arrivée de Lucien Bouchard à la tête du Parti québécois et comme premier ministre du Québec, une nouvelle vision a semblé s'imposer dans les rela-tions fédérales-provinciales. À la souveraineté intransigeante d'un Jacques Parizeau, on peut opposer la défense des intérêts du Québec d'un Lucien Bouchard qui propose certes la souveraineté-partenariat, mais qui est également prêt à conclure des ententes avec le fédéral lorsque le Québec peut en tirer profit (comme dans le cas de la forma-tion de la main-d'oeuvre). Toutefois, cet esprit d'ouverture peut aussi se refermer en fonction d'un appui trop manifeste d'Ottawa et des autres provinces à la ligne dure à l'égard du Québec. Lucien Bouchard doit aussi composer à la fois avec les militants du PQ qui ne partagent pas tous cette nouvelle vision et avec la population québé-coise qui n'endosse pas encore majoritairement le projet souverainiste.

INTRODUCTION

In recent years, Quebecers have been asked almost annually to give their opin-ions on the Canadian federation. In October 1992, they expressed their views through a referendum on the Charlottetown Accord, which they rejected with a no vote of 56.7 percent. A year later, they elected 54 Bloc Québécois (BQ) MPs (giving the party 49.3 percent of the vote), to defend the interests of Quebec and promote sovereignty in Ottawa. In September 1994, they chose the Parti Québécois (PQ) to form their provincial government with 77 MNAs (with 44.8 percent of the vote). In October 1995, Quebecers opted to remain in Canada by a narrow majority of 50.6 to 49.4 percent and a record voter turnout of 93.5 percent. This result contrasts with the referendum of 1980, when 20 percentage points separated the two sides (voter turnout that year was 85.6 percent).

Most recently, in the federal election of June 1997, Quebecers sent a rather ambiguous message. Certainly the Bloc Québécois continues to hold a large majority of the Quebec seats, but caucus membership has declined from 54 in 1993 to 44 in 1997, and voter support has slipped from 49.3 to 38 percent. Meanwhile, the Liberal party of Jean Chrétien has made mild progress, but has not substantially increased its proportion of seats or votes. Rather, it was the Conservative party of Jean Charest which attracted a good number of voters from the Bloc in 1997. These were "soft" nationalists who were attracted by the theme of "national reconciliation" or were troubled by the Bloc's internal divisions and its performance in Ottawa, although the Conservatives failed to make a significant breakthrough in Quebec. Even though the Bloc continues to be prominent on the federal political scene in Quebec, the party is weaker than in 1993. This may foreshadow difficulties for the Parti Québécois in the next provincial election and in a future referendum, since the support for sovereignty, as measured by the vote obtained by the Bloc, is the lowest managed by a sovereignist party for more than 20 years.

Following the failures to renew Canadian federalism in 1990 and 1992, and the unwillingness of the rest of Canada to amend the constitution so Quebec could assent to the *Constitution Act, 1982*, the country faced an impasse once again. These failures have led to strong reactions from Quebec, which sent a clear message to Canadian federalists: the support for the Bloc Québécois in two federal elections, the victory of the Parti Québécois provincially, and, above all, the near-victory in the referendum. These events suggest that the failure of constitutional reforms could cause the break-up of the country.

Facing this impasse, and finding themselves unable to amend the constitution, politicians have explored other ways of renewing the federation. If the constitutional route is closed, there remains room for administrative agreements. Since the 1993 election, this clearly has become the approach preferred by Jean Chrétien and the provincial premiers.[1] Even Lucien Bouchard has engaged — sometimes hesitantly — in this form of negotiation to achieve benefits for Quebec. In contrast, Jacques Parizeau did not use this option during his short time as premier.

Considering this negotiation of administrative agreements with the federal government, has the arrival of Lucien Bouchard as leader of the Parti Québécois brought a new approach to Quebec's relations with the federal government? Before answering the question by exploring the non-constitutional approach to federal-provincial relations, it is important to consider, as background, two important events which have influenced political life in Quebec and Canada in the 1990s, and to contrast the two sovereignist leaders, Parizeau and Bouchard. In the final part of this chapter, we will outline some factors that could influence the future of Quebec, and thereby affect the future of the Canadian federation.

BACKGROUND: TWO POLITICAL TURNING-POINTS

Considering the recent events of Quebec political life, we can note two major factors which changed the course of things. First, the defeat of the Meech Lake Accord in June 1990 was strongly resented in Quebec, strengthening the sovereignty movement and almost giving it a victory in the 1995 referendum. We do not need to look beyond this — especially the rejection of the Accord's recognition of Quebec as a "distinct society" — for reasons for the strength of sovereignist sentiment at the start of the 1990s. We must also remember that the progression of sovereignty-association since 1989 followed several events which generated strong reactions in Quebec. In December 1988, the Supreme Court declared that the requirement of unilingual French signs violated the Quebec and Canadian Charter of Rights. Then Quebec decided to use the notwithstanding clause to pass a new sign law, and, apparently in response various cities — mostly in Ontario — saw demonstrations against the French language and declared themselves English-only during the fall of 1989. As well, the premiers of Manitoba, Newfoundland, and New Brunswick threatened not to ratify the Meech Lake Accord unless significant amendments were forthcoming.[2] Analysts of this period submit that the progress of various sovereignist options was highly sensitive to contemporary events.[3] We will return to this later in the chapter.

We must also consider the arrival of Parizeau as the leader of the PQ in 1988 and his replacement by Bouchard in 1996. Parizeau has always promoted a *"pur et dur"* ideal of independence, tirelessly repeating that it is essential to speak of independence "before, during, and after elections" — never hiding this goal for electoral reasons and always making it the ultimate objective of the sovereignist movement.

After support for sovereignty peaked at 58 percent in 1990 (support for sovereignty-association peaked at 70 percent in November of that year), nationalist fervour declined, with support for sovereignty stalling at around 40 percent in 1994 and early 1995.[4] After he had postponed the referendum from spring to fall of 1995, Parizeau agreed in June to a compromise to try to increase support for the sovereignty cause: he signed an agreement with Bouchard and Action Démocratique leader, Mario Dumont, adding the idea of partnership to that of sovereignty. This is reminiscent of René Lévesque's idea of sovereignty-association, which had caused a great deal of tension within the sovereignist camp years earlier.

Despite the "instantaneous" rise in support for sovereignty in June 1995, the gains soon slipped away, and it seemed that sovereignists could not hope for the yes vote to exceed 45 percent.[5] An abrupt change occurred during the referendum campaign, when on 7 October 1995 Parizeau introduced Bouchard as the leader of Quebec's negotiation team in the event that the sovereignists won the referendum. Bouchard rapidly gained a high profile in the media, and at the same time he personified the partnership option. This option would mute the most harmful consequences of separation and softened the hard line position of Parizeau on independence. The more moderate Bouchard took over as the uncontested leader of the sovereignist forces, a leader who many francophone Quebecers could identify with.

What lessons for the future can we draw from these two turning points? The first of these was an unprecedented rise in support for the sovereignty option in the early 1990s, and its decline in the years that followed. One lesson emerges right away: Quebecers' sensitivity to the events of the moment causes support for sovereignty to fluctuate[6] in accordance with the importance of these events for Quebec, its distinct character, and its French-speaking majority.

The second turning point relates to the role of Lucien Bouchard in the Quebec political scene, first as leader of the Bloc Québécois, then as leader of the PQ, and finally as premier of Quebec. Unlike Parizeau, who was firmly committed to the idea of independence, Bouchard embodied moderation and the notion of partnership as well as sovereignty, and he even reflected a certain ambivalence felt by a large number of francophone Quebecers. The cold, rational thinker was replaced by a more passionate and emotional leader. This shift dramatically changed the political landscape of Quebec and the province's relationship with the federal government.

TWO CONTRASTING VIEWS OF SOVEREIGNTY

For Jacques Parizeau, who became a sovereignist after a conference in Banff in 1967, there were certain lessons to draw from the 1980 referendum. These were to not take for granted a link between sovereignty and association, and to not ask for a mandate simply to negotiate such an agreement between Quebec and Canada. This explains why Parizeau made his convictions widely known after he became PQ leader in 1988 and especially during the second referendum campaign:

> I abandoned these recurrent hesitations, the peculiar constitutional ideas and delaying tactics, and supported two simple formulae. Firstly, the Parti Québécois is sovereigntist before, during, and after an election, and sovereignty is our *raison d'être*. Secondly, a referendum must be held to achieve a mandate for a sovereign Quebec; this referendum will be called soon after we form the government.[7]

Even after signing the tripartite agreement of 12 June 1995, Parizeau continued to say that the ultimate goal was sovereignty rather than partnership. This is "a flexible formula to define the kind of economic relations that Quebecers want to maintain with Canada" until English Canada takes a clear position on the matter. Moreover, he asked whether there would be a third formula after association and partnership. It might be necessary, he concluded.[8]

In short, we may classify Jacques Parizeau as a *"pur et dur"* sovereignist, for whom the goal of sovereignty is always paramount, even without association or partnership. This highly uncompromising position contrasts with that of Lucien Bouchard, who is more wavering and doubtful. Parizeau aims at a single objective: sovereignty. While Bouchard shares the same goal, his faith is less steady. Yet he better reflects the ambivalence of the Quebec population.

Although he was once a Liberal, Lucien Bouchard joined the PQ in the early 1970s. A friend of Brian Mulroney, Bouchard wrote speeches for him and helped to prepare the Conservative Party program in the 1984 election.[9] Named Canada's ambassador to France in 1985, he entered electoral politics as a Conservative candidate in a by-election in June 1988. Two years later, he resigned from Mulroney's Cabinet and from the Conservative caucus, to protest the amendments proposed to the Meech Lake Accord as part of an effort to persuade provincial legislatures to ratify it. He concluded his resignation letter with these words:

> It is definitely better to have honour in disagreement than agreement in dishonour. Anyway, nothing would be worse than dishonour in disagreement, which I believe will be reserved for those who try, in vain I do believe, to convince Quebec to come to a conference to be trapped into final, humiliating concessions.[10]

After the resignation, the Bloc Québécois was born in Ottawa and Bouchard became involved in the sovereignty movement — the same Bouchard who had agreed to support the *"beau risque"* card announced by René Lévesque, a new orientation that led Parizeau at that time to leave the PQ as both minister and MNA.

The routes travelled by the two leaders are very different. Once he became a sovereignist, Parizeau never wavered in his ideology, always embodying the *"pur et dur"* face of sovereignty. On the other hand, Bouchard's nationalist convictions and his will to defend the interests of Quebec led him to found the Bloc Québécois, which obtained unexpected success in the 1993 election. Then he entered the 1995 referendum campaign, and would later become leader of the PQ and premier in January 1996. Although sovereignty is important for him, not everything is reduced to this single question. Above all, sovereignty must be achieved on terms that are acceptable for Quebec's entire population.

One of these conditions involves partnership. For Parizeau, the goal is sovereignty, with or without partnership; for Bouchard, partnership is more closely linked to the sovereignist project. Although he pledged in 1990 to "remain in politics to work for the sovereignty of Quebec,"[11] clearly he has not travelled in a straight line. If there is one constant in his trajectory, it is his faithfulness to the aspirations and interests of Quebec. At present, this trajectory carries Bouchard toward a sovereignist position, but this is a sovereignty based on a European model of partnership and the preservation of Canada's economic structure.[12]

With support from Mario Dumont, Bouchard virtually imposed this policy of partnership on Parizeau prior to the 1995 referendum. This agreement of 12 June, it is useful to note, has two important differences from previous projects of the PQ. First, the idea of a treaty on economic partnership adds a number of provisions to the kinds of agreements the PQ had previously indicated it would pursue, namely shared customs and currency and free circulation and mobility of labour. The new provisions deal with internal trade, international trade, Canadian representation in international affairs, transportation, defence policy, financial institutions, budgetary and fiscal policies, environmental protection, and postal services. More than a simple treaty of economic partnership, this proposal would reshape relations between Quebec and Canada in a confederal union covering numerous areas of activity.

This agreement also breaks new ground in its proposals for shared political institutions. To the three traditional bodies outlined in previous PQ documents — a council, a secretariat, and a tribunal — the agreement adds a parliamentary assembly. This would be comprised of Quebec and Canadian representatives nominated by their respective legislatures and would make recommendations to council and approve resolutions. This proposition takes the partnership concept closer to the European model that Bouchard had discussed previously. This is not to say that institutions based on a partnership of two members would necessarily be any more harmonious than one of six, twelve, or fifteen.[13]

A further subject remains to be explored: the identity of Quebec. For Parizeau, "anyone who wishes to be a Quebecer can be." Of course, Quebecers are of diverse backgrounds, but "neither race, nor colour define them, it is language." From this definition, Parizeau therefore recognizes that anglophone rights would be maintained in a sovereign Quebec, although he follows this by adding "Perhaps it would be preferable, in this case, to add nothing and bring ourselves closer in line with what English Canada wishes to do with regard to francophones outside Quebec."[14] However, he stresses that a people who know who they are does not abandon the principle of equality of rights of all citizens, and that therefore a sovereign Quebec would respect its minorities.

While Bouchard shares Parizeau's views on the question of defining the identity of Quebecers primarily in terms of language, he has, however, disassociated himself from the idea of tying the rights of anglophones in Quebec to those of francophones outside the province. These rights are not to be bargained, says the present leader of the PQ, who follows René Lévesque in opposing a reduction of the rights of anglophones in Quebec. In a speech to anglophone representatives in Montreal's Centaur Theatre on 11 March 1996, Bouchard firmly stated:

> As a sovereigntist and as premier of Quebec, I believe that it is my duty to solemnly reaffirm our commitment to preserving the rights of the anglophone community at present, and in a sovereign Quebec. They shall continue to administer their schools, their colleges, and their universities; have access to courts and government in English; have access to social services and health care in their language; have radio and television in English.[15]

He added this forceful sentence: "When you go to the hospital and you are suffering, you may need a blood test, but certainly not language control."

In sum, Parizeau's uncompromising position on sovereignty contrasts with the consistent defence of Quebec's interests by Bouchard, who believes that these interests would be best defended, in practice, in a sovereign Quebec that will reach agreement on an economic and political partnership with Canada. Sovereignty is not a panacea to Bouchard; it must be achieved under the best possible conditions for Quebec. To him, it has become a necessity for Quebec in the wake of the failures of the *"beau risque"* idea and the Meech Lake and Charlottetown Accords. Such a position resonates not only with the nucleus of but also with more moderate, "softer" nationalists, for whom independence is not an absolute necessity, but rather an option that may become necessary if other alternatives fail.

Bouchard's record of more varied thinking, doubts, and ambivalence reflect the feelings of Quebecers, especially francophone Quebecers, better than the certainty and uncompromising nature of Parizeau. This is revealed in a series of polls in 1995-96 about voting intentions. Polls taken between June and October, while Parizeau led the party, showed the PQ's support averaging 46 percent. Polls between October 1995 and May 1996, with Bouchard's name as PQ leader, found party support averaging 54 percent. These results clearly demonstrate the attraction of the new PQ leader, with the PQ increasing its lead over the Liberal Party.[16]

A NEW VISION?

Meanwhile, two major tasks await the Bouchard government. First, it must clean up the province's public finances and completely eliminate its deficit by the year 2000, and do this while maintaining the social security net. In 1993, while he was leader of the Bloc, he spoke of a crisis in Canadian public finance: "the question is not about whether or not we will some day have to restore order to public expenditures. Rather, we must ask ourselves what is the most equitable way of doing so. And who will decide for Quebecers, the federal government or our government?"[17]

In keeping with this, fighting the deficit remains a priority — virtually an absolute necessity — for the Bouchard government, for two reasons. First, the government must end the uncontrolled increases in public expenditures and the resulting deficit. Second, an independent Quebec would be in a better position to assume responsibility for its share of the Canadian debt. This responsible financial management is not only necessary in the short term, but it will also make the government better equipped to face the economic up-heavals which will inevitably follow secession. Overall, good financial management in the present will be seen as an indicator of future management practices by the inquisitive eyes of credit agencies.

The other major task of the Bouchard government is to defend the interests of Quebec within the Canadian federation (while awaiting sovereignty). In this light, Bouchard must look for agreements with the federal government that help Quebec to gain powers or alter conditions which are seen as being unacceptable. This provides a context in which we may analyze the agree-ment recently reached with the federal government to do with labour force training (or more exactly, a Canada-Quebec agreement relating to the labour market). Certainly there have been calls for such an agreement from all socio-economic sectors of Quebec. But Chrétien's Liberal government was not eager to conclude such an agreement only with Quebec, because of the risk that it would be interpreted elsewhere in Canada as a concession or a step toward special status for the province. By concluding an agreement with other prov-inces, this objection could be met. But the federal government was also anxious to reach an agreement before the 1997 federal election to show Quebecers that federalism could function effectively and flexibly.

From Quebec's perspective, such an agreement, first proposed by the gov-ernment of Jean Lesage in the 1960s, had become an absolute necessity. Conditions appeared more favourable following the 1995 referendum, since the federal government felt it had to make efforts to accommodate Quebec. For Quebec, the situation had also changed following the departure of Parizeau and his replacement by Bouchard. The latter prefers negotiated solutions to endless confrontation, as is witnessed by the holding of socio-economic sum-mits involving public and private sector leaders. Bouchard also prefers to avoid what he calls "the politics of the worst" by following a strategy of refusing to make any agreements in order to demonstrate that Canadian federalism can never work. According to him, such politics is always "the worst of politics."

The accord reached with Quebec conveys a recognition of asymmetrical federalism within the framework of an administrative agreement. The asym-metry lies in the fact that four provinces are content with a formula of co-management or participation in the federal program, while four of the other provinces (Alberta, Manitoba, New Brunswick, and Quebec) have obtained total jurisdiction in labour training. As well, the asymmetry is evident in the Quebec accord which distinguishes itself from those of other provinces on one point (through an exchange of letters between the relevant ministers). In line with Bill 101, French is recognized as the official language in public administration; services are offered first in French, but on request they are then given in English throughout Quebec. This contrasts with the federal government's bilingualism policy requiring services in both official languages, but only where demand justifies it. The Quebec agreement also differed from others on another point which was, however, subsequently modified. Even though the accord is of indeterminate length, the level of financing was assured for specified time periods: five years in the case of Quebec, and three years in the case of other provinces. The other provinces' financing was later increased to five years to meet the level for Quebec (at the time of writing, this change was not yet official).

Concluded shortly after the federal election was called, this agreement generated little reaction as attention rapidly shifted to other events of the election campaign: job creation, deficit reduction, maintaining social programs, and Canadian unity (including discussion of "Plan B," which specified the conditions for the attainment of sovereignty). These issues quickly eclipsed the agreement on labour training, kept in step with a "Plan A" stressing negotiations with Quebec and the other provinces, and changes to the Canadian federation.

For the federal government, a priority was to prove that Canadian federalism was flexible and that reform of the federation was possible through administrative agreements. Meanwhile, the Quebec government was delighted by the gains achieved, but also underlined that Quebecers had been waiting 30 years for this reform. At the same time, it wanted to show that it was capable of negotiating a partnership with Canada in the future. Neither government really attained its short-term objective. On the other hand, at the political level, it may be useful to retain from this agreement the spirit of openness that was shown by both sides. Without giving up the possibility of "Plan B," the federal government can come to an understanding with the provinces about a transfer of powers. In the meantime, while continuing its quest for independence, Quebec may reach an accord with the federal government.

The spirit of openness and cooperativeness was also seen when Bouchard agreed to participate in Team Canada, led by the prime minister, to seek out economic markets in Asia. Certainly the premier of Quebec risked playing into the hands of defenders of federalism, a risk Parizeau had previously been unwilling to take. With the economy still weak, Bouchard preferred to take this chance if it offered the prospect of significant economic gains for Quebec. Again, we can say that, for him, defending the interests of Quebec is more important than just defending the idea of independence.

However, we cannot forget that Bouchard is also the leader of the Parti Québécois. Elected without opposition to lead the party after the resignation of Parizeau, Bouchard was not welcomed with the same enthusiasm by all party members. Some of them viewed him, and continue to view him, suspiciously: he was an MP and minister for the Conservatives in Ottawa, they think that he is too soft and too conciliatory toward the federal government, he practically imposed the idea of partnership during the 1995 referendum, he broadened this idea of partnership in both economic and political respects, and he imposed budgetary restraint in health care, social services, and education — while the PQ has always defined itself as a social democratic party. In sum, the new leader, without deep roots in the party, fundamentally changed its orientation: the idea of sovereignty was now accompanied by a broader partnership, and the social democratic character was weakened by the fight against the deficit. Given these circumstances, we can better understand the serious warning the party activists gave to their leader at the party's 1996 convention: they gave him a vote of confidence of only 76.9 percent, which amounted to a call for him to exercise caution.[18] We must not forget, then, that the PQ leader, also the premier of Quebec, operates with a narrow margin in which to manoeuvre — one that is more likely to shrink than expand.

Accordingly, the spirit of openness evident earlier can end quickly if the federal government decides to stress "Plan B," thereby forcing the Quebec government to avoid further negotiations, raise the ante, and make it more difficult to reach any agreement. In other words, if the federal government firmly adopts "Plan B," this can only lead to Quebec withdrawing from negotiations and a hardening of the positions of both sides.

It is within this context that we can analyze the failure of negotiations for a new family insurance system which Quebec had wanted to establish by January 1998. This is considered a key element of the Bouchard government's family policy. The system would allow access to personal income during maternal and parental leave, compensating for the limitations of the federal employment insurance program. To do so, the Quebec government asked the federal government to assume the additional costs and to consider the income as non-taxable. The two governments were unable to reach agreement on these two points and ended their negotiations, making it impossible to implement the program on schedule. In sum, Quebec wanted to create its own parental leave policy, by using the right to withdraw from the federal program as provided in federal law, and by doing so, considered that it had the right to fully recover its contributions to the federal program (not just the equivalent benefits withdrawn by parents in Quebec). At present, negotiations have stopped, but it is uncertain whether they have come to a complete halt, especially if both sides soften their positions somewhat.

The situation is different, however, where the Canadian social union is concerned. Since the premiers' meetings in Jasper in 1996 and in St. Andrews in 1997, the provincial goverments have wished to become more involved in this area, and have arrived at a compromise between the richer and poorer provinces. Their agreement recognizes the formal presence of the federal government in the social sphere and its capacity to define and establish "national standards" in areas of provincial jurisdiction, provided that the provinces participate. Bouchard has completely rejected this approach on the grounds that the constitution designates the social sphere as within provincial jurisdiction, and that the federal government's financial contributions in this area do not give it the right to impose national standards. This position had already been defended by other Quebec premiers, both Liberal and PQ. It was difficult for Bouchard to follow a different route because he had to consider the views of PQ activists. On this issue he had very little room to manoeuvre and did not dare to go outside it.

Overall, we can see that Bouchard has shown a spirit of openness toward the federal government in certain sectors, but the hardening of federal positions and the constraints imposed on him by party activists sometimes prevent him from maintaining this spirit. This is similarly evident when the premiers of the other provinces try to provide the Quebec Liberal Party with ammunition by recognizing "the unique character of Quebec society" and say they hope that the party will win the next election. How is it possible to work with other premiers who openly support your political opponent and hope you lose the next election?

WHAT OF THE FUTURE?

Quebecers, as we observed previously, are very sensitive to the way that events unfold: their support for sovereignty tends to rise during periods of crisis and fall during periods of calm. If this premise is correct, it is necessary to watch the political situation for the next two or three years, between now and the next provincial election and (if the PQ is reelected) the next referendum.

From Ottawa's perspective, two kinds of events could influence future support for sovereignty. First, the pursuit of "Plan B" amounts to a hard-line approach regarding Quebec and could generate strong reactions from its population, primarily among francophones. For instance, the next judgement of the Supreme Court on the legality of a unilateral declaration of independence could induce negative reactions in Quebec, arousing sovereignist fervour. Similarly, if Ottawa fails to recognize a majority yes vote in the next referendum, this would be perceived (and is already perceived) by many as an undemocratic act at the very moment when the sovereignist movement can pass the threshold of 50 percent of the vote. Nor should we forget that the partition movement arouses great hostility among Quebecers. Overall, then, past political-constitutional crises have had an impact on support for sovereignty, and these crises resulted from major events and untimely declarations by political leaders.

We must also take note of the presence of the Reform Party in the House of Commons, where it is now the official opposition, as well as its role outside Parliament. Its firm support for the principle of equality of all the provinces and its refusal to recognize Quebec as a distinct society should assist the sovereignist movement. However, it is highly likely that recognition of distinct society status, if it ever occurs, will have little impact in Quebec — since it will take place too late, have its meaning weakened, and only be concluded after endless negotiations. The lack of recognition remains important since Quebecers perceive it as a rejection of their province's uniqueness by the other provinces. This rejection, then, has more impact than recognition would. It is important enough that the sovereignty movement will benefit if the Reform Party continues to reject the "distinct society" concept.

The following remarks, written by Jeffrey Simpson near the end of the last federal election campaign, summarize the situation well:

> The Bloc and Reform feed off each other.... Quebec, under siege from a hostile, uncomprehending rest of Canada has for many years been a favourite depiction by secessionists. The arrival of Reform in Ottawa as official opposition will make that depiction even easier, given what Reform has said during the campaign about Quebec leaders.[19]

But sensitivity to the moment cannot explain everything: it is more useful for explaining short-term changes in mood than long-term trends. The latter certainly have more significance for Canadian unity than events of the moment, without denying their importance.

In this regard, two observations should be made. The first concerns the mobilization of Quebecers around events that might produce anger or indignation. We should note that it is becoming increasingly difficult to mobilize Quebecers against interventions or attacks by the federal government. A majority of Quebecers already believe that the federal government should have a say in a referendum question, and that more than 50 percent plus one of the votes are necessary to declare sovereignty. As well, it is growing more difficult to stir up indignation by simply recalling the patriation of the constitution in 1982 without Quebec's consent, or the defeat of the Meech Lake Accord in 1990. The memory of these events has faded with the passing of time (it has been 15 years since the patriation) and a weariness resulting from the many constitutional debates which resolved nothing.

But we should not assume that this weariness is a permanent and irreversible element of Quebec political life. If the federalist camp wants it to be, the sovereignists can still mobilize the Quebec population following major events which are perceived as unfavourable to Quebec's interests. It is, therefore, less the references to past events than the impact of new ones that aids the sovereignist movement. Similarly, the references to past events must be linked to personalities who are still playing a role in politics (e.g., connecting Jean

Chrétien to the repatriation of 1982 and the defeat of the Meech Lake Accord) if the sovereignists wish to have a real impact.

The second observation is more fundamental and deals with the support for sovereignty. The sovereignist movement begins with a base of about 35 percent of the electorate. To this, we can add 5 to 10 percent of voters who generally support the sovereignist option. Added to this fairly stable number, the support of others will often vary from poll to poll in response to political events. In this manner, 54.8 percent of Quebecers were favourable to sovereignty when it was accompanied by an offer of economic and political partnership with the rest of Canada, in the month following the 1995 referendum. Eighteen months later, in May 1997, no more than 42.9 percent expressed the same opinion.[20] However, between November 1995 and August 1996, an average of 52.4 percent of Quebecers supported sovereignty-partnership; on average only 46.4 percent took the same position between September 1996 and May 1997. More recently, a poll published on 30 August 1997 showed support for the sovereignist option at 45.4 percent. The president of Léger and Léger explains the decline by saying that some past supporters of sovereignty are now undecided and they are dissatisfied with the Bouchard government's cuts to expenditures and services.[21]

What conclusions can we draw from these numbers? Support for sovereignty, or more precisely, sovereignty-association (today referred to as sovereignty-partnership) usually lies between 40 and 50 percent. It is only after important events such as the defeat of the Meech Lake Accord in 1990 or the near-victory in the 1995 referendum that support passes the 50 percent mark. It stays at this level for a short time, and then declines. Therefore, it is difficult to mobilize consistently a majority of Quebecers in support of the sovereignty-partnership option. In these circumstances, Quebec may not find it easy to attain sovereignty and negotiate the kind of economic and political partnership that it might like, even after a majority vote for sovereignty. Such a majority would seem too volatile and unstable to provide a solid basis for sovereignty. In my opinion, the percentage of support (what level of majority?) is less important than the solidity and stability of this support; the latter will be the key factor in a referendum, because the principle of majority rule includes the risk of it turning quickly against supporters of sovereignty when they become a minority.

In pursuing the sovereignist cause, Bouchard must therefore take into account some factors that point in different directions: that Quebecers are sensitive to political events, yet it is nonetheless difficult to mobilize Quebecers against past federal actions; and that support for sovereignty-partnership sometimes exceeds the 50 percent mark, but is frequently below that level.

Overall, we may conclude that Jacques Parizeau and Lucien Bouchard embody two very different faces of sovereignty. The former represents the uncompromising, even dogmatic, vision of sovereignty; the latter appears more conciliatory, more open to agreements and more concerned with reaching an economic and political partnership with the rest of Canada. These two visions both enjoy support among Quebecers. But if Bouchard represents the softer vision of the sovereignist option, he must take into account different realities, some of them unavoidable — such as the facts that not all the PQ's members share his vision and that the Quebec population does not give majority support to the sovereignist option (most of the time). Bouchard must therefore constantly navigate between the two constraining realities that push him in different directions: to harden his position to strengthen his leadership within the party; or to show a spirit of openness and to negotiate agreements with the federal government to build support for his cause among the population as a whole. Has the change from Parizeau to Bouchard brought a new vision of sovereignty? Yes, but...

This "but" indicates that there are heavy constraints on the Bouchard government. With this in mind, how can we evaluate the non-constitutional approach to modifying Canadian federalism? First, we must stress that the actions of the Quebec government vary from issue to issue. The government cannot accept the current terms of the Canadian social union, as this would imply official recognition of federal intervention in matters of provincial jurisdiction. However, it can negotiate agreements on labour training and even eventually a family insurance program since the province's jurisdiction in these matters is officially recognized. If Quebec is likely to benefit from such ventures, the Bouchard government is willing to pursue them.

However, Bouchard's government cannot always do this. When the federal government takes a hard line toward Quebec, or when provincial premiers openly wish for his electoral defeat, it becomes more difficult for the government to open negotiations with anybody. In this case, Bouchard probably will adopt a harder line, at least until the next provincial election. While Lucien Bouchard undeniably embodies a new vision of sovereignty which contrasts with Jacques Parizeau's, he cannot cede mastery of the political game to others, especially if this causes his own defeat.

NOTES

1. This applies at least until the Calgary declaration of 14 September 1997, when the nine provincial premiers from the rest of Canada, along with the two territorial leaders, agreed on a new "Canada Clause," in which they recognized the "unique character of Quebec society" as well as recognizing equality of citizens, equality of the provinces, Aboriginal Peoples, bilingualism, and the country's multicultural character. This declaration is subject to consultations in each province according to rules that vary from one province to another.

2. See Edouard Cloutier, Jean H. Guay and Daniel Latouche, *Le virage. L'évolution de l'opinion publique au Québec depuis 1960 ou comment le Québec est devenu souverainiste* (Montreal: Quebec/Amerique, 1992), pp. 62-66.

3. Ibid., p. 67.

4. The factual material presented here draws on the work of Denis Monière and Jean H. Guay, *La bataille du Québec. Troisième épisode: 30 jours qui ébranlèrent le Canada* (Montreal: Fides, 1996), pp. 181-202.

5. Adopting a "realistic"method (rather than a proportional one) to estimate the views of the "discreet" or non-respondents, the average support for the yes side in 15 polls published between 23 August and 12 October 1995 was 45 percent. (Support for the yes side saw a slight increase at the end of September.) From the moment when the "Bouchard effect" became evident, support for sovereignty-partnership increased to 48.2 percent based on an average of the eight following polls. (The last two polls saw the yes side at 49.5 percent and 49.8 percent.) This method of estimating the distribution of support of "discreet respondents" (those who refuse to respond) was developed by Pierre Drouilly. It allocates three-quarters of this group to the no side and one-quarter to the yes side. See Pierre Drouilly, "Le référendum du 30 octobre 1995: une analyse des résultats," in *L'année politique au Québec 1995-1996*, ed. Robert Boily (Montreal: Fides, 1997), pp. 119-43.

6. It should be noted that the sovereignist camp (like the federalist camp) is able to count on a base of support of about 35 percent of the electorate.

7. Jacques Parizeau, *Pour un Québec souverain* (Montreal: VLB éditeur, 1997), p. 38.

8. Ibid., p. 348.

9. Lucien Bouchard, *À visage découvert* (Montreal: Boréal, 1992), pp. 137-57.

10. Ibid., p. 325.

11. Ibid., p. 334.

12. Under the direction of Lucien Bouchard, *Un niveau parti pour l'étape décisive* (Montreal: Fides, 1993), pp. 87-95.

13. For a more detailed analysis of these institutions in a new Canadian framework, see Réjean Pelletier, "Les arrangements institutionnels d'un nouveau partenariat" (especially the section entitled "Un partenariat d'égal à égal") to appear in Roger Gibbins and Guy Laforest (eds.), *Pour sortir de l'impasse* (Montreal: Institut de recherche en politiques publiques, 1998).

14. Parizeau, *Pour un Québec souverain*, p. 350.

15. Lucien Bouchard, "Vivre ensemble, avant, pendant et après le référendum," notes for a speech by Premier Bouchard to the anglophone community of Quebec, Montreal, 11 March 1996, pp. 6-7.

16. The factual material presented here draws on Édouard Cloutier and Yann Strutynski, "L'opinion publique québécoise," in *L'année politique au Québec 1995-1996*, ed. Boily, pp. 108-11.

17. Under the direction of Bouchard, *Un nouveau parti pour l'étape décisive*, p. 48.

18. According to the PQ's statutes, at the first convention after a general election, there will be a vote of confidence in the leader, whether or not he or she is newly-elected.

19. Jeffrey Simpson, "Postelection scenarios, none of them encouraging,"*The Globe and Mail*, 28 May 1997, p. A28.

20. These results of these polls on sovereignty-partnership were published at different times by *Le Journal de Québec*. They have been published with the permission of *Le Journal de Québec*- Groupe Léger and Léger.

21. The poll was published in *The Globe and Mail*, 30 August 1997, p. 1.

12

Searching for Plan A: National Unity and the Chrétien Government's New Federalism

Robert Howse

Malgré les plaintes disant que le gouvernement de Chrétien manque d'une vision positive du futur de la fédération, le gouvernement fédéral a en fait pris un nombre d'initiatives pour renouveler et renforcer le fédéralisme. Celles-ci comprennent la négociation réussite d'une Entente d'échange interne avec les provinces, d'importants premiers pas vers la restructuration de l'union sociale, la création d'une agence d'inspection alimentaire nationale, et la négociation d'un arrangement rationnel pour livraison des programmes au sujet du marché du travail avec les provinces. Quoique ces efforts puissent sembler dérisoires quand jugées à l'encontre des attentes créées par les politiques mégaconstitutionnelles, ils sont un moyen de renforcer l'union canadienne en tant que communauté associative, formées de citoyens individuels dont les sentiments d'appartenance à la communauté sont basés sur des valeurs et des principes partagés, sur des buts et des objectifs partagés, et sur des intérêts partagés et réciproques, ces derniers reflétés dans les rapports économiques et sociaux parmi des individus à travers le pays. Cette idée de communauté associative est conforme à une allégeance parallèle à des communautés d'identités constituées par un langage commun ou autres liens sous politiques parmi les gens. Cela dépends aussi, cependant, sur un lien direct entre l'individu et la communauté associative canadienne, lequel est sans intermédiaire de la part de ces autres communautés d'identités. La déclaration de Calgary apporte le risque que les efforts apportés pour renforcer la communauté associative canadienne, seront encore une fois mélangés dans des politiques d'identités — ceci est une tentation qui devrait être évitée autant que possible. Plutôt, le défi principal est de mieux engager les individus et les organisations non gouvernementales dans des initiatives pour renforcer la communauté associative canadienne.

INTRODUCTION

Whatever the views of the proverbial "ordinary Canadian,"[1] media pundits, opposition politicians and constitutional experts have been relentless in pestering the federal government to develop a plan to "save Canada" — Plan *A*, as it has now come to be known. Despite the grandiose failure of what Peter Russell has described as "mega-constitutional politics"[2] in the Canada round, there is no shortage of new proposals being generated that purport to restructure fundamentally the Canadian federation in the cause of unity. These include André Burelle's European Union-inspired scheme of co-determination in *Le Mal canadien*; Tom Courchene's ACCESS; and Gordon Gibson's original Plan *A*. Further "solutions" to the purported unity crisis are being worked on by a group of individuals oddly named the Group of 22, and by the Business Council on National Issues.

The grand and comprehensive aspiration of most of these schemes indicates that the authors have learned little or nothing from the Charlottetown debacle — once acquired, a taste for mega-constitutional politics seems hard to shake off. Yet despite the high risks, mega-constitutional politics often sets the implicit (and sometimes explicit) standard against which more modest, more subtle, incremental changes to the working of the federation are judged and found wanting.

Against this tendency, there is much to be said for judging the Chrétien government's record on federalism on its own terms, that is, not as a timid and unsatisfactory attempt at some kind of comprehensive national unity project, but rather as based on *an alternative vision* to that of mega-constitutional politics. This entails viewing the evolution of the Canadian federation as advanced best not by "throwing the dice" and the manufacture or exploitation of crisis, but through step-by-step evolution of federal practice to reflect changing realities and evolving conceptions of justice. This vision is underpinned by an understanding of the institutional sophistication and complexity of the Canadian constitutional order, which adapts and changes through multiple channels and processes, including the political practice of federal-provincial relations, formalized intergovernmental agreements and the judicial interpretation of the constitution.[3] Even the major innovation of the *Charter of Rights and Freedoms* in 1982 can be seen as the culmination of an increasing rights orientation in Canadian political culture, expressed in provincial human rights codes, and a series of constitutional decisions that inferred the protection of civil liberties from the general character of the Canadian constitution and the Canadian form of government. Similarly multilculturalism and its constitutional entrenchment were less a product of some ideal model of Canadian society, but a response to the reality of its changing shape. Likewise the amendment to the constitution in 1982 giving provinces increased control over their natural resources emerged from a context of difficult political bargaining and interaction between the provinces and the federal government, not from an academic's or bureaucrat's conception of an ideal, rational division of powers.

On the basis of this more institutionally subtle and complex vision of how the federation evolves, the Chrétien government can claim some important achievements, although these will doubtless seem paltry to those still trapped in the mindset of mega-constitutional politics. The government has success-fully pursued and achieved a major agreement with the provinces on the removal of barriers to internal trade; it has restructured its policy role in la-bour market training, developing agreements with the provinces that get the federal government out of the service delivery end while vindicating the na-tional interest through performance-based, negotiated national standards; the government has begun to reimagine the Canadian social union, working with the provinces under the umbrella of the Ministerial Council for Social Policy Renewal and already achieving concrete results in the area of child poverty.[4] A new national institution, the Canadian Food Inspection Agency, has been created, consolidating and rationalizing important functions within the fed-eral government while providing a new institutional framework for interjurisdictional cooperation.

If this were not enough, the government has — in the Speech from the Throne and the second *Red Book* of the Liberal Party — given itself the task, during the second mandate, of further enhancing mobility within the Cana-dian economic and social union, and pledged on 26 February 1996 to "work with the provinces and the private sector" to achieve "a much more open agree-ment" on internal trade.

If the federal government has not neglected the task of strengthening the Canadian community, it has been labouring at some disadvantage because its vision of the Canadian community has remained largely unarticulated. Per-haps as a reaction to unrealistic and grandiose schemes, the government has consciously decided to portray its activity as muddling through or making the federation work better.

In this chapter, I propose a vision of Canadian community that makes sense for the twenty-first century; a vision nevertheless rooted in the major trans-formations in the Canadian polity that have occurred in the last 25 years, from the introduction of bilingualism to the holding of a national constitutional referendum; and a vision that vindicates the general intuitions behind the sig-nificant but incremental changes to federalism that the government has sought to achieve over the last five years. Because this is not a partisan effort, it will also entail criticisms of federal practice, although not from the perspective of mega-constitutional politics.

CANADA: WHAT KIND OF COMMUNITY?

The search for Canadian community has often, if not usually, been defined in terms of finding a Canadian identity. This is hardly surprising since, in impor-tant ways, the entire agenda of nation-building has been a response or a reaction to those who do seem to know who they are — Americans on the one hand, and francophone Quebecers on the other. English Canadians have sought a nation that would look like, and compete with, what others understood by a national community — one based on a Canadian *identity*.

At least as a response to Quebec nationalism, this has been a self-defeating process, because, rooted in language and culture, french Quebec as a community of *identity* appears obviously more authentic and compelling than Canada, where the markers of identity — a few symbols and few distinctive public policies — seem much weaker and more tenuous. If Canada, in the strong sense, were to be a democratic community of identity it would need to be a community reflecting the language, culture, and so on, of the majority — therefore, crudely speaking, English-Canadian. And this is precisely why many Quebecers, including many who care for Canada, have seen attempts to strengthen Canadian nationalism as a threat to the existence of Quebec as a community of identity. How can one have allegiance to Quebec as a community of identity, and also be a *Canadian* nationalist, when nation is defined in cultural or linguistic terms?

The predominant answer to this dilemma has been to conceive Canada, not as a nation at all, but a "community of communities," as "two nations" or — perhaps including the Aboriginal Peoples — several nations. Canada is not itself a community of identity but a kind of shell or umbrella for many identities. This was most clearly manifested in the so-called "Canada Clause" of the Charlottetown Accord, which recognized all manner of collective identities, as if one added up the sum of these and arrived at Canada.

Yet these notions of "community of communities" or "two (or more) nations" are merely vapid formulas, at least in defining what makes Canada itself a *community*. They are based on the outlook that, if we somehow could solve all provincial and regional, or other group grievances, then national unity would magically appear on the horizon.[5] But a community cannot be defined, much less justified, in such negative terms. One sometimes hears of couples who go into marriage therapy, making heroic efforts to solve all their grievances and complaints, but then discover — after working out the most delicate and complex *modus vivendi* — that they no longer love one another, that there no longer exists a community of interest and feeling.

How then to begin thinking about Canada as a community of interest and feeling that is, nevertheless, compatible with allegiance by its members to other communities of identity, yet more than the aggregate of these other communities? In fact, there are ways of belonging to a political community that do not implicate a shared *identity* that has been forged through some pre- or sub-political bond between the majority of individuals that constitute the community. Because of the obsession with identity politics, these other conceptions of belonging or allegiance have been underexplored in Canadian political and constitutional discourse.

One of these ways of belonging is expressed in the idea of constitutional patriotism, developed by the German philosopher Jürgen Habermas.[6] This denotes an idea of citizenship and allegiance based upon shared values and principles, typically embodied in a liberal democratic constitution. A further kind of belonging, also not based on identity, is denoted by association for shared ends. This entails not simply the sharing of abstract values and principles but active association for the realization of specific projects or goals — saving the environment or eliminating child poverty, for example.[7] In addition, a sense of belonging can evolve and crystallize through what Joseph Weiler calls "long term peaceful relations with thickening economic and social intercourse"[8] — interaction and intermingling of individuals, with shared or complementary economic, social or cultural interests. When Canadians trade across the country, move for reasons of work or study, maintain friendships that cross provincial, regional, and linguistic boundaries, they affirm the reality of this form of belonging to a Canadian community. All three of these ways of belonging are associative rather than identity-based — they are premised on the will of *individuals* to live together and interact, whether based on shared values, or shared goals, or shared, or complementary interests. Thus, Canada as an associative community is not a compound of other communities or collectivities, but a community of individual citizens, who may have parallel allegiances to communities of identity, but whose association as *Canadians* need not be mediated through those other identity-based communities.[9]

Political theorists have often viewed these non-identity-based forms of belonging as somehow weak or inadequate as a basis for national unity. Thus, Will Kymlicka suggests that shared values are not sufficient to produce "social unity," but a shared identity is required as well.[10] Yet these claims are rarely documented properly. In some contexts, even shared values or ideology have been enough to create the kind of social unity that causes people of different nationalities to fight in wars and risk their lives — North Americans did not fight in the second world war on the basis of a shared national identity, but in significant measure for the cause of freedom and democracy. Still, it may well be true that shared identity is often the *easiest* way to produce strong forms of allegiance to the community, unconstrained or unqualified by whether the community serves values, goals, or interests that can be rationally articulated and debated. Associative communities, by contrast, rarely sustain the "my country, right or wrong! variety of patriotism" — the community continually has to justify the allegiance of its members in exemplifying or serving the values, ends, and interests that are shared or overlapping, and this is always a matter of democratic argument and debate, in which at the limit the community itself and its reason for being are *en jeu*. But is social unity of the unconditional kind really an appropriate foundation for a liberal democratic federation? Perhaps it is a *desirable* feature of associative communities, that they are unlikely to be plagued by the forms of extremism characteristic of unreflective and unconditional attachment to a community of identity.

The attempt to address national unity through megaconstitutional politics has invariably led to an emphasis on the recognition of group identity — different groups struggle to have communities of identity constitutionally recognized and protected. The Canadian nationalist counter-reaction is to argue for Canada itself as a community of identity — thereby increasing the threat to other communities of identity within Canada. But facilitating associative forms of belonging to the Canadian community need pose no such threat, provided this is done carefully. To be sure, *any* meaningful direct allegiance to an associative community that transcends particular identities is a threat to extreme forms of nationalism or collectivism that seek to *absolutize* a single community of identity as the central, predominating locus of human allegiance. But, once we understand properly the distinction between identity-based and associative community, the question, for example, as to whether Quebecers are Canadians or Quebecers first need never again be asked — one's primary attachment to Quebec as a community of identity need not conflict with an attachment to Canada as an associative community. There may, of course, be disagreements between these two communities on specific policies, for communities of identity do overlap with communities of association — both may have a legitimate stake in areas like social and economic policy, and may have a different perspective on these matters. But these conflicts are not conflicts of *allegiance* as such.

Managing the co-existence of an associative Canadian community with communities of identity is perhaps the most fundamental challenge of liberal democratic governance in Canada. Pierre Trudeau had a tendency to formulate this in terms of a competition of allegiances, implying that a fully emancipated member of the Canadian community of association would no longer need or would be jettisoning a community of identity — like growing up and leaving home.[11] Yet communities of identity provide a permanent and vital support for the projects we have as autonomous agents, and for the ends that we may wish to pursue as members of communities of association: they constitute a significant part of what Robert Putnam calls "social capital."[12] This is a point that Will Kymlicka has elaborated in arguing for the importance of cultural context in the free self-development of the individual.[13]

At the same time, communities of identity (if they are genuinely liberal and democratic, and do not practise ethnic cleansing) usually have minorities within them who do not share the identity on which the community is based in quite the same way as the majority — perhaps because the identity of the minority has been acquired rather than being predetermined in the way that identities are often thought to be, or because they belong *as well* to some other community of identity. Moreover, communities of identity must deal with the reality that their members are likely to have multiple or plural identities — whether through marriage, and family background, or because characteristics such as gender or religion cross-cut with those elements of identity upon which the *community* of identity is based (e.g., majority language). If, then, communities of identity are to manage properly the inevitable challenge of pluralism, they must draw on some of the strengths that are likely to be exhibited by the associative community, particularly the use of universal frameworks of rights and norms as a basis for cooperation among people who are different.

In sum, the relationship between communities of identity and associative community — between different kinds of belonging — is not intrinsically one of competition, but rather of balance between the distinctive strengths and weaknesses of two different kinds of human affiliation or attachment. This balance would be lost, if one were to attempt Canadian unity by turning Canada itself into a community of identity *or* if one were to conceive the Canadian community merely as a compound of different communities of identity, each of which mediates the relationship between its own members and the Canadian union as a whole.[14]

THE CONSTITUTION AS A FRAMEWORK FOR ASSOCIATIVE COMMUNITY

It is quite remarkable to what extent the original and evolving architecture of the Canadian constitution can be understood as a framework for a community of association, where living together is based on shared values, common goals, and thickening or evolving economic and social intercourse between citizens. The federal powers over trade and commerce, over areas that relate to the common infrastructure required for economic and social intercourse such as interprovincial transportation, aviation, telecommunications, and broadcasting, as well as the provisions on federal works and undertakings are all relevant to this understanding. They give to the federal government, which is democratically responsible for the entire community, the responsibility for ensuring the means for economic and social intercourse among its members. Other provisions, such as the prohibition of internal tariff barriers in section 121, and the mobility rights[15] and equalization[16] provisions of the *Constitution Act, 1982* reflect the fact that not only the protection of free intercourse through negative rights to move and to trade, but governance mechanisms as well, are needed to facilitate thickening economic and social intercourse among Canadians.[17]

The broader relationship between the original and evolving architecture of the constitution and the idea of Canada as a community of association has been grasped in a variety of Supreme Court judgements: for example, in *S.M.T. (Eastern) Ltd. v. Winner*, Rand J. suggested that "To be a citizen of Canada must be a dynamic reality that extends beyond the realm of political and legal institutions to the vital aspects of one's material existence ... [The] freest possible access to the national market should be inherent to Canadian citizenship and therefore secured in the Constitution."[18] More recently, LaForest J., in the cases of *Morguard* and *Hunt* has articulated the relationship between economic union and the idea of Canadian citizenship.[19]

In policy and constitutional debates over the last decade or so, the connection between economic union and the idea of Canada as a community of association has nevertheless frequently been obscured. In various ways, the economic union "agenda" has become identified with a *laissez-faire* outlook, or a conservative economic platform more generally. In the Canada round of constitutional negotiations, the idea of a social union was introduced in the first instance to counter this *laissez-faire* version of the economic union, as if it were premised upon a different and opposed ideological outlook.[20] Thus, what might have been an opportunity for broadening the concept of economic union into a fuller notion of the requirements of a community of association was largely lost. However, as was acknowledged at least as early as the Rowell-Sirois Commission, portability and comparability of social benefits could facilitate movement of people across Canada — when people do not move because they lose the degree and kind of social support provided by the community that they are exiting, we have an impediment to labour mobility in Canada, one of the most important dimensions of the Canadian community of association.[21]

More controversially, the viability of an associative community can be argued to depend, not only on economic and social mobility, but also upon the realization of a conception of distributive justice among its members — this may include the conception of a minimum level of social welfare as a right of citizenship[22] and also a notion about sharing the benefits and burdens of the association equitably. Both dimensions can be found in section 36 of the *Constitution Act, 1982*, which commits the federal and provincial governments to providing reasonable levels of public services, wherever citizens may live in the country, and also gives the federal government a role and responsibility in equalization.[23] There is, I believe, a special case for norms about social equality in an associative community. In communities of identity, people almost naturally see their likeness to other members, since membership is defined by some pre-political common characteristic, language, ethnicity, culture, regional customs and history, etc. Hence, such communities can afford unusual degrees of social and civic inequality, without necessarily risking the sense of community itself — in fact, communities of identity have often been caste societies. But communities of association depend on a *civic* bond between their members, and this bond is both practically, as well as theoretically, difficult to sustain in the absence of equality of opportunity and meaningful rights to participate in the social and economic intercourse of the community. This does not necesarily translate into a convincing case for welfare rights, but it does suggest at a minimum that one cannot be indifferent to the emergence of vast discrepencies in the social protection enjoyed by citizens in different localities, if one wishes to sustain the idea of common citizenship that underlies the associative community.

THE FEDERAL ROLE

Democratically elected by the Canadian people as a whole, it would be inconceivable if the federal government did not have a major role in evolving the institutions, norms, and policies needed to sustain and develop Canada as an associative community. As already suggested, many of the federal government's explicit competences go to facilitating economic and social intercourse among citizens. But, as the only public authority democratically responsible to the members of the association itself, the federal government's responsibility in sustaining and facilitating the community naturally exceeds the normal pursuit of discrete public policy goals within well-circumscribed competences. The government cannot be indifferent to the impact of policy outcomes of other orders of government on the sustainability of the associative community. At a formal juridical and constitutional level, this can be accounted for through the elasticity of federal general powers of Peace, Order and Good Government and Trade and Commerce, especially as recently interpreted by the Supreme Court.[24] But given the precarious constitutional status of these powers prior to the recent jurisprudence, the federal government tended to rely very extensively on the spending power to sustain its overall role in facilitating the community of association.

The use of the spending power provided necessary leverage to achieve certain results. But in various ways it also weakened or failed to strengthen the community of association. By paying substantial parts of the bill, the federal government was able to impose conditions on other governments that helped sustain the associative community, but the ease of doing so obviated a more subtle policy dialogue, or the need to state explicitly, and to win agreement on the shared values and principles, and the shared goals or ends, informing the union. Moreover, there were problems in realizing the associative community that could hardly be solved through spending, such as various regulatory barriers to internal trade, and these remained inadequately addressed.

As well, the federal role in sustaining the associative community was entangled with a command and control view of what governments do, despite the fact that here in essence its function is facilitative of intercourse among citizens, and is one that cannot by its nature be performed without engaging the confidence and resources of other actors. Thus, in securing the social union through national standards in the Canada Assistance Plan, in fact, the federal government sought to prescribe modes of delivery, or forms of programming, as if operating within an exclusively federal jurisdiction; this was even more the case with labour market training, where the government actually involved itself in creating and managing the detail of programs within individual communities.[25] Labour mobility concerns, and the relationships between macroeconomic policy, trade, labour markets, and adjustment gave the federal

Government a legitimate policy *stake* — provincially driven approaches might not satisfactorily reflect the need to retrain workers for jobs *elsewhere* in Canada, and might pose new barriers to mobility, through residency reqirements, etc.[26] But the manner of federal intervention relfected an inadequate appreciation of the extent to which the quality of the outcomes must depend on the engagement and support of other actors — whether provincial governments, with their responsibility for labour markets and education, or trade unions and community associations, critical sources of social capital.

THE CHRÉTIEN STYLE OF FEDERALISM

The Chrétien government has been cautious and bold at the same time in defining its role in sustaining Canada as an associative community of association. On the one hand, it has retreated from unilateralist or hierarchical approaches to sustaining the Canadian community of association; on the other hand, it has been much more insistent than previous governments have often been on the evolution of explicit principles and norms as a framework for association and it has defended vigorously the value of mobility, which is crucial to thickening economic and social intercourse among citizens.

THE ECONOMIC UNION

The federal government, through relentless moral pressure on the provinces (but not the heavy-handed use of carrots and sticks) encouraged the conclusion of a comprehensive statement of principles and norms for economic mobility within Canada, the Agreement on Internal Trade (the AIT). Harsh criticisms have been levelled at the agreement from the perspective of free trade — it contains many exceptions or loopholes, it is not legally-binding and often represents an agreement to engage in further negotiations, many of which have made little progress.[27] In fact, there is much to be said for the positive appreciation of the agreement by, for instance, Bruce Doern, who sees it as an unprecedented attempt at providing a general normative framework to structure the interaction of governments with a view to a particular set of pan-Canadian objectives.[28]

However, the agreement has largely failed at engaging citizens — the members of the Canadian associative community — in those processes. This is a view also articulated by Knox in his contribution to this volume. The loose institutional frameworks envisaged by the agreement are largely intergovernmental in character. Its language, largely borrowed from international trade arrangements, is inscrutable to the non-expert citizen. Indeed, it does not reflect the economic union as a characteristic of Canadian citizenship but rather merely as a free trade arrangement. Access to dispute settlement for individual citizens has been curbed through a screening process.[29] It is significant that one area where progress is being made in realizing the AIT blueprint is labour mobility, where a degree of dynamism has been achieved through the engagement of non-governmental actors such as unions and regulatory and licensing bodies for trades and professions. As well, the entitlements under this chapter of the AIT have been effectively publicized, and the dispute settlement process internal to this chapter stands out in its capacity to allow individual citizens the opportunity to challenge barriers to mobility.

The federal government could do much more to engage citizens in the AIT exercise, without changing the text of the agreement. For example, in cooperation with various business and labour associations, and other stakeholders, it could seek to disseminate much more information about the provisions of the agreement, explaining these in terms of a citizen's charter of economic mobility rights, and their relationship to the overall architecture of Canada as a community of association. The secretariat itself could be transformed into a much more proactive organization,[30] with a mandate for dialogue and interaction with the public — obviously, this would require the support of the provinces and territories.[31]

THE SOCIAL UNION

The dismantling of the Canada Assistance Plan (CAP) was widely interpeted as the first stage in federal withdrawal from an active policy role in social assistance. However, it is becoming evident that this was really the first stage in a much more careful but also more explicit redefinition of the federal stake in social policy outcomes in terms of social mobility, and perhaps also distributional equity (with a reconceptualization of equalization), as well as a rethinking of the means appropriate to vindicating such a policy stake.

It is significant that the one CAP condition that remained was a prohibition on residency requirements, reflecting the core value of mobility, and equally significant that, when British Columbia flouted this prohibition, the federal government held its ground, achieving a negotiated settlement that actually entailed placing mobility on the intergovernmental social policy agenda.[32] The mobility principle was thus recognized to entail some kind of broader set of principles and norms that address divergent levels of social protection, and costs and benefits to provincial societies of inward and outward migration from other parts of Canada.[33]

It is easy to misinterpret[34] the fact that the federal government has placed less emphasis on explicit carrots and sticks in playing its role as ultimate democratic guarantor of the community of association — allowing, for instance, the provincial Ministerial Council to take the initiative, in the first instance, in developing proposals on principles and norms to govern the evolution of the Canadian social union. This does not constitute federal withdrawal. All the actors are aware of the federal government's continuing financial role in sustaining the social union; that if it wishes, it can choose the path of disentanglement, substituting a unilateral policy role through the tax system; and that the government gains legitimacy and credibility from being elected by the Canadian people as a whole.[35] When federal officials communicate the federal policy stake in sustaining the social union, it can reasonably be presumed that the provinces do not simply hang up the phone on them. What the Chrétien government has rightly rejected is a *macho* style of federal-provincial relations that brought discredit to the federal role, however legitimate in principle.[36] In sum, one can walk softly, while still carrying a big stick.

Finally, the federal government has discovered resources other than large grants of money with which to pursue its legitimate policy stake in the social union. For example, the government has a unique database, from federal tax information to mobility across Canada — probably essential to the settlement of disputes concerning the burdens and benefits of interprovincial migration. This last insight goes, of course, beyond the social union context, and will be discussed below in connection with the Canadian Food Inspection Agency initiative.

LABOUR MARKET TRAINING

The restructuring of the federal role in labour market training has almost always been presented, at least in the media, as an example of decentralization. This is ironic, because in its agreements with the provinces, the federal government has moved closer to a structure for accountability for results than it had ever achieved when it was acting as a direct purchaser of training.[37] The agreements foresee the development of a national methodology by the *federal* government to establish national results levels for the programs, determined in accordance with criteria that include return to employment of Employment Insurance clients. The process of evaluation of results is to be overseen by a joint federal-provincial evaluation committee.[38] Future federal funding is to be adjusted on the basis of the results.

By establishing a national methodology, the federal government will in fact be able to create a kind of competition between provinces — which are the more, and the which less, successful in achieving results with the programs will be evident, and those more successful can obviously be rewarded with greater funding in the future. Moreover, from the perspective of the associative community, it is important to note that the agreements prohibit residency requirements as a condition of access training benefits. This facilitates interprovincial labour mobility, by allowing an individual to move into any province in Canada where he or she believes that a training program is available that will meet specific needs, or where it is possible to obtain a job, once trained or retrained. Moreover, because the performance of the programs is defined in terms of criteria that do not refer to the *provincial* labour market, but reemployment generally, the provinces do have an incentive to provide training, even where the trainee may find reemployment elsewhere in Canada — no such incentive would exist in the case of purely provincial programs defined in terms of intraprovincial criteria for success. In sum, to the extent that the federal role in sustaining the Canadian associative community is implicated in labour market training, the federal government has been able to better define, and will probably be better able to vindicate this role in the future, through its agreements with the provinces. At the same time, in removing itself from direct provision and detailed program design, the federal government will be better able to exploit the social capital of other communities, some of which may be communities of identity, in the development of integrated networks for training, education, retraining, and job search.

THE CANADIAN FOOD INSPECTION AGENCY

Food inspection is an area where executive federalism was particularly unsuccessful in generating effective cooperation and concerted action by the various levels of government.[39] I believe the initiatives of the federal government in this area display particularly well some of the characteristics of the Chrétien approach to federalism already mentioned, but especially the tendency to more carefully and precisely conceptualize the federal government's own policy stake and role *at the same time as more effectively engaging other responsible actors, including the provinces.* Thus, in the case of food inspection, the federal government proceeded simultaneously on two fronts: reorganizing and refocussing its own often diffuse involvement in the area through the consolidation of the direct federal role in a new agency, while at the same time undertaking a variety of federal-provincial initiatives, in close consultation with industry and consumer interests, one success of which is the National Dairy Code. The government never lost sight of, and indeed more clearly conceived, its own policy stake as the government representative of all Canadians, with responsibilities for international and internal commerce in agricultural products (the latter engaging the associative community); it brought to the intergovernmental table its own expertise and vision of the future of food inspection, given globalization and developments in best regulatory practice. In sum, the federal government, while not attempting to *impose* its vision, never lost sight of its distinctive role and competencies, and its responsibility as government of *all* Canadians; it did not recede into the position of just another government in a co-determination processs. And indeed, the government — rightly in my view — resisted the temptation to turn the Canadian Food Inspection Agency into a formal co-determination mechanism with the provinces. The agency remains a federal entity, but also provides a forum for more effective links and joint initiatives with the provinces and indeed other stakeholders in the overall food inspection system, but this has not been solidified into formal joint-decisionmaking.

CONCLUSION

The Chrétien government has evolved a new way of doing federalism in Canada, shifting the focus away from the politics of identity toward the support and development of the Canadian associative community. It has combined a more carefully and explicitly defined articulation of the federal government's role as a national government, with the gradual evolution of a set of subtle instruments more capable of engaging other actors, whether provinces, the private sector, or other communities, while also responding to the limits of traditional command and control styles of federal intervention. The government has wisely steered clear of attempting to use federal powers to assert a strong Canadian nationalism that would somehow "compete" with Quebec nationalism. Instead, it has focused on a strengthening of the associative community of Canadians through the evolution of the Canadian economic and social union — which does not threaten or compete with communities of identity, but as the labour market training example shows, can actually exploit their social capital in the achievement of pan-Canadian goals.

As the example of the economic union most clearly illustrates, however, where the government has to some extent failed has been in the engagement of citizens directly in the the new federalism. The idea of associative community is, of course, in its essence the idea of a community of citizens, not governments.[40] The government should define more clearly the new federalism in terms of a context of engagement with a wider range of actors than just provinces. This need not involve the development of new and grandiose structures — the stimulation of public debate, the education of citizens about the constitutional foundations of the associative community, the provision of information about rights and entitlements provided through intergovernmental agreements, whether the AIT or the labour market training accords, all serve to engage citizens directly in the new federalism, without the need to devise novel decisionmaking structures at odds with established understandings about the lines of governmental accountability. This is all part of developing an ethos of *citizenship* appropriate to an associative community, as an alternative to the construction of a Canadian *identity*. Indeed, in the development of this ethos a greater self-consciousness of the extent to which Canada does function as an associative community is important, and the federal government should consider providing a regular report on free movement in Canada, using its unparalleled statistical resources to document, in an accessible fashion, the multiple links and contacts, economic, social, educational, and so on, that bind us as an associative community, a community of *citizens*. At the same time, inasmuch as new formal structures *are* being created, for instance for dispute settlement in the case of principles or norms governing the social union, direct access for citizens is vital to the concept of Canada as a community of association.[41]

Finally, the federal government must continue to retain its own distinctive policy stake in the Canadian associative community; it is not merely a facilitator of interprovincial cooperation to sustain that community, but the *democratic* authority that is uniquely responsible for that community in itself. Part of the answer to the democratic deficit that has plagued the European Union as well as executive federalism in Canada, an answer that the Europeans do not unfortunately have easily available to them, is that in Canada there is one government that is at the intergovernmental table with a claim to represent the *entire* community. Contrary to the suggestion of André Burelle,[42] the traditional European co-decision model cannot be easily analogized to Canadian federalism, because that model supposes that each deciding partner represents some particular community constituting part of a whole, while no partner is present representing the European *demos* itself. Despite its initial promise, strengthening the European Parliament has not succeeded in correcting the democratic deficit of European executive federalism, simply because the Parliament does not have its own executive, ultimately responsible to the European *demos*, which can directly participate in the co-decision process among representatives of national governments.

A closely related point is that the federal government, just as it should avoid locking into a rigid co-decision framework for conducting intergovernmental relations, should also avoid the elevation, if that is the right word, of intergovernmental negotiations on the social union or further economic union negotiations, into a kind of pseudo-constitutional process where the attempt is to recast, through non-constitutional means, the division of powers. As the labour market accords illustrate, the federal government has flexible means at its disposal to restructure its involvement in areas where rebalancing is appropriate given policy substance. On the other hand, pseudo-constitutionalism, as for instance, entailed in the full-blown version of the Courchene *ACCESS* proposal is likely to once again re-engage the politics of identity, making national unity if anything more elusive.[43] It is possible to seek agreement on the norms and principles governing the social union, without any political statement about the extent or limits on federal or provincial *powers* — the existing powers are simply re-affirmed (as in the AIT) remain the same, but the focus is on articulating the *lignes directrices* for some foundational elements in the Canadian associative community, which inform the interaction of governments and their relationship to citizens.

The federal government has also supported recognition of the distinctiveness of Quebec, one community of identity within the Canadian federation, and in so doing it has not avoided altogether the dangers of entangling identity politics with the challenge of strenthening the Canadian associative community. However, such recognition does not in itself entail a conflict with the idea of Canada as an associative community — as long as it is not undertaken in a manner that suggests that the associative community itself is constituted by two (or more) nations as communities of identity, rather than by citizens of all identities. The call for consultations on national unity in the declaration that emerged at the September 1997 Premiers' Meeting in Calgary based on a framework consisting of general principles will require a carefully crafted federal response. The principles in their ambiguity and uncertain interrelationship reflect the land mines of identity politics — thus all provinces have "equal status" while Quebec has a "unique character" and Canada's "gift of diversity" includes "a multicultural citizenry drawn from all parts of the world." This is an invitation to become mired once again in the intractable task of sorting out how abstract constitutional recognition of very different kinds of identities and communities of identity can be consistent with equality of citizens. The thrust of this chapter suggests that the federal government should instead place the emphasis on concrete measures to better manage the co-existence of communities of identity with the Canadian associative community. The Labour Market Agreement with Quebec is precisely an example of such a concrete measure, reflecting the distinct needs of the province in this area, without trying to make a general statement about the place of Quebec in Canada, or how, for example, that place differs from or is similar to the place of various aboriginal communities. Similarly, the complex, and often difficult process of negotiating self-government arrangements with individual aboriginal communities, however frustrating and unjustifiably slow, has shown considerably more promise than the effort to define a constitutional "right" to aboriginal self-government, and the relation of this right to federal and provincial powers and to the *Charter of Rights and Freedoms*. In sum, far from ignoring the important challenge of allowing communities of identity their appropriate place within Canada, the federal government should continue to respond to this challenge in ways that avoid the politics of group *recognition*, which is how constitutional identity politics have been cast from Meech Lake on. The idea of Quebec's distinctiveness or unique character should be viewed, then, as a principle among others to inform concrete policy-making where the federal government and Quebec government have shared or overlapping interests, and not as a substitute for the symbolism of constitutional recognition.[44]

In its future initiatives to sustain and evolve the Canadian community of association, the federal government will rightly not be returning to command and control methods of unilateralism. It will be acting increasingly with and through other stakeholders — which means taking account of their views and interests in the shaping and reshaping of policy. But there are times when it will be more appropriate to engage directly with citizens or the private sector rather than with other governments; times when the appropriate approach is bilateral arrangements with individual governments, which could become trilateral if other organizations become involved (for example, in alternative service delivery); and at yet other times a full-blown multilateral intergovernmental process. By avoiding a global approach to the definition of powers and decision-rules the federal government maintains this kind of flexibility, and preserves the full range of possibilities inherent in its unique role and responsibility as the government of Canadians as a whole — of a sovereign *demos* or people.

NOTES

1. A recent *Globe*/Environics poll found that a majority of the population was generally supportive of the Chrétien government on the issue of unity, 56 percent nationwide with 45 percent in Quebec (reflecting close to the entire federalist population of the province). *The Globe and Mail*, 4 August 1997, p. A1.

2. See Peter Russell, *Constitutional Odyssey: Can Canadians Become a Sovereign People?* (Toronto: University of Toronto Press, 1995), ch. 11.

3. See the suggestion by Katherine Swinton that Canada's constitutional order "is continuously being restructured through various mechanisms such as intergovernmental agreements, tax and spending policies and judicial decisions." Katherine Swinton, "Concluding Panel," in *Seeking a New Canadian Partnership,* ed. F.L. Seidle (Montreal: Institute for Public Policy, 1994), p. 203.

4. See Kenneth Battle, *Transformation: Canadian Social Policy, 1985-2001* (Ottawa: Caledon Institute of Social Policy, 1997), pp. 31-32.

5. This is the perspective behind Kenneth McRoberts' diatribe against Pierre Trudeau; Kenneth McRoberts, *Misconceiving Canada: The Struggle for National Unity* (Oxford: Oxford University Press, 1997); see my review of this book and McRoberts' response, *Policy Options*, October 1997, pp. 44-48.

6. Jürgen Habermas, "Citizenship and National Identity: Some Reflections on the Future of Europe"*Praxis International* 12, 1 (1992).

7. See, for instance, Aristotle, *Politics*, Book I (Oxford: Clarendon Press, 1916).

8. Joseph H.H. Weiler, "The State 'über alles'," Harvard Jean Monnet Working Paper 6/95 (Cambridge, MA: Harvard Law School). The basic argument of my chapter owes much to this paper, and to a related conversation with Professor Weiler.

9. This conception is developed in the discussion of Canadians as a democratic people in R. Howse and A. Malkin, "Canadians are a Sovereign People: How the Supreme Court Should Approach the Reference on Quebec Secession," *Canadian Bar Review* 76 (1997): 197-200.

10. Will Kymlicka, *Multicultural Citizenship* (Oxford: Oxford University Press, 1995).

11. Indeed, there is a cosmopolitan position that goes further than Trudeau and questions whether any positive moral value attaches at all to association based on shared identity, as opposed to a shared universal humanity. See the essay by Martha Nussbaum, in *For Love of Country* (Boston: Beacon, 1996). This is the position erroneously attributed to Trudeau by McRoberts, *Misconceiving Canada,* for instance.

12. Robert Putnam, *Making Democracy Work: Civic Traditions in Modern Italy* (Princeton: Princeton University Press, 1993).

13. Will Kymlicka, *Multicultural Citizenship* (Oxford: Clarendon, 1995).

14. As Charles Taylor, for instance, proposes in "Shared and Divergent Values," in *Reconciling the Solitudes: Essays on Canadian Federalism and Nationalism* (Montreal: McGill-Queen's University Press, 1993), pp. 182-84. Taylor's notion of Canadian identity, for Quebecers for instance, "passing through" or being mediated by their primary community of identity should be contrasted with Weiler's conception of a "civic, value-driven demos *co-existing side by side* with a national organic-cultural one," Weiler, "The State 'über alles'," p. 46.

15. *Charter of Rights and Freedoms*, section 6

16. *Constitution Act, 1982,* section 36.

17. This draws on work in progress of the author and Stevan Pepa, "Trade, Mobility and the Future of the Economic Union," University of Toronto, Faculty of Law, 1997.

18. [1951] S.C.R. 887.

19. *Morguard Investments Ltd. v. DeSavoye* [1990] 3 S.C.R. 1077 and *Hunt v. T & N plc.*

20. The argument that social and economic union are intrinsically linked is developed in Robert Howse, *Economic Union, Social Justice, and Constitutional Reform: Towards a High and Level Playing Field* (Toronto: Centre for Public Law and Public Policy, York University, 1992); see particularly the critique there of the economic efficiency perspective on the union at 12-15.

21. See Keith Banting, *The Welfare State and Canadian Federalism* (Montreal: McGill-Queen's University Press, 1982).

22. See M. Jackman, "The Protection of Welfare Rights Under the Charter," *University of Ottawa Law Review* 20 (1988): 305.

23. See Robin Boadway, "Federal-Provincial Relations in the Wake of Deficit Reduction" in *Canada: The State of the Federation 1989,* ed. R. Watts and D. Brown (Kingston: Institute of Intergovernmental Relations, Queen's University, 1989). See also Robert Howse, "Another Rights Revolution? The Charter and the Reform of Social Policy in Canada" in *Redefining Social Security,* ed. P. Grady, R. Howse and J. Maxwell, (Kingston: School of Policy Studies, Queen's University, 1995) and "Find New Ways to Secure our Social Union," *Policy Options*, June (1996).

24. *R v. Crown Zellerbach Canada Ltd.* [1988] 1 S.C.R. 401; *General Motors of Canada v. City National Leasing* [1989] 1 S.C.R. 641. For a detailed analysis of these decisions and their impact on Canadian federalism, see Robert Howse, "Subsidiarity in All But Name: Evolving Principles of Federalism in Canadian Constitutional Law" in *Contemporary Law Droit contemporain: Canadian Reports to the 1994 International Congress of Comparative Law, Athens,* ed. H.P. Glenn (Cowansville, Qué.: Yvon Blais,1995), pp. 712-21.

25. For an elaboration of this point, see Howse "Find New Ways to Secure our Social Union."

26. See R. Howse, *Economic Union, Social Justice and Constitutional Reform,* pp. 107-08.

27. See, for example, the comments of Armand de Mestral in *Getting There: An Assessment of the Agreement on Internal Trade,* ed. M.J. Trebilcock and D. Schwanen (Toronto: C.D. Howe Institute, 1995), pp. 95-98.

28. Bruce Doern, "Rules about Rules," paper presented at conference on "Globalization and the Canadian Regulatory State," Carleton University, May 1997.

29. This last criticism is developed in detail in Robert Howse, "Between Anarchy and the Rule of Law: Dispute Settlement and Related Implementation Issues in the Agreement on Internal Trade," in *Getting There,* ed. Trebilcock and Schwanen.

30. On the possibilities for strengthening the secretariat, see Daniel Schwanen, *Drawing on Our Inner Strength: Canada's Economic Citizenship in an Era of Evolving Federalism,* Commentary no. 82 (Toronto: C.D. Howe Institute, 1996).

31. These kinds of proposals are to be found in Robert Howse, *Securing the Canadian Economic Union: Legal and Constitutional Options for the Federal Government,* Commentary, no. 81 (Toronto: C.D. Howe Institute, 1996).

32. Human Resources Development Canada, "Prime Minister and Premier Clark Settle BC Residency Dispute: "The Prime Minister and the Premier agreed that a national multilateral process, with all parties consulted on its design, would advance everyone's interest in protecting and promoting mobility in Canada. The Government of Canada will raise the issue with all the provinces and work toward a national solution in two years," press release, 6 March 1997.

33. The emphasis the government has placed on mobility in a number of contexts is quite consistent with its (implicit) vision of Canada as a community of association. The freedom, and practical capacity, of each citizen to associate with others throughout Canada is precisely what permits Canada to be a community of association. Thus, in the Speech from the Throne the government clearly stated that "the Government with continue to protect and promote unhampered social mobility between provinces and access to social and other benefits, and will work with the provinces to identify new and mutually agreed approaches." Speech from the Throne to Open the Second Session Thirty Fifth Parliament of Canada, February 27, 1996. The Speech from the Throne contains a parallel commitment to "work with the provinces and the private sector to achieve a much more open agreement."

34. Thus, for example, Roger Gibbins has chosen to characterize the policy moves in question almost exclusively in terms of decentralization and a shift to inter-governmental decisionmaking. See Roger Gibbins, *Time Out: Assessing Incremental Strategies for Enhancing the Canadian Political Union*, Commentary no. 88 (Toronto: C.D. Howe Institute, 1997).

35. The negotiation of the Canada Child Tax Benefit represents an excellent illustration of this; the federal government is both fully committed to working *with* the provinces, but also vigorously insistent that its own policy stake, as the government of all Canadians, be recognized; the government will want to ensure, for example, adequate commitments that an enhanced federal benefit will lead to provincial reinvestment in programs that effective deal with the needs of low-income families with children, that is, that the moral hazard problem is addressed. See Battle, "Transformation: Canadian Social Policy, 1985-2001," p. 33.

36. Perhaps the clearest example were the dealings between certain western provinces and the Trudeau government around the National Energy Program.

37. On the accountability and performance problems of federal training programs see generally Robert Howse and Marsha Chandler, "Industrial Policy in Canada and the United States," in *Degrees of Freedom,* ed. K. Banting, G. Hoberg and R. Simeon (Montreal: McGill-Queen's University Press, 1997), and the studies cited therein.

38. *Canada-Alberta Areement on Labour Market Development*, sections 7-8. I have used this agreement as the example for purposes of this chapter.

39. The following draws on Robert Howse, "Reforming the Canadian Food Inspection System: An Opportunity to Build a New National System," in *Alternative Service Delivery: Sharing Governance in Canada* , ed. R. Ford and D. Zussman (Toronto: Institute of Public Administration of Canada and KPMG Centre for Government, 1997), pp. 138-50.

40. See Howse and Malkin, "Canadians are a Sovereign People."

41. The Courchene ACCESS proposal, despite the use of ombudsmen within provincial communities, would duplicate the shortcoming of the AIT in this respect, through screening of citizen or other private actor (e.g., corporation) complaints both with respect to the social and economic union. This would hardly be mitigated by the fact that under Courchene's system *government* complaints as well would have to pass through screening. See Thomas Courchene, "ACCESS: A Convention on the Canadian Economic and Social Systems" in *Assessing ACCESS: Towards a New Social Union,* ed. D. Cameron (Kingston: Institute of Intergovernmental Relations, Queen's University, 1997), pp. 106-07.

42. André Burelle, *Le mal canadien: essai de diagnostic et esquisse d'une thérapie* (Montreal: Fides, 1995).

43. In this sense, André Burelle's reaction to ACCESS is instructive; once powers and formal decisionmaking capacities get on the table, the temptation to raise the old canards of identity politics becomes irrestible. André Burelle, "Canada Needs a Political and Cultural as well as a Social and Economic Covenant," in *Assessing ACCESS,* ed. Cameron.

44. Thus the intergovernmental affairs minister, Stéphane Dion, while an academic, cast the distinct society notion in terms of responding to genuine distinct needs posed by the position of Quebec as a linguistic community of identity, not in terms of abstract recognition of a "people" or nation. This distinguishes Dion from those like Charles Taylor and Guy Laforest who have conceived the issue in terms of group recognition. See Stéphane Dion, "Explaining Quebec Nationalism," in *The Collapse of Canada?* ed. R.K. Weaver (Washington, DC: Brookings Institution, 1992).

IV

Chronology

13

Chronology of Events July 1996 – June 1997

Melissa Kluger

An index of these events begins on page 363

5 July 1996 *Health Policy*	After a meeting with his Alberta counterpart, Health Minister Halvar Jonson, the federal health minister, David Dingwall, says Ottawa will not give Alberta the $3.6 million it was penalized during a dispute over health fees. Last October, Ottawa began withholding $422,000 per month in transfer payments to Alberta for allowing private clinics to charge fees to patients.
8 July 1996 *Aboriginal Peoples*	Justice George Adams rules that a native band in Sarnia can pursue a class action suit against corporations and individuals in order to settle a land-claims dispute. The Chippewas have claimed ownership to an area known as the Cameron Lands.
9 July 1996 *National Unity*	Prime Minister Jean Chrétien announces the establishment of The Canada Information Office. Heritage Minister Sheila Copps will utilize a $20-million budget to inform Canadians about federalism — promoting the Canadian identity and national unity. Copps says the office will enable Canadians to learn more about one another through such activities as cross-country exchanges.
9 July 1996 *Agriculture*	Agriculture Minister Ralph Goodale says he wants to end the debate about the future of the Canadian Wheat Board.

A federal panel proposes that the Wheat Board, which has a monopoly over Prairie grain sales, should continue to market all grains except feed barley, which should be placed on the open market. Farmers on both sides of the debate are unhappy with the panel's recommendations. Supporters of the board say the proposed changes will put farmers at risk for increased prices, while those in favour of privatization say the suggestions are not drastic enough. Goodale says he will consult with western Canada's farmers before going ahead with any of the recommendations.

10 July 1996
Aboriginal Peoples

At the annual meeting of the Assembly of First Nations, Indian Affairs Minister Ron Irwin announces that Ottawa will be providing $98.5 million to improve water and sewage treatment on Indian reserve lands. Despite these extra funds, Chief Ovide Mercredi criticizes the Liberals for failing to carry out their election promises which included a new housing program and increased land-claims settlements.

19 July 1996
Aboriginal Peoples

The Labrador Inuit Association agrees to talks with Ottawa and the Newfoundland government, which will speed-up a 19-year-old land claim involving more than 5,000 Inuit in northern Labrador.

22 July 1996
Emergency Aid

Flood victims in eastern Quebec who lost homes, businesses, and loved ones, are assisted by the province's establishment of a $200-million fund and Ottawa's contribution of about $150 million. In early July, 12,000 people were evacuated from their homes in the Saguenay-Lac St. Jean, North Shore, and Charlevoix regions in order to escape flash floods in the area. Quebec Premier Lucien Bouchard praises Ottawa for its quick response to the emergency.

22 July 1996
Agriculture

Alberta launches a legal challenge in the Federal Court of Canada against the monopoly held by the Canadian Wheat Board over the sale of wheat and barley. The challenge is one of many responses to Agriculture Minister Ralph Goodale's call for opinions regarding the role of the export agency and the possibility of putting some type of barley on the open market. In contrast to Alberta's legal challenge, Saskatchewan Agriculture Minister Eric

Upshall announces that he wants to fight to preserve the Wheat Board as an institution that continues to serve Canadians.

22 July 1996
Fisheries

Federal Fisheries Minister Fred Mifflin approves a deal struck by the bilateral Pacific Salmon Commission, allowing natives from Washington State to catch about 50,000 fish bound for British Columbia. BC Premier Glen Clark attacks the deal and says his province will attempt to block it. The deal comes only a week after Ottawa had agreed to discuss the possibility of giving the provinces more say in the fisheries.

24 July 1996
Education

A bill aimed at reforming Newfoundland's church-run education system passes unanimously in the provincial legislature. The bill's provisions include reducing the provinces 27 religious school boards to ten, centralizing control over construction of new schools, and establishing a French-language school board. Some of the more controversial issues, such as parental choice of schools and transportation arrangements, will not be resolved until after public consultations in the fall, assuming the constitutional amendment is passed.

25 July 1996
Aboriginal Peoples

Indian Affairs Minister Ron Irwin announces that federal spending for native communities will be increased by $140 million over the next five years. The funds will be directed toward a new housing program to improve living conditions on reserve lands.

26 July 1996
Sovereignty

BC Intergovernmental Relations Minister Andrew Petter says an internal federal government memo, regarding the growth of separatism in British Columbia, is an encouraging sign that his province is being heard in Ottawa. The memo shows a growing feeling that the federal government is insensitive to BC's concerns and an increasing separatist sentiment based on economic growth and geographic isolation. The memo cites an Angus Reid poll taken in 1995 which reported that 12 percent of British Columbians support separatism.

31 July 1996
Environment

The Ontario government releases a discussion paper proposing to cut the number of provincial environmental regulations almost in half. Federal Environmental Minister Sergio Marchi says he is concerned that deregulation will threaten national environmental standards. Marchi is also sceptical of the Ontario government's claim that streamlining the system will not be harmful to the environment.

6 August 1996
Premiers

Catherine Callbeck announces her resignation as premier. Callbeck's Liberal government had won all but one seat in the 1993 election and she was planning to call another election. A public opinion poll showed that her party's popularity was waning. While Callbeck says she has achieved the goals that her government had set, it was time to make way for a successor who "better reflects the current wishes of the people."

7 August 1996
Emergency Aid

Quebec Premier Lucien Bouchard announces that Quebec will give $100 million to rebuild homes, businesses, and farms that were destroyed or damaged in July by flooding in the Sageunay region. Ottawa announces a contribution of $300 million.

12 August 1996
Environment

Federal Environment Minister Sergio Marchi says he wants to work with the provincial government to find a "community-based" solution for cleaning up toxic tar ponds in Sydney, Nova Scotia. Decades of steel-making has resulted in 700,000 tonnes of sludge and has created one of Canada's worst environmental catastrophes.

19 August 1996
Health

Federal Health Minister David Dingwall tells delegates at the Canadian Medical Association's annual meeting that Ottawa will not accept a dual health-care system since it privileges Canadians based on their ability to pay. The delegates pass a resolution which calls for public discussion on new ways to fund health care, but do not endorse a two-tiered system.

22 August 1996
Premiers – Annual Conference

Health care is a central issue as premiers call for a restructuring of national standards and joint management of social policy at their conference in Jasper, Alberta. With the exception of Quebec Premier Lucien Bouchard, the premiers agree to establish a council to rewrite the rules controlling social programs. The premiers disagree about whether provinces who violate the standards should be fined. Alberta Premier Ralph Klein, whose province was docked $3.6 million for failing to comply with the new standards, argued against the penalty while other premiers favoured the rule as a means to maintain quality health care across the country. Aside from social policy, the premiers decided to develop a three-year plan for rebalancing federal and provincial powers, to press Ottawa for $2-billion national infrastructure program, to lobby Ottawa for a fairer tax system, and to support Canada's efforts dealing with foreign overfishing.

22 August 1996 *Disputes*	Quebec Premier Lucien Bouchard and Nova Scotia Premier John Savage agree to let federal regulators decide the route of a natural gas pipeline running from Sable Island gas field of Nova Scotia to New England. Bouchard says it would be more economical to run the line through Quebec, while Savage sees this as an attempt to divert Nova Scotia's royalties. Savage warns that Canada should not endanger the pipeline by putting it in a part of the country that could become independent.
27 August 1996 *Language*	As his government is about to begin a hearing into Bill 40 to bring back the Commission de protection de la langue française, Premier Lucien Bouchard calls for understanding on the topic of Quebec's language laws. The language debate was rekindled by English-rights activist Howard Galganov who announced his plan to air his complaints about language laws to business leaders in New York next month.
8 September 1996 *Sovereignty*	Quebec Premier Lucien Bouchard says another referendum will not be held until after the next election in order to focus on the economy and jobs.
10 September 1996 *Health*	Health ministers say a new national agency will be established within a year to control Canada's blood system. While the new agency is supposed to be national, Quebec Health Minister Jean Rochon says his province is looking to establish its own system.

| 11 September 1996 *Aboriginal Peoples* | Indian Affairs Minister Ron Irwin is accused by Chief Ovide Mercredi of trying to impose his opinion on what is good for Canada's natives. Irwin has proposed changes to the *Indian Act* which Mercredi feels may result in the loss of reserve land. |

| 12 September 1996 *Lieutenant-Governor* | Former Senator Jean-Louis Roux is sworn in as Quebec's new lieutenant-governor with little enthusiasm from Premier Lucien Bouchard. Prime Minister Jean Chrétien chose Roux without consulting the province. |

| 18 September 1996 *Constitution* | Saskatchewan Premier Roy Romanow, New Brunswick Premier Frank McKenna, and Newfoundland Premier Brian Tobin call for a new round of constitutional talks. Romanow wants Canada to recognize Quebec's historic demands and the distinctive nature of the province. Quebec Premier Lucien Bouchard says he is currently focusing on his province's economic problems, rather than constitutional issues. |

| 24 September 1996 *Energy* | Reform Leader Preston Manning suggests that Ottawa decrease its equalization payments to Quebec and give the money to Newfoundland as compensation for the Churchill Falls power deal which grants Hydro-Québec 90 percent of the Fall's 5,428 megawatts of power at pre-1970s prices. According to Newfoundland Premier Brian Tobin the deal translates into $70-$80 million annual earnings in Newfoundland and $750 million in Quebec. Tobin wants Quebec to renegotiate the contract to direct a greater share of the profits to his province. |

| 26 September 1996 *Sovereignty* | Ottawa is seeking advice and clarification from the Supreme Court of Canada regarding the legalities of separation. Justice Minister Allan Rock wants to establish the ground rules prior to the next referendum by asking the court to answer the following questions: |

- Can the Government of Quebec take the province out of Canada unilaterally?
- Is there a right of self-determination under international law?
- If there is a conflict between domestic and international law on the question, which one takes precedence in Canada?

26 September 1996 *Senate*	Prime Minister Jean Chrétien appoints Nova Scotia lawyer and Liberal party organizer Wilfred Moore to the Senate to replace retired Allan MacEachen, bringing standings in the upper house to 51 Liberals, 50 Conservatives, and three independents.
26 September 1996 *Gun Control*	Ontario, Manitoba, Saskatchewan, and the Yukon say they will intervene in a challenge filed by Alberta against Ottawa's decision to establish a national firearms registry. The five governments claim that federal Justice Minister Allan Rock's gun control legislation, which makes registration of firearms mandatory, is unconstitutional and will not reduce criminal activity.
27 September 1996 *Aboriginal Peoples*	Despite threats of protest from native chiefs, Indian Affairs Minister Ron Irwin says Ottawa will go ahead with legislation to amend the *Indian Act*. Native leaders voted 24 September to reject the amendments and to create their own committee to discuss the Act.
1 October 1996 *Education*	The Council of Ministers of Education announces a new set of national tests to assess the level of skill and knowledge of students across the country. The tests, to begin next year, will focus on mathematics, literacy, and science in order to measure trends in curriculum and teaching. Although education is a provincial responsibility, Ottawa has aided in the project by investing $4.5 million over the last three years.
2 October 1996 *Quebec*	Former Quebec Premier Robert Bourassa, 63, dies in Montreal. Bourassa, who brought his Liberal Party to power in 1969, became Quebec's youngest premier at the age of 36.
3 October 1996 *Fisheries*	The proposal for a new *Fisheries Act* is tabled in the House of Commons by Fisheries Minister Fred Mifflin. Under the new Act, provinces would take more responsibility for the protection of fish habitats in their area, and fisheries ministers would be able to negotiate with the industry according to regional management needs rather than adhering to federal regulations.
3 October 1996 *Welfare*	BC Supreme Court Justice John Spencer strikes down the provincial government's controversial 90-day residency

requirement for welfare recipients. The new rule, estimated to save approximately $25 million a year, was announced November 1995 to compensate for a decrease in transfer payments to the province. Ottawa reacted by withholding $46 million in transfer payments, saying that BC had violated the Canada Assistance Plan.

4 October 1996
Canada Pension Plan

At a meeting of federal and provincial finance ministers, Ontario's Ernie Eves leads Quebec, BC, Manitoba, and Saskatchewan in a threat to upset Ottawa's plans for overhauling the Canada Pension Plan, including the proposed hike in employer and employee contributions, if the government fails to reduce Unemployment Insurance premiums. It is expected that the Employment Insurance fund will be $5 billion in the black at the end of this year and twice that in two years. Business wants to see these earnings returned to the economy as an incentive for job creation.

10 October 1996
Premiers

Keith Milligan, minister of transportation and public works, is sworn in as Prince Edward Island's new premier.

10 October 1996
Fisheries

Following BC Fisheries Minister Corky Evans' call for aid, his federal counterpart, Fred Mifflin, announces that Ottawa will soon be able to help the BC coastal communities that have been devastated by the decline in salmon fishing. The report of the provincial Job Protection Commission says that 7,800 jobs were lost in fisheries, at a cost of $245 million to the BC economy. To ease the economic situation, Ottawa is considering a proposal to hire unemployed workers to work at rehabilitating salmon streams that have been damaged by forestry and urbanization.

10 October 1996
Taxes

Finance Minister Paul Martin says that three Atlantic provinces can make books tax-exempt when the provincial sales tax is merged with the federal goods and services tax next April, but that Ottawa will not cover the cost. Without posing a threat to the GST harmonization plan, Nova Scotia, New Brunswick, and Newfoundland will be able to offer a partial refund to cover the provincial share of the proposed 15-percent blended levy.

10 October 1996 *Education*	The final report issued by Quebec's commission on the state of education says that the role of religion in school should be diminished, that full-time kindergarten should be provided, and that funding to private schools should be reduced. While Education Minister Pauline Marois could not commit to all of the recommendations, she did reiterate that the government hopes to replace the current religious school boards with boards based on language.
10 October 1996 *Labour*	The Quebec government announces its plan to pass legislation which will make it easier for Ontario workers to get construction jobs in Quebec. Currently over 4,000 Quebec residents work on construction sites in Ontario while only a few hundred Ontario residents work on sites in Quebec.
15 October 1996 *Energy*	Newfoundland Premier Brian Tobin releases a secret document which he says proves Quebec acknowledged it is reaping unfair profits from the Churchill Falls power contract which it signed with Newfoundland in 1969. The agreement has allowed Hydro-Québec to buy energy from the Labrador project and sell it at ten times the original price. Tobin argues that the contract can and should be renegotiated, while Hydro-Québec and the Quebec government have made it clear that they have no plans to reopen the deal.
16 October 1996 *Constitution*	A draft of a new constitutional proposal is tabled in the Northwest Territories legislature. The proposal was motivated by a fear that the North would become a fragmented political structure unless native and mainstream governments find a way to work together. The draft suggests that beginning in 1999, when the new territory of Nunavut is created, over one-third of seats in the western-Arctic legislature should be reserved for Aboriginals.
18 October 1996 *BC-Federal Relations*	Relations between the British Columbia and federal governments were improved after a meeting in Vancouver between Premier Glen Clark and Prime Minister Jean Chrétien. The leaders agreed on a new national cost-shared infrastructure program, while agreeing to disagree on BC's residency requirement for new welfare recipients and on

proposals to revise the Canada Pension Plan. In addition, Ottawa offered BC a bigger role in the management of the fishery.

21 October 1996
Industrial
Development

Prime Minister Jean Chrétien announces an $87-million interest-free loan to Bombardier Inc. The money is granted to the Montreal-based company for the development of a new 70-seat passenger jet which is expected to create and maintain 1,000 jobs. Reform MPs object to the government's decision to allocate one-quarter of its new Technology Partnerships Canada fund to the project, pointing out that Bombardier has received almost $1.2 billion from Ottawa over the past 15 years.

28 October 1996
Aboriginal Peoples

The federal government is condemned by Alberta Premier Ralph Klein, Saskatchewan Premier Roy Romanow, and national aboriginal groups for its declining commitment to native social programs. Ottawa claims it is only responsible for covering welfare costs for reserve Indians and wants to shift the economic burden of some aboriginal social programs to the provinces. Grand Chief of the Assembly of First Nations, Ovide Mercredi, is concerned that if native issues are handed over to the provinces then natives would receive fewer services. Ottawa currently spends approximately $700 million a year on welfare for reserve Indians.

29 October 1996
Aboriginal Peoples

A plan to relocate the remote community of Davis Inlet to the Labrador mainland is met with overwhelming support in a referendum. More than 97 percent of the ballots favoured the agreement between the Innu and Newfoundland and federal governments, in which the province will turn over land at Sango Bay to provide health and education services to the community afflicted with such problems as poor sanitation and housing. The transfer, estimated to cost Ottawa $70 million, will provide the community with running water, sewers, and access to the mainland.

6 November 1996
Fisheries

Fisheries Minister Fred Mifflin responds to BC's call for help by announcing that Ottawa will spend "whatever it costs" to provide short-term job relief to thousands of salmon fishery workers who have been displaced as a result of poor salmon runs and fleet reduction.

14 November 1996 *Language*	Louise Beaudoin, Quebec's minister responsible for the French Language Charter, announces new language policies for civil servants. The objective of the 30 new rules, which restrict the use of languages other than French by civil servants, is to send a message to immigrants that they must become part of the francophone majority. Services that were bilingual prior to the new policies will still be provided in either language but anglophones will now have to request English service.

14 November 1996
Lieutenant-Governor

A motion to abolish the position of lieutenant-governor is tabled by Premier Lucien Bouchard. Bouchard calls the post a colonial relic and says that if it cannot be abolished, Quebec should at least have the power to make its own appointments. The issue was sparked by Chrétien's appointment of Jean-Louis Roux, a federalist, as the Quebec's new lieutenant-governor. On 5 November, Roux admitted that he had worn a swastika and participated in anti-conscription protests when he was a student at university, giving sovereigntists an impetus to demand his resignation. While Chrétien assured Roux he did not have to step down, he resigned the next day, apologizing to Jews and veterans for his actions.

18 November 1996
Elections

The ten-year-old Liberal government is replaced by the Conservatives in PEI's election. The Tories take 18 of the Island's 27 seats, the Liberals hold onto only eight and, for the first time, a seat goes to an NDP representative. Conservative leader Pat Binns suggests that PEI's dissatisfaction with the Liberals comes as the result of its ties to the federal government and its unpopular policies.

20 November 1996
Industrial
Development

After taking criticism from the West about its $87-million loan to Montreal-based Bombardier Inc., the federal government provides a $30-million loan to British Columbia's Ballard Power Systems Inc. The money will go to the development of environmentally-friendly fuel cells to provide electric power to homes, hospitals, and industry.

20 November 1996
Environment

Provincial and federal environment ministers agree in principle to unify Canada's environmental standards. Although
the details are not yet worked out the accord would set
common requirements for each province on issues such
as air, water, and soil quality.

21 November 1996
Aboriginal Peoples

The Canadian Royal Commission releases its report on
Aboriginal Peoples. The report indicates that Canada risks
violence unless it gives its natives a new deal, including
new lands, resources, respect, and real self-government.
Recommendations include an increase in government
spending to improve housing, health, education, and employment opportunities for natives; an aboriginal
parliament; and an independent tribunal to oversee and
accelerate land claims. The commission says that spending money will lead to healthier and more productive
aboriginal communities.

26 November 1996
Elections

Changes to the *Elections Act* pass in the Commons. Under the revised Act, voting hours will be staggered across
the country so that voters in the west can cast their votes
before results in the east have decided the election.

27 November 1996
Education

The Senate approves a revised version of Newfoundland's
original constitutional amendment to reduce the role of
churches in the school system. Since the Senate cannot
kill a constitutional amendment once it is passed by Commons a second time, Justice Minister Allan Rock says the
original amendment will return to the House for its final
passage. The change to Newfoundland's school system
follows a provincial referendum in which 54 percent of
voters supported the proposal. The process of constitutional amendment is necessary because the change involves
conditions that were set out when Newfoundland joined
Canada in 1949.

27 November 1996
Social Programs

A national program to fight child poverty is supported, in
principle, by federal and provincial social services ministers, but provincial representatives are waiting to see how
much the program will cost before making a commitment.
Federal Human Resources Minister Pierre Pettigrew says
bureaucrats have been asked to brainstorm on ways in

which the two orders of government can work together to fight child poverty and to bring those ideas to their January meeting.

29 November 1996
Sovereignty

The Supreme Court of Canada receives applications from Saskatchewan, Manitoba, and the two territories to intervene in Ottawa's constitutional reference on Quebec separation. Quebec lawyer Guy Bertrand, Quebec's Grand Council of Cree, the Algonquins of Barrier Lake, and other groups also hope to come before the court during the hearing expected next summer. Meanwhile, the Quebec government says it will not participate in the case.

2 December 1996
Leadership

Bloc Québécois Leader Michel Gauthier steps down.

3 December 1996
Agriculture

Agriculture Minister Ralph Goodale introduces legislation that would change the way the Canadian Wheat Board operates. Most significantly, it would end the Wheat Board's monopoly over Prairie grain sales.

6 December 1996
Social Programs

Federal Minister of Human Resources, Pierre Pettigrew, and Alberta's minister of advanced education and career development, Jack W. Ady, sign an agreement that transfers the responsibility for labour market development to the province. The $317 million deal is part of Ottawa's decision to offer all provinces and territories opportunity to take responsibility for the design of active labour market development measures for Employment Insurance Clients. Under the new deal, all services for the unemployed will be under one roof in the hope that more people will have access to employment programs.

7 December 1996
Sovereignty

The Quebec Liberal Party takes a new stand on the constitution in order to reduce the threat of separation. The party proposes that Quebec's distinct society status should be entrenched in the constitution with a clause that requires courts to recognize its unique position. The proposal also includes a guarantee of three Quebec judges on the Supreme Court, provincial priority over shared jurisdiction with Ottawa, and the ability to limit Ottawa's spending power in provincial jurisdictions. Liberal Leader Daniel

Johnson says that if Canada adopts the proposal and thereby shows that change is possible, another divisive sovereignty referendum could be avoided.

9 December 1996 *Education*	Newfoundland introduces changes to its education laws in the House of Assembly. Under the changes, parents will be asked what type of religion they want their children to be taught and the majority responses will determine the religious designation of each school. Education Minister Roger Grimes wants to run an interdenominational school system, but also respects the rights of single denominations to have their own schools.
12 December 1996 *Aboriginal Peoples*	Indian Affairs Minister Ron Irwin is booed from the public gallery as native leaders express their discontent for the newly revised *Indian Act*. Native leaders accuse the government of failing to consult them, as well as failing to fulfill the recommendations outlined by the Royal Commission on Aboriginal Peoples.
12 December 1996 *Lieutenant-Governor*	Prime Minister Jean Chrétien appoints Lise Thibault as Quebec's new lieutenant-governor. Thibault, disabled-rights activist and television personality, is to replace Jean-Louis Roux who resigned last month. Like Roux, Thibault is also an acknowledged federalist but she says she will keep politics out of her new position. Chrétien also appointed Hilary Weston, Toronto businesswoman and author, as Ontario's lieutenant-governor, and medical scientist Dr. A.M. House to the position in Newfoundland.
13 December 1996 *Social Programs*	New Brunswick signs a $237 million accord to take over job training and other employment services from the federal government.
17 December 1996 *Industrial Development*	Federal Industry Minister John Manley announces that Montreal-based Bombardier Inc. will receive more federal assistance. The company will use the additional $57 million in its de Havilland division for research and development on the Dash 8-400. The project is expected to create up to 1,000 jobs and advance Canada's aerospace industry.

19 December 1996 *Demography*	Statistics Canada reports that the first six months of 1996 saw a net loss of 12,792 residents moving from Quebec to other provinces. Premier Lucien Bouchard does not attribute the high migration levels to Quebec's uncertain future, but rather to English-speaking Quebecers who have the mobility to leave for economic reasons. Liberal Leader Daniel Johnson is concerned that it is language policies that are causing the exodus from Quebec.
3 January 1997 *Language*	English-rights crusader Howard Galganov announces he is dissolving his campaign for English-minority language rights due to lack of financial support from anglophones. Galganov first attacked the provincial language laws by boycotting stores that did not have English on their signs. Later, he took his grievances to Wall Street but failed to draw much attention to the issue.
4 January 1997 *Unity*	Ottawa launches a 12-part French-language series on a Quebec network to advertise government services and programs which are available to Canadians. Critics say the commercials have been introduced to increase Liberal popularity in Quebec, while a representative from the Human Resources Department denies any political motivation.
7 January 1997 *Infrastructure*	Ottawa announces that it wants to extend its job-creating infrastructure program for a fourth year by offering the provinces an extra $425 million. Treasury Board President Marcel Massé predicts the extension could lead to up to 2,500 new projects, giving rise to as many as 20,000 jobs in areas that will improve Canada's roads, sewers, and other infrastructures.
9 January 1997 *Fisheries*	Federal Fisheries Minister Fred Mifflin announces that Ottawa is going ahead with its plans to cut the BC salmon stock in half and to permit fishers to buy a licence for more than one area. Ottawa will provide $5 million to help troll and gillnet fishers stack licences and $8 million to assist those whose fishing gear has been rendered useless under the new licensing regulations. BC Fisheries Minister Corky Evans criticizes Ottawa's plan and says he wants to see control over fisheries put into provincial hands.

| 10 January 1997 Industrial Development | Ottawa lends Pratt and Whitney Canada Inc. of Longueuil, Quebec $147 million to enable the US-owned aerospace firm to maintain its engine production in Canada. |

10 January 1997
Industrial
Development

Ottawa lends Pratt and Whitney Canada Inc. of Longueuil, Quebec $147 million to enable the US-owned aerospace firm to maintain its engine production in Canada.

17 January 1997
Taxes

Ottawa and three Atlantic provinces try to sort out some of the controversial aspects of a plan to harmonize provincial and federal sales taxes. Under the new plan, the 15 percent levy will be buried in consumer prices but retailers will be able to mark the cost before and after taxes on their price tags. Businesses in New Brunswick, Newfoundland, and Nova Scotia are concerned that the blended tax will put the provinces at a disadvantage because prices will be inconsistent with national advertising.

17 January 1997
Energy

Quebec Premier Lucien Bouchard agrees to "exploratory talks" with Newfoundland Premier Brian Tobin regarding the Churchill Falls power contract. On 19 November, Tobin had warned that if Quebec separates it will lose the contract.

17 January 1997
Sovereignty

Chief Justice Antonio Lamer gives permission for 13 groups to intervene in the federal government's court reference on whether or not Quebec can secede unilaterally. Saskatchewan and Manitoba are the only two provinces that will intervene, along with the territories which will be arguing largely for native rights.

20 January 1997
Trade

Team Canada returns home after a 12-day trade mission to Asia made up of about 400 business representatives and nine premiers, including Quebec Premier Lucien Bouchard. While Bouchard maintains that the mission has not changed his separatist goals, he did keep internal politics out of the trip in order to focus on bringing jobs into the country. But other interprovincial disagreements did arise. Manitoba Premier Gary Filmon and British Columbia's Glen Clark criticized New Brunswick Premier Frank McKenna for attempting to lure business from other provinces into his own. The team signed a total of over $2 billion in deals with Thailand, South Korea, and the Philippines.

23 January 1997
Education

In an attempt to reflect changing demographics and improve efficiency, Quebec hopes to produce a constitutional amendment which would allow denominational school boards to be replaced by linguistic boards. The proposal is met with dissent from some sovereigntists who are concerned that by doing so Quebec will be forced to acknowledge the 1982 constitution which the province never signed. Quebec Premier Lucien Bouchard says that Quebec will be amending the 1867 *British North American Act,* rather than the revised *Constitution Act,* 1982.

25 January 1997
Health

A resolution is passed at the Parti Québécois' national council meeting to limit health care in English to those areas in which the anglophone population is over 50 percent. On 31 January Bouchard argues that his government provides satisfactory health-care service in English.

28 January 1997
Social Services

Canada's social services ministers agree in principle to adopt a plan to ensure that child benefits are not limited to those on welfare, but extended to the working-poor. According to the plan, Ottawa will increase its contribution to the child tax benefit and provincial welfare payments for children will be decreased. Money saved by the provinces will be used by them to design and deliver aid to poor families with children in a manner that fosters work incentives through programs such as day care and school lunches.

29 January 1997
Health

Provincial and territorial health ministers release a report titled *A Renewed Vision for Canada's Health System* which says medicare should be preserved but changes should be made to the universal system. The report calls on Ottawa to establish a panel of experts to assist in settling disputes which arise over medicare rules and transfer payments. In addition, the provinces call for a new interpretation of the *Canada Health Act* in order to give provinces a greater role in health-care decisions.

4 February 1997
Health

Health Minister David Dingwall welcomed the report of the National Forum on Health, *Canada Health Action: Building on the Legacy,* which maps out a long-term plan for reforming the health-care system and improving the health of Canadians. The report notes that maintaining the five principles of the *Canada Health Act* are critical to preserving medicare while flexible enough to accommodate organized reforms.

7 February 1997 *Infrastructure*	Alberta is the first province to sign on to the federal government's new infrastructure offer. Both the provincial and municipal governments will match the $35 million provided by Ottawa in order to improve roads, sewers, and bridges. It is estimated that the deal will create 1,800 jobs.
12 February 1997 *Education*	Prime Minister Jean Chrétien says Ottawa needs evidence that there is a consensus among Quebecers to move from religious-based school boards to linguistic boards before a constitutional amendment can be made. Members of Alliance Quebec, an English-rights lobby group, want to ensure that the constitution entrenches the rights of anglophones to their own schools and school boards — a request that Quebec Premier Lucien Bouchard has rejected. A constitutional amendment is necessary because the denomination school boards are protected under the 1867 *British North America Act.*
18 February 1997 *Budget*	Federal Finance Minister Paul Martin tables the pre-election budget in the Commons. He announces that while the government plans to focus on bringing down the deficit, an additional $1 billion a year will be invested in social programs. The deficit is now at a 15-year low and Martin predicts that by 1998-99, for the first time in almost 30 years, Ottawa will not have to borrow money. Martin says there will not be cuts to taxes since he does not want to "jeopardize the basic values of Canadians." He also introduces a new child tax credit for working-poor families, created in cooperation with the provinces, which will cost Ottawa $600 million. Prime Minister Jean Chrétien comments that this is a "down payment on social justice." Martin also announces that Ottawa will spend $425 million for an infrastructure program designed to encourage provinces to improve roads, bridges, and sewers. Other highlights include:

- a $225 million Youth Employment Strategy to create jobs and internships for 139,000 students;
- $300 million over three years to be invested in improving the delivery of better health services to Canadians; and
- selective tax cuts for low-income families, charities, the disabled, students, and parents saving for their children's future education

21 February 1997 *Trade*	Quebec Premier Lucien Bouchard announces that he will lead his own trade mission to China in November and to Latin America next year. Bouchard plans to focus on Quebec's economy and on building business connections both with Canadian provinces and the rest of the world.
24 February 1997 *Aboriginal Peoples*	Native leaders are outraged by Ottawa's failure to act on at least some of more than 400 recommendations set out in the Royal Commission on Aboriginal Peoples' report. The report calls on the government to increase its spending by $1.5 to $2 billion annually in order to improve aboriginal housing, health, and employment opportunities over the next two decades. Indian Affairs Minister Ron Irwin says Ottawa has already acted on some of the recommendations and that it would be too expensive to implement any of the others. Native Chief Ovide Mercredi says that in order to be heard, Indian leaders will participate in a one-day protest by slowing traffic on the Trans-Canada Highway.
28 February 1997 *Sovereignty*	Ottawa presents its argument to the Supreme Court of Canada regarding Quebec's right to separate. The argument, which is the most formal condition Ottawa has ever made in the long-standing sovereignty debate, is that Quebec must use the constitution to take its leave.
28 February 1997 *Justice*	At a meeting of Canada's justice ministers, federal Minister of Justice Allan Rock says Ottawa will not provide Quebec with the $77 million it has requested in order to retroactively fund its young offender services. The program reflects Quebec Justice Minister Paul Begin's belief that through rehabilitative measures, young offenders can be returned to society rather than being put in jail.
7 March 1997 *Immigration*	Ottawa announces that most provinces will receive more immigrant resettlement payments from a new fund of about $63 million a year. The new money has been introduced to correct an imbalance in the allocation of federal immigration funds. Under the new program federal dollars for immigration services will be allocated more appropriately, according to the immigration rates of each province. The announcement followed a meeting on 6 March in which Citizenship and Immigration Minister Lucienne Robillard

promised British Columbia an additional $22.4 million for services to assist BC-bound immigrants. The promise prompted Premier Glen Clark to end the province's controversial welfare-residency requirement.

11 March 1997
Elections

Premier Ralph Klein and his Conservative government return to power after a landslide victory in the Alberta election. The Tories formed another majority government with 63 of the 83 seats in the legislature. The Liberals won 18 seats and the NDP won two.

15 March 1997
Elections

Gilles Duceppe is elected as the new leader of the Bloc Québécois.

20 March 1997
Taxes

Legislation for a new blended sales tax is passed in the House of Commons. The BST, which merges the federal GST and provincial sales taxes into one, will go into effect 1 April in Newfoundland, New Brunswick, and Nova Scotia. The single 15 percent levy will make those items formerly taxed at both the federal and provincial level less expensive, while making goods and services which were previously exempt from provincial sales taxes more costly.

20 March 1997
Premiers

John Savage announces his resignation as Nova Scotia's premier. During his time as premier, Savage and his Liberal Party introduced a number of unpopular changes in the province including drastic health reforms, a wage freeze for civil servants and the blended sales tax. Savage hopes that by electing a new leader the Liberals will have a better chance at maintaining their popularity.

24 March 1997
Budgets

Quebec's budget for 1997-98 is announced by Finance Minister Bernard Landry. Landry says his government plans to cut $2 billion of its provincial deficit and to eliminate it entirely by 1999-2000. In his budget, Landry announces a 15 percent personal income tax cut for households that earn under $50,000. The cut is financed mainly by raising the provincial sales tax one percentage point to 7.5 percent. Other highlights of the budget include: raising vehicle-registration fees, increasing the cost of cigarettes, spending half a billion dollars to stimulate private sector investment and cracking down on black market activity — specifically construction, alcohol, and tax evasion.

24 March 1997
Social Programs

At a meeting in Ottawa, Prime Minister Jean Chrétien and Newfoundland Premier Brian Tobin sign a $308 million labour-market accord. Newfoundland is the third province to sign onto the deal, but unlike the devolution agreements with Alberta and New Brunswick, Newfoundland's program will be co-managed with Ottawa.

25 March 1997
Budgets

BC's Finance Minister Andrew Petter introduces the 1997-98 provincial budget. Petter promises to increase spending on health and education while cutting last year's $395 million deficit in half. A balanced budget is predicted for 1998-99 and surplus of $110 million for the following year. In order to avoid raising taxes, Petter has proposed a series of fee hikes on such things as fishing licences, cellular phones, and safety inspections.

25 March 1997
Agriculture

Federal Agriculture Minister Ralph Goodale announces that 62.9 percent of barley growers voted in favour of keeping the Wheat Board and asks farmers to respect the outcome of the survey.

26 March 1997
Education

The Parti Québécois tables a resolution in the provincial legislature requesting the amendment of section 93 of the *British North America Act* to allow a change from religious to linguistic school boards. Premier Lucien Bouchard hopes that the amendment will be passed at the federal level before the next federal election, in order to put the reforms into motion by September 1998.

14 April 1997
Unity

Only a day before the Liberals are expected to call a federal election, the party is bombarded with criticism for the way it has handled national unity. Lawyer Guy Bertrand, granted intervenor status in Ottawa's constitutional reference on Quebec separation, says the Liberal government has failed to maintain the country's constitutional rights and wants the government to put up a stronger fight against separation. Meanwhile, former Prime Minister Brian Mulroney tells an audience in Toronto that the Liberals have failed to deal with Quebec's historic grievances and says constitutional talks must be reopened. By

ensuring the province's language and culture in the constitution, Mulroney says a vote in favour of independence
will be avoided. But the premiers of Ontario, British Columbia, and Alberta disagree with Mulroney and say they
have no plans to reopen constitutional talks.

15 April 1997
Education

The Quebec National Assembly votes unanimously in favour of a motion which asks Ottawa to amend the
constitution to allow the province to move from religious
to linguistic-based school boards. The opposition supported the motion after it was adjusted to allow the
English-speaking minority to govern their own schools.
The motion stipulates that the constitutional change is
being made to the original *British North America Act,*
rather than the *Constitution Act,* 1982, which Quebec has
not signed.

17 April 1997
Fisheries

Fisheries Minister Fred Mifflin announces that 1 May will
see the reopening of a small east coast cod fishery. In 1993,
about 40,000 fishermen were put out of work when Ottawa closed the ailing groundfishery. It is estimated that
the reopened fisheries will bring in $10 million to New-
foundland's fishers and provide thousands of them with
jobs.

18 April 1997
Aboriginal Peoples

First Nations Chief Ovide Mercredi is told that Prime
Minister Jean Chrétien will be unable to meet with aboriginal leaders before the federal election. Chrétien assures
Mercredi that the recent report of the Royal Commission
on Aboriginal Peoples is being studied, but Mercredi wants
to see action on the commission's recommendations and
says that native leaders will keep after Chrétien throughout the election period. On 17 April natives across Canada
rallied on streets and highways to protest poverty on native reserves and the government's failure to respond to
the royal commission recommendations.

21 April 1997
Social Programs

Prime Minister Jean Chrétien and Quebec Premier Lucien
Bouchard sign a labour market agreement, in which Ottawa agrees to provide Quebec with almost $3 billion over
five years from the Employment Insurance Account.

21 April 1997 *Budget*	Treasurer Stockwell Day introduces Alberta's third consecutive surplus budget. Cuts to social spending and a booming economy have enabled the reelected Conservatives to cut $3.45 billion from the debt over the past three years. It is expected that the province will reap a surplus between $154 million to $744 which will go toward increased social spending.
22 April 1997 *Education*	Ottawa tables a motion put forward by Quebec to move from religious to linguistic-based school boards in the province. While it appears that Ottawa is working to give Quebec the constitutional change it has requested, critics have charged that the motion is nothing more than an empty gesture since Parliament will be dissolved when the election is called.
25 April 1997 *Unity*	Prime Minister Jean Chrétien makes unity the priority in his election campaign. In a speech at the Canadian Club in Toronto he says, "Keeping Canada united is the single most important duty and responsibility of a national government and of a prime minister." Chrétien says he plans to use step-by-step measures to improve relations with all provinces.
26 April 1997 *Election*	The Bloc Québécois unveils its party platform which attacks the Liberals for failing to bring down unemployment rates, promises to press Ottawa to compensate Quebec for its blended sales tax, and calls for the end of funding directed toward the promotion of Canadian unity.
26 April 1997 *Justice*	A bill aimed at easing Quebec's motorcycle gang wars is rushed through Parliament and given royal assent. Over the past three years, battles between the Hell's Angles and the Rock Machine over Quebec's fruitful drug trade have resulted in at least 48 deaths.
27 April 1997 *Election*	Prime Minister Jean Chrétien calls a national election. Chrétien and the Liberals face criticism from other party leaders for calling the 2 June election after being in office for only three and a half years.

30 April 1997
Flood Relief

Manitoba braces for a major flood as residents of Winnipeg upgrade their defences against the looming natural disaster. About 2,000 soldiers have come from across Canada to help communities build dikes and evacuate the threatened areas. Reform Leader Preston Manning criticizes Prime Minister Jean Chrétien for going ahead with his federal election call while Manitoba is in a state of emergency. Chrétien says that according to a previously-unused election rule, the 2 June date could be postponed for 90 days if the Chief Electoral Officer believes it is necessary. Meanwhile, candidates in Manitoba are postponing their campaigns in order to help their communities build sandbag dikes.

6 May 1997
Budget

Ontario's Conservative government releases its $57 billion budget for 1997-98. The budget reduces spending by $2.3 billion and brings the deficit down to $6.6. billion from last year's $7.5 billion and is expected that the books will be balanced by 2000-2001. Ontario Finance Minister Ernie Eves introduces phase two of his three-year plan – which cuts provincial income taxes by 22.5 percent and says the federal government should follow suit. The tone of the budget suggests serious strains in the relations between Queen's Park and Ottawa, reflected in Eve's statement that his government will explore the possibility of setting up its own income tax collection system independent of Ottawa. Other budget highlights include:

- a $124 million drop in education spending, but $650 million available for building and renovating schools;
- $250 million raised by universities and colleges will be matched by the government for tuition assistance; and
- $40 million promised last year for child care will not be spent, but will be used for a low-income tax credit.

7 May 1997
Sovereignty

A Quebec City journalist reports that, in his new book, Jacques Parizeau says he had planned to separate his province from Canada only days after a yes vote in the 1995 sovereignty referendum. Parizeau quickly denies the report and claims that the journalist twisted his words. Regardless of Parizeau's actual intentions, the release of his book has done nothing to help Bloc Québécois leader Gilles

Duceppe's already faltering election campaign. The book is ammunition for other leaders who are using it as evidence that separatists cannot be trusted.

12 May 1997
Election

Party leaders participate in the English federal election debate. National unity is a major issue, but discussion also covers tax cuts, health care, unemployment, and the effectiveness of Parliament. On 13 May, the French election debate is cut short when moderator Claire Lamarche collapses and is taken to hospital. The discussion ends just as Prime Minister Jean Chrétien is asked what he would do if, in another referendum, Quebec voted by 50 percent plus one in favour of sovereignty. On 15 May it is announced that party leaders will have another opportunity to participate in the French-language debate which will focus solely on the issue of national unity.

13 May 1997
Emergency Aid

The Globe and Mail reports that as Manitoba's devastating flood waters recede, the province faces over $150 million in damages. Manitoba is paying flood claims of up to $100,000 and Ottawa has sent $25 million in aid. In addition, citizens across the country have donated over $12 million to local charities.

15 May 1997
Health

Federal Health Minister David Dingwall threatens to amend the *Canada Health Act* in order to prevent the opening of a private health-care clinic in Alberta. The new facility, expected to be opened in July, will cater its private medical services to the Workers' Compensation Board, Americans, native groups, and private corporations. Dingwall is surprised the facility has not met with dissent from the Alberta government, which has been penalized by Ottawa for charging patients extra fees.

2 June 1997
Election

The Liberals win a slim majority in the federal election, marking the first time the party has won successive majorities since the 1950s. The Liberals took 155 of 301 seats, owing a large part of their success to overwhelming support from Ontario, where the party captured 101 of 103 seats. Both the NDP and Conservative Party regained party status with 21 and 20 seats respectively; many of which were won in Atlantic Canada. Meanwhile support for the Bloc Québécois slipped from 54 to 44 seats. As a result, the Bloc lost its status as official Opposition and was replaced by the Reform Party, which won 59 seats in the west.

Members elected by province/territory and party:

	Lib	Ref	BQ	NDP	PC	Ind	Vac
Newfoundland (7)	4	0	0	0	3	0	0
PEI (4)	4	0	0	0	0	0	0
Nova Scotia (11)	0	0	0	6	5	0	0
New Brunswick (10)	3	0	0	2	5	0	0
Quebec (75)	26	0	44	0	5	0	0
Ontario (103)	101	0	0	0	1	1	0
Manitoba (14)	6	3	0	4	1	0	0
Saskatchewan (14)	1	8	0	5	0	0	0
Alberta (26)	2	24	0	0	0	0	0
BC (34)	6	24	0	3	0	0	1
Yukon/NWT (3)	2	0	0	1	0	0	0
Total (301)	*155*	*59*	*44*	*21*	*20*	*1*	*1*

	1997	*1993*	*1988*
Liberals	155	177	83
Reform	59	52	0
Bloc Québécois	44	54	0
New Democrats	21	9	43
Progressive Conservatives	20	2	169
Independent	1	0	0
Vacancies	1	0	0
Totals	*301*	*295*	*295*

6 June 1997
Language

The Quebec National Assembly votes 63-24 to bring back the Commission de protection de la langue francaise. The bill was introduced last year by Language Minister Louise Beaudoin in order to reestablish the commission, which ensures that everything in Quebec meets the stipulations of Quebec's French Language Charter. The commission was established by the first Parti Québécois but abandoned in 1993 by the late Premier Robert Bourassa.

11 June 1997
Cabinet

Reelected Prime Minister Jean Chrétien names his new Cabinet. He announces that the emphasis of this Cabinet will be on balancing the budget, improving and expanding the health-care system, and providing for Canada's children. A number of the positions went to left-of-centre Liberals including Sergio Marchi in international trade, David Collenette in transport, and Allan Rock as health minister. Paul Martin was reappointed as finance minister. Sheila Copps maintained her heritage portfolio but lost her position as deputy prime minister to MP Herb Gray.

19 June 1997
Unity

Premier Lucien Bouchard says that Canada would inevitably accept a partnership with an independent Quebec in order to ensure payment of the debt and trading opportunities. Members of the Parti Québécois agree in general that if another sovereignty referendum was cast in their favour they would proclaim sovereignty regardless of whether or not Canada agrees to a partnership. Bouchard predicts that the federal election, which displaced the Bloc Québécois as official Opposition, will further the sovereignty movement.

19 June 1997
Infrastructure

At a meeting of transportation ministers, the federal minister, David Collenette, tells his provincial counterparts that there will be no money to improve Canada's highways until the federal budget is balanced. For each of the past two years Ottawa has provided $300 million in order to improve efficiency and safety on Canada's roads.

24 June 1997
Unity

The new federal justice minister, Anne McLellan, tells the *Sun* that Canada can no longer be held "hostage" to separatists and that Quebec must clarify the process and implications of independence. McLellan adds that in the instance of a yes vote, Quebec could be partitioned to allow certain areas to stay within Canada. Separatists, in reaction to her statement, accuse McLellan of pandering to the west.

Note: The principal source for this chronology was *Canadian News Facts*. Other sources included *The Globe and Mail* and federal web sites.

Chronology: Index

Queen's Policy Studies
Recent Publications

The Queen's Policy Studies Series is dedicated to the exploration of major policy issues that confront governments in Canada and other western nations. McGill-Queen's University Press is the exclusive world representative and distributor of books in the series.

School of Policy Studies

Lone-Parent Incomes and Social-Policy Outcomes: Canada in International Perspective,
Terrance Hunsley, 1997
Paper ISBN 0-88911-751-9 Cloth ISBN 0-88911-757-8

Social Partnerships for Training: Canada's Experiment with Labour Force Development Boards, Andrew Sharpe and Rodney Haddow (eds.), 1997
Paper ISBN 0-88911-753-5 Cloth ISBN 0-88911-755-1

Reform of Retirement Income Policy: International and Canadian Perspectives,
Keith G. Banting and Robin Boadway (eds.), 1996
Paper ISBN 0-88911-739-X Cloth ISBN 0-88911-759-4

Institute of Intergovernmental Relations

Canadian Constitutional Dilemmas Revisited, Denis Magnusson (ed.), 1997
Paper ISBN 0-88911-593-1 Cloth ISBN 0-88911-595-8

Canada: The State of the Federation 1996, Patrick C. Fafard and Douglas M. Brown (eds.), 1997
Paper ISBN 0-88911-587-7 Cloth ISBN 0-88911-597-4

Comparing Federal Systems in the 1990s, Ronald Watts, 1997
Paper ISBN 0-88911-589-3 Cloth ISBN 0-88911-763-2

John Deutsch Institute for the Study of Economic Policy

The Nation State in a Global/Information Era: Policy Challenges, Thomas J. Courchene (ed.),
Bell Canada Papers no. 5, 1997
Paper ISBN 0-88911-770-5 Cloth ISBN 0-88911-766-7

Reforming the Canadian Financial Sector: Canada in a Global Perspective,
Thomas J. Courchene and Edwin H. Neave (eds.), 1997
Paper ISBN 0-88911-688-1 Cloth ISBN 0-88911-768-3

Policy Frameworks for a Knowledge Economy, Thomas J. Courchene (ed.),
Bell Canada Papers no. 4, 1996   Paper ISBN 0-88911-686-5

Available from:
University of Toronto Press, 5201 Dufferin St., North York, On M3H 5T8
Tel: 1-800-565-9523 / Fax: 1-800-221-9985

The following publications are available from:

Institute of Intergovernmental Relations
Queen's University, Kingston, Ontario K7L 3N6

Tel: (613) 545-2080 / Fax: (613) 545-6868
email: iigr@qsilver.queensu.ca

Securing the Social Union: A Commentary on the Decentralized Approach,
Steven A. Kennett, forthcoming
ISBN 0-88911-767-5

Assessing ACCESS: Towards a New Social Union, Proceedings of a symposium held at
Queen's University, 31 October-1 November 1996, 1997
ISBN 0-88911-591-5

Equalization on the Basis of Need in Canada, Douglas M. Brown, 1996
ISBN 0-88911-585-0

The New Face of Canadian Nationalism, Roger Gibbins, 1995
ISBN 0-88911-577-X

Integration and Fragmentation: The Paradox of the Late Twentieth Century, Guy Laforest
and Douglas M. Brown (eds.), 1994
ISBN 0-88911-567-2